DRY TORTUGAS

UNIVERSITY PRESS OF FLORIDA

Florida A&M University, Tallahassee
Florida Atlantic University, Boca Raton
Florida Gulf Coast University, Ft. Myers
Florida International University, Miami
Florida State University, Tallahassee
New College of Florida, Sarasota
University of Central Florida, Orlando
University of Florida, Gainesville
University of North Florida, Jacksonville
University of South Florida, Tampa
University of West Florida, Pensacola

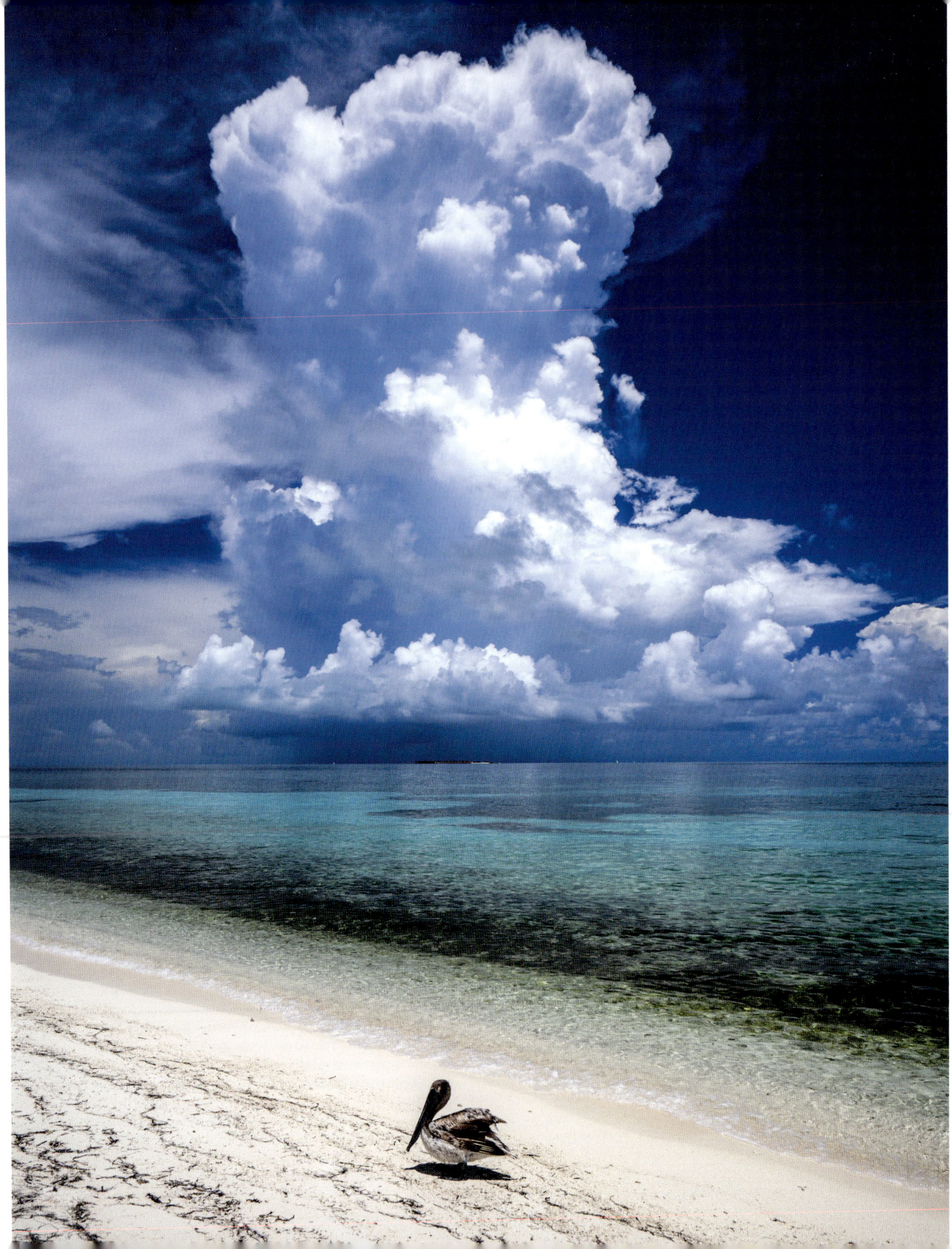

Dry Tortugas

Stronghold of Nature

Ian Wilson-Navarro

UNIVERSITY PRESS OF FLORIDA

Gainesville · Tallahassee · Tampa · Boca Raton
Pensacola · Orlando · Miami · Jacksonville · Ft. Myers · Sarasota

Funding for this publication was provided through a grant from Florida Humanities with funds from the National Endowment for the Humanities. Any views, findings, conclusions or recommendations expressed in this publication do not necessarily represent those of Florida Humanities or the National Endowment for the Humanities. As the non-profit, state affiliate of the National Endowment for the Humanities, Florida Humanities supports programs and resources that explore the history and culture of Florida and encourage a lifelong appreciation of literature, literacy, and learning.

Published in the United States of America. Printed in Korea.

29 28 27 26 25 24 6 5 4 3 2 1

Library of Congress Cataloging-in-Publication Data
Names: Wilson-Navarro, Ian, author.
Title: Dry Tortugas : stronghold of nature / Ian Wilson-Navarro.
Other titles: Stronghold of nature
Description: 1. | Gainesville : University Press of Florida, [2024]
Identifiers: LCCN 2024011355 | ISBN 9780813079127 (hardback)
Subjects: LCSH: Natural history—Florida—Dry Tortugas National Park. | Natural history—Florida—Florida Keys. | Fort Jefferson (Fla.)—Pictorial works. | Dry Tortugas National Park (Fla.)—History. | Florida Keys (Fla.)—History. | BISAC: PHOTOGRAPHY / Subjects & Themes / Regional (see also TRAVEL / Pictorials) | TRAVEL / Pictorials (see also PHOTOGRAPHY / Subjects & Themes / Regional)
Classification: LCC F319.F69 W55 2024 | DDC 508.759/41—dc23/eng/20240327
LC record available at https://lccn.loc.gov/2024011355

The University Press of Florida is the scholarly publishing agency for the State University System of Florida, comprising Florida A&M University, Florida Atlantic University, Florida Gulf Coast University, Florida International University, Florida State University, New College of Florida, University of Central Florida, University of Florida, University of North Florida, University of South Florida, and University of West Florida.

University Press of Florida
2046 NE Waldo Road
Suite 2100
Gainesville, FL 32609
http://upress.ufl.edu

To my mom and dad for encouraging me to pursue my passions,
for none of this would have been possible without them.

Thank you to the National Parks Arts Foundation for providing the initial opportunity to create work in this very special place. This book project would not have been possible if it weren't for being awarded their Dry Tortugas Artist Residency.

CONTENTS

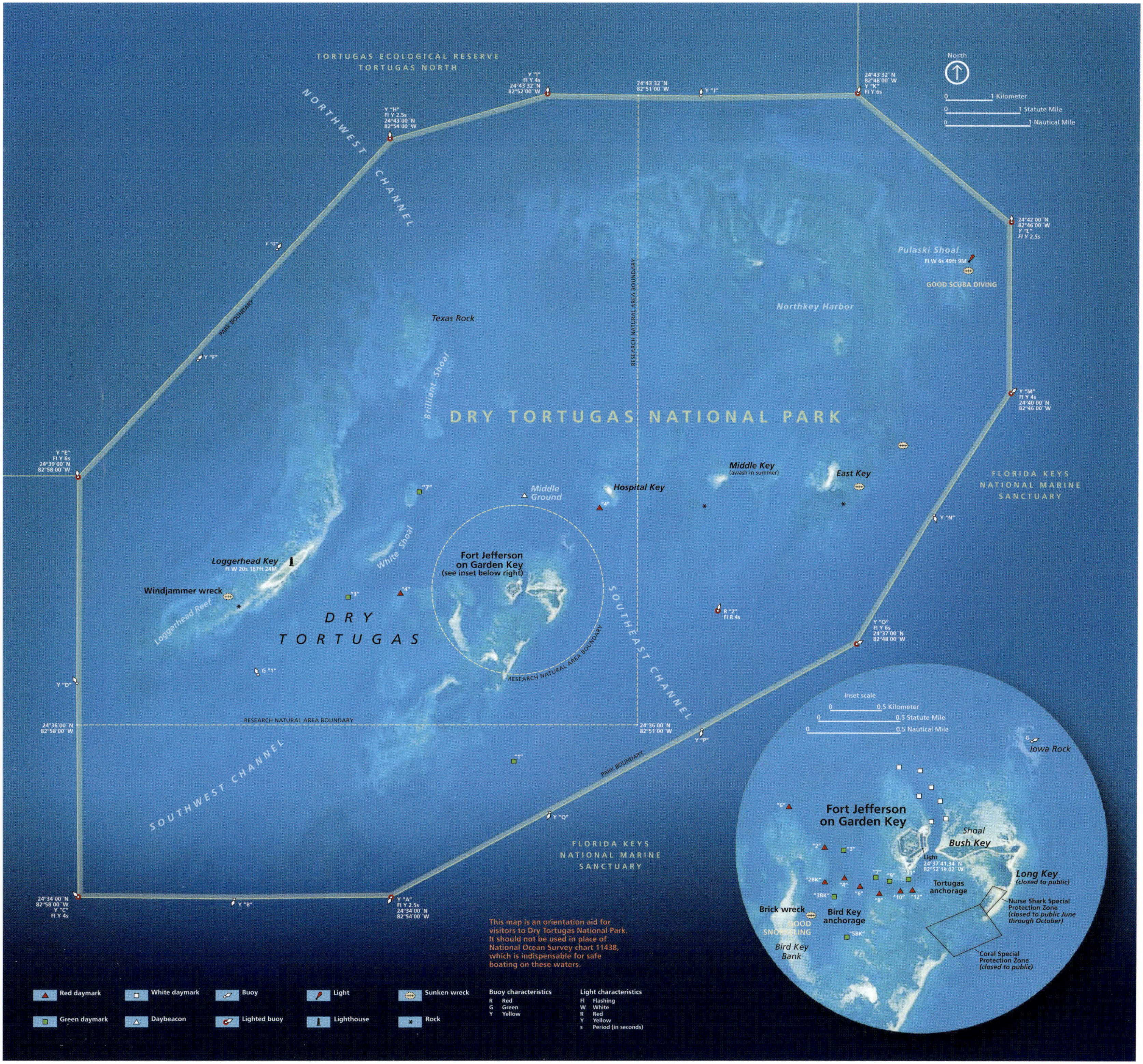

TORTUGAS ECOLOGICAL RESERVE
TORTUGAS NORTH
NORTHWEST CHANNEL
North
1 Kilometer
1 Statute Mile
1 Nautical Mile
Pulaski Shoal
GOOD SCUBA DIVING
Northkey Harbor
Texas Rock
Brilliant Shoal
RESEARCH NATURAL AREA BOUNDARY
PARK BOUNDARY
DRY TORTUGAS NATIONAL PARK
Middle Key
(awash in summer)
East Key
Hospital Key
Middle Ground
FLORIDA KEYS
NATIONAL MARINE
SANCTUARY
White Shoal
Loggerhead Key
Windjammer wreck
Loggerhead Reef
Fort Jefferson
on Garden Key
(see inset below right)
DRY
TORTUGAS
SOUTHEAST CHANNEL
SOUTHWEST CHANNEL
FLORIDA KEYS
NATIONAL MARINE
SANCTUARY
Inset scale
0.5 Kilometer
0.5 Statute Mile
0.5 Nautical Mile
Iowa Rock
Fort Jefferson
on Garden Key
Shoal
Bush Key
Long Key
(closed to public)
Tortugas
anchorage
Nurse Shark Special
Protection Zone
(closed to public June
through October)
Brick wreck
GOOD
SNORKELING
Bird Key
anchorage
Bird Key
Bank
Coral Special
Protection Zone
(closed to public)
This map is an orientation aid for
visitors to Dry Tortugas National Park.
It should not be used in place of
National Ocean Survey chart 11438,
which is indispensable for safe
boating on these waters.
Red daymark
White daymark
Buoy
Light
Sunken wreck
Green daymark
Daybeacon
Lighted buoy
Lighthouse
Rock
Buoy characteristics
R Red
G Green
Y Yellow
Light characteristics
Fl Flashing
W White
R Red
Y Yellow
s Period (in seconds)

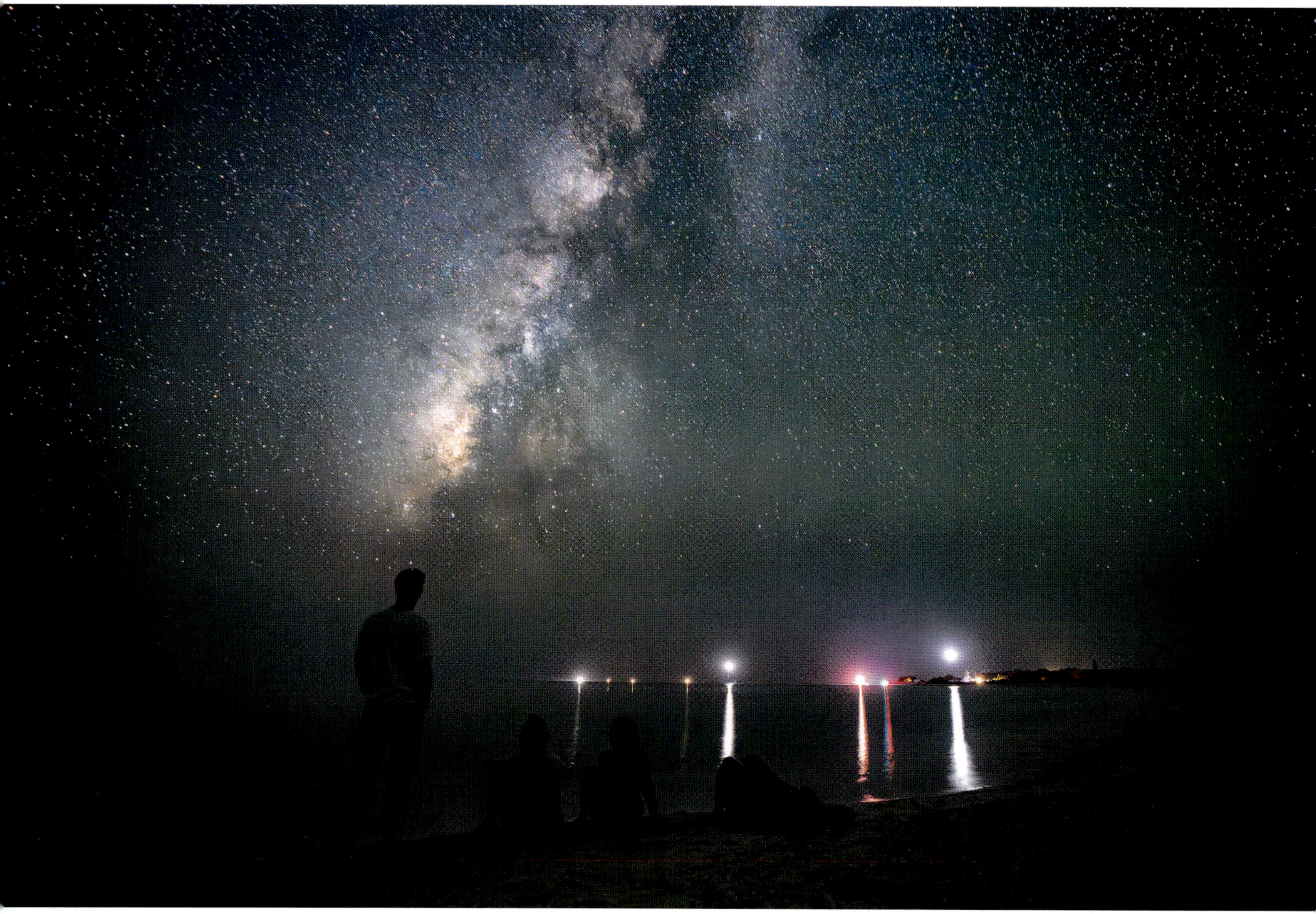

Introduction

IAN WILSON-NAVARRO

Florida Keys—where land and sea interlace to create a mosaic of ecosystems. This unique group of islands is my home and has shaped me into the person I am today. Born to a Nicaraguan mother and an American father, I was fortunate to grow up in a place where the beauty of nature seamlessly blended with diverse cultures and traditions.

Some of my earliest memories take me back to fishing off a dock in Key Largo, at the old bayside home my family used to rent. It became a hub of adventure and exploration for my brother and me. As kids, we spent endless hours casting our lines into the waters of Blackwater Sound, hoping to reel in a prized catch. Mangrove snapper, spotted sea trout, and the occasional tarpon were the rewards we sought. It was during those moments of anticipation and excitement that our deep and lasting connection with the ocean and its bountiful treasures was forged.

When people inquire about my upbringing in the Keys, I describe it as a quintessential small-town American experience, but with a twist. While we enjoyed the familiar aspects of suburban life such as playing sports and attending school dances, our weekends took on a distinctively different flavor. We would immerse ourselves in the waters, embracing the ecosystems that make the Florida Keys a true paradise.

I learned to snorkel among the vibrant corals of Molasses Reef and, together with my family, would venture far offshore to a place known as Floyd's Wall for thrilling fishing expeditions. We would kayak across the tranquil seagrass flats of John

Pennekamp State Park and often conclude our days at the Rodriguez Key sandbar. The Upper Keys became our playground, where nature served as both our teacher and our friend. It is a common statement among those who grew up in the Keys that they learned to drive a boat before they ever drove a car, and I can attest to the truth of this statement. We learned to navigate the waters, read the winds and tides, and adapt our plans according to the ever-changing weather conditions. These experiences fostered my deep respect for the environment and instilled in me a profound sense of gratitude for and harmony with the natural world.

Over time, I began to notice changes occurring in the Keys, changes similar to those marring other precious places. The stories told by older generations about what the region used to be like became a common refrain. I found myself becoming desensitized to these tales, hearing them repeatedly: "There weren't so many people"; "There were more fish"; and "The coral was everywhere." But as time went on, I started witnessing these differences firsthand. The baseline was shifting right before my eyes, subtly but clearly. It wasn't an overnight transformation, although at times it felt that way. To truly grasp the changes, one had to pay attention to day-to-day and month-to-month fluctuations. Slowly but surely, I noticed things that seemed amiss or were missing altogether.

During my high school years when I was learning to spearfish, I witnessed the average size of hogfish decrease. Soon after, the regulations changed, with the minimum size for keeping hogfish increasing from twelve to sixteen inches within the four years I attended Coral Shores High School. The short-spine sea urchins I used to find under rocks along the shoreline seemed to vanish overnight. And more recently, the stony corals, including the brain corals I cherished swimming over, are increasingly affected by the lethal stony coral tissue loss disease (SCTLD), which has reduced the populations to a point where some consider them functionally extinct. These unfortunate examples are just a few of many.

The disheartening truth is that I found myself falling more in love with a place each year while simultaneously becoming increasingly aware of its decline. The more I observed, the more I yearned for an opportunity to experience what the Keys might have looked like before my time, to understand what they were like before human influence left its mark. A time machine would be ideal: to travel back fifty years or, better yet, 1,000 years, to witness and learn from the Tequesta and Calusa Indians, the original inhabitants who lived in harmony with the ecosystem. One can only imagine what that existence might have been like and the resources they shared for thousands of uninterrupted years.

In August 2021, an opportunity presented itself. My friend Austin Armstrong and I were granted a unique artists' residency, allowing us to live off-grid in the Dry Tortugas National Park. I had visited this small archipelago, located seventy miles west of Key West, once before with my father, and I was aware of its enchanting seascapes and, compared with the rest of the Florida Keys, its relatively pristine ecosystems. This gave us the chance to reside on Loggerhead Key, the largest island in the archipelago, for a whole month, with the sole purpose of creating art inspired by the park's natural beauty, I as a photographer, Austin as a Gyotaku printmaker. Although not a time machine, it was the next best thing in our minds.

Austin and I wholeheartedly agree that our month on Loggerhead Key was one of the most profound experiences we have ever had. With usually only one or two other individuals on the island, typically natural resource employees working with the park, we had the pleasure of fully embracing its entirety. We would wake up at sunrise and often join their two-mile hike around the island to help survey the loggerhead and green sea turtle nests laid the night before. Depending on the weather, we would decide whether to snorkel the reefs just off the shoreline, the most famous being Little Africa, or take our small dinghy over to Garden Key, where fishing was permitted within a one-mile radius, in search of dinner and photo opportunities. One of our proudest achievements that month was supplementing half of our protein with fish we had caught ourselves, a testament to the health and abundance of the fishery in the national park.

Whenever we submerged ourselves in the water, we immediately noticed a substantial difference in the number and size of the fish. They were larger and more abundant than fish outside of protected areas. Mutton snapper, hogfish, spiny lobster—these charismatic species that grace menus throughout the Keys—were plentiful here, and it felt reassuring to know that they were completely protected in much of the park. Nearly 50 percent of the Dry Tortugas is off-limits to fishing, and even anchoring is prohibited in the quadrant surrounding Loggerhead Key.

As I write this, two years have passed since that residency, and I have returned to the park several times on separate occasions. I consider myself incredibly fortunate to have experienced this place on such an intimate level, given that most people only get to glimpse it for a brief window during the day.

Living, working, and photographing in the Dry Tortugas presents unique challenges. Its remote location limits access to the typical amenities found closer to the mainland. As a photographer primarily focused on an underwater national park, I relied on my life experiences to document this remarkable place as best as I could. Aside from a few shots, most of the photographs featured in this book were captured through human-powered energy. I had to rely solely on my own two feet as I hiked the islands and often found myself floating in a kayak, covering an average of ten miles a day, or diving beneath the ocean surface on a single breath of air in search of subjects worth documenting. Traveling light was a necessity. Sometimes getting dinner had to take priority over capturing the perfect shot. Despite these challenges, I wouldn't change a thing. Even as I jot down these notes, floating in my kayak just off the front of Fort Jefferson, I am reminded of the moments when I hesitated to capture an image without a reliable dive buddy by my side, partly due to the presence of the healthy and very curious shark population found here. This park allowed me to discover more about myself, my capabilities, and sometimes my limitations, than any other experience thus far in my life.

Time spent in the Dry Tortugas is always liberating. I find myself laughing often, embracing a life free from the digital handcuffs of the modern world. I have had the privilege of sharing stories with people from all over the world, forming connections that transcend language and cultural barriers. And as the night sky unfolds above us, we gather under the canopy of the Milky Way, sipping rum and immersing ourselves in the sheer wonder of the universe.

In a world where nature is increasingly threatened, it is vital to raise awareness about the fragility of our ecosystems. The Florida Keys, despite their allure and natural abundance, are not immune to the challenges posed by human impacts and environmental degradation. It is my mission to document the changing landscape, the struggles faced by our reefs and fisheries, and the urgent need for conservation. Through my photographs, I hope to contribute to the collective efforts of preserving this extraordinary ecosystem.

My upbringing in the Florida Keys has left indelible impressions on my life, heart, and artistic endeavors. I have learned not to take their wonders and beauty for granted. The experiences I have accumulated here have fueled my passions for photography and conservation. I am immensely grateful to have been raised in a place where the natural world is not just a backdrop to, but an integral part of, our lives. In my love for the Florida Keys, I have found my calling: to capture their beauty, vulnerability, and resilience through my photographs, hopefully inspiring others to join in efforts to protect and preserve these extraordinary and pristine ecosystems so that their splendor endures for generations to come.

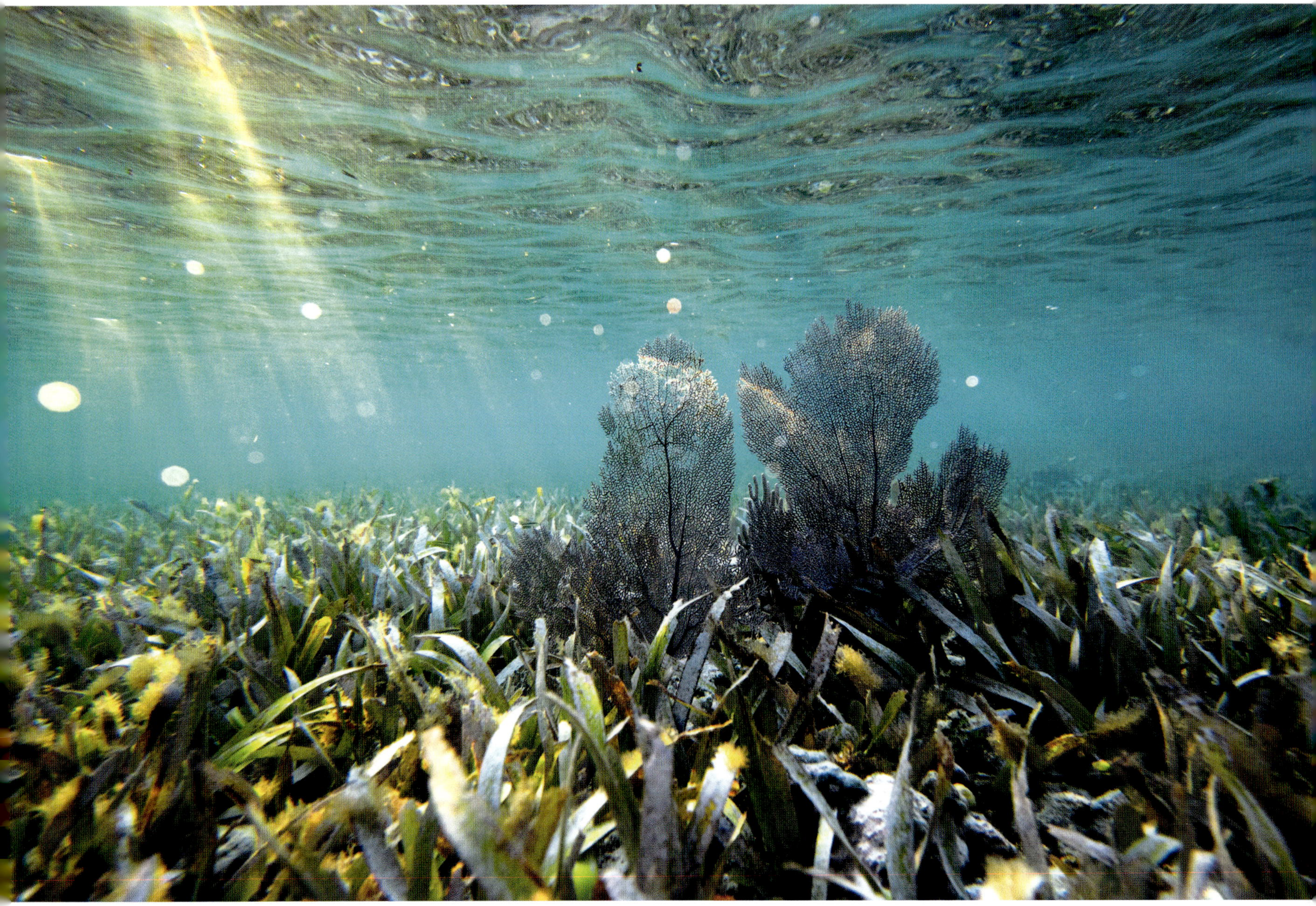

1

Interconnectivity

Sanctuary, Park, Reserves

SARAH FANGMAN

The first time I laid eyes on Dry Tortugas National Park was in 2006 from the deck of the 180-foot NOAA research vessel *Nancy Foster,* when I was on board serving as dive master for two weeks of coral research. After ten days of intense operations, our commanding officer, inspired by the beauty of the setting, dropped anchor and called for shore leave. As chefs prepared a barbecue meal on deck, the crew launched a tender boat, and we explored the waters around the fort—a magical memory shared by all who have had the privilege of making port at Garden Key.

Today, my privilege is leading a team that works closely with the National Park Service to maintain the legacy of Dry Tortugas through professional disciplines that range from science and education to buoy maintenance and facilities operations. It is always a good day when I see the Dry Tortugas tender *Fort Jefferson* at our sanctuary pier, restocking supplies for park service staff who live there full-time.

As a technicality, the park is not part of NOAA's Florida Keys National Marine Sanctuary. Its perimeter resembles a doughnut hole at the western end of our 3,800 square-mile boundary, a man-made demarcation unrecognized by sea life that transits freely between. In science, this intersection of domains is called interconnectivity, and it is no accident that waters inside and outside the park's boundary are protected by two federal jurisdictions.

The deep coral reefs of the Tortugas are the crown jewel of Florida Keys National Marine Sanctuary, healthier and more abundant than anywhere else in the Florida Keys. The remoteness of the Dry Tortugas has allowed habitats there to remain healthier than in similar environments, primarily because they are so lightly used.

Accessible only by boat or seaplane, Dry Tortugas is among the least visited sites in the national park system. Yet, this remoteness places it at the headwater of the entire Florida Keys, an upstream barometer and incubator.

The region is a hot spot for biodiversity, and many of the ecologically and economically important species reproduce there before their larvae are carried by water currents to the Florida Keys and southeast Florida, helping maintain populations of these key species throughout Florida's coral reef. The reverse is also true, as these same currents bring larvae of fish and other creatures to the Tortugas from both the Gulf of Mexico and the Caribbean Sea.

Clean, clear water and powerful ocean currents fuel the diversity of life in the region, and more than four hundred species of reef fish inhabit the region, including all species of grouper. Research suggests some tuna species may use the Tortugas as a spawning ground, and about forty species of sharks pass through the region. Between the park service and sanctuary, ours is a shared responsibility for protecting key resources vital to the economic and environmental future of the region.

Bordering the national park boundary is an area in the sanctuary called Tortugas North Ecological Reserve. Nearby is Tortugas South Ecological Reserve. These zones, embracing more than 180 square miles combined, are managed by the sanctuary with special regulations for protecting diverse habitats, including seagrass beds, coral reef habitats, and hard-bottom areas.

By designating these areas as ecological reserves, the sanctuary prohibits fishing or harvesting of marine life by any means. Anchoring, touching, or standing on corals is also prohibited, and even transiting the areas by boat may require a permit. More than twenty years now after these regulations went into effect, their establishment has proven worthy of the original design, and the benefits spill over into the park.

A scientific study examining how these ecological reserves affect both the marine life of the region and the people whose livelihoods depend on them found that overfished species such as black and red grouper and yellowtail and mutton snapper increased in presence, abundance, and size inside the reserve and throughout the entire region, including the Dry Tortugas National Park. Spawning aggregations of commercially valuable species that had been depleted outside the reserve began to reform inside the reserve. Downstream, commercial catches of reef fish in the region increased. By establishing protected areas, marine reserves and economically viable fishing industries can coexist, as the health of our economy is tied to the health of our oceans.

Federal protections were also required to save the region's namesake turtles, which were decimated by commercial fishing in the late 1800s and early 1900s. Of the seven turtle species protected under the U.S. Endangered Species Act (which turned fifty years old in 2023), five are native to our waters: hawksbill, green, loggerhead, leatherback, and Kemp's Ridley. While these turtles are now protected from capture, we must remain ever vigilant on their behalf. The sanctuary is proposing to expand protections of some nesting areas that beckon females to return year after year, like a lighthouse showing the way home. Florida Keys National Marine Sanctuary, recognizing the importance of these reptiles to our region, has commissioned two of our work vessels, *Leatherback* and *Hawksbill,* the latter drawing attention to a species that is among the top ten most endangered in the world. Because these turtles utilize park and sanctuary waters, protections in one area benefit the other, reinforcing why our shared efforts are so important.

Part of the sanctuary's mandate is to preserve maritime resources, defined as anything of historical, cultural, archaeological, or paleontological significance greater than fifty years old. The majority of these resources remain undiscovered, primarily because time has rendered them part of the natural seascape, and they do not look as we expect them to appear. Not far from the park lies an underwater history as rich as the fort itself, including the watery graves of ships that sank during World Wars I and II.

The guiding principle of maritime heritage is to "take only pictures, leave only bubbles," and it is wise advice, indeed, for visitors who may happen upon historical resources. The recent discovery of burial sites from the Dry Tortugas hospital island, now underwater, is a modern-day example of just how much of our past remains to be rediscovered.

The Florida Keys of today are a chain of fossilized coral reefs more than 100,000 years old. From just south of Miami, extending west to Dry Tortugas, these remnants are a reminder of the self-renewing power of nature. Through federal agencies like NOAA's Office of National Marine Sanctuaries and the National Park Service, humankind has assumed a share of responsibility for preserving the Keys ecosystem, so that future generations of scientists, divers, snorkelers, fishers, and boaters can experience the same sense of wonder and joy that fell over me from the deck of the *Nancy Foster* so many years ago.

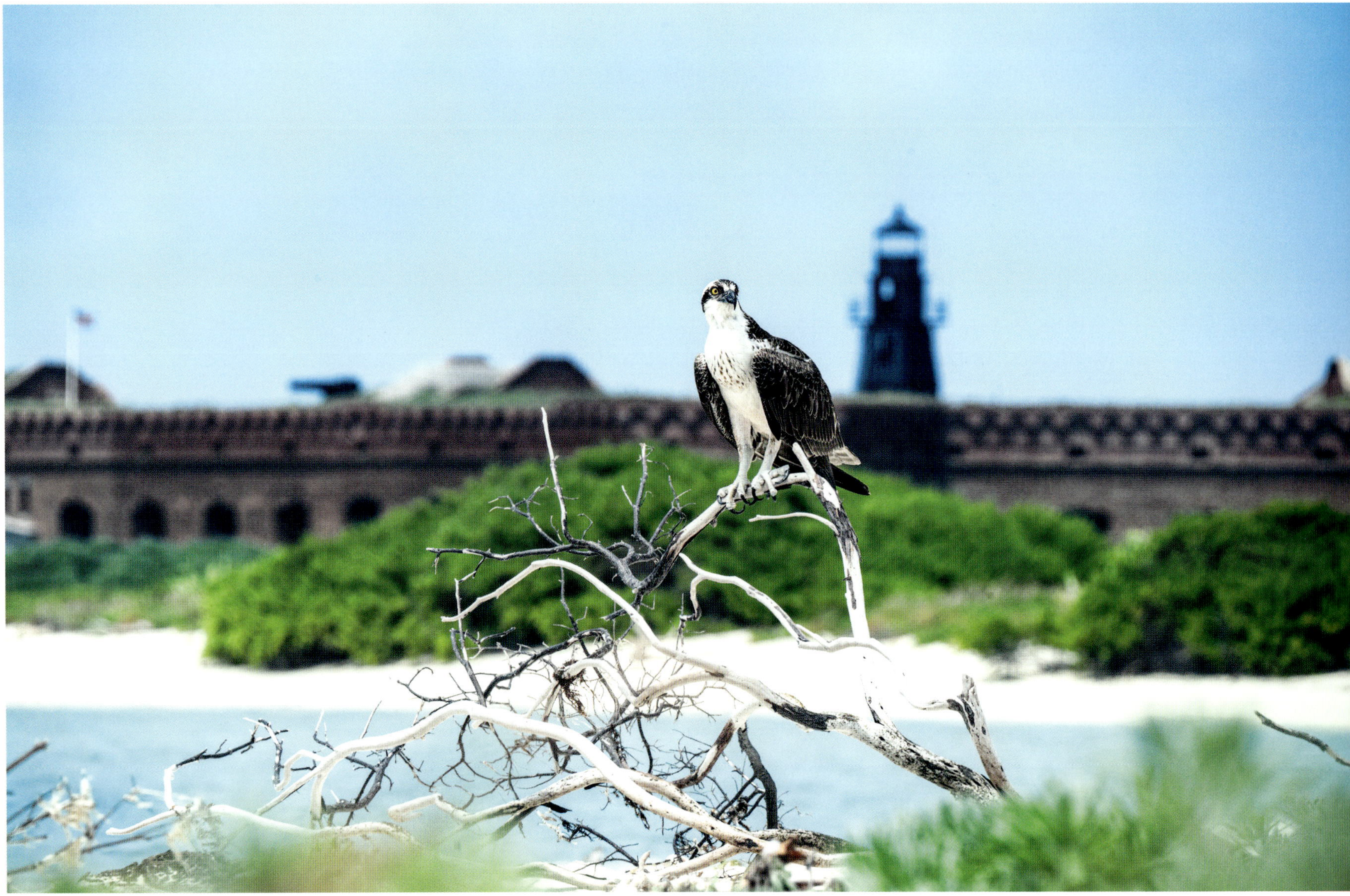

2

The Gibraltar of America

A Short History of the Dry Tortugas

CORI CONVERTITO

The islands and surrounding waters of Dry Tortugas National Park are an enchanted place with a rich, storied history. Lying at the entrance to the Gulf of Mexico and on vital shipping lanes, the unassuming islands figure prominently in several chapters in the history of the fledgling United States. Remote as the islands are, they were nevertheless advantageous to a range of mariners including Native Americans, West Indies pirates, Bahamian and New England fishermen, army and navy personnel, Key West shrimpers and wreckers, and global adventurers.

Geographically, the islands and the patch reef that surrounds them are the westernmost segments of the Florida Keys, positioned roughly sixty-eight miles to the west of Key West. The islands are near the southwestern edge of the Florida Platform, a plateau on which the landmass of Florida is perched. Fluctuations in sea level across many geological eras meant that, for a time, the Dry Tortugas were fully above water and formed part of the Florida landmass. When sea level reached its current position, much of the land was covered by water, leaving visible a string of islands that we now know as the Florida Keys.

Native Americans were likely the first peoples to use the Dry Tortugas steadily for fishing and foraging. Multiple tribes of Indigenous people—including the Tequestas, Calusas, and Seminoles—visited the islands to catch turtles, fish, and lobster. They utilized the shells of conchs as shovels, weapons, and other functional tools. The absence of natural fresh water, however, made permanent settlement unachievable.

The relatively undisturbed islands would evolve with the arrival of European explorers, beginning with Juan Ponce de León in 1513. Serving as governor of the eastern province of Hispaniola on behalf of the Spanish government, Ponce de León explored the present-day island of Puerto Rico in pursuit of gold. Encouraged further by the Spanish Crown, Ponce de León landed near what is now St. Augustine and explored the peninsula's coastline, although he mistakenly believed that the landmass was an island. His coastal survey included the Florida Keys archipelago.

From a distance, the chain of the Florida Keys reminded Ponce de León of men who were suffering, so he named them Los Mártires (the Martyrs). He and his expedition reached the Dry Tortugas on June 21st and claimed the islands for the Spanish Empire. There they captured giant sea turtles, Caribbean monk seals, and hundreds of seabirds. Ponce de León and his shipmates named the group of islands Las Tortugas, "the turtles" in Spanish, referencing the throngs of sea turtles they harvested in the area to sustain them during their voyage.

Ponce de León is also credited with identifying the Gulf Stream, a powerful natural force that could propel ships from the West Indies toward Europe. News of the Gulf Stream quickly circulated among colonists and merchants in the West Indies and Europe, as did information on the bountiful provisions accessible in Las Tortugas. Spanish explorers heeded Ponce de León's testimonials and began using the islands as a strategic location when traveling along Florida's Gulf Coast. Because the islands were nestled between the Gulf of Mexico and the Atlantic Ocean, the Spanish considered the Dry Tortugas an essential navigational marker that indicated when their vessels should begin turning toward the Gulf Coast. The nearest city to the Tortugas was Havana, reinforcing the Spanish claim in the region. Cuban mariners frequented the area to catch fish, hunt turtles and birds, and trade with Indigenous peoples, conveying all goods to the Havana market.

The Spanish were not alone in colonizing the Americas. The British, French, and Portuguese were likewise eager to seize settlements. The Florida Straits and the Dry Tortugas became heavily trafficked by ships carrying goods to and from the New World. It was these explorers and merchants who, realizing that the islands lacked fresh drinking water, changed their name to the "Dry" Tortugas to reflect this deficit.

As maritime traffic increased, so did the number of pirates who hoped to capture merchant ships transporting lucrative cargo. They, too, made use of the strategic location and resources that the Dry Tortugas afforded. The majority of pirates in the eighteenth and nineteenth centuries enjoyed haven in Cuba and Hispaniola, not far from the Dry Tortugas. Lying in wait for ships to use the Gulf Stream, pirates in their shallow drafted vessels were able to make chase from the remote location. But the lack of fresh water that had distressed explorers also precluded any hope for a permanent pirate retreat.

Remarkable changes were afoot for the Dry Tortugas when the United States formally acquired Florida from Spain in 1821 with the ratification of the Adams-Onis Treaty. Once the peninsula, including the Florida Keys, was counted as American soil, the federal government deemed it prudent to fortify the islands and to mark their location along the Florida Reef with a series of lighthouses. Congress appropriated money to erect lighthouses in the Dry Tortugas—one on Garden Key in 1825 (with a replacement in 1858) and another, more powerful lighthouse at Loggerhead Key in 1858. Multiple lighthouses were intended to aid vessels navigating the reef and the Florida Straits.

The U.S. military likewise recognized the geographic significance of the Dry Tortugas, specifically the natural deepwater anchorage that could benefit the country's expanding Navy. U.S. Naval Lieutenant Josiah Tattnall, who surveyed the islands in 1829, pointed out that any nation occupying the Tortugas would control navigation in the Gulf of Mexico. Following the maritime difficulties experienced with the British during the War of 1812, the United States was determined not to be vulnerable to sea attacks. Large-scale brick fortifications erected around America's coasts offered protection for strategic shipping channels against foreign attack and provided operations headquarters and training facilities to all branches of the military.

Accordingly, Congress appropriated over $800,000 for this ambitious seacoast defensive system, a plan referred to as the Third Tier System that lasted from 1816 to 1867. Third System forts were large structures with myriad guns concentrated in tall, thick masonry walls. By the completion of the Third System in 1867, forty-two forts safeguarded all major harbors along America's coastlines. This included an immense fortification on Garden Key in the Dry Tortugas.

In 1846, the U.S. Army Corps of Engineers initiated construction on Fort Jefferson, named in honor of America's third president. Construction plans made it the largest fort in the country's coastal defense system. The edifice's great size was necessary to support all the cannons, ammunition, personnel, material, water, and food needed to withstand a protracted naval siege, seeing as reinforcements would not be readily available. Lieutenant Horatio G. Wright, the fort's first construction engineer, laid out the lines of a hexagonal structure with walls standing fifty feet high and eight feet thick. It was designed for 450 guns in three tiers and expansive enough to garrison 1,500 soldiers. Over 16 million bricks went into the construction of Fort Jefferson. The original tan bricks on the lower two tiers came from brickyards near Pensacola before Florida seceded from the Union during the Civil War. After Florida left the Union in 1861, the red bricks along the top of the fort's walls were shipped from Maine, a distance of nearly 2,000 miles.

As it had done during the construction of other forts, the Army Corps of Engineers relied heavily on the use of enslaved laborers to erect the edifice. Key West residents immediately rented out their slaves as fort-construction laborers at a cost of $1.12 a day—a fee that was paid directly to the slaveowner.

Building progress was slow. Cargoes bound for the site were lost when the ships carrying them were wrecked on the reefs; hundreds of the enslaved and free laborers who were working on the fort died of disease or sunstroke; and at one point, what little work had been accomplished was wiped out by a powerful hurricane. By the time the Civil War commenced, work on the three-quarter-mile ring of brick was only partially completed.

On January 18, 1861, news arrived at Fort Jefferson that Florida had seceded. The strong federal presence in the Dry Tortugas destined the islands to remain under Union control for the duration of the conflict. Troops occupied the garrison throughout the Civil War, but beyond a few shots at passing Confederate blockade-runners, soldiers saw no action. Rather, Fort Jefferson saw usefulness as a military prison, chiefly for captured Union deserters.

Following the Civil War, construction efforts continued, with particular attention given to the completion of the officers' quarters and barracks. However, the invention of the rifled cannon during the war had rendered Fort Jefferson (like almost all masonry forts), practically obsolete as a bastion, as its thick walls could now be penetrated by this advanced weaponry. By 1888, the military usefulness of the structure had waned, and the cost of maintaining it, as a result of frequent hurricane damage and the corrosive and debilitating tropical climate, could no longer be justified. That year, the U.S. Army turned the fortification over to the Marine Hospital Service to be managed as a quarantine station.

The Dry Tortugas achieved renewed importance during the Spanish-American War, where the greater part of the fighting took place in and around Cuba. American seamen were treated for injury and illness at the makeshift hospital, but no structural or armament upgrades were undertaken. The U.S. Navy did, however, fabricate a coaling station on Garden Key, as its proximity to Cuba offered a distinct maritime advantage in supporting the war effort. Its coaling station included piers, docks, conveyor belts, and large coal sheds. Many of these relics are still visible today.

When a strong hurricane struck the Dry Tortugas in October 1910, it damaged Fort Jefferson so severely that the decision was made to effectively relinquish control of the structure and the surrounding islands. Even the coaling station was abandoned by the military, and any items of value were removed from the site. Only a few people remained in the Dry Tortugas, one of whom was the lighthouse keeper responsible for lights at both Garden Key and Loggerhead Key.

The desertion of the islands by the military only enhanced the area's allure for mariners, fishermen, and Key West residents. Many frequented the area in search of tranquility, to gather provisions, pursue scientific investigations, and enjoy exploration. A recurring visitor in the 1930s was famed author and Key West resident Ernest Hemingway, who sailed his boat the *Pilar* to the Dry Tortugas and Garden Key in search of game fish. Birdwatchers and hunters also found the islands a lively center for research and observation during migration periods. Nesting seabirds received attention from President Theodore Roosevelt who, in 1908, declared the Dry Tortugas a bird reserve with the purpose of protecting the birds and their eggs from hunters and poachers. A quarter century later, Franklin Roosevelt, who had visited the islands prior to being elected president, set aside Fort Jefferson as a national monument in 1935. The monument was expanded in 1983 to encompass not just the garrison but also the surrounding islands. Eventually, in 1992, the monument was officially redesignated as Dry Tortugas National Park by an act of Congress.

Since 1935, the National Park Service has been dedicated to preserving the Dry Tortugas for the enjoyment of visitors, who are fascinated by the region's incredible history, culture, wildlife, and ecology. Today's visitors to the Dry Tortugas National Park encounter tremendous diversity in its combination of historic structures, bountiful patch reefs, picturesque low-lying islands, fascinating wildlife, and an unmitigated tranquility that exists few other places on earth.

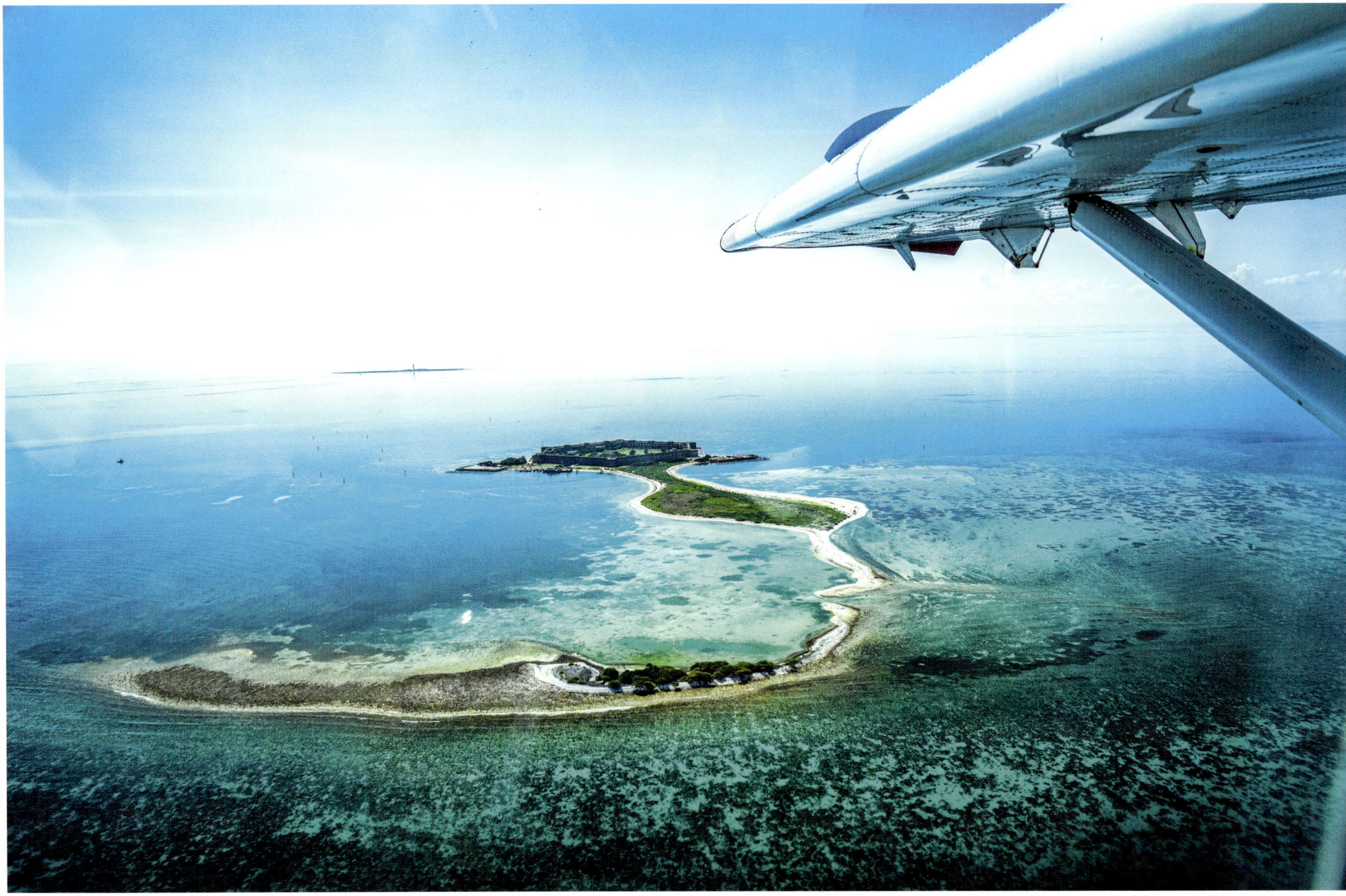

3

Nexus

This Place of Many Meanings

CURTIS HALL

The Tortugas are identified by one of our nation's oldest place-names. Over five centuries of recorded history, since Ponce de León's 1513 arrival, and even further back into prehistory with the islands' Indigenous peoples, the Tortugas have been many things to different generations of visitors. Places of shelter, provision, struggle, demise, and perseverance. Places of defense, imprisonment, research, freedom, and recreation. A UNESCO International Biosphere Reserve, a national monument, and one of the Florida Keys original tourist attractions. The Tortugas are positioned at a nexus of open ocean currents and provide a confluence of early human history, natural resources, and scientific discoveries at America's most remote national park in the contiguous United States.

Dry Tortugas National Park (DTNP) is a true marine park with nearly 98 percent of the park submerged beneath the beautiful azure waters of the Atlantic, Gulf of Mexico, and Caribbean ecosystems. Terrestrial features make up just over 1 percent of the park, but the geomorphology of the islands is constantly shifting. Islands break apart and re-form or make new ones depending on strong storms and currents. Rising sea level has claimed a few islands.

The shallow water and perilous reefs surrounding the islands are also home to over three hundred historic shipwrecks. In 1742, the British ship HMS *Tyger* ran aground on the reefs of the Tortugas while attempting to blockade and intercept Spanish ships departing from Cuba. The crew quickly fortified Garden Key with shipboard artillery to defend against Spanish foes. Thus, the Tortugas could mean simultaneously sustenance or death for early mariners.

In the nineteenth century on Garden Key, life at Union-controlled Fort Jefferson in the southernmost part of the United States was challenging. Supplies needed to build Fort Jefferson and nourish soldiers came from northern states and could take months to arrive. Often, food was rotten or spoiled by the time it reached the Tortugas. Shallow coral reefs located in the middle of open oceans provided a strategic advantage to fortify defensive positions in the Tortugas. However, many ships full of supplies, also ran aground on those reefs within view of the fort. Over 80 percent of soldiers and prisoners were also hospitalized there during the 1860s and '70s. Many soldiers and laborers succumbed to illnesses and were laid to rest on islands surrounding Garden Key. In the fall of 2022, National Park archeologists discovered structural remains of a submerged hospital and a nearby headstone for day laborer John Greer. This active archeological site has led to additional discoveries, confirming that shipwrecks are not the only thing claimed by the sea in the Tortugas.

The most complete shipwreck in the park is the historical Norwegian ship *Avanti.* This three-masted windjammer-class sailing ship was nearly the size of a football field, and in January 1907 it ran aground on reefs surrounding Loggerhead Key in the early morning hours during a fierce winter storm. The *Avanti* was born during a transitional period in shipbuilding history. Shipbuilders had switched from wooden to iron hulls but had not yet moved from sails to steam propulsion. With its iron hull and trio of masts, *Avanti*'s construction embodied this transitional phase. Little remains of hundreds of history's wooden sailing ships that came to rest in the Tortugas, but the *Avanti*'s story differs. Corals need a hard substrate, such as a large iron hull, on which to establish a home and grow. Not only did the *Avanti* run aground on a vibrant coral reef, but, by becoming herself a platform for the reef to expand on, she has become a historico-cultural ecosystem over a century of natural marine processes. Divers and snorkelers can observe corals from horizontal and vertical perspectives at this wreck. The Windjammer Reef site is in twenty feet of seawater, and the bow section of the *Avanti* transitions from the seafloor to the surface, providing homes for hundreds of iconic subtropical marine species.

People often ask whether shipwrecks in the park contain treasures. The true treasure of historic shipwrecks lies not in precious metals or stones but rather in connecting us with centuries-old maritime history, human struggle and perseverance, and beautiful submerged resources. Having places in our national parks to experience a convergence of amazing cultural and natural resources is something to be treasured. In that regard, yes, shipwrecks in the Tortugas all contain treasures of the past for the enjoyment of present and future generations.

The origins of scientific research and discovery in the Tortugas predate the Civil War. In 1851, noted Harvard biologist Louis Agassiz conducted undersea coral reef mapping to identify hazards for commerce. Louis and Alexandra Agassiz, early pioneers in oceanography, inspired a young prodigy named Alfred Mayer. Mayer wanted to establish a marine laboratory in the United States to rival research being conducted in Europe. In the early 1900s he petitioned the Carnegie Institute in Washington to fund marine biology in the Tortugas, and in 1904 the first tropical marine biology laboratory in the United States was established on Loggerhead Key. The Carnegie-Tortugas Marine Lab operated for over thirty years during a foundational period of innovative natural science. Over two hundred research *Papers from the Tortugas Laboratory* (as the multivolume series is called) were published, and many are still referenced by scientists today. If you enjoy the underwater photographs in this book, they too have historic connections to discovery in the Tortugas. In 1927 the first underwater color photograph was taken and published by researchers at the Carnegie-Tortugas Marine Lab.

Modern science at the park is often conducted through collaborations with other federal, state, and nongovernmental organizations. DTNP is currently home to the longest ongoing shark research in history. Wes Pratt and a team of researchers led by Nick Whitney have been tagging and monitoring nurse sharks at the Tortugas for over thirty-three years while publishing scientific papers on their work. USGS (United States Geological Survey) has a biology team led by Kristen Hart, who maintains a field site at DTNP. Hart's group conducts significant turtle research, which helps park supervisors develop effective management strategies for endangered sea turtle species. USGS's Isla Kuffner is conducting multiple studies on endangered elkhorn corals at the park. Most recently, she and a team of researchers employed new strategies for mitigating the effects of coral bleaching and for preserving impacted species. The Florida Fish and Wildlife Conservation Commission (FWC) is also currently conducting the most comprehensive study on hogfish to date. Florida International University maintains a seagrass monitoring program, and Duke University has been tagging and conducting bird research in the Dry Tortugas for over a decade.

Revered as one of the great ornithological wonders of the world, the Dry Tortugas have long been a destination for naturalists, including John James Audubon, who spent time here in 1832. Historically, the Dry Tortugas are home to the only colony of masked booby birds in the United States and site of the nation's largest annual rookery for magnificent frigatebirds. Geography places the Tortugas in both the Atlantic and Mississippi flyways, making the islands a mecca for migratory species and a delight for bird-watchers. Annually, between February and September, visitors can witness more than 80,000 sooty terns and brown noddies as they roost in their breeding grounds. Once sooty terns fledge and leave the nest, they fly continuously for the rest of their lives until returning to the Tortugas to mate, nest, and once again touch land after traveling there from as far away as the west coast of Africa. Given the Tortugas' abundant avian species in relation to their scant landmass, it is little wonder that birds were the first of the Tortugas' animals to receive federal protections from President Theodore Roosevelt in 1908.

Historically, the Dry Tortugas have been places of tragedy, perseverance, recovery, discovery, and freedom. Although times and circumstances have changed, these verities from past centuries recur today. In September 2022, the Dry Tortugas were directly impacted by the powerful category 4 Hurricane Ian—a catastrophe resulting in critical infrastructure damage that will take years to repair. Less than one month later, the Dry Tortugas became a key destination for Cuban migrants seeking asylum from rapidly deteriorating socioeconomic conditions in their own country. On New Year's Day 2023, seeking freedom through an unauthorized form of immigration, migrants landing at the Tortugas exceeded all the park's capacities and resources. Sheer numbers of migrants forced an immediate closure of the park—a first in our history—but the situation also affirmed modern connections to the Tortugas' past as a place of refuge and survival.

Though facing challenges, many of the park's natural resources remain resilient. Hurricane Ian decimated Long Key and the slow-growing black mangroves, home of magnificent frigatebirds. Many frigatebirds sought new habitats in the Marquesas Keys, then later returned to Long Key for breeding season. Coral disease, aggravated by the hottest ocean temperatures in recorded history, has brought about coral bleaching, mortality, and shifting reef conditions with new species of hydroids and macro-algae, which can deprive corals of a vital food-synthesis source: sunshine. Year after year, we are seeing an increase in plastic waste washing up onto sensitive habitats in the Tortugas, and microplastics in the marine environment have negative impacts on sea turtles and fish. Even so, in August 2023, with a few weeks still remaining in nesting season, researchers recorded the highest number of turtle nests in the history of the park. Nature is resilient, especially if we aid in recovery, minimize our negative impacts, and create young stewards for these special places.

It bears saying again: the Tortugas have been many different things to generations of people over many centuries. Experiencing the Tortugas creates a sense of going back to a time when fish were larger and more abundant, corals more vibrant, and things built to last. I invite you to slow down and see the Tortugas not only with your eyes, but also with your imagination. The Tortugas can be magical. I began visiting the Dry Tortugas as a young child with my father, and I've now had the opportunity to work there for nearly a decade. Among the struggles that accompany efforts to preserve the Tortugas, I still experience numerous moments of unimaginable awe. For instance, in August 2023, dinoflagellates (motile single-celled algae) accumulating in the moat around Fort Jefferson, when disturbed, produced bioluminescence. On one particularly clear night, new moon conditions transformed the moat into a reflection pool for the Milky Way galaxy. While sharing the sight with a colleague, we got into a lighthearted debate about which lights in the moat were reflected stars and which were bioluminescent fish trails. We both stopped to laugh at the context of our debate and agreed—all argument aside—that the moment itself simply couldn't get any better. Later that same night, as we sat on the beach, loggerhead hatchlings began to emerge from their nests. As the hatchlings made their way into the water they, too, fluoresced with bioluminescence. Just when you think it can't get any better, a glowing baby sea turtle comes along to broaden your perspective.

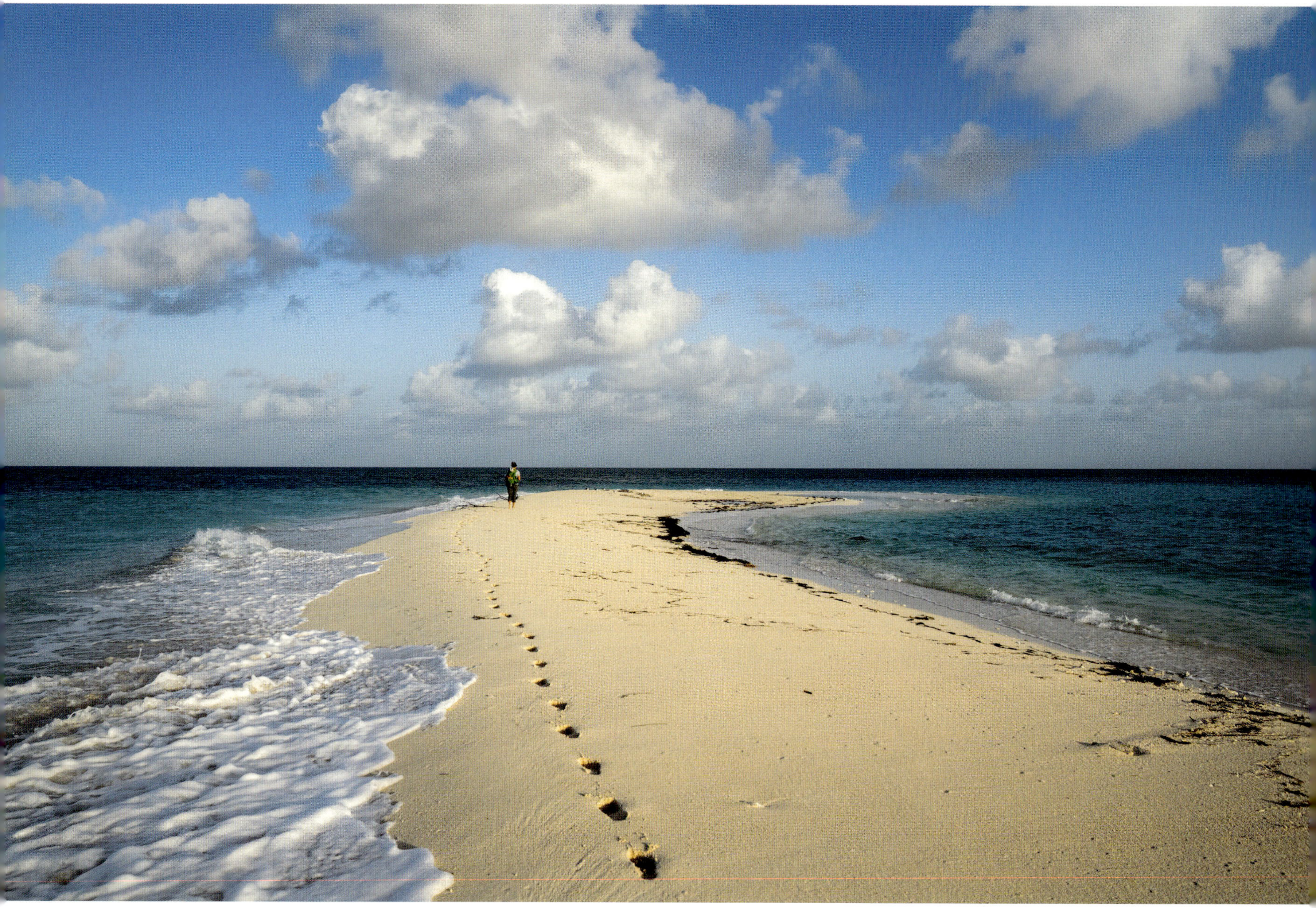

4

Tortugas

The Florida Keys' Keys

NANCY KLINGENER

The Keys are Florida distilled. All the challenges facing the state happen there first. A small landmass, fragile ecosystems, and high demand make for a great tourism destination but a tough place to live. There's almost no affordable housing. Pollution leaches out into nearshore waters, because nowhere is far from shore. Some of our several dozen endangered species, like the Key deer, can be found no place else on the planet and are surviving on a couple square miles. It's one of the most vulnerable spots in the nation to sea level rise, so we're starting to see sunny-day flooding during king tides. Looked at closely, living in the Keys is preposterous. We pipe in all our fresh water 150 miles from the mainland. We truck out all our garbage and recycling. We get our power from the mainland via a tie-line. We rely on a single highway, whether we're going to the grocery store or to Miami. We insist on living in the bullseye of the Atlantic hurricane zone, where the highest ground is less than twenty feet above sea level, and the storms can come at us from the Atlantic or the Caribbean or the Gulf of Mexico.

If the Keys are the preposterous Cassandra-land of Florida, the Tortugas are the ultimate expression of that, the highest-proof distillation of a place that likes its booze. Navigators put "Dry" on the name of the islands to let everyone know there was no fresh water. It's hot and salty, and there's even less freeboard than the rest of the Keys. Some of the islands shape-shift on a regular basis, rearranged by storms and currents or disappearing entirely. Archaeologists recently identified a cemetery that is now underwater. In less than two hundred years, the gravestones have been submerged like a subtropical Atlantis.

Its strategic location at the mouth of the Gulf of Mexico, spitting distance from the Caribbean, is obvious. You can see why a young United States, bolstering its coastline while expanding its interior, would want to stake its claim. Still, Fort Jefferson looks like a mirage every time you approach it. It doesn't seem possible that humans created this massive structure, essentially by hand.

I first visited the Tortugas in 1991; it took five hours to get to the park because there was not yet regular ferry service. We traveled via one of the party fishing boats booked by the Mudd family. It was part family reunion, part publicity event in the family's long-running quest to clear the name of Fort Jefferson's most famous prisoner, Dr. Samuel Mudd. I was a young newspaper reporter, recently assigned to the Keys bureau, and this kind of story was one of the best benefits of the job. Dr. Mudd's grandson, ninety-year-old Richard Mudd, was on the trip, and I took a melancholy photo of him looking out the window of Dr. Mudd's cell. Mudd was imprisoned at Fort Jefferson in 1865 after he was convicted as a conspirator in the assassination of President Abraham Lincoln. Dr. Mudd set the broken leg of John Wilkes Booth, who had injured himself jumping from Lincoln's box to the stage after shooting the president. Mudd was initially sentenced to life, but President Andrew Johnson pardoned and released him in 1869. Despite appeals to the Army (Mudd was convicted by a military tribunal) and the federal courts, the original conviction stands.

As focused as I was on the story, I was blown away by the beauty of the gigantic brick fort and its parklike interior, as well as by the idea of getting 16 million bricks there in the age of (mostly) sail and of people surviving on this scrap of sand in pre-industrial conditions. And I was blown away by the clarity of the water and the health of the corals I could see, compared to the water around Key West. I returned as often as I could in the years after, especially once regular ferry service started. It's one of Florida's most beautiful places, which is why it's now protected as a national park with some of the undersea areas an ecological reserve: no fishing allowed. It's why people pay a lot of money to spend a short time out there, and the ferry and seaplane are sold out weeks in advance.

I've stayed in the park overnight, camping, and even a couple times in the fort itself. The tranquility when the ferry pulls away and the seaplane takes off and you are left with the park staff and a few fellow campers is unmatched.

It's also the ultimate expression of how the Tortugas, like the Keys, like Florida, have evolved from a place of hardship and struggle—where the mosquitoes might drive you insane if the alligators don't kill you—to the exclusive paradise portrayed in tourism ads and Instagram photos, a place that many people want but fewer can reach. This beautiful, tranquil, brick structure was built with slave labor and used as a prison. People died there, of yellow fever and in attempts at escape. Emily Holder, who lived at the fort during the Civil War with her physician husband, wrote in her diary that it was "hardly a pleasant thought that we were inside of a prison, not knowing who were desperadoes and who were not, without any means of protecting ourselves against them." And when yellow fever arrived, "it was terrible beyond description to be hemmed in by those high, literally red-hot brick walls with so much suffering sickness."

Even though the Tortugas are a now a national park, these islands will never be a high-volume, high-comfort destination. That seems right for a place built as a fortress and used as a prison. For all of our military determination and, now, conservation intentions, we cannot deny the realities of the environment and the changes brought by storms, tides, currents, and a rising sea. The Tortugas are beautiful and harsh, seductive and hostile. Depending on one's perspective, it's the end of Florida. Or the beginning.

Photographs

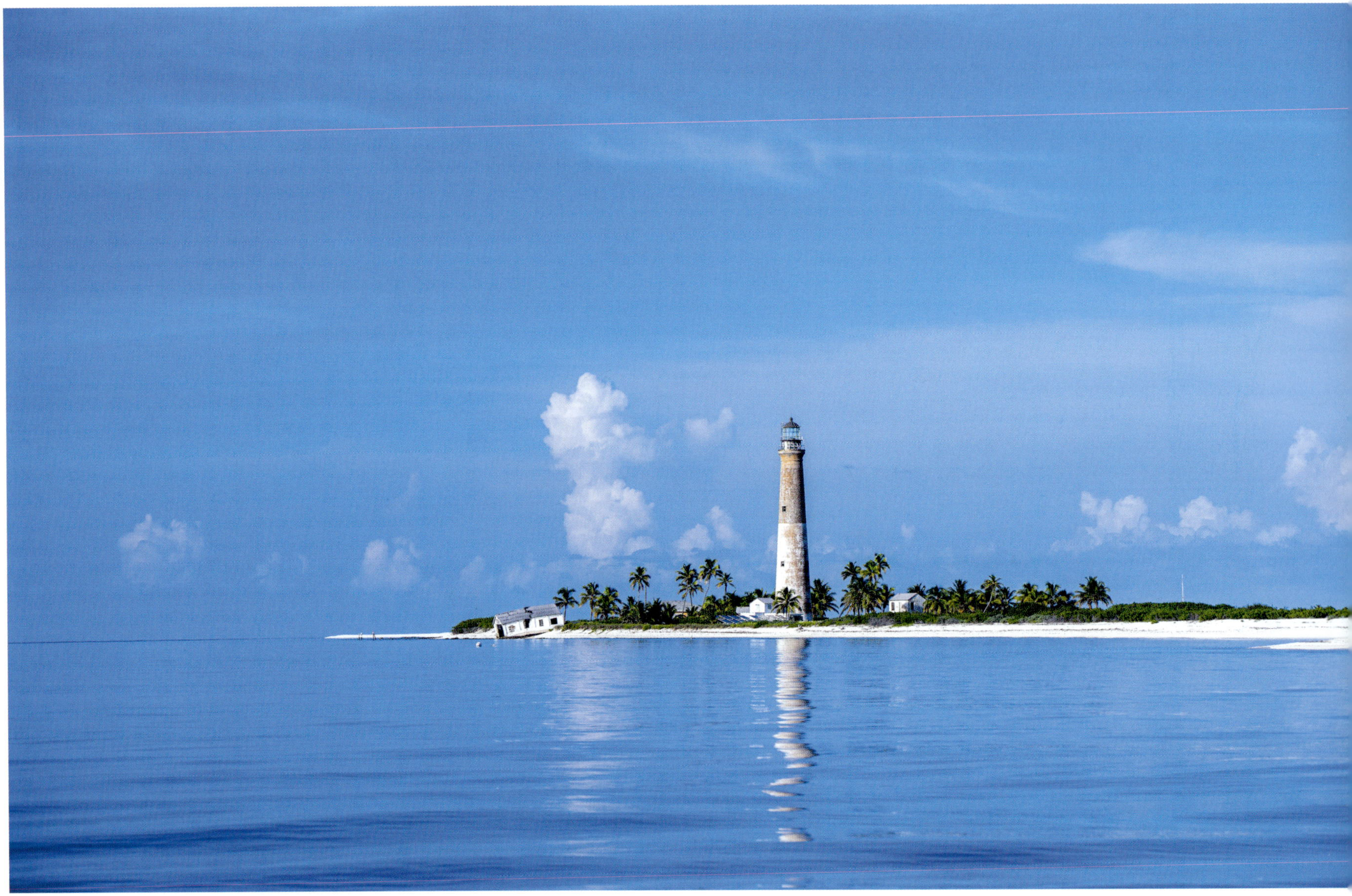

Loggerhead Key pre–Hurricane Ian.

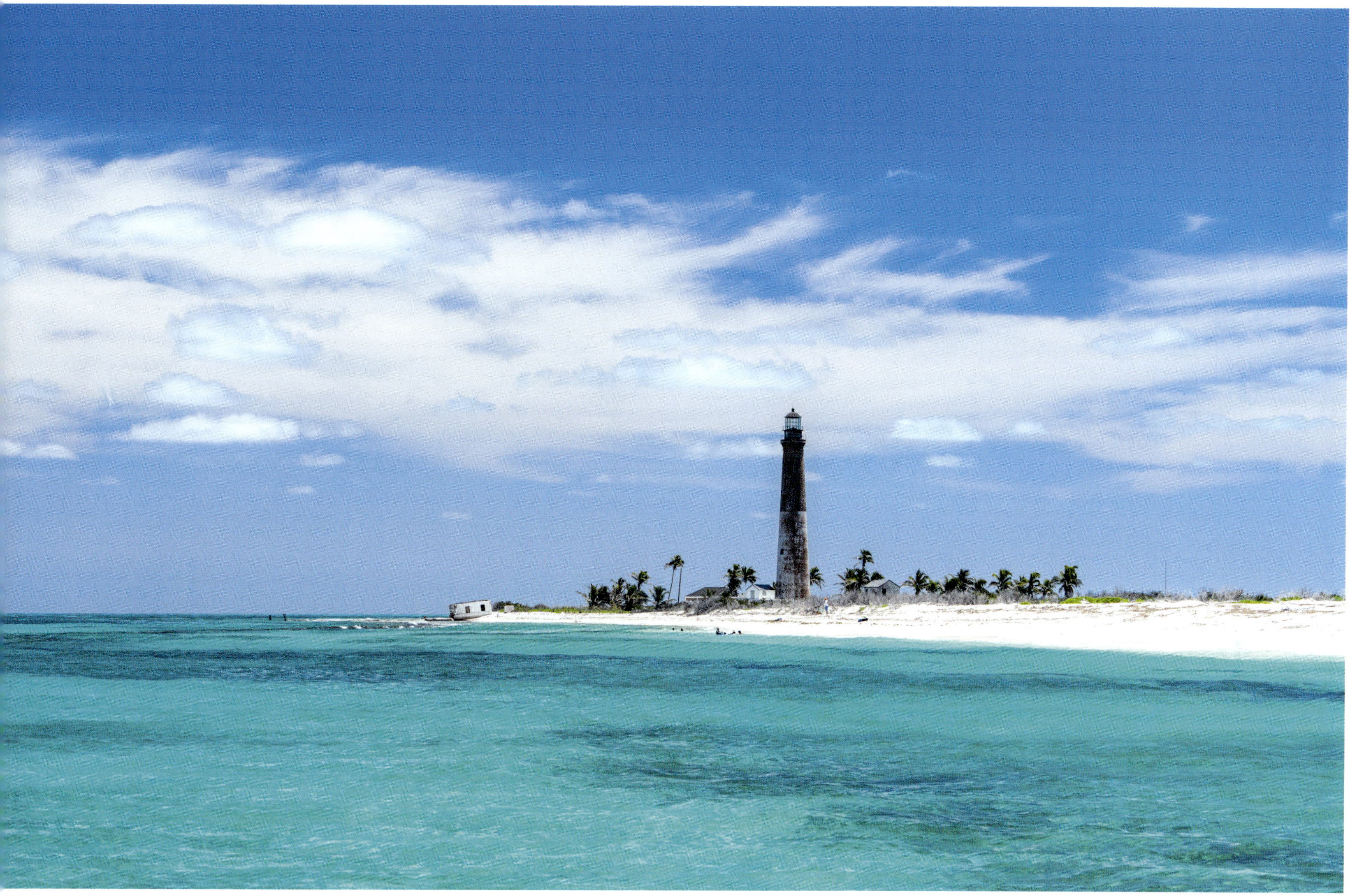

Loggerhead Key post–Hurricane Ian.

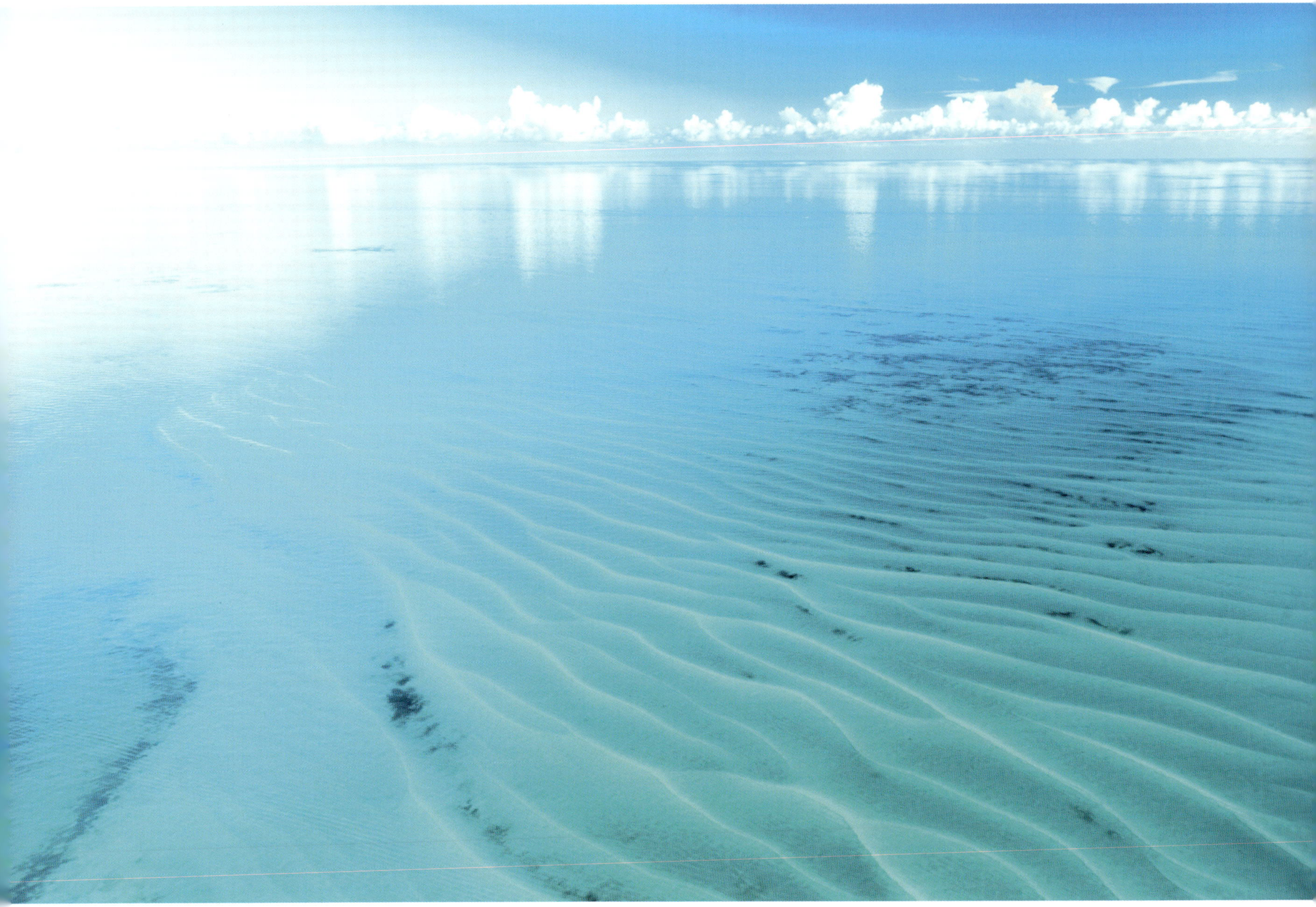

On route to the Tortugas, an area known as the Quicksands
is seen from the air.

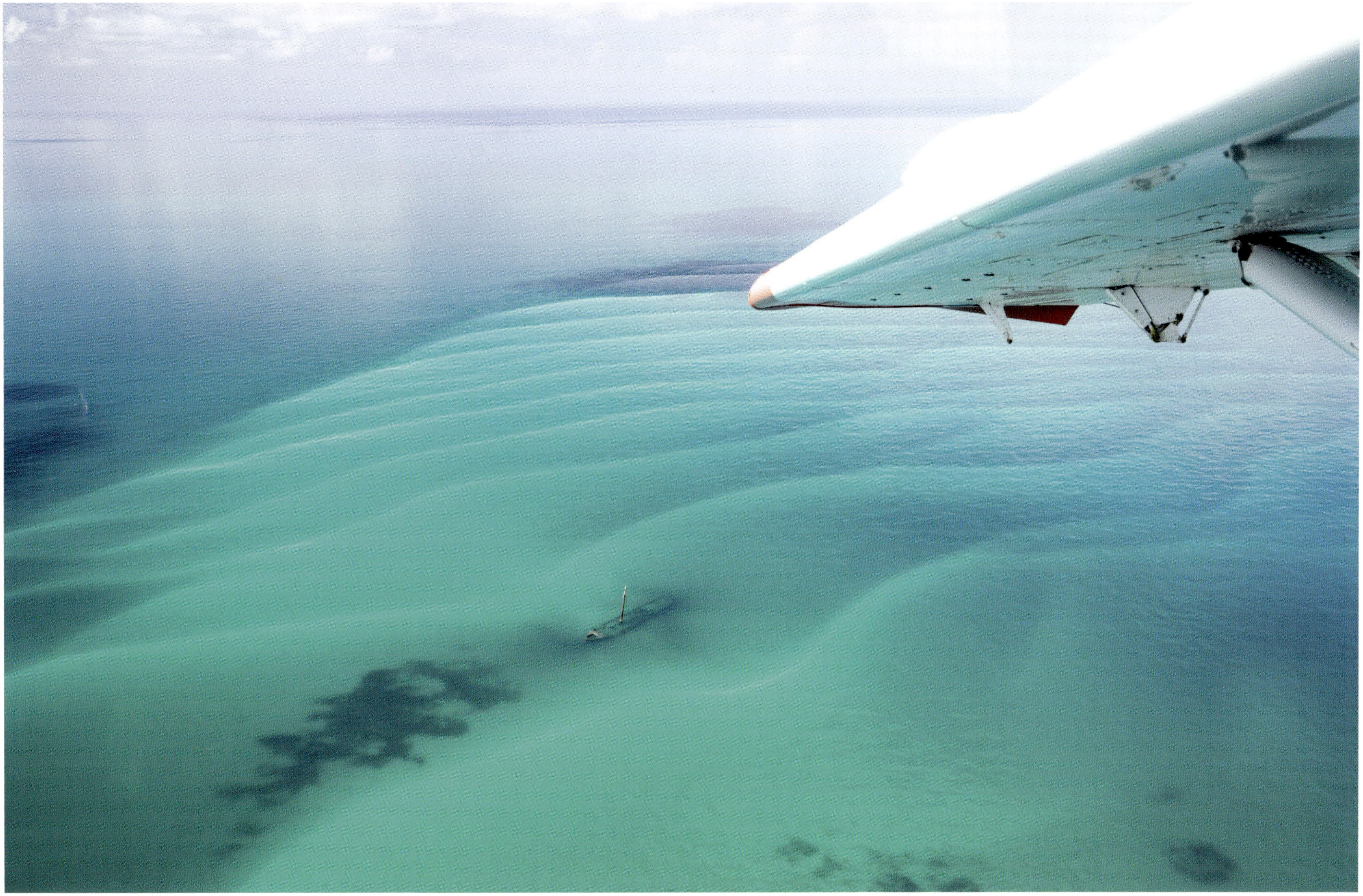

Aerial view of the wreck of the *Arbutus.*

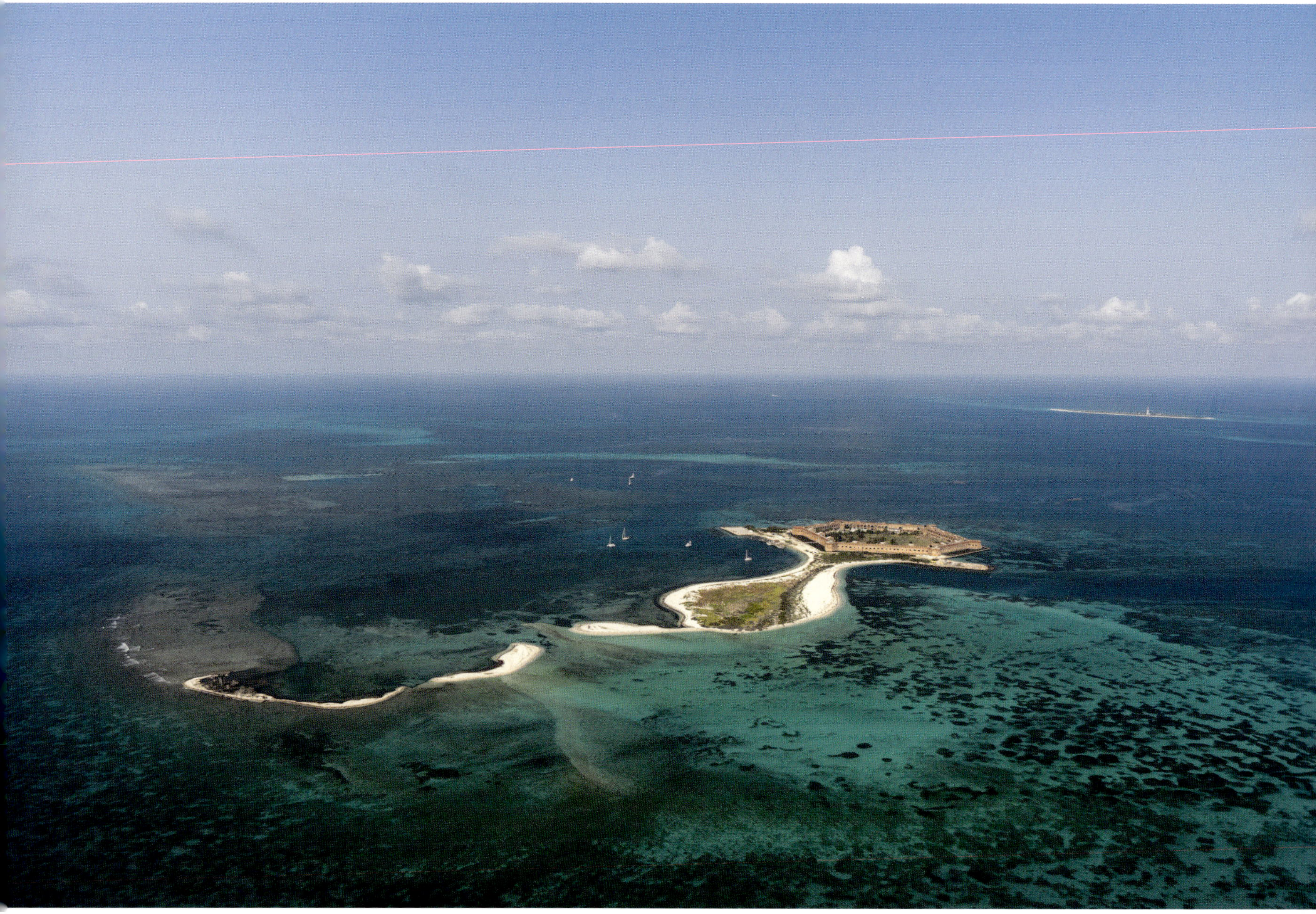

First look at Dry Tortugas on approach.

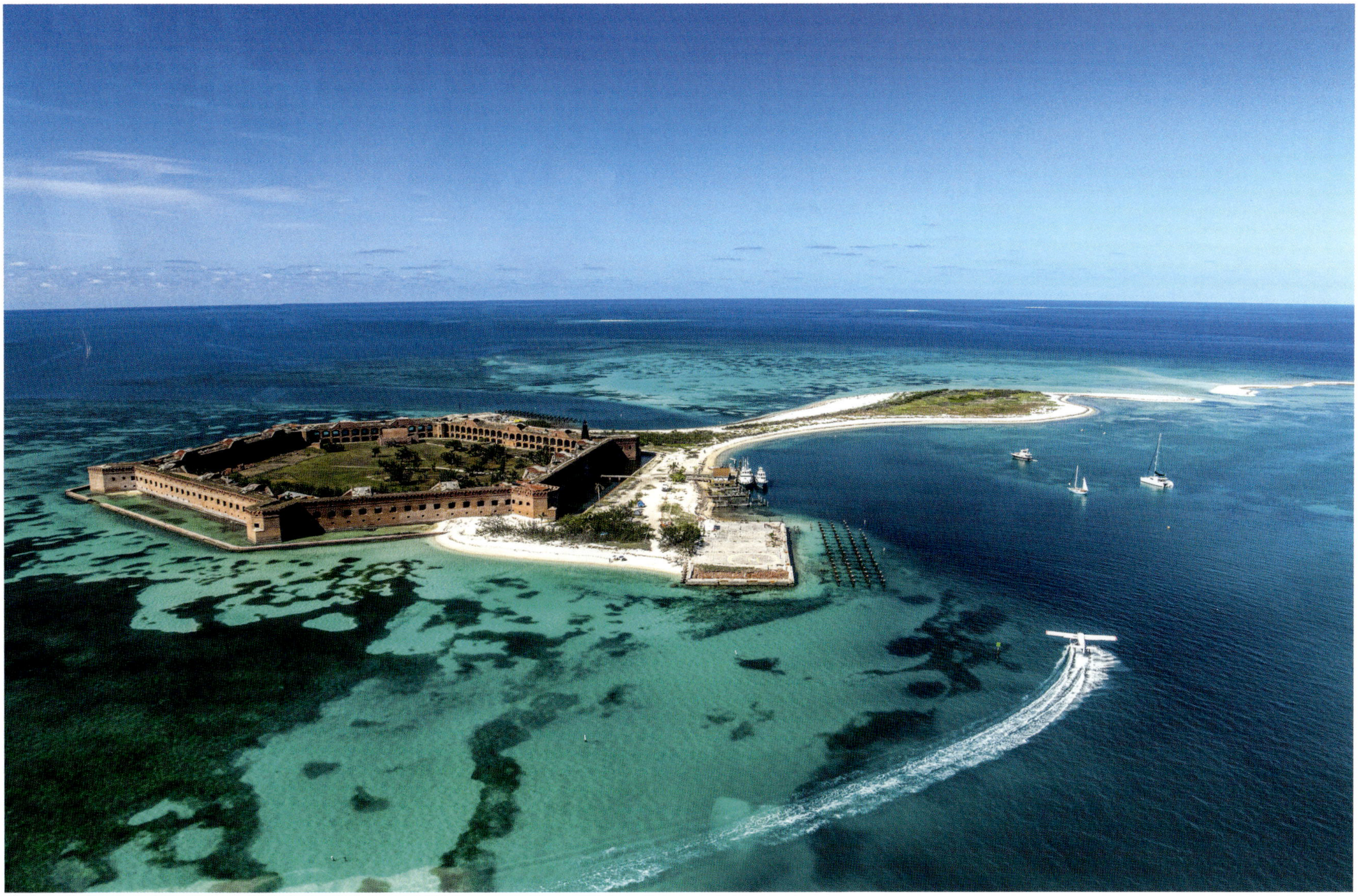

Fort Jefferson on seaplane descent.

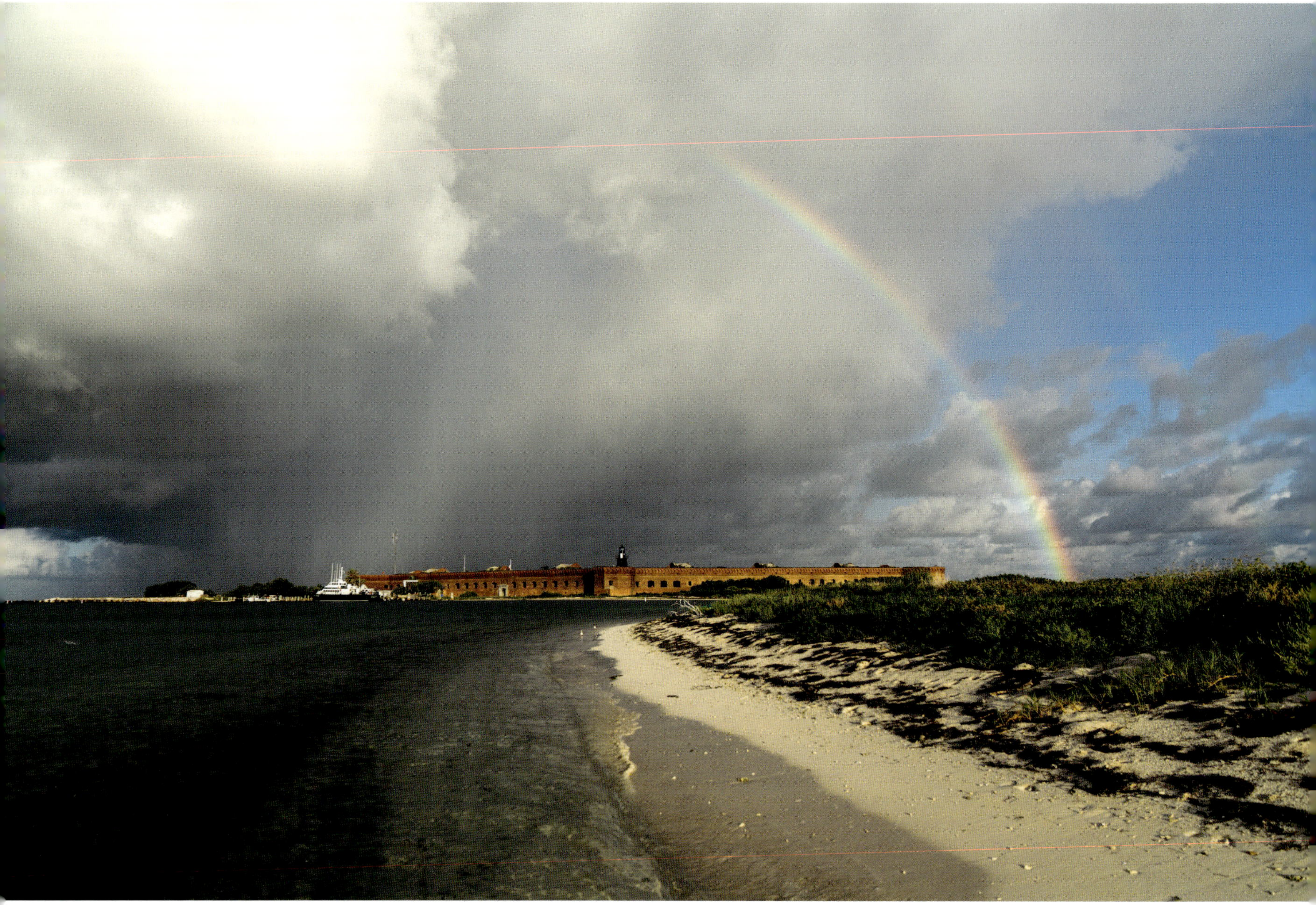

A rainbow opens up over Fort Jefferson.

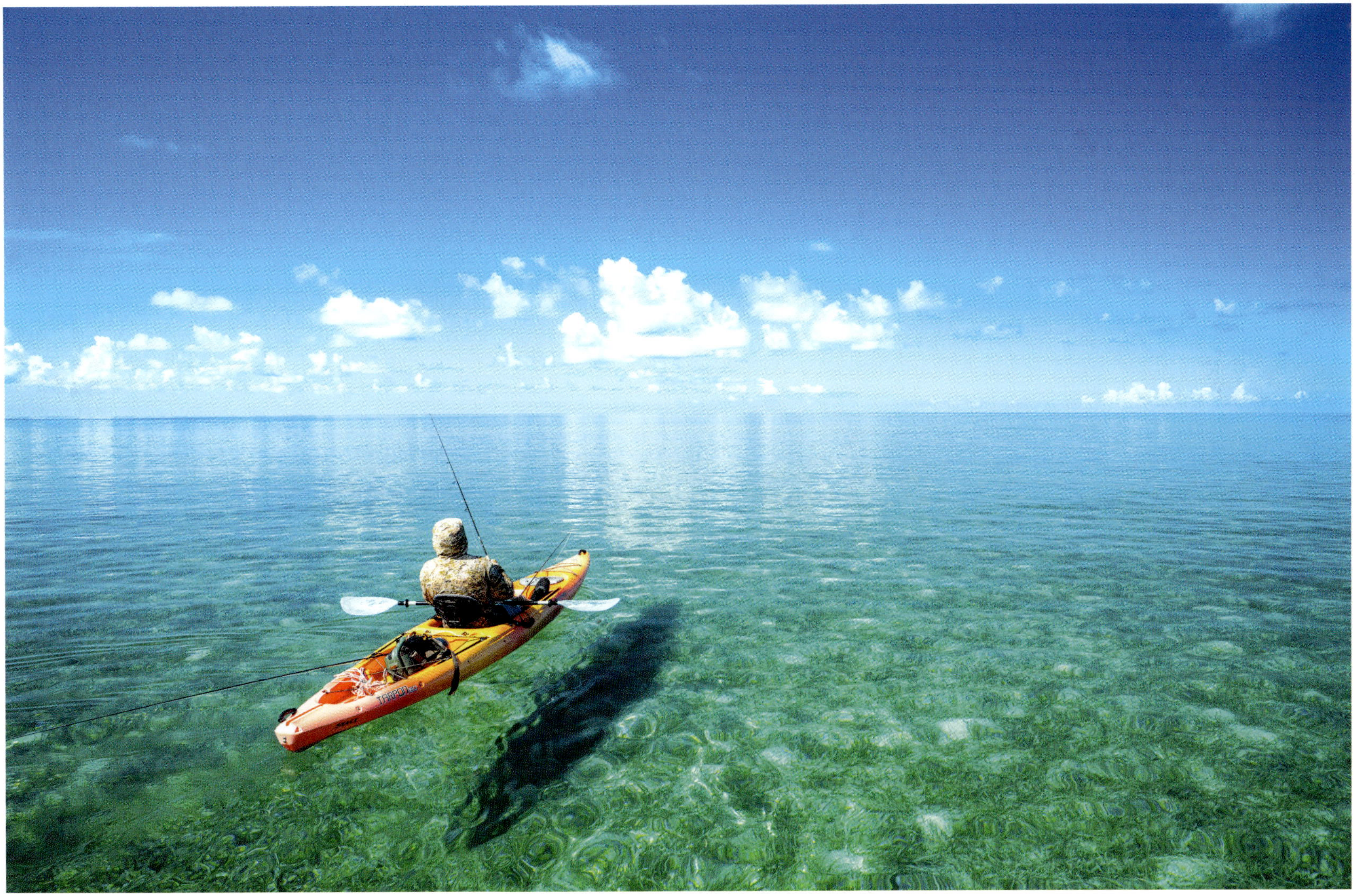

Kayaking over the expansive seagrass flats surrounding Garden Key.

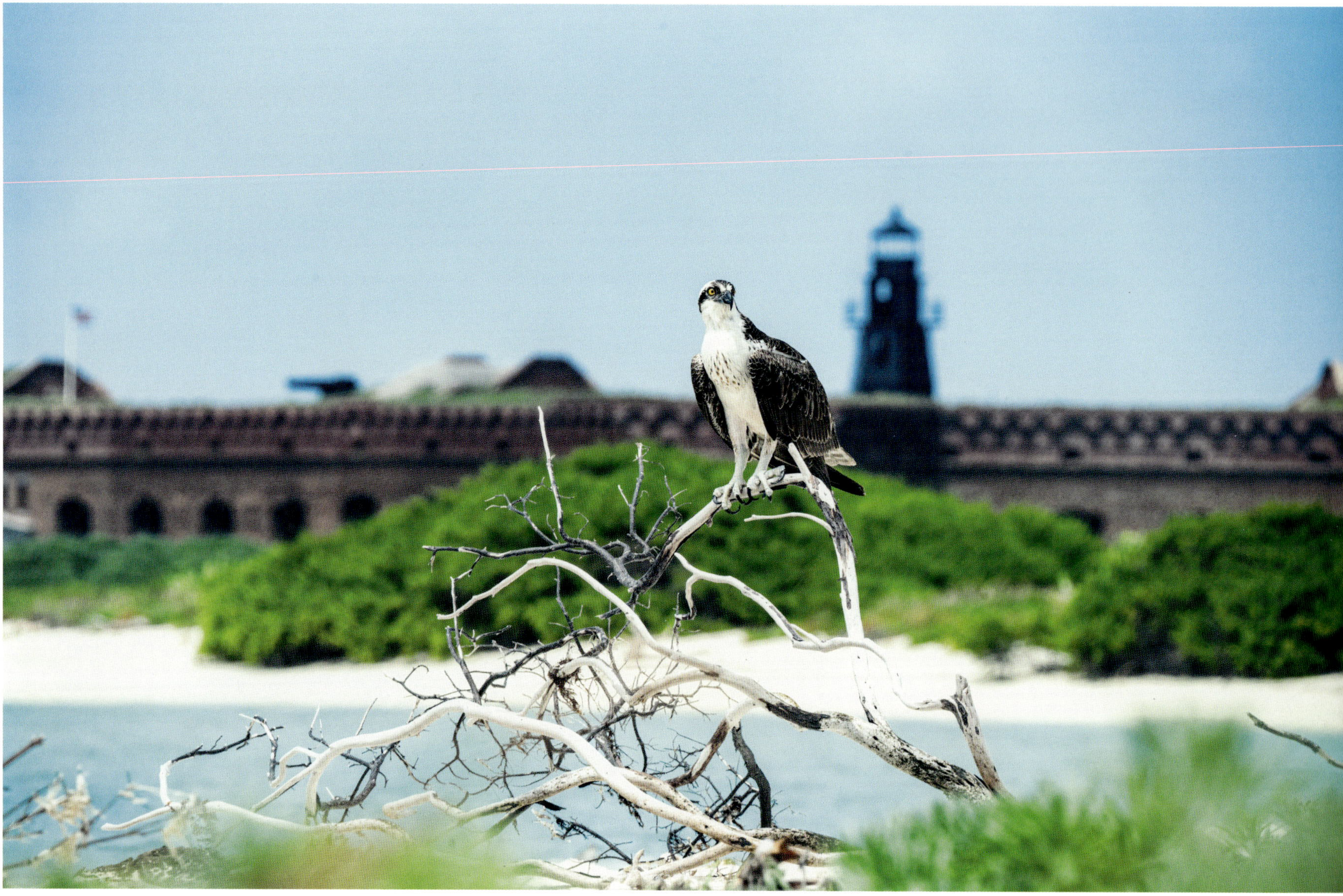

An osprey (*Pandion haliaetus*) perched and actively scanning for its next meal.

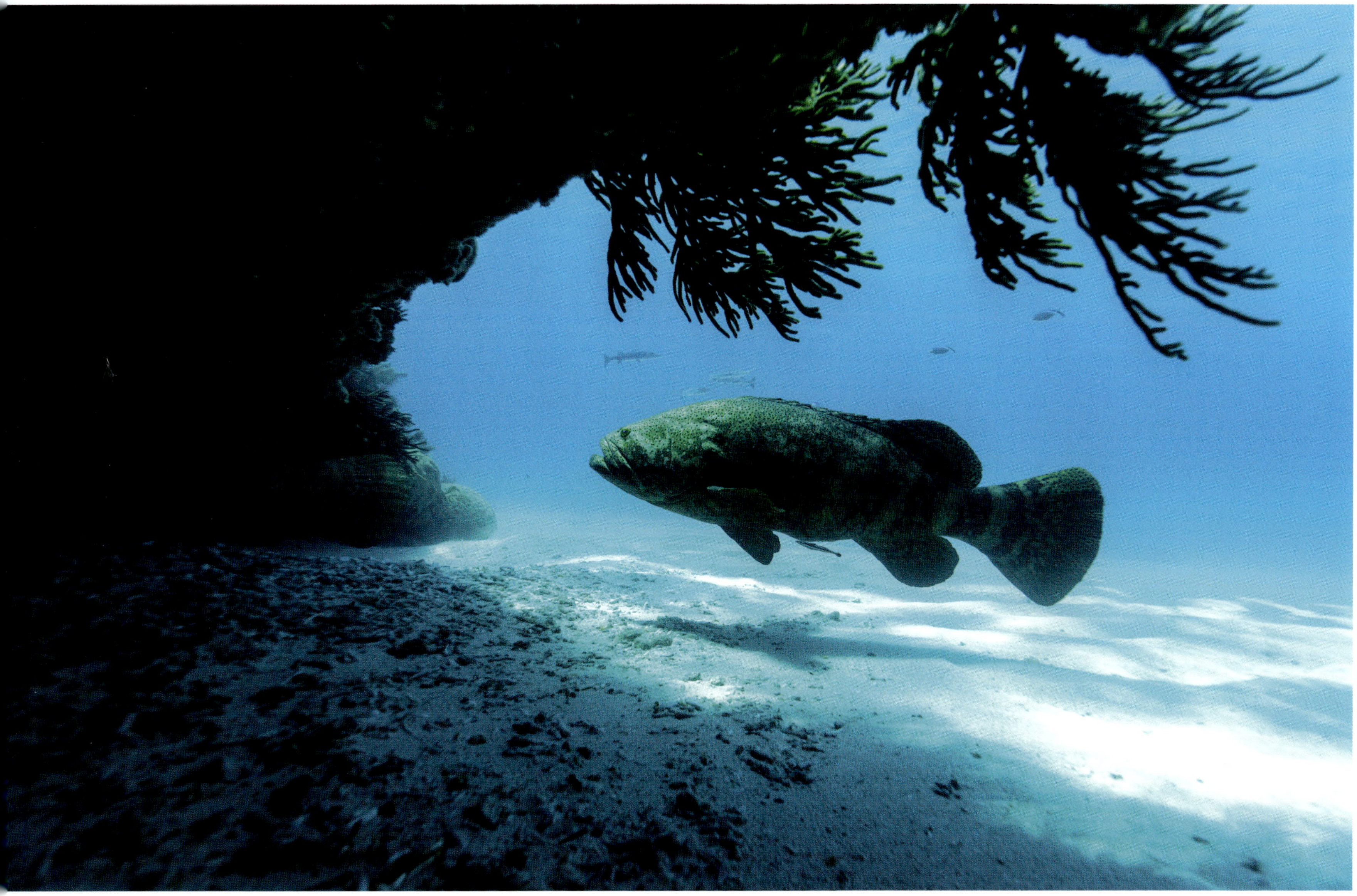

A goliath grouper (*Epinephelus itajara*) rests in the shadow of the Windjammer Reef wreck. Located a mile southwest of Loggerhead Key, this wreck site comprises the remains of the large Norwegian ship *Avanti,* which sank in January 1907 en route from Pensacola to Uruguay.

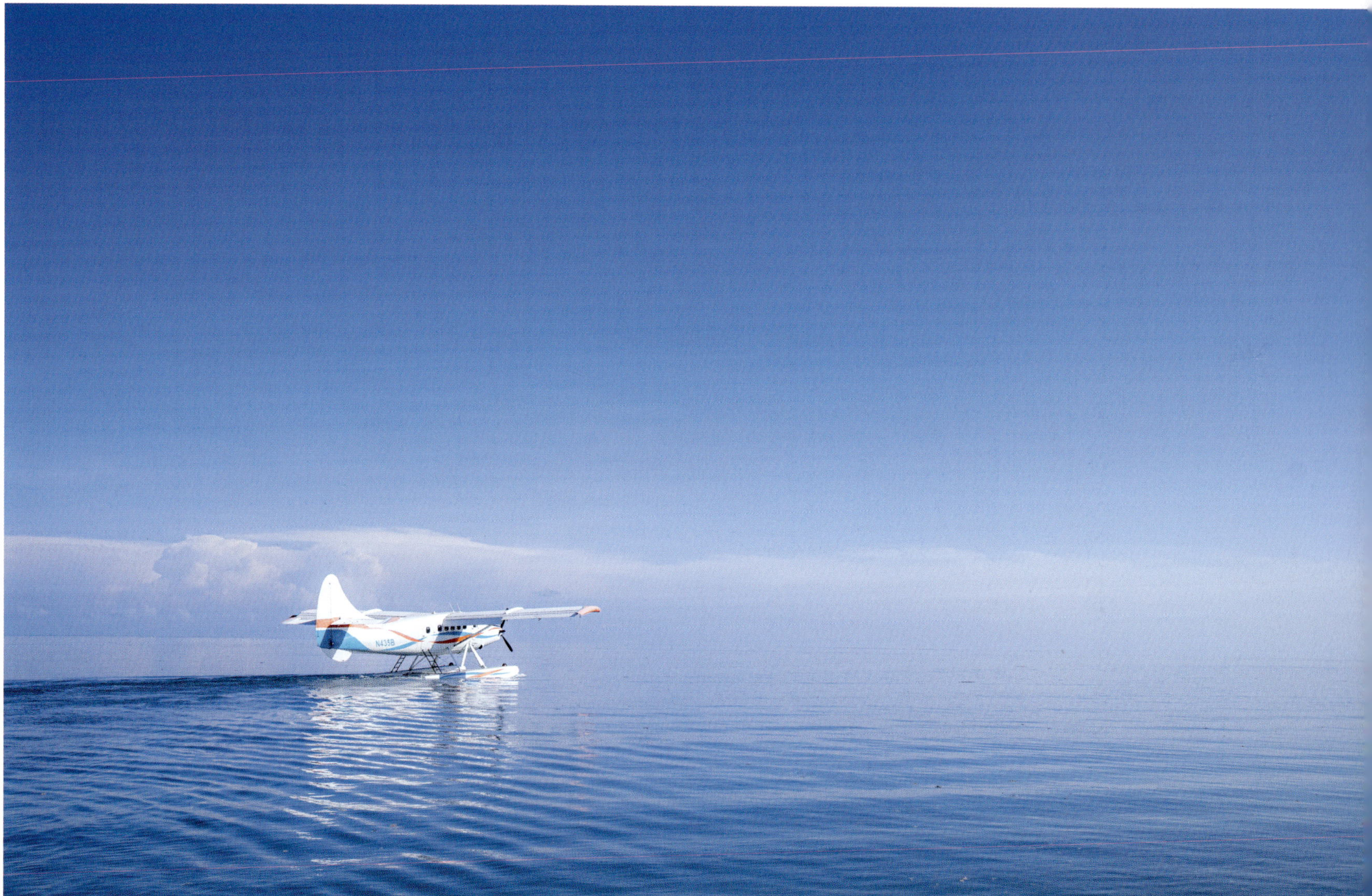
A seaplane prepares for takeoff.

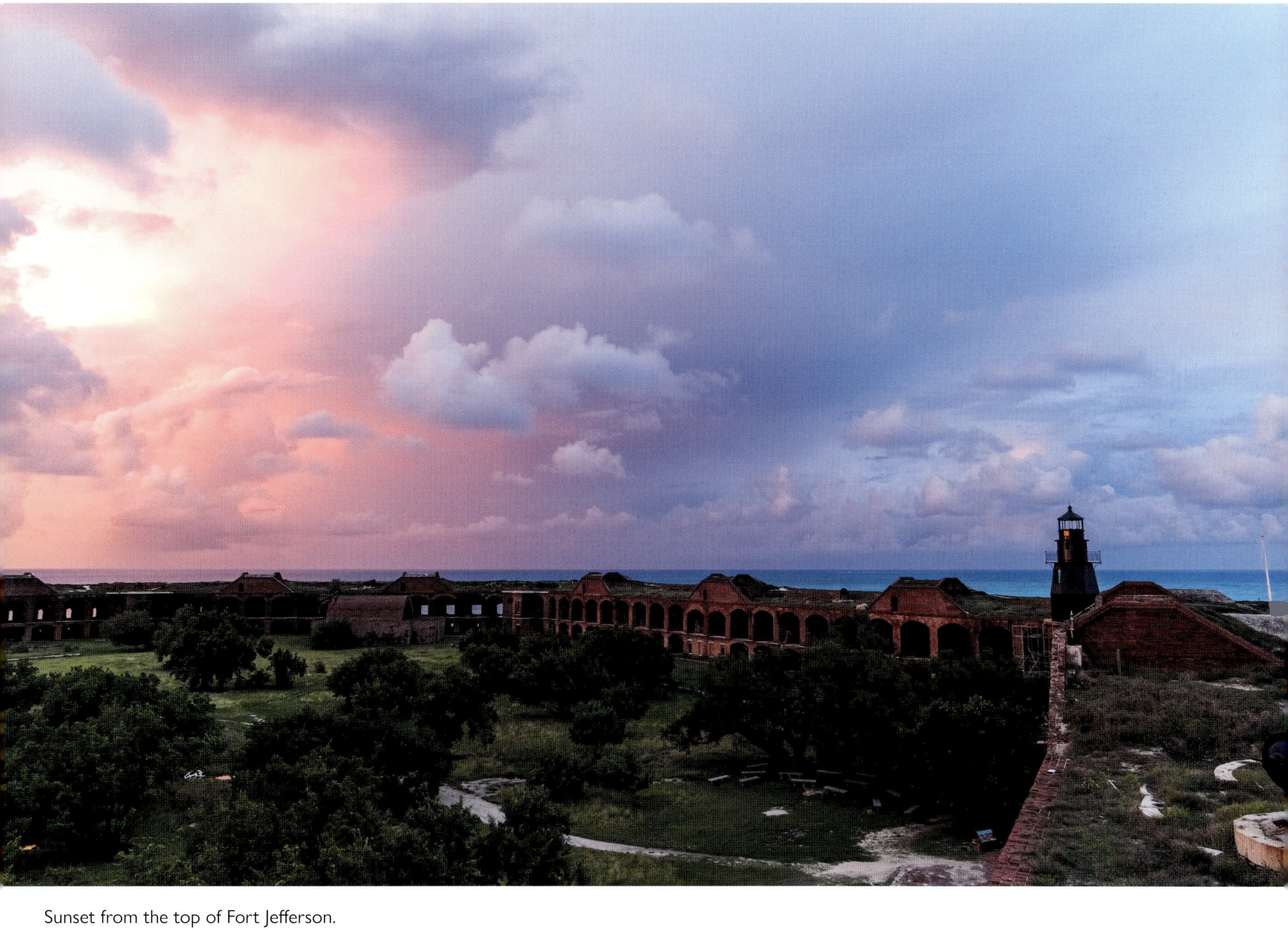

Sunset from the top of Fort Jefferson.

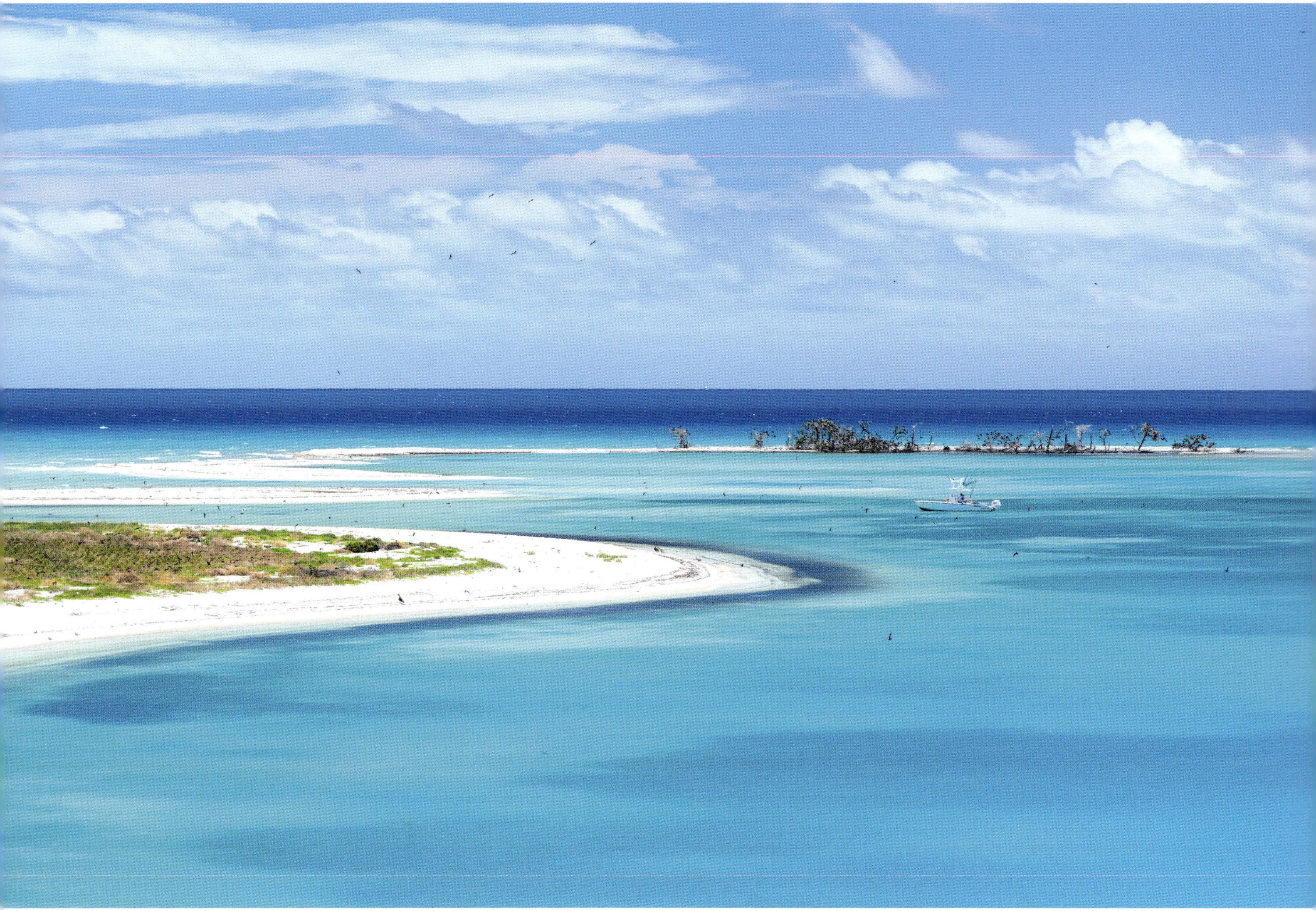

Tortugas blues.

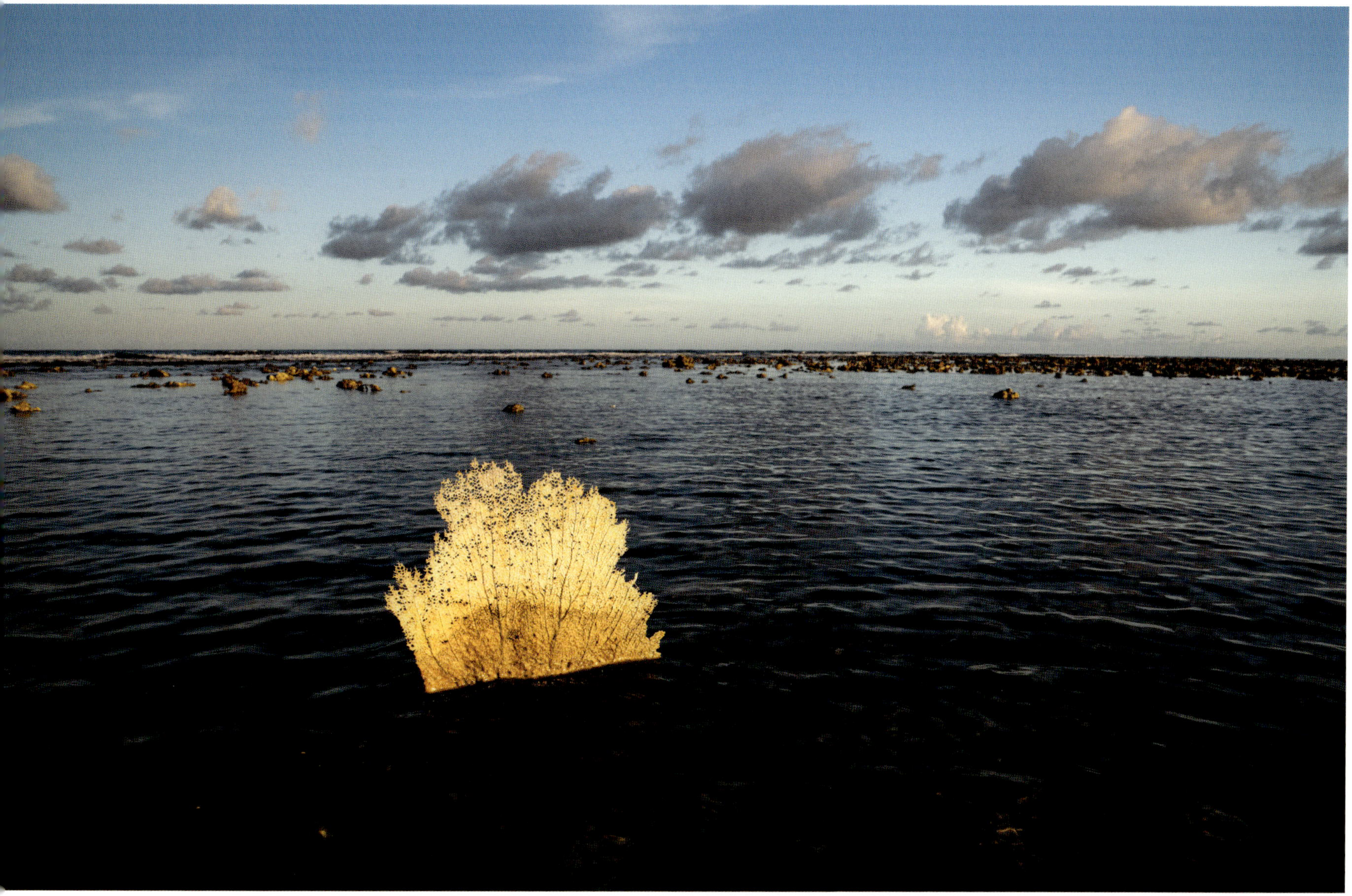

A sea fan (*Gorgonia ventalina*) reflects a golden sunset's light.

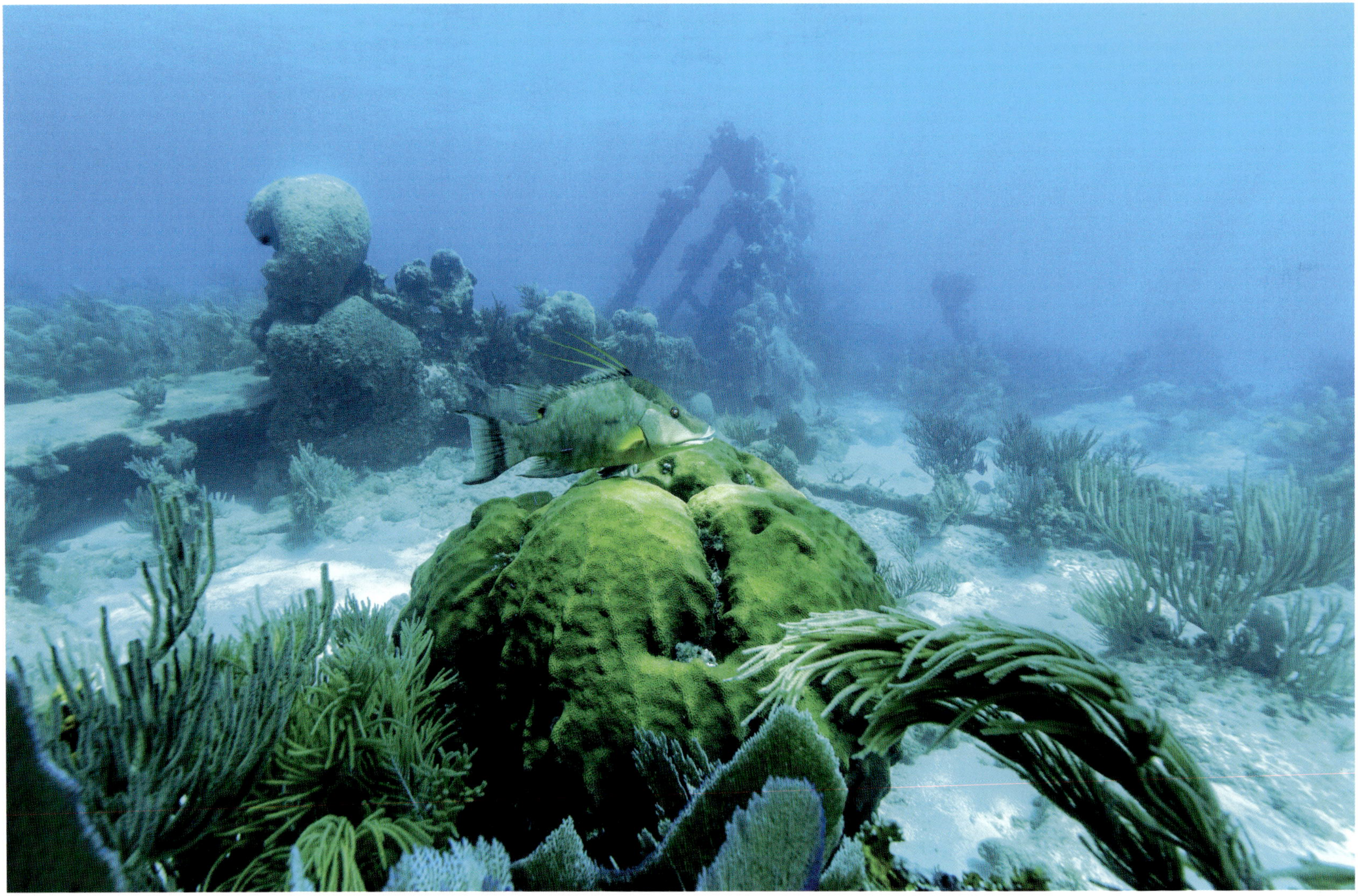

A hogfish (*Lachnolaimus maximus*) posted over a boulder coral.

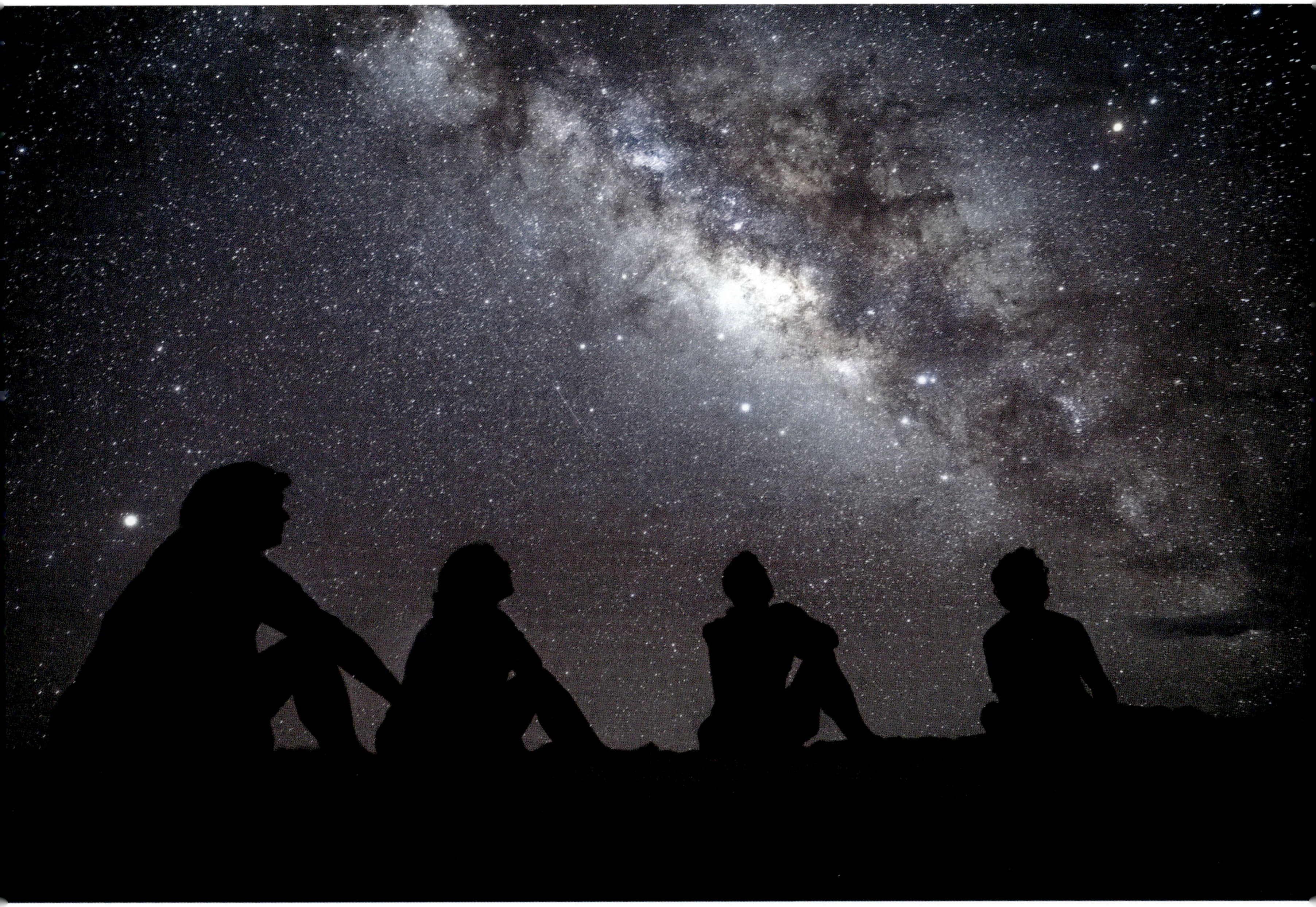

A group of friends takes in the wonder of the Milky Way.

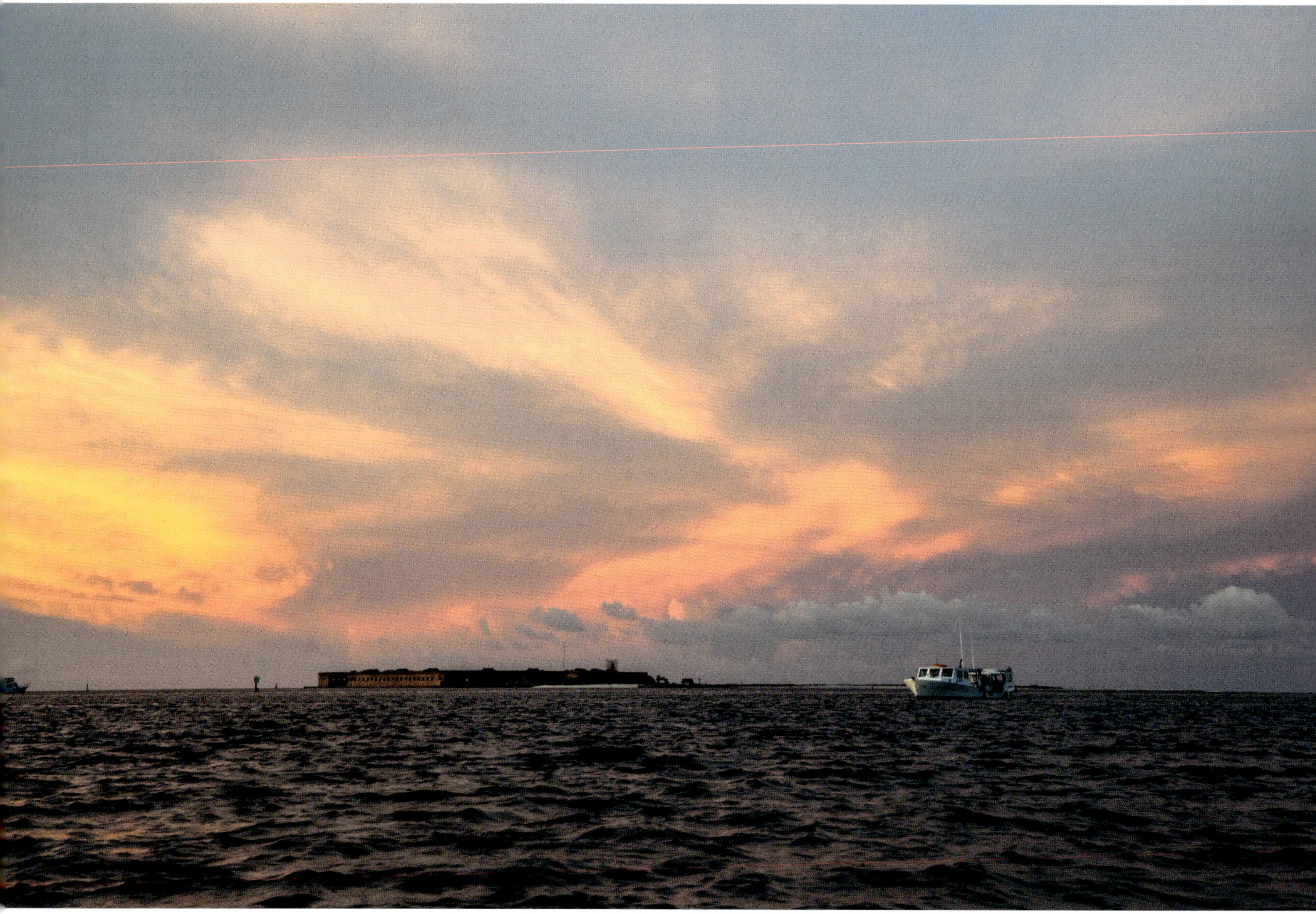

Sunset as seen from the Bird Key Harbor anchorage.

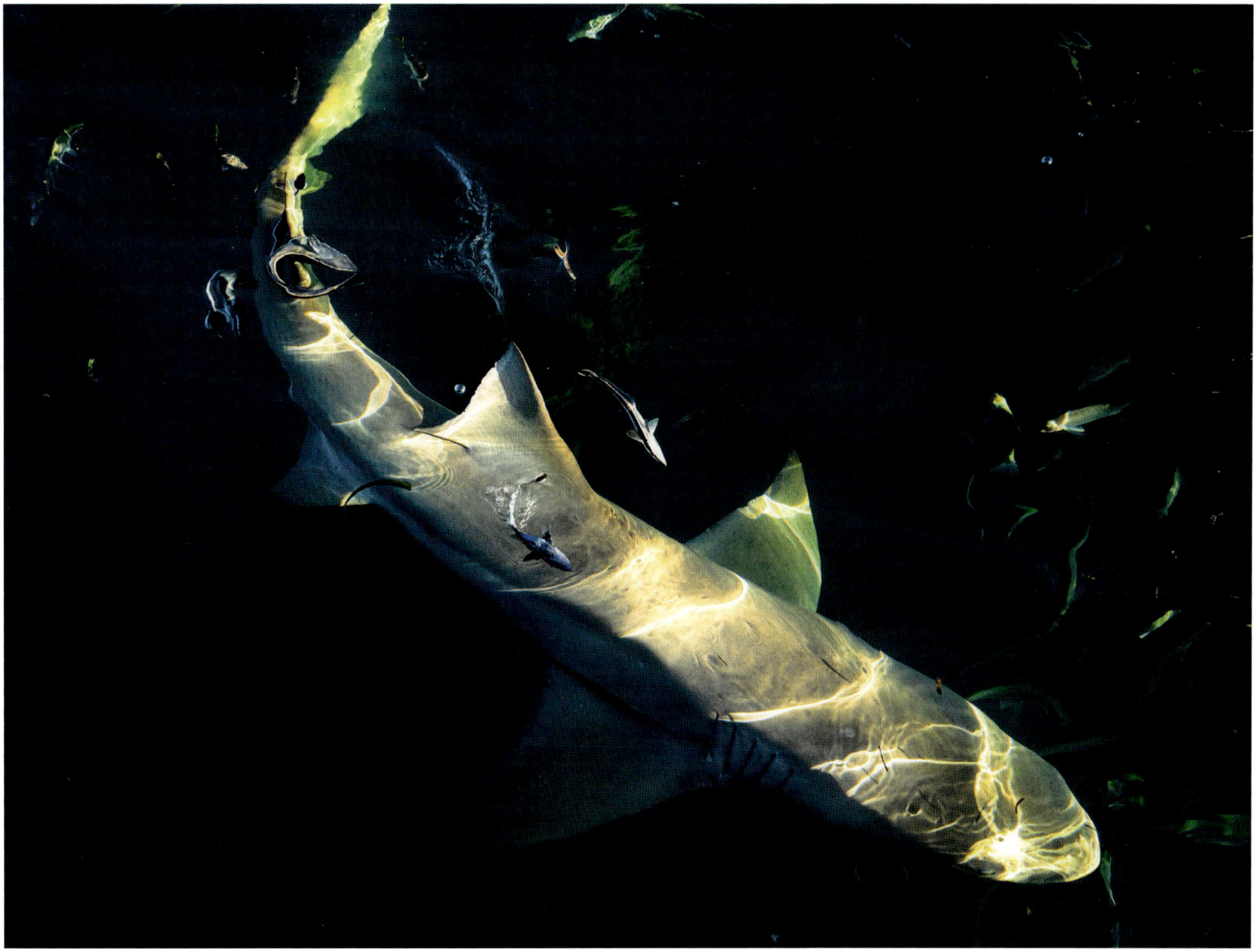

Feeding time.

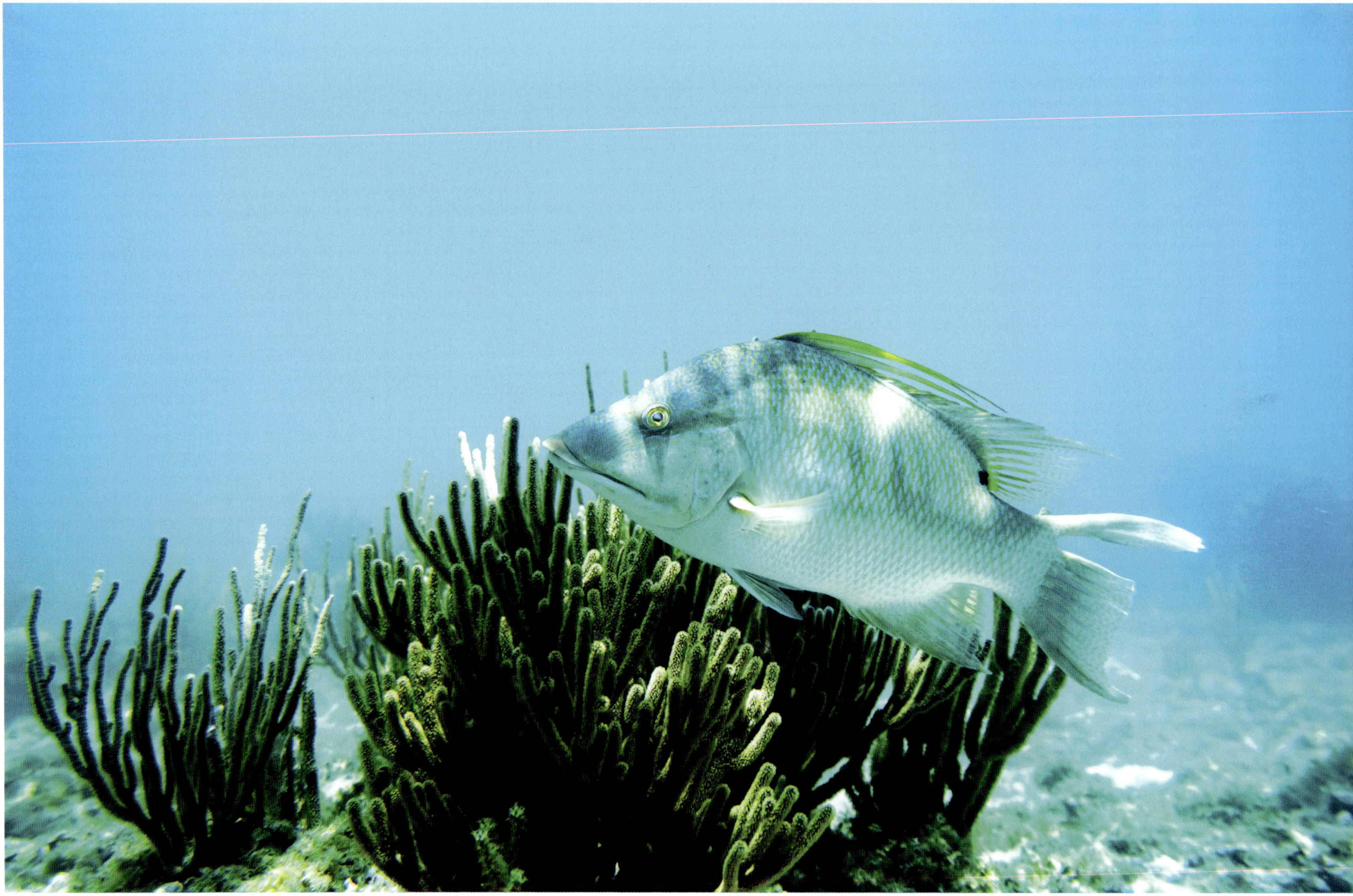

A resplendent hogfish.

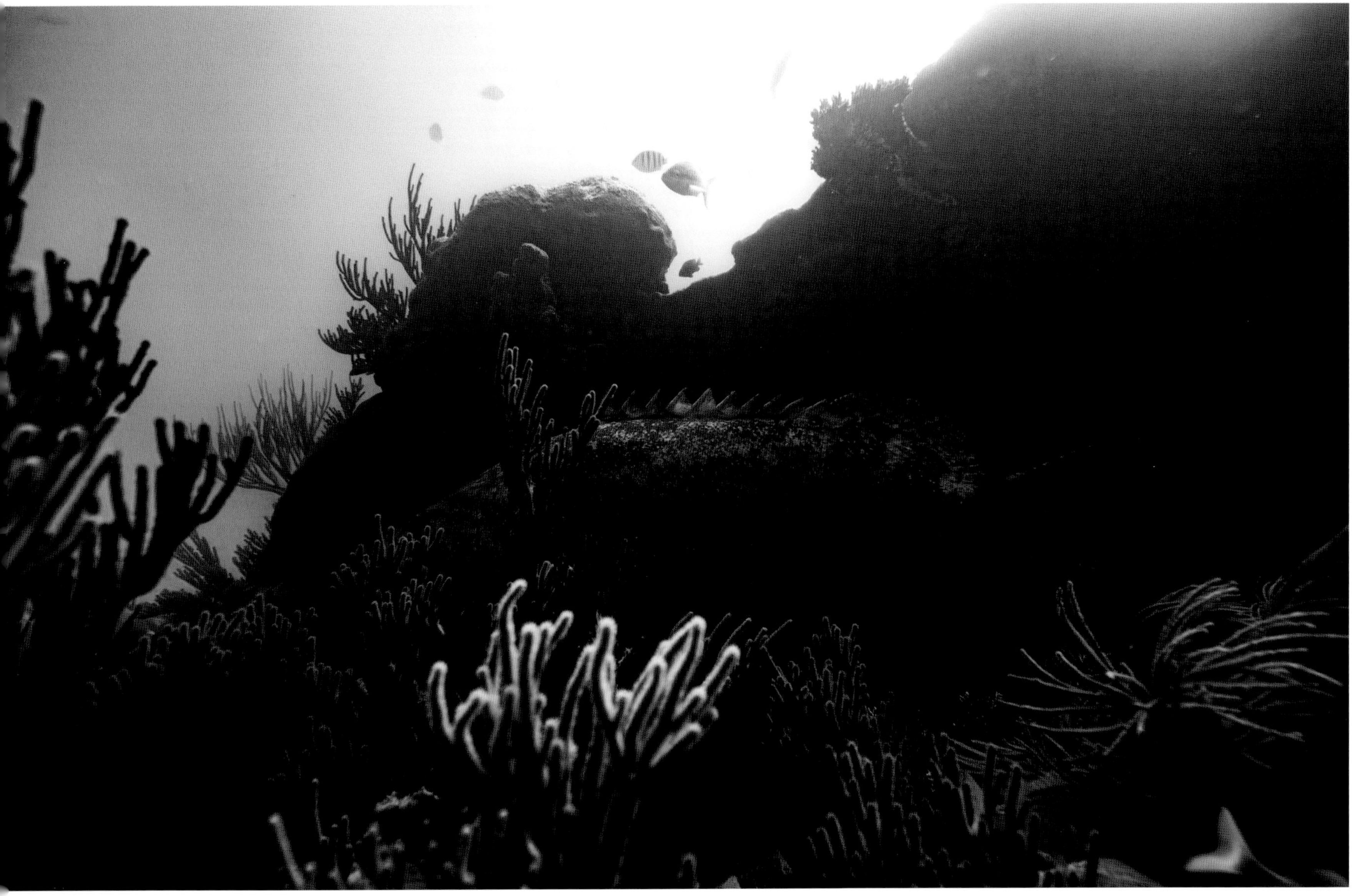

The outline of a goliath grouper pokes up from behind some soft corals.

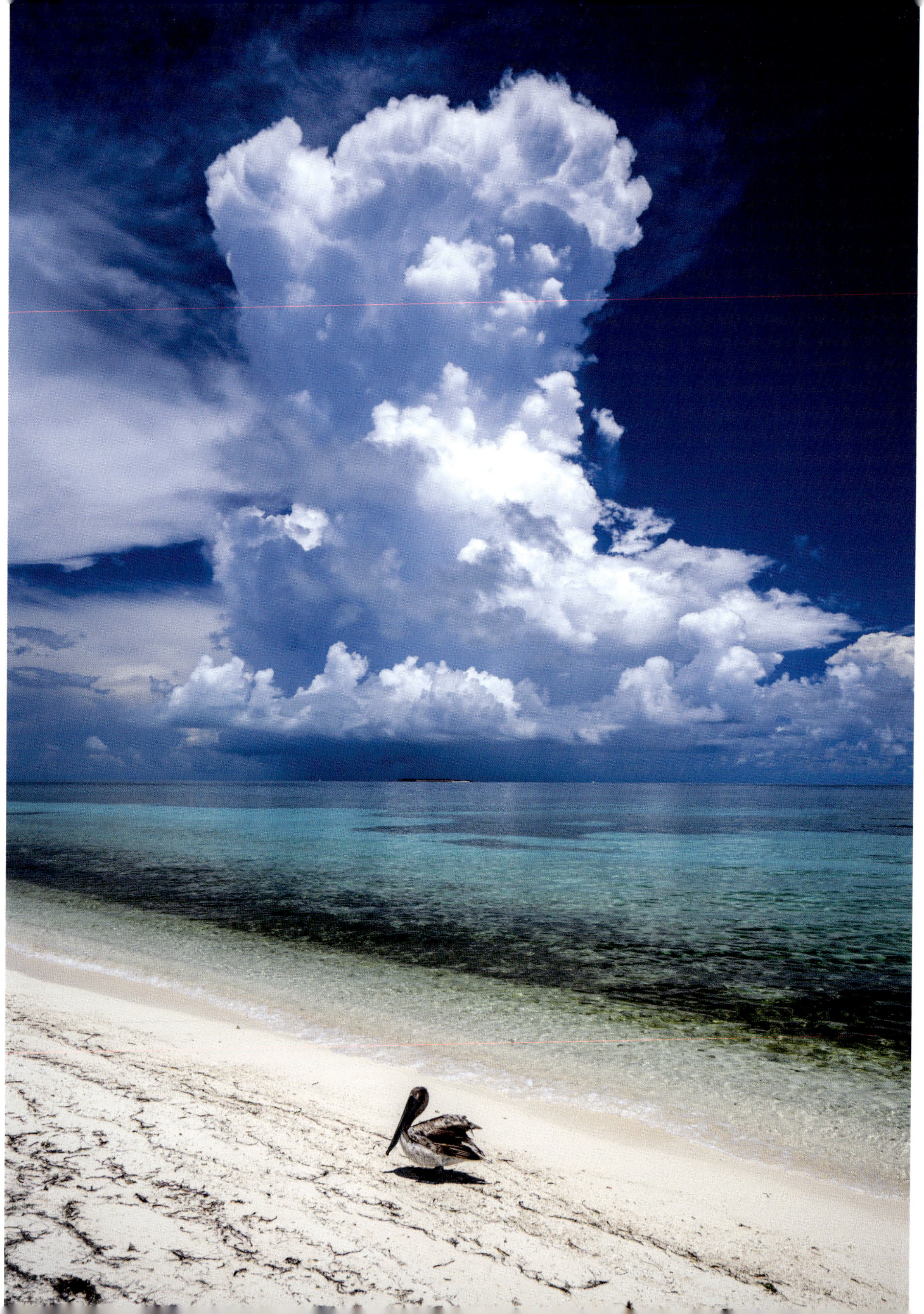

Midday blues off
Loggerhead Key.

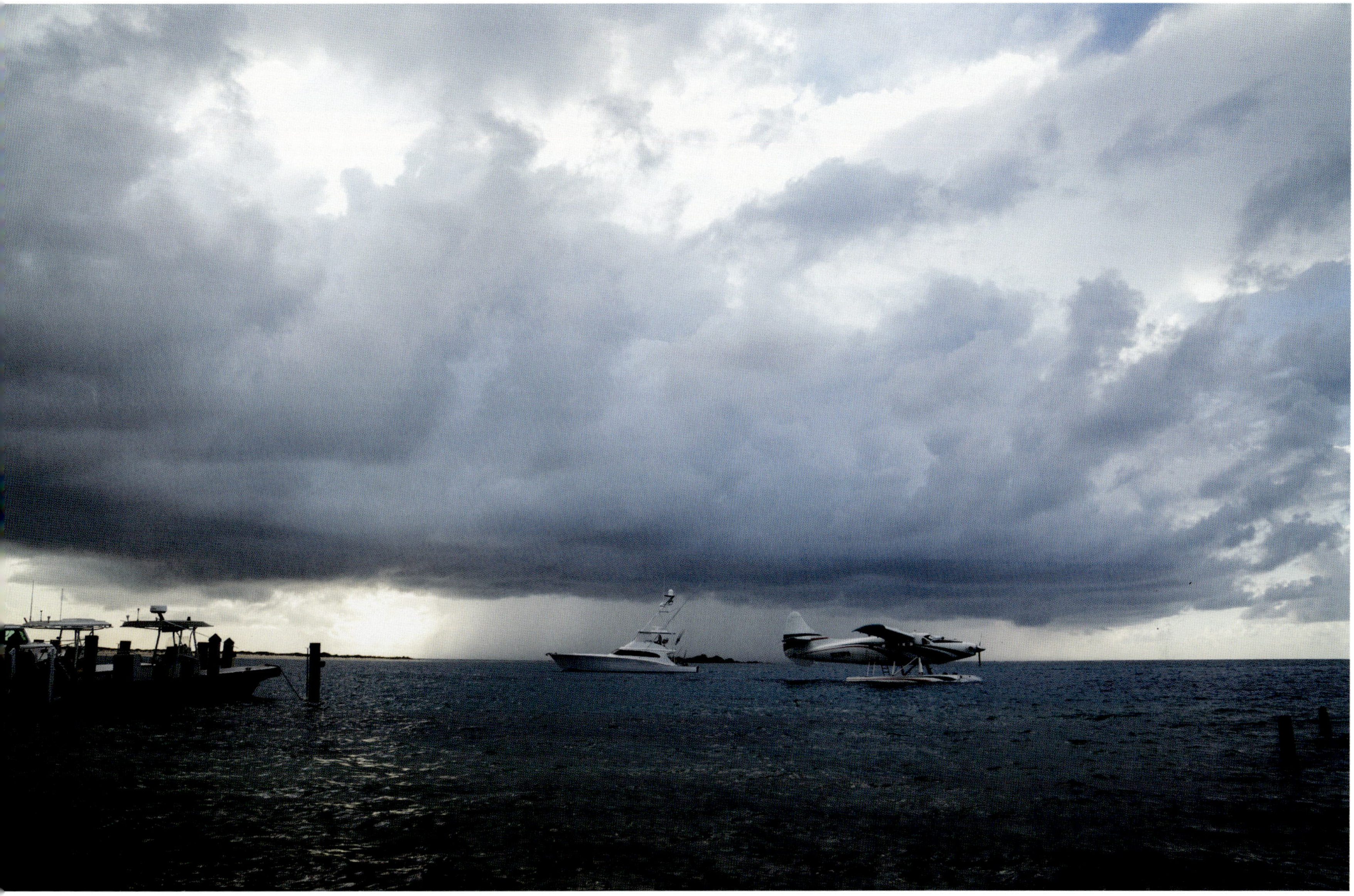

There are two ways to get to the Tortugas: by boat or by plane. Both methods, in different ways, offer unique opportunities for experiencing the park.

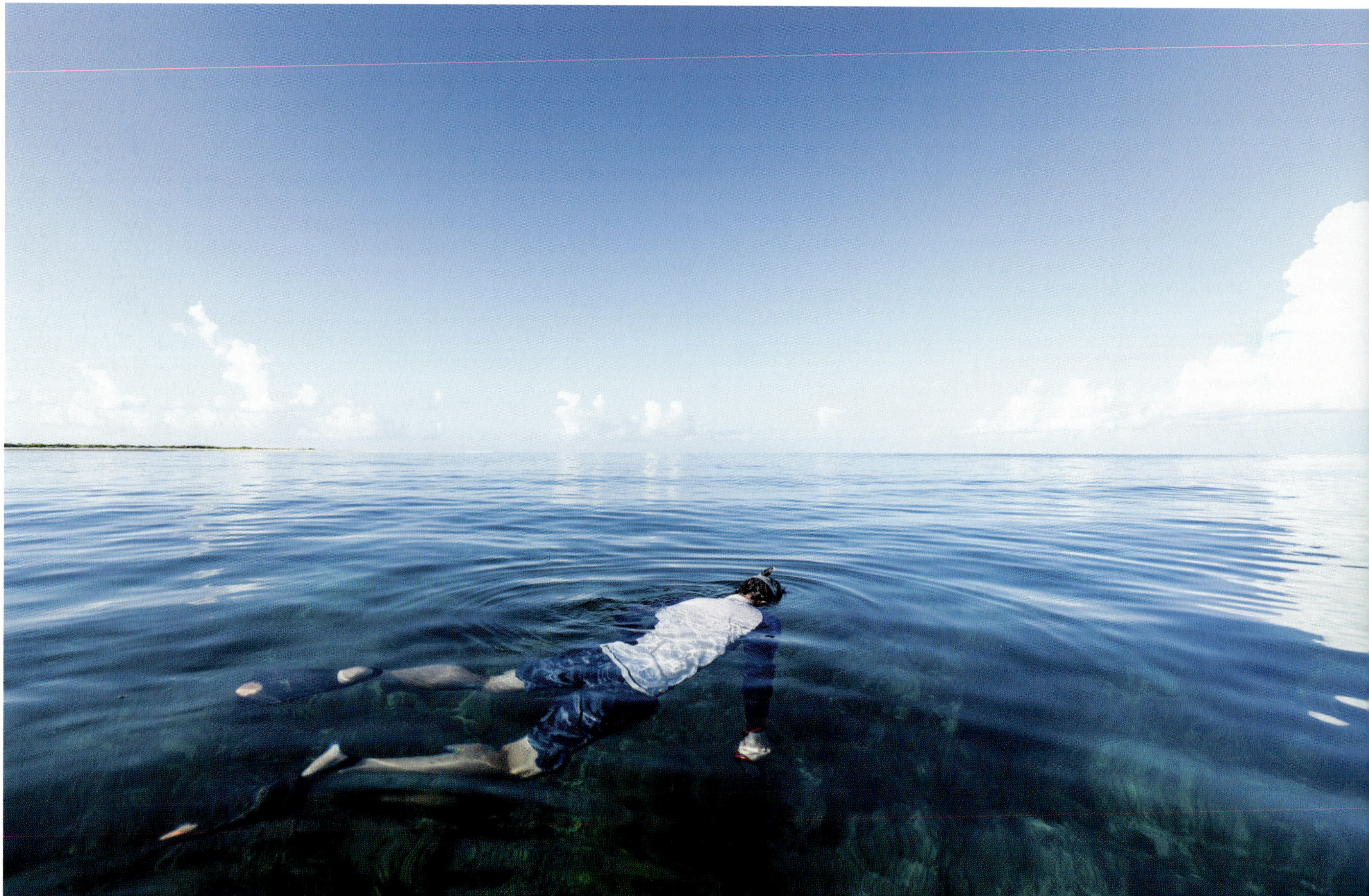

A snorkeler takes in the views of Little Africa Reef.

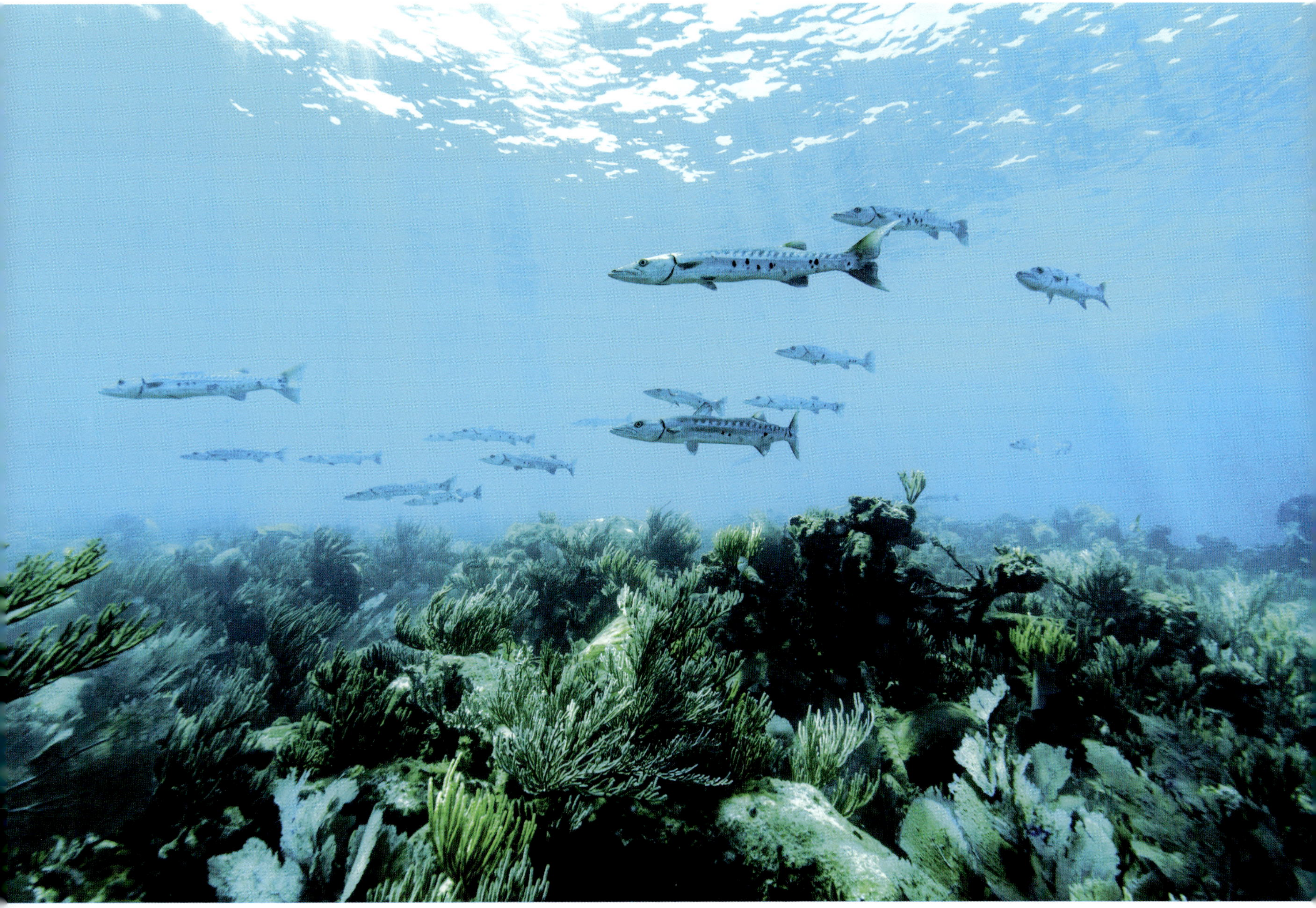

A school of barracuda (*Sphyraena barracuda*) floats in the current over the Windjammer Reef southwest of Loggerhead Key.

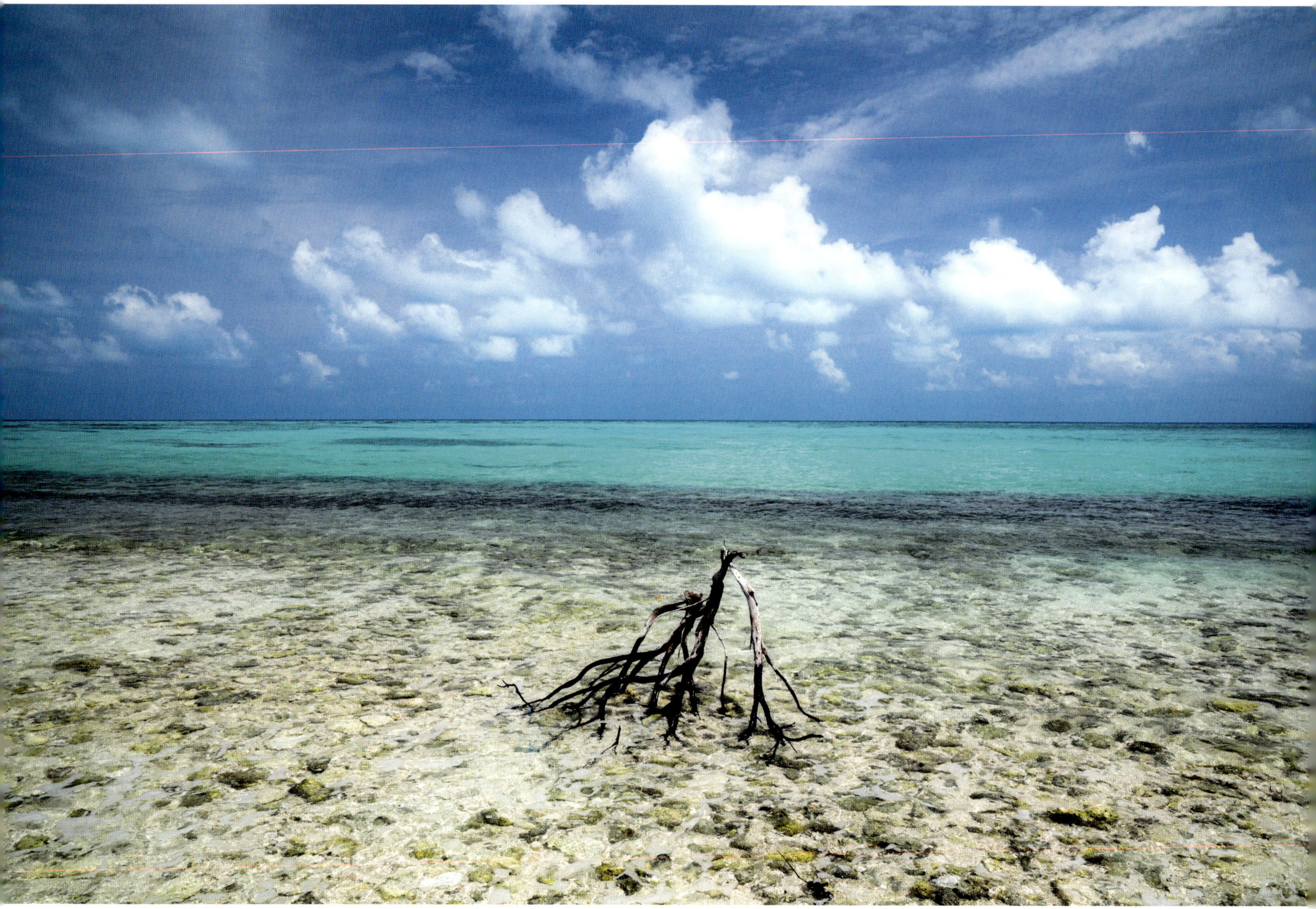

Remnants of past shorelines live on as a reminder of how the Tortugas' islands have shifted over time.

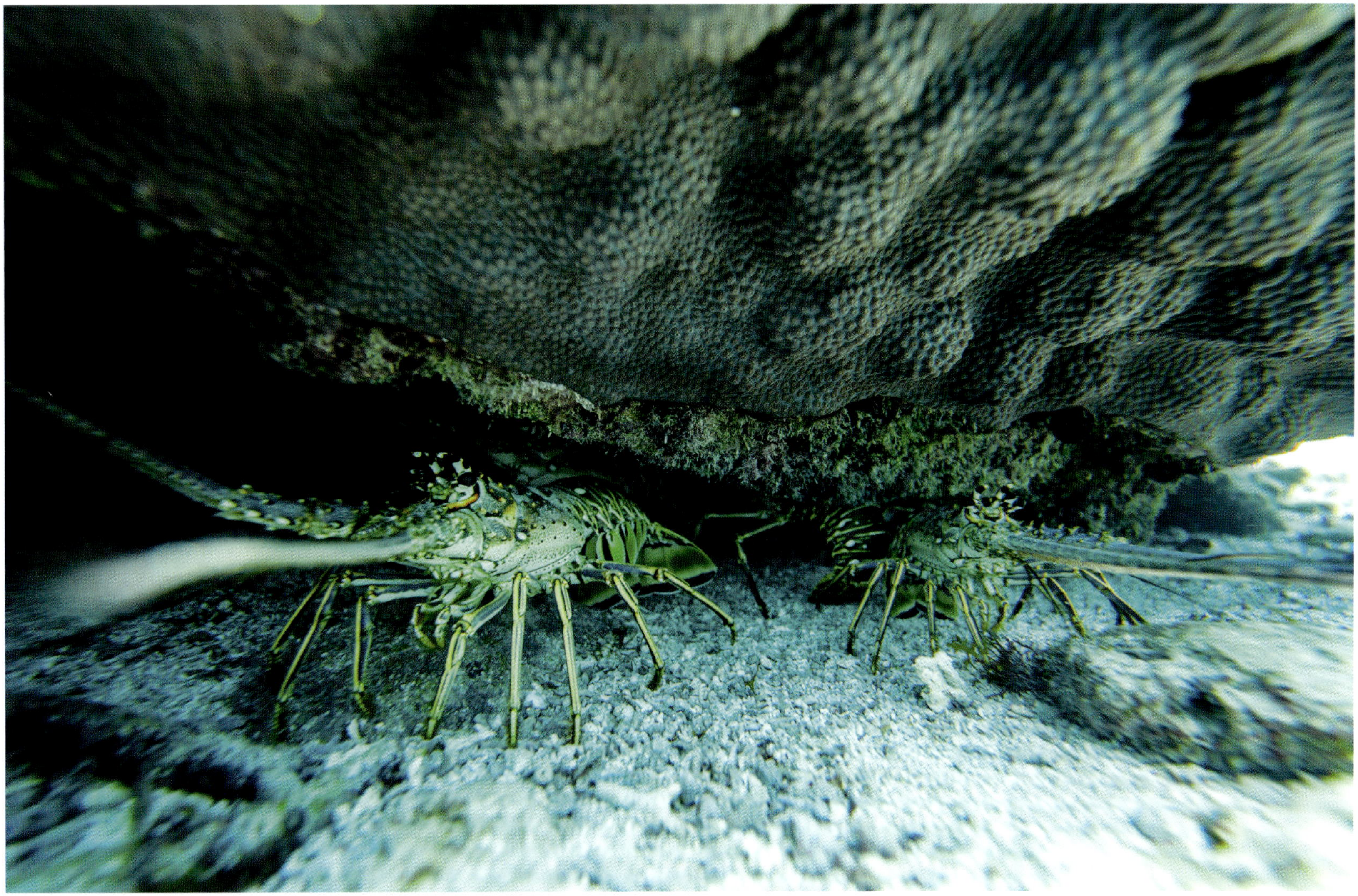

Spiny lobsters (*Panulirus argus*) squeeze in tight under a boulder star coral (*Orbicella annularis*).

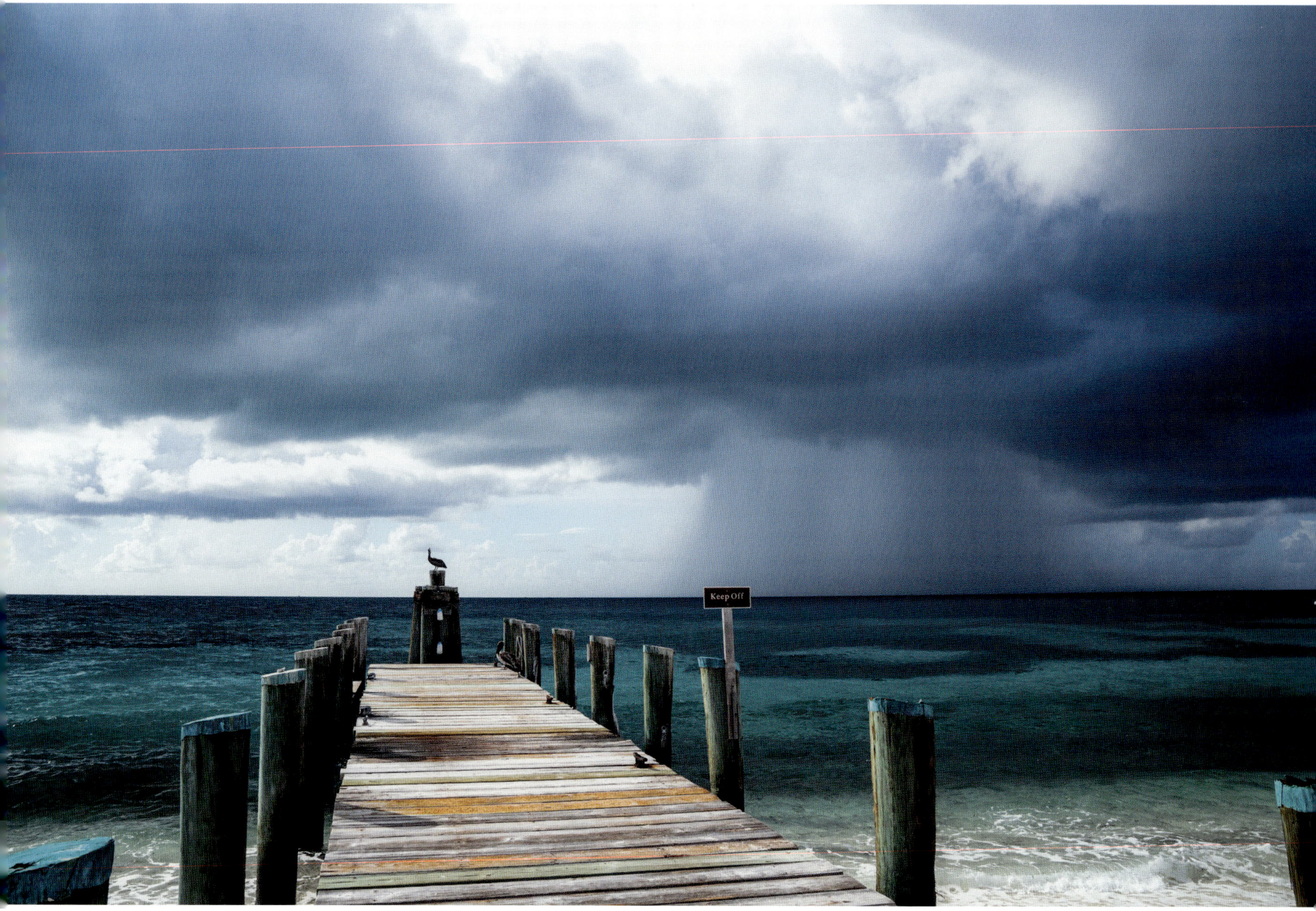

Passing storms as seen from the Loggerhead loading dock.

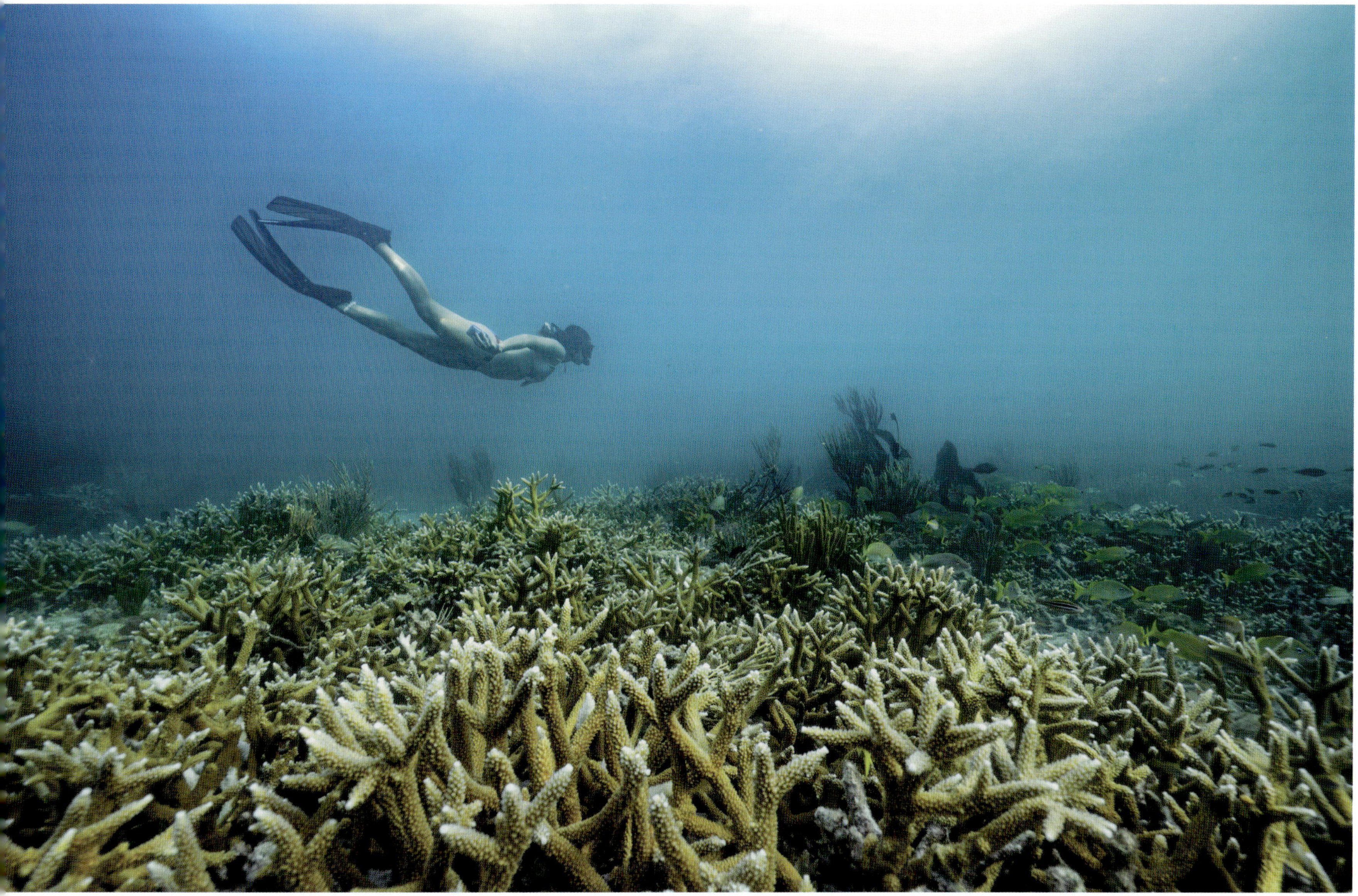

A swimmer dives down to get a better look at a beautiful thicket of staghorn coral (*Acropora cervicornis*).

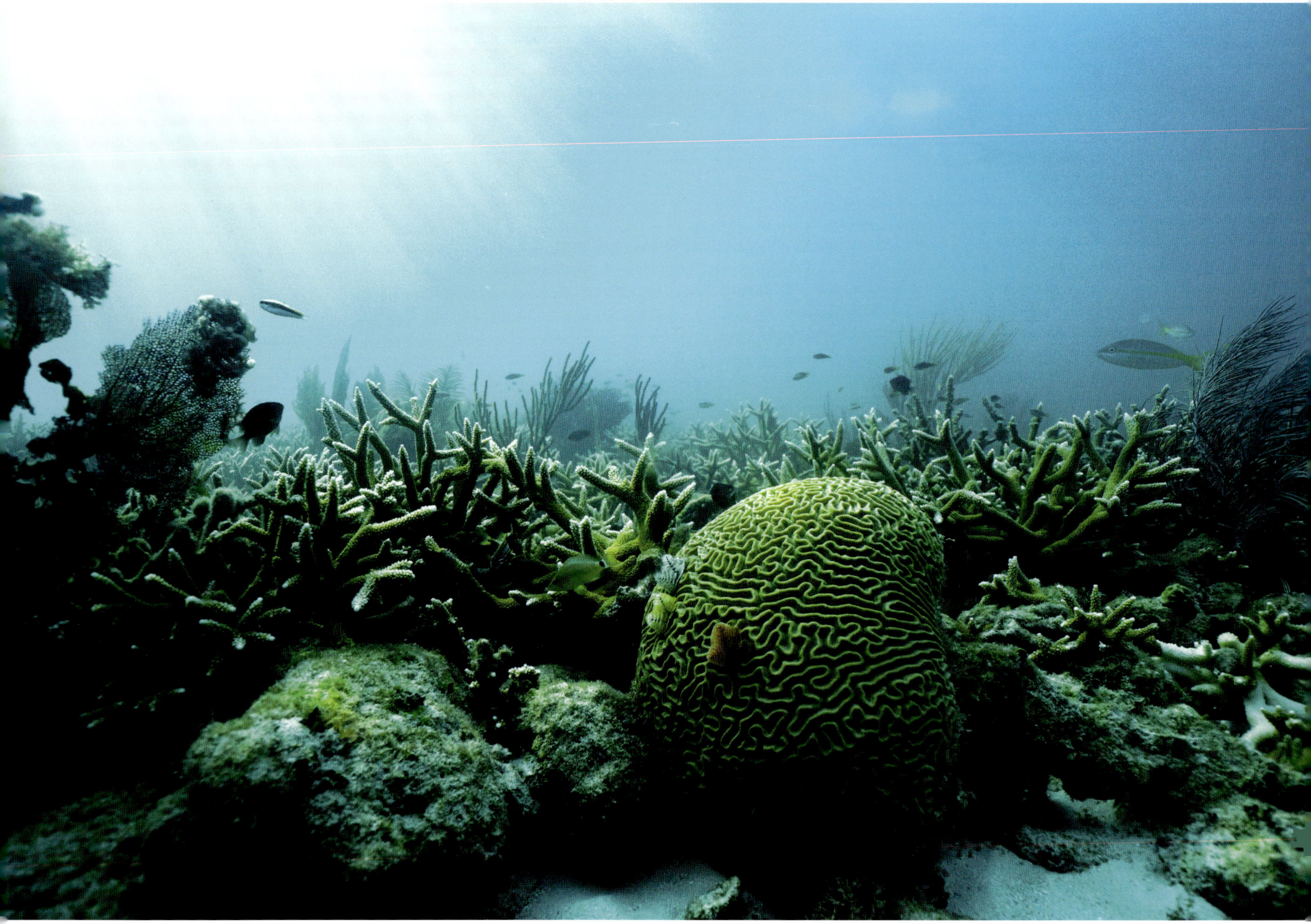

Brain corals (*Platygyra lamellina*) and staghorn corals.

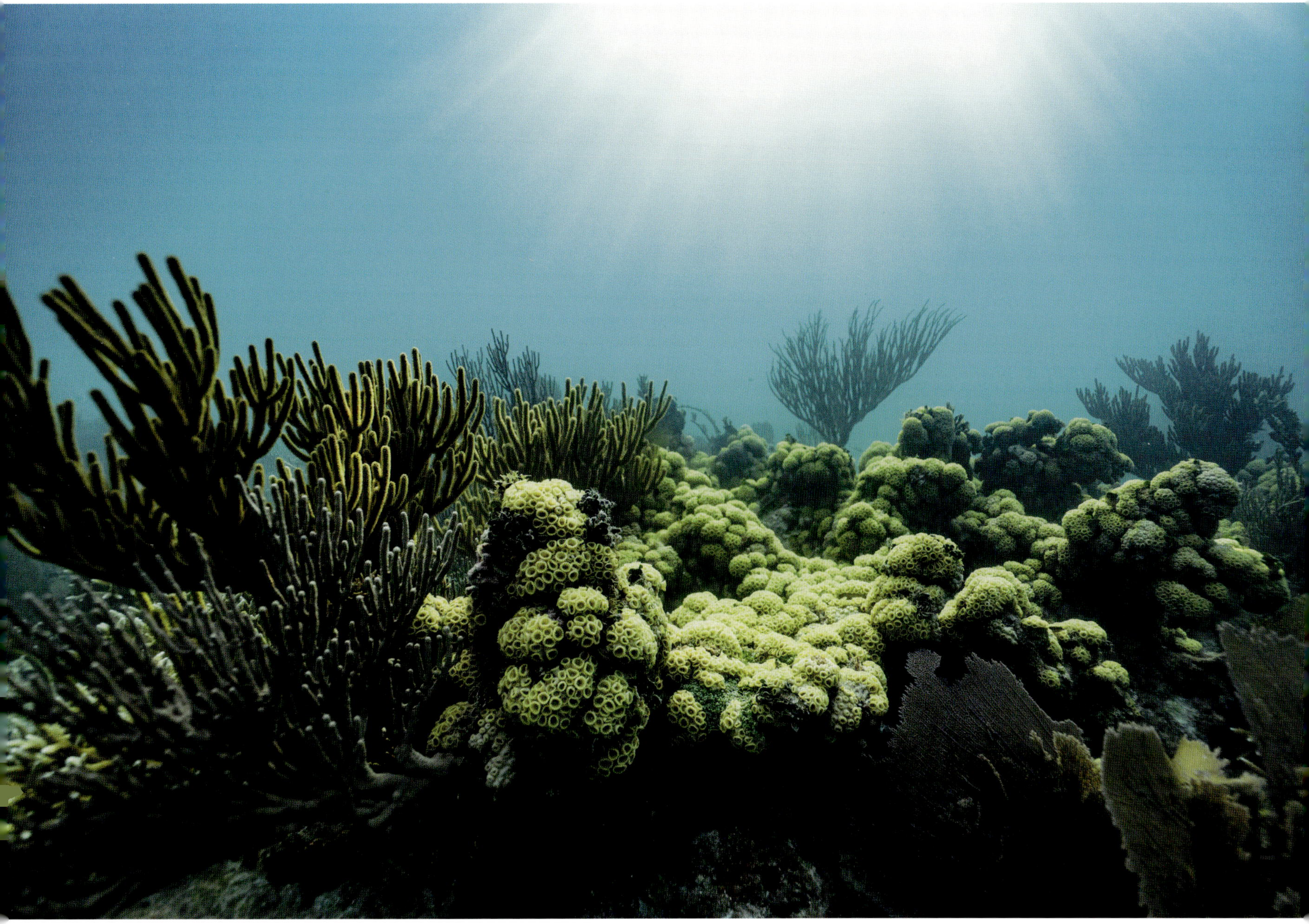

White encrusting zoanthid (*Palythoa caribaeorum*). Zoanthids are related to corals, sea anemones, and jellyfish.

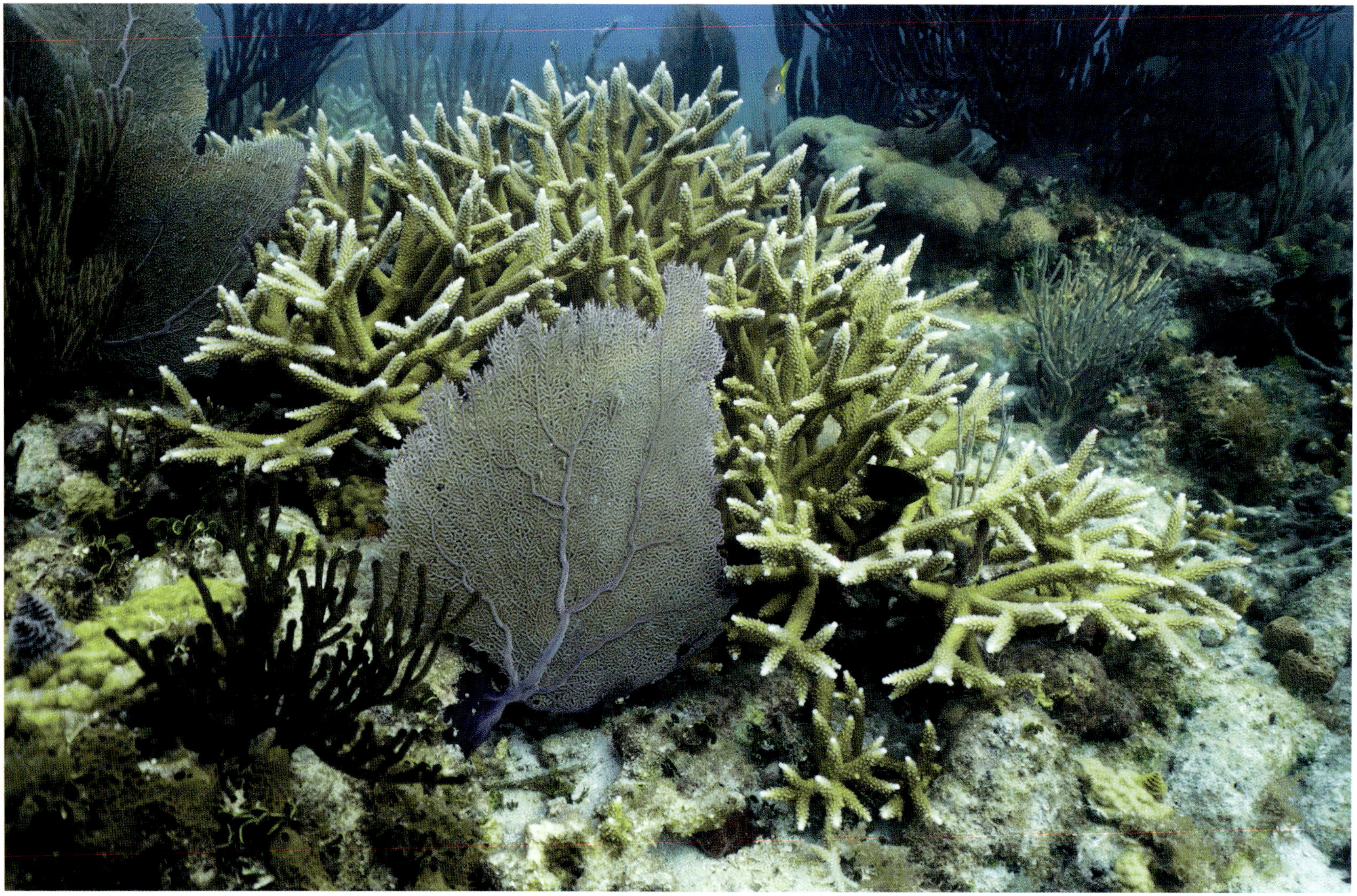

Staghorn coral clusters around a common sea fan.

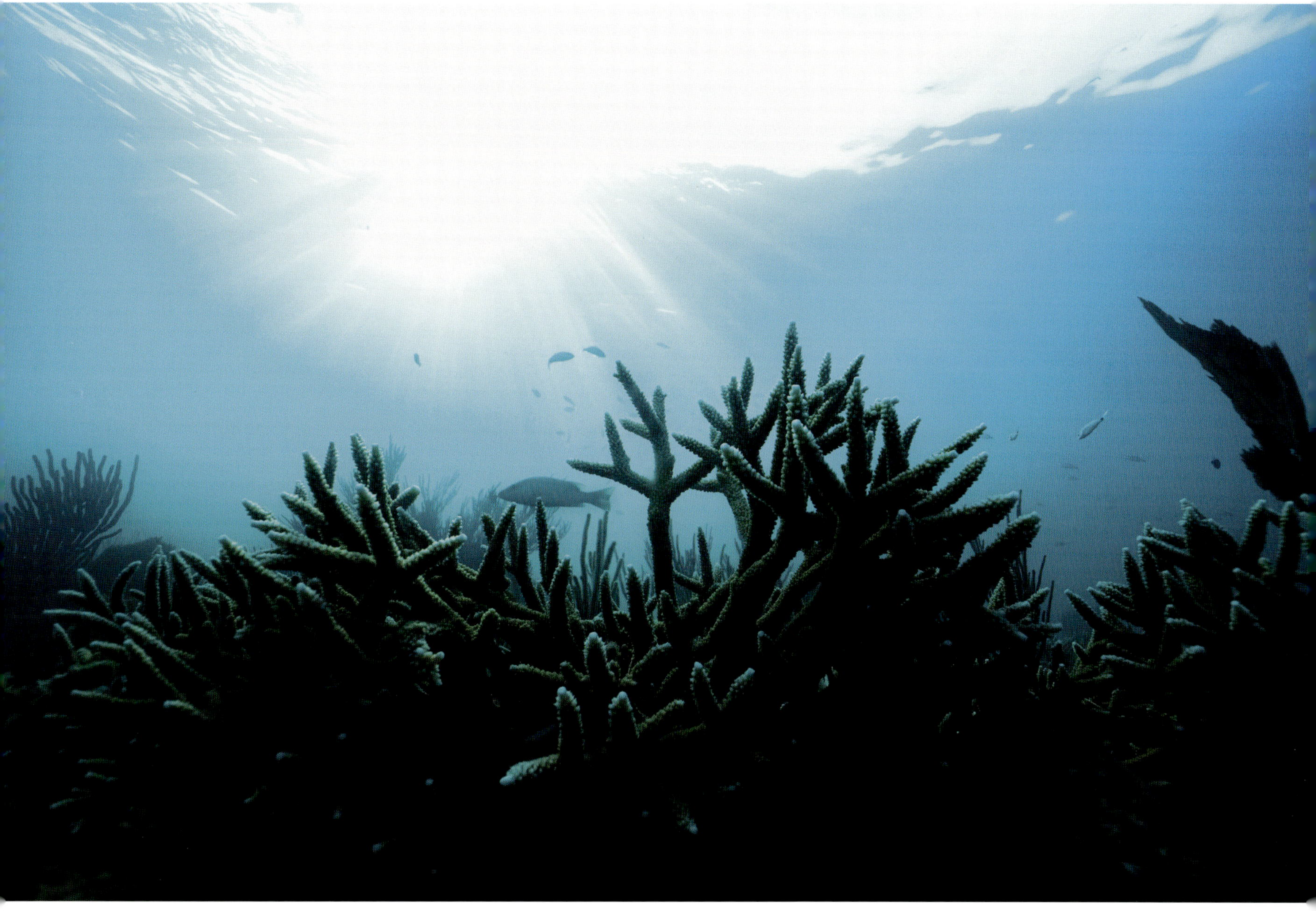

Staghorn coral silhouettes.

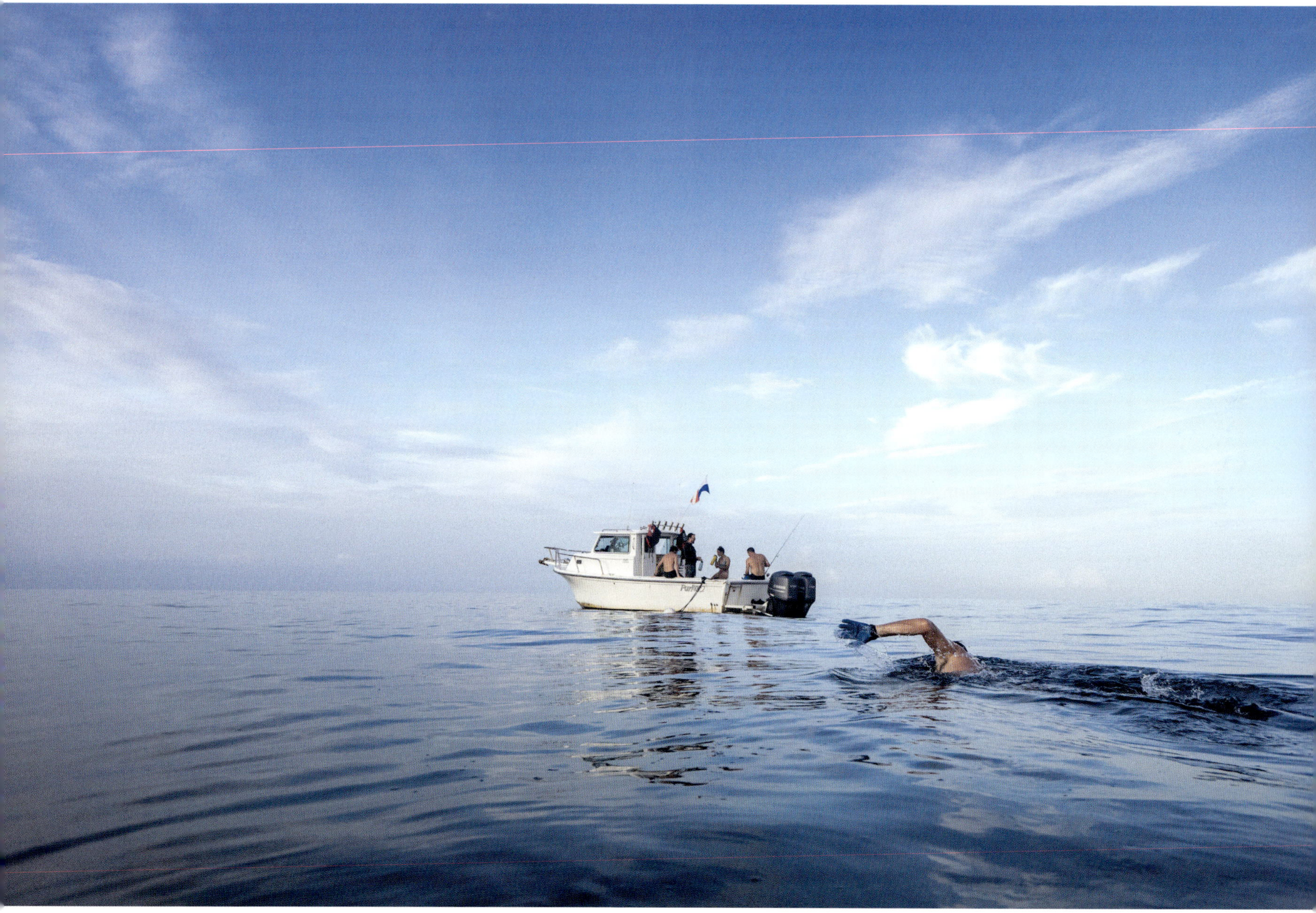

A swimmer heads back to the boat after a successful coral survey.

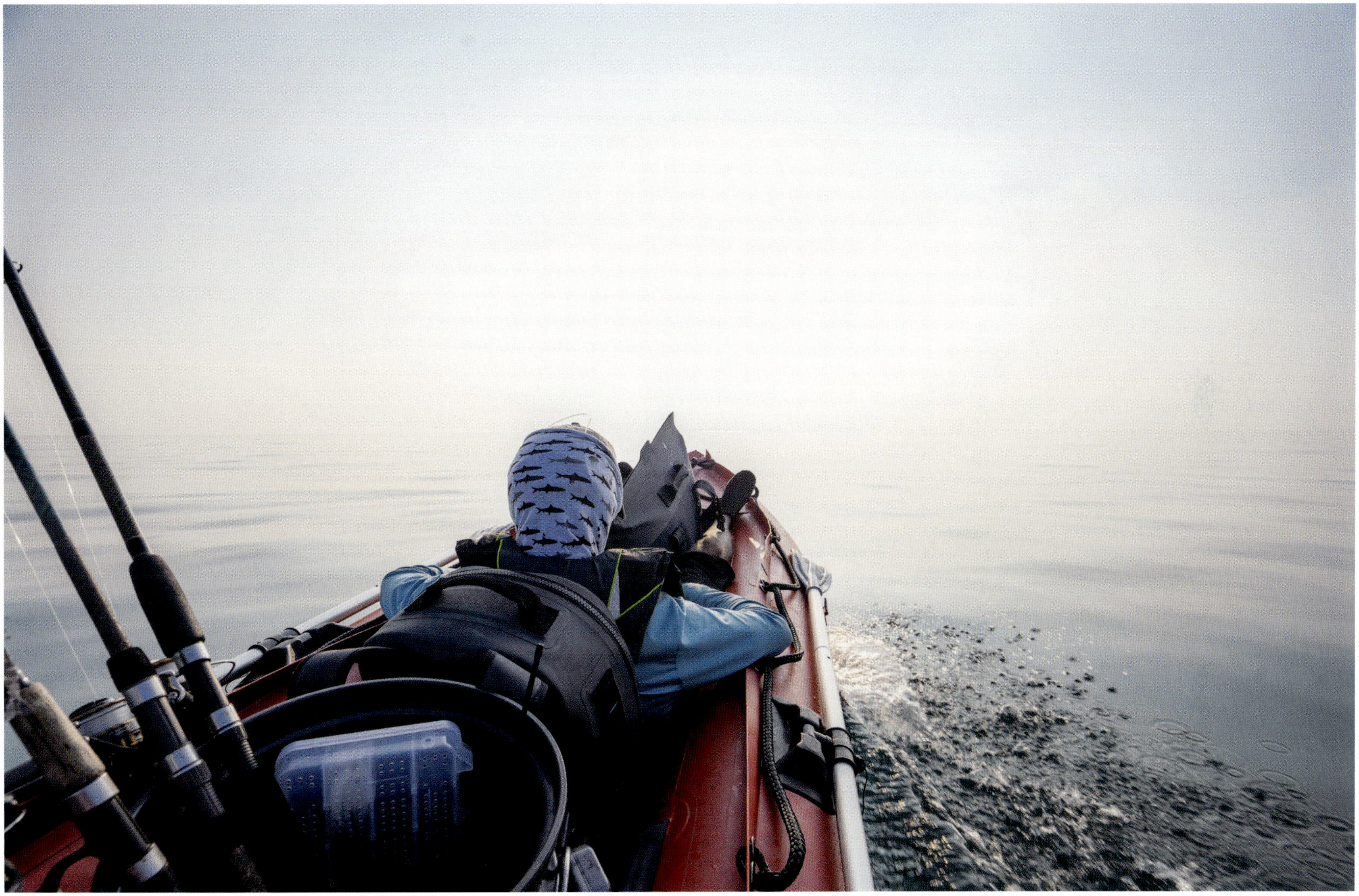

It's three miles from Garden Key to Loggerhead; boaters in small crafts can only hope for good weather and light winds to make for an easy crossing.

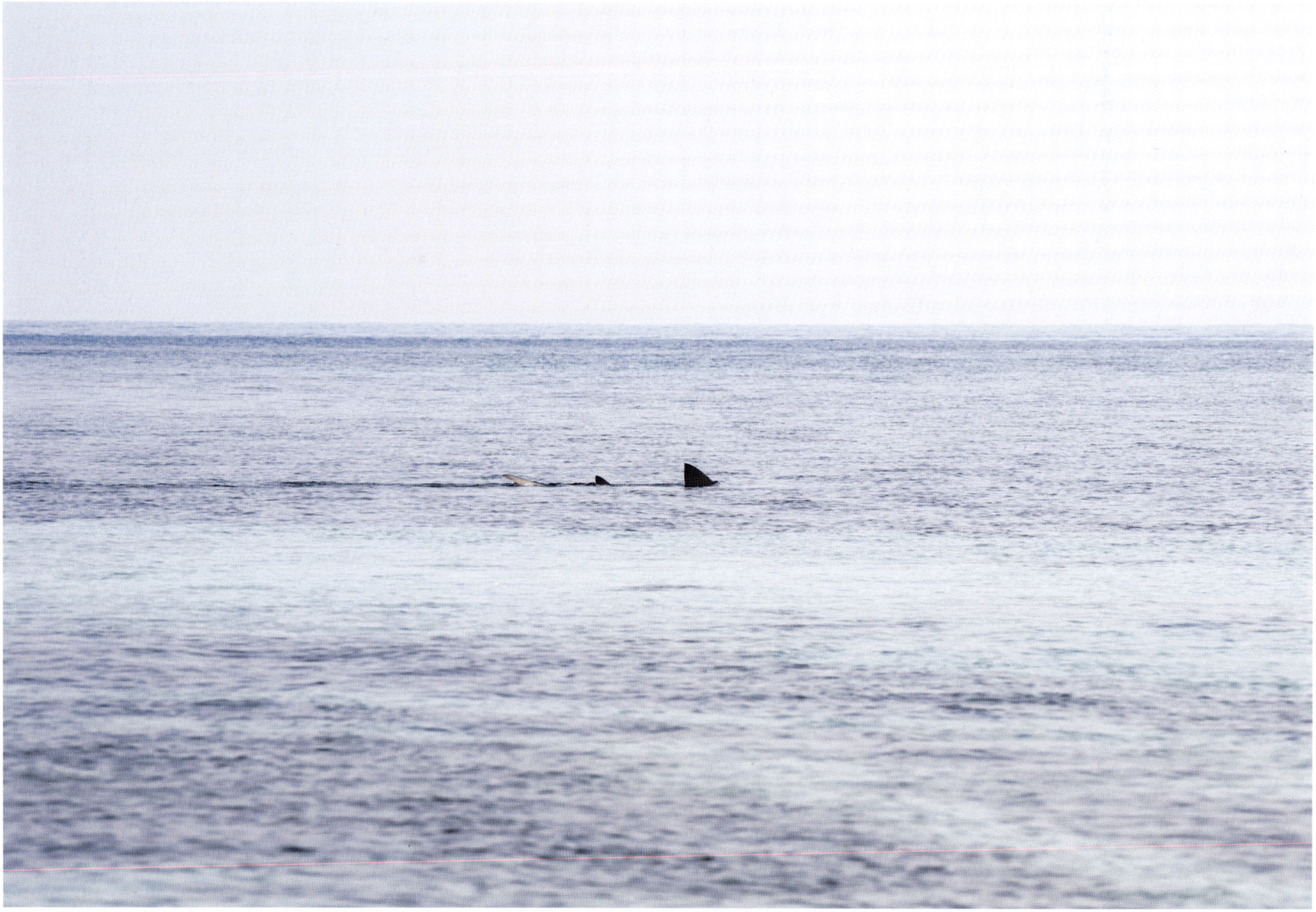

A large shark, probably a big bull (*Carcharhinus leucas*), swims off Loggerhead Key, dorsal fins breaking the water.

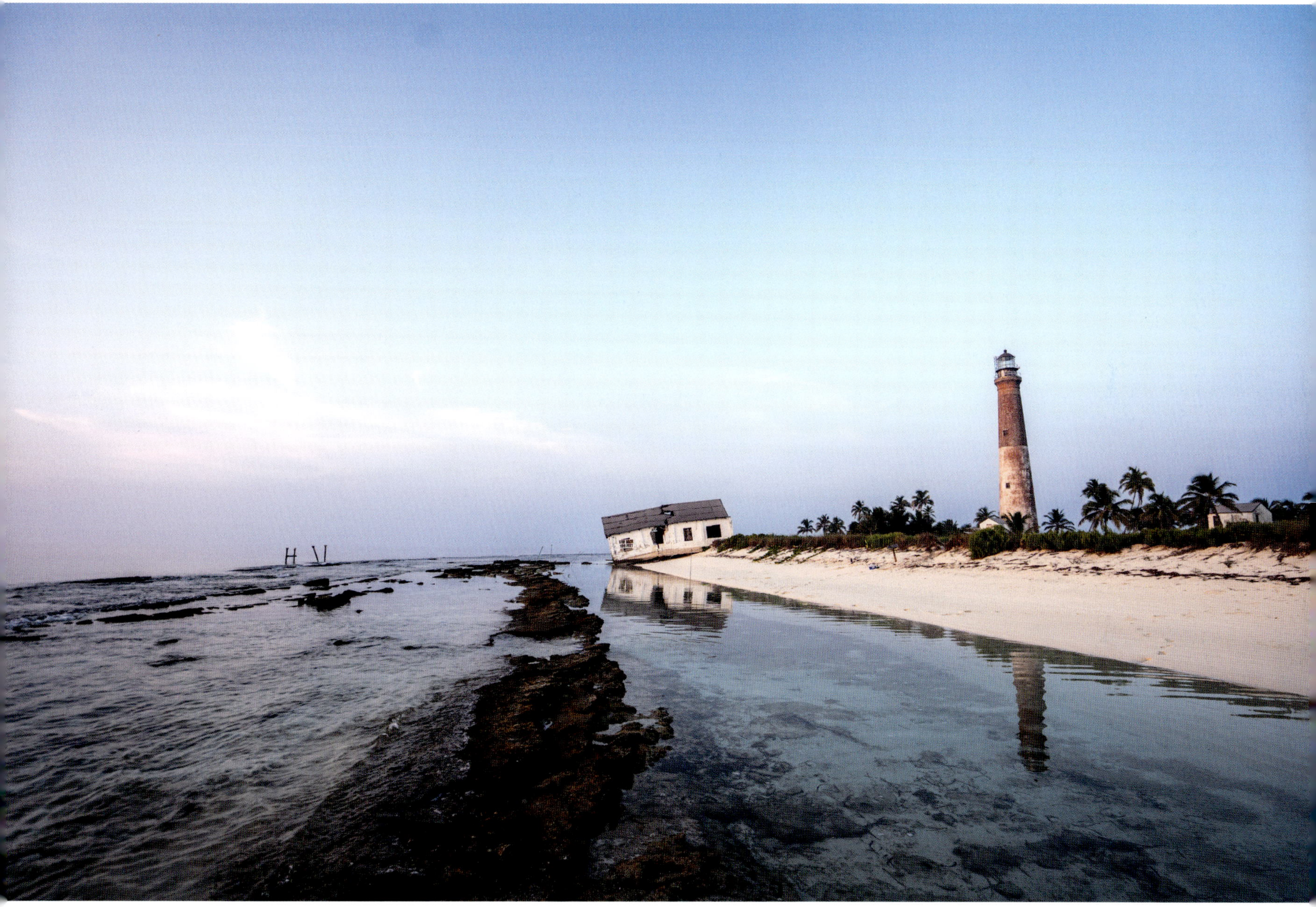

West side of Loggerhead Key and the old boathouse. The boathouse's position at water's edge is the result of erosion that over time has pushed back the original shoreline.

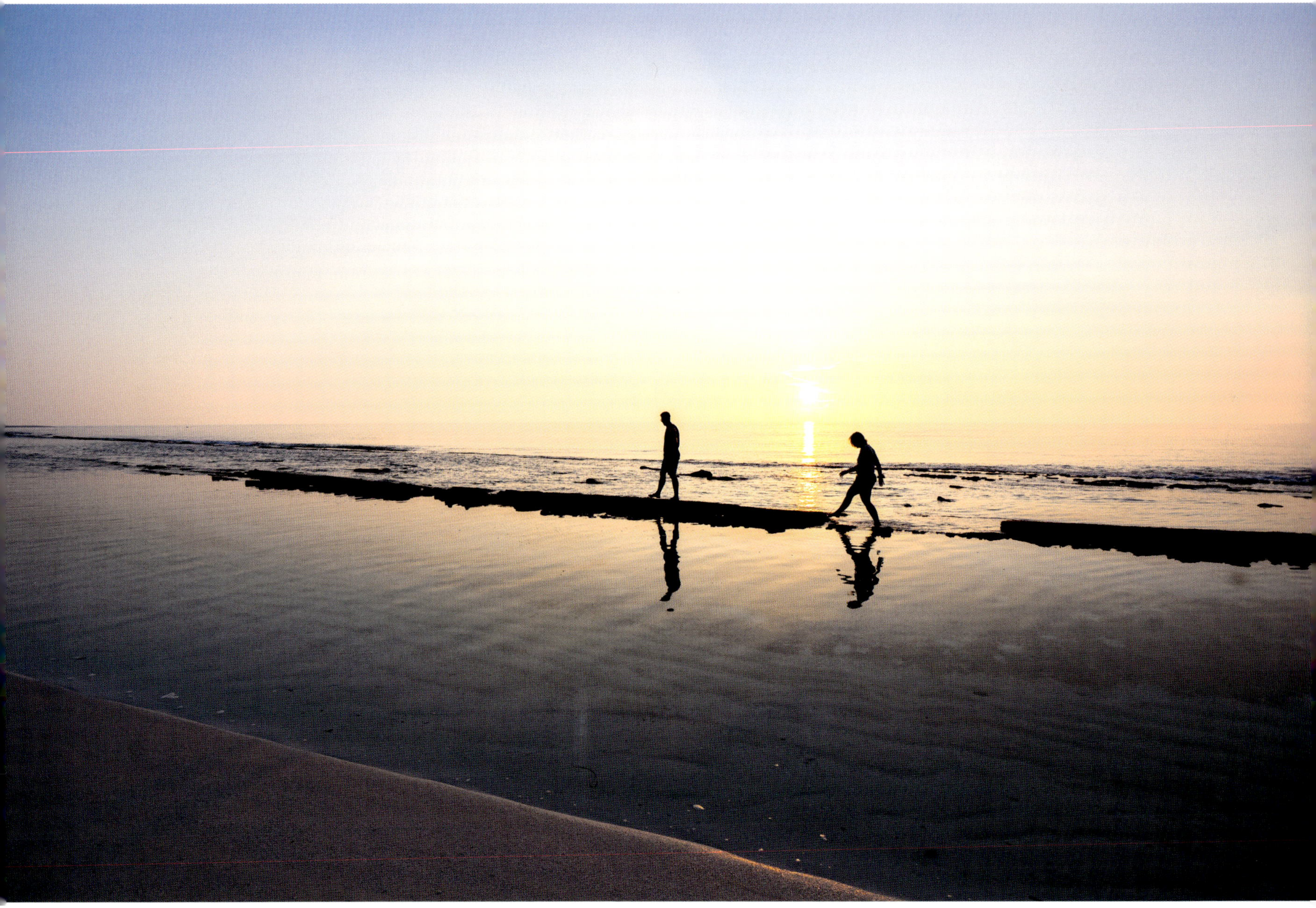

Park interns take a leisurely stroll at sunset.

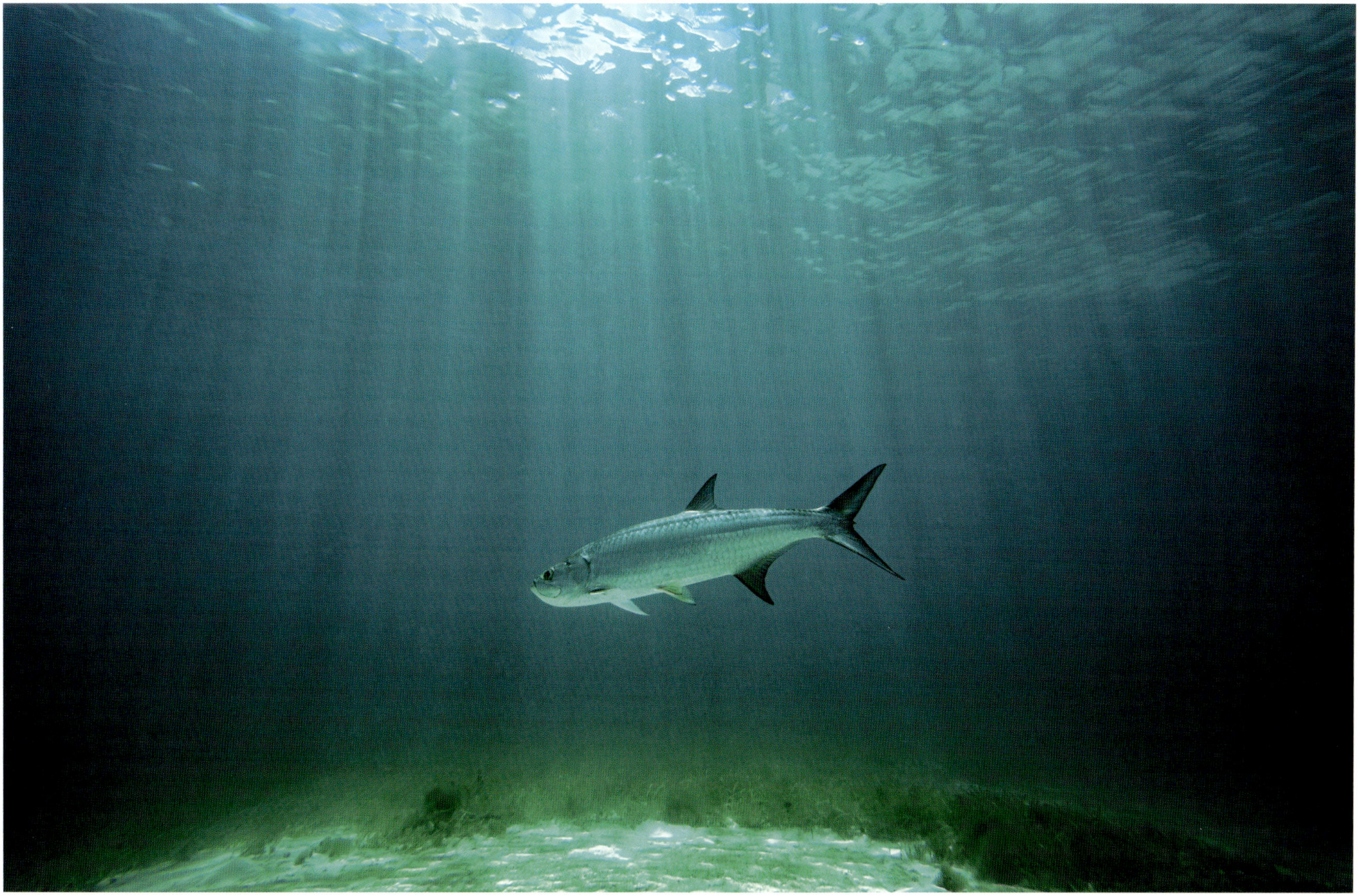

A tarpon (*Megalops atlanticus*) basks in the light.

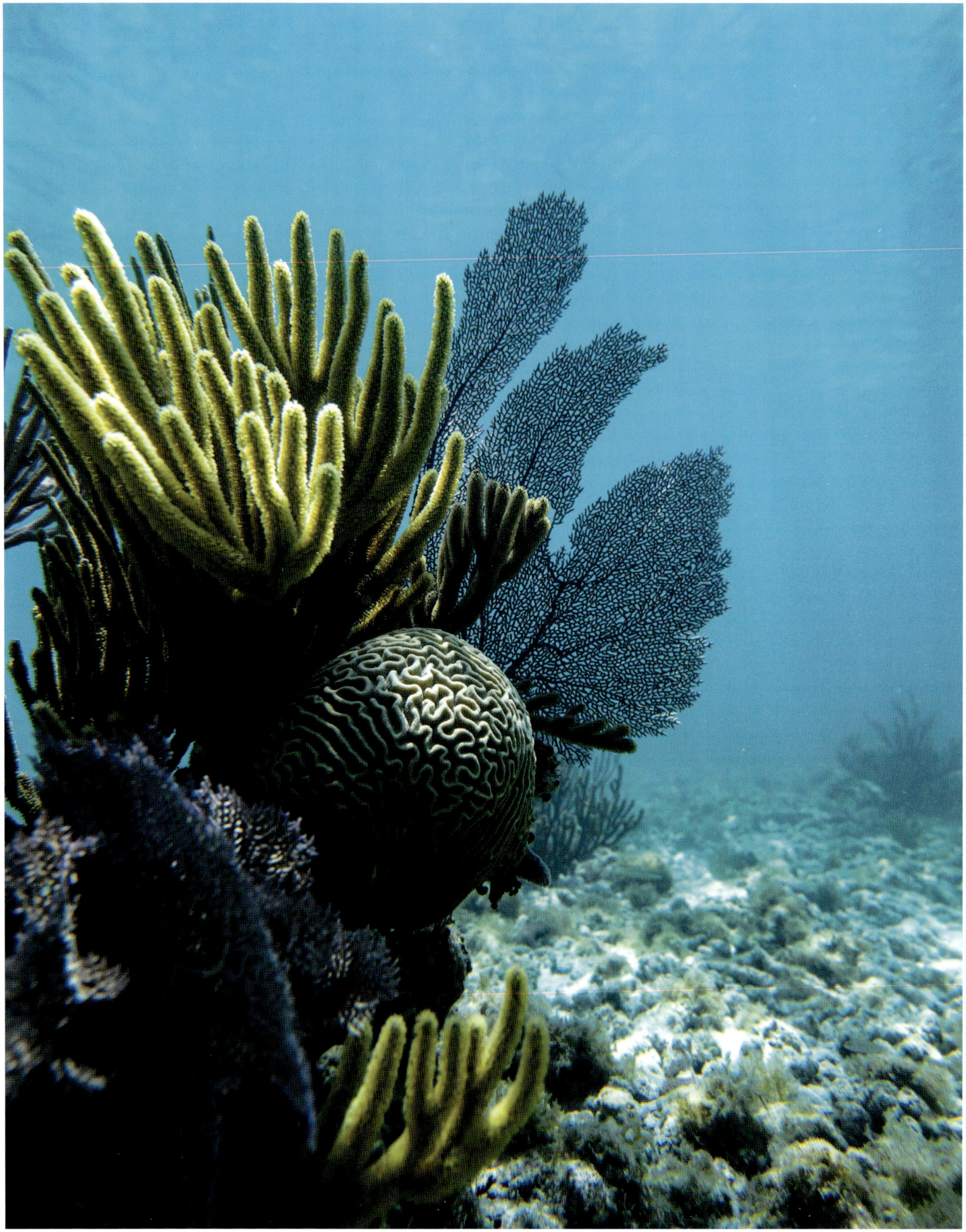

The foundations of the Caribbean reefs are stony and soft corals. Pictured here are three of the most common: sea fan, brain coral, and gorgonian soft coral.

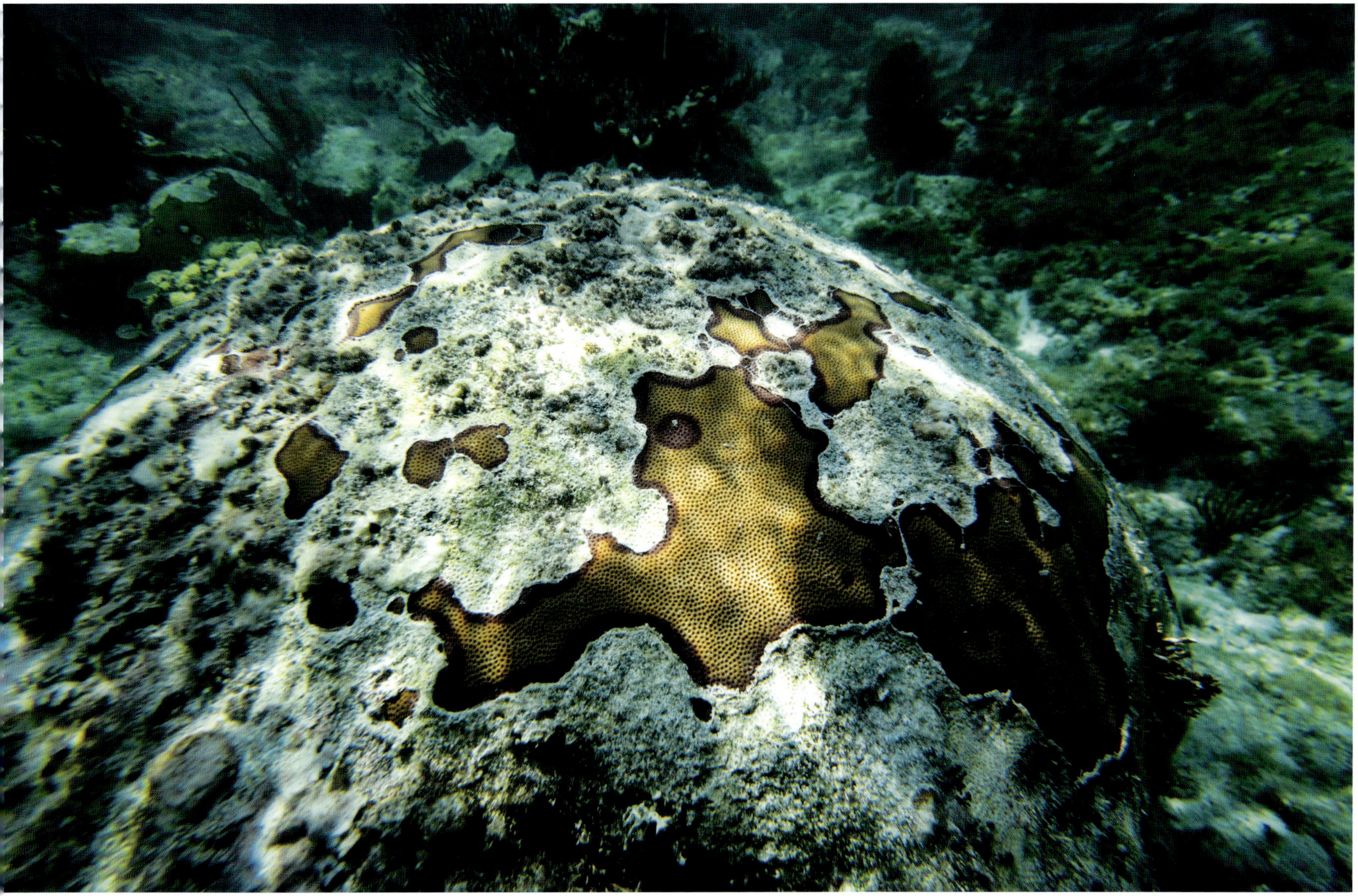

A coral disease spreads over a boulder star coral.

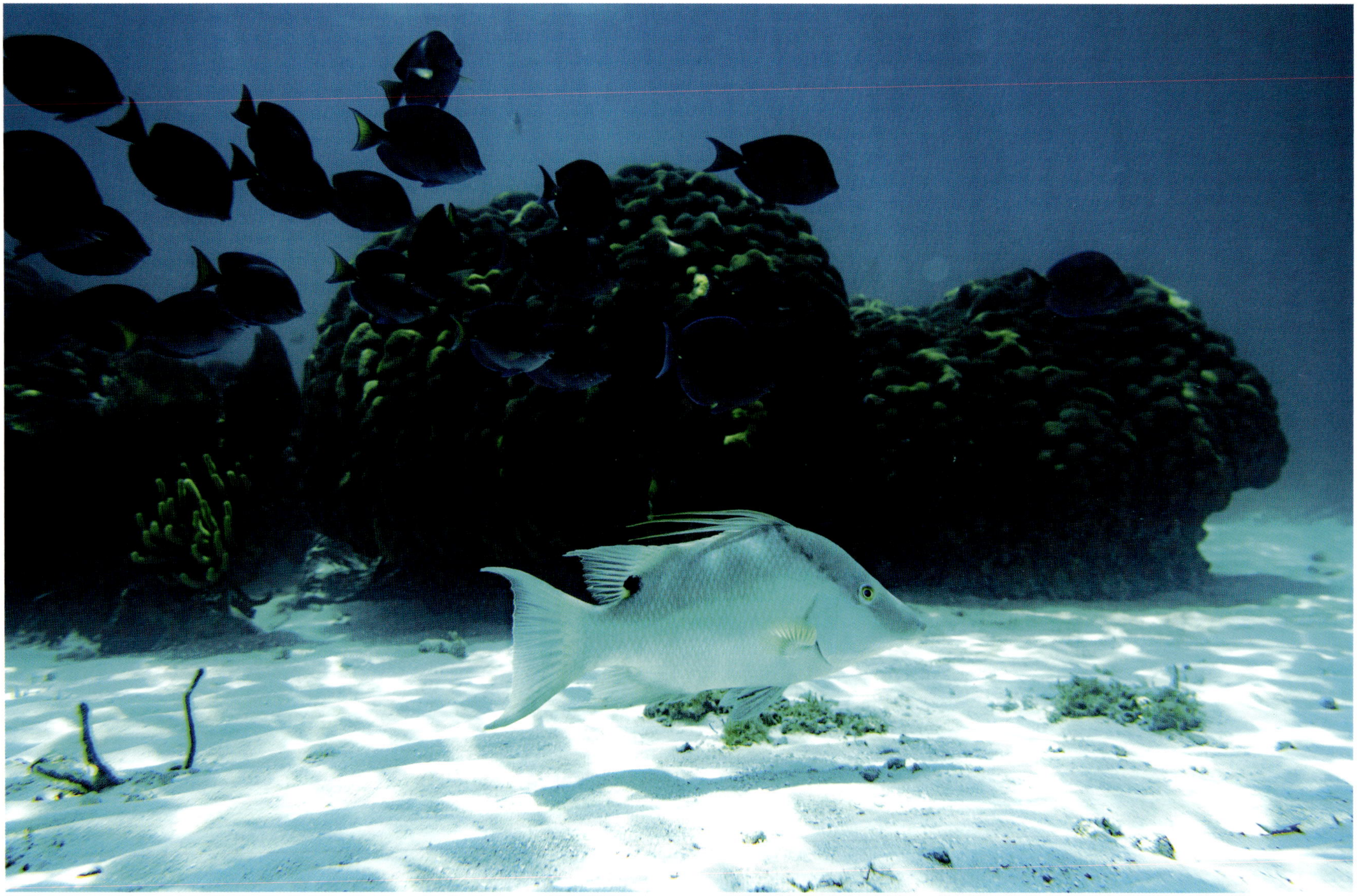

A hogfish navigates a small patch reef off Loggerhead Key.

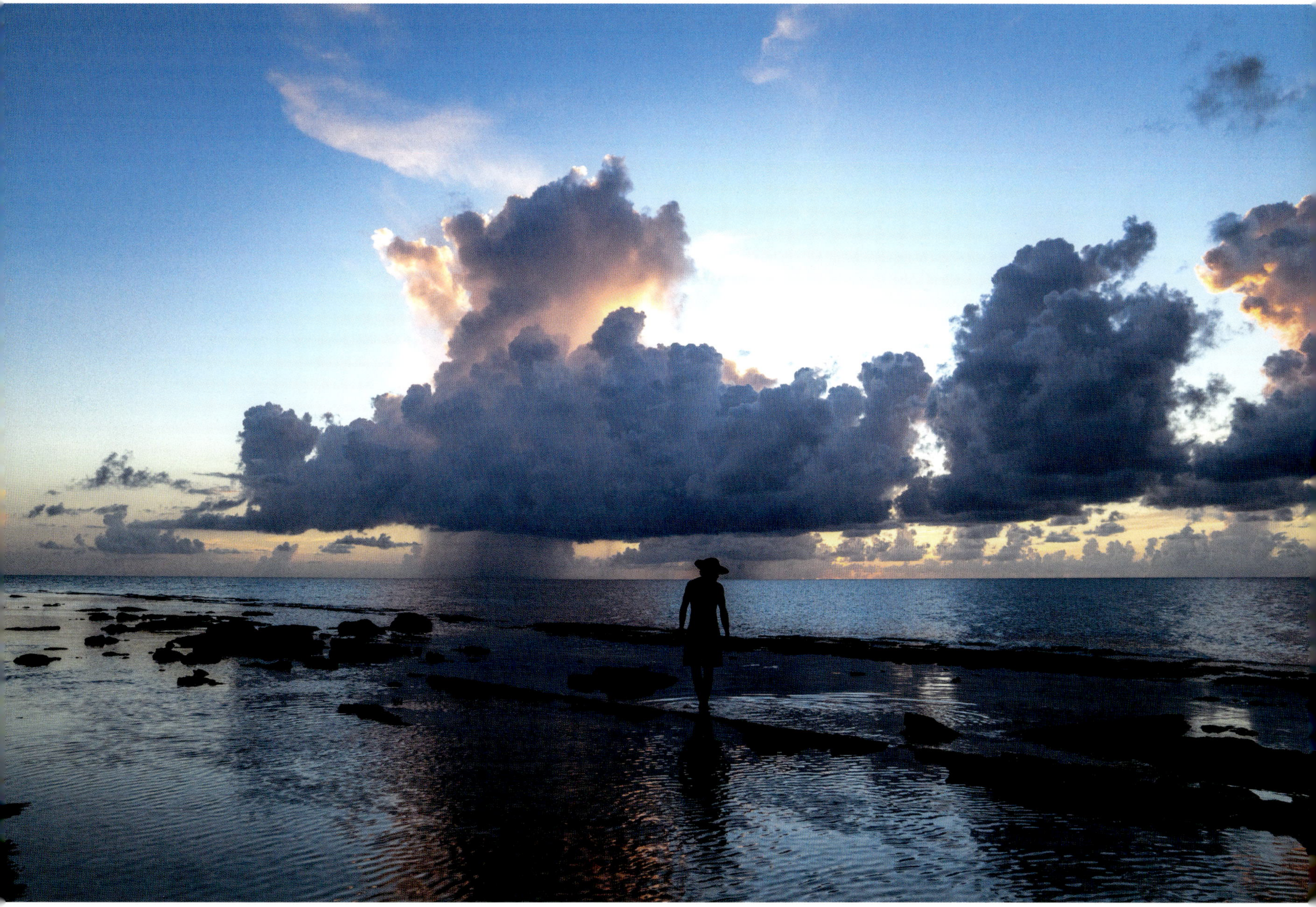

Late evening tide-pooling; you never know what you might find out here.

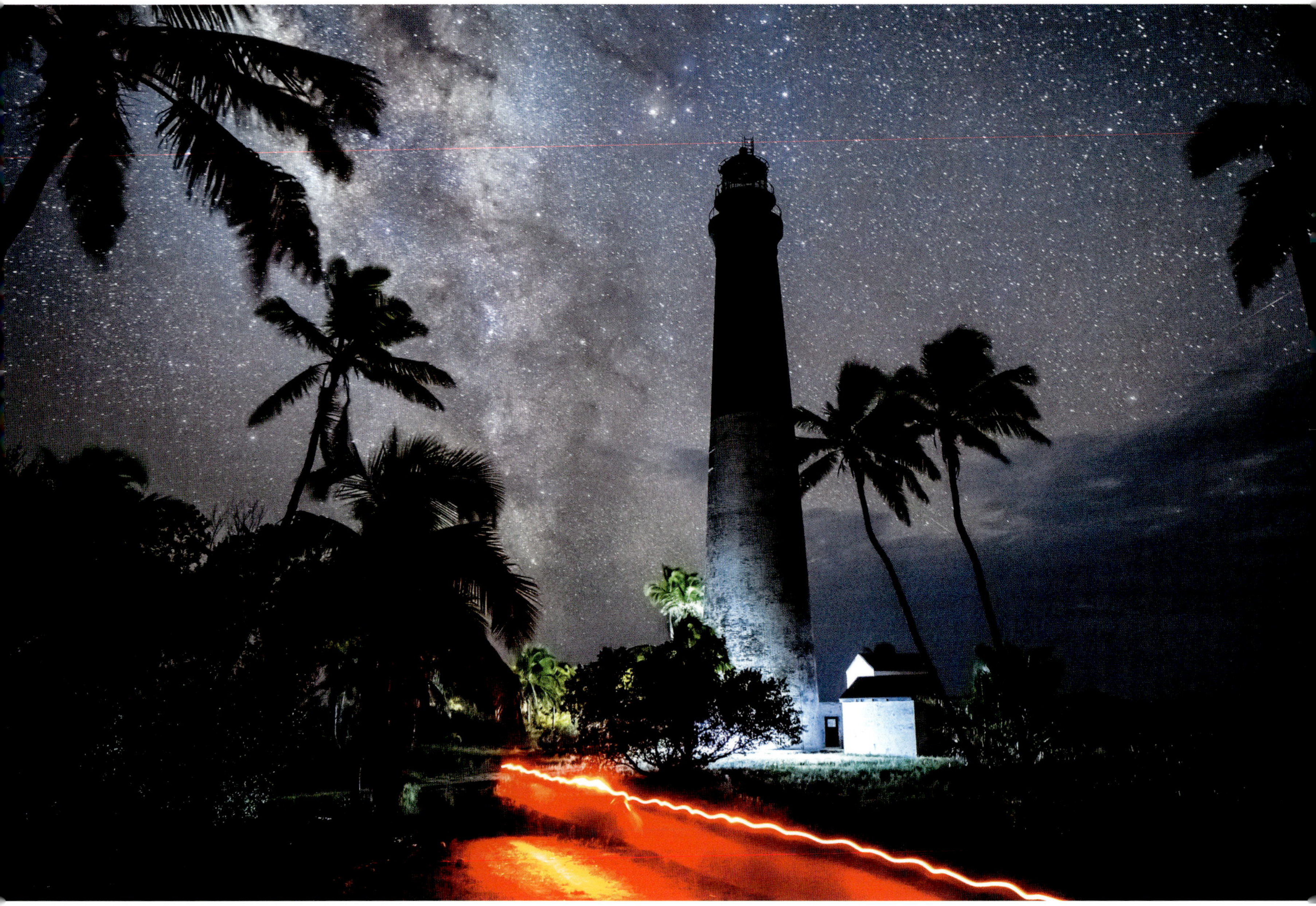

Loggerhead Key lighthouse under the Milky Way.

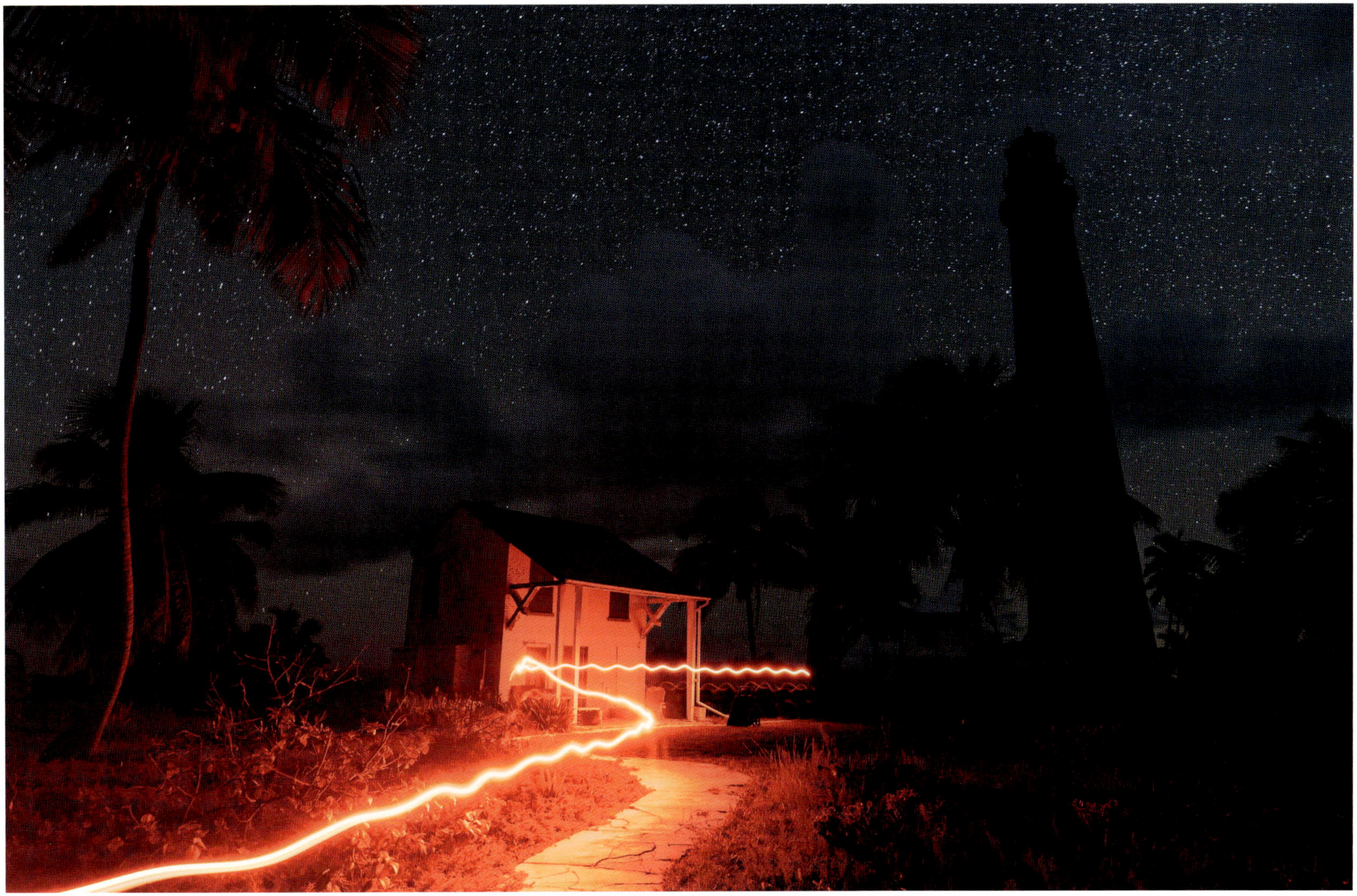

The old lighthouse keeper's home, now turned into staff housing for visiting scientists and volunteers.

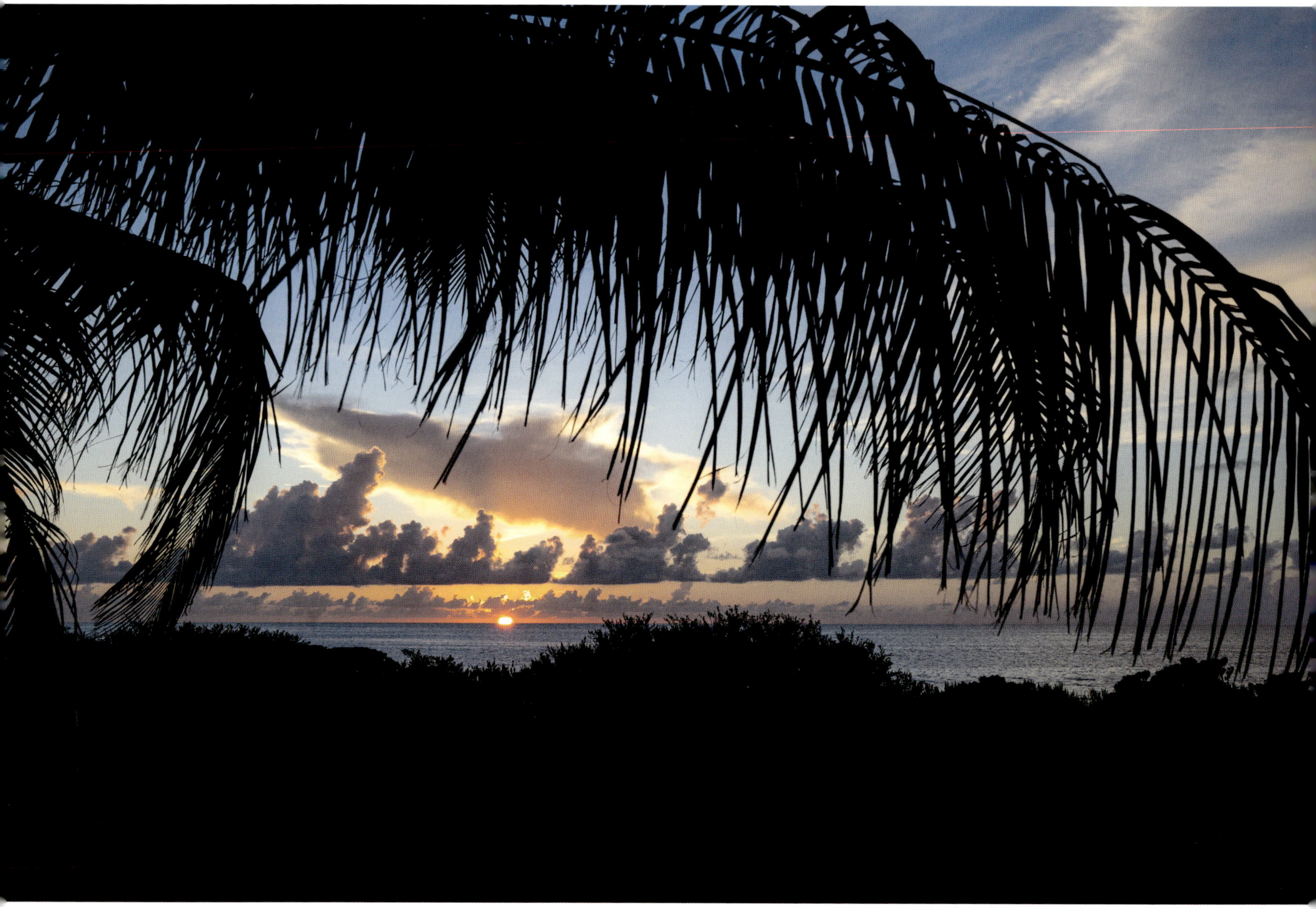

A classic Florida Keys sunset.

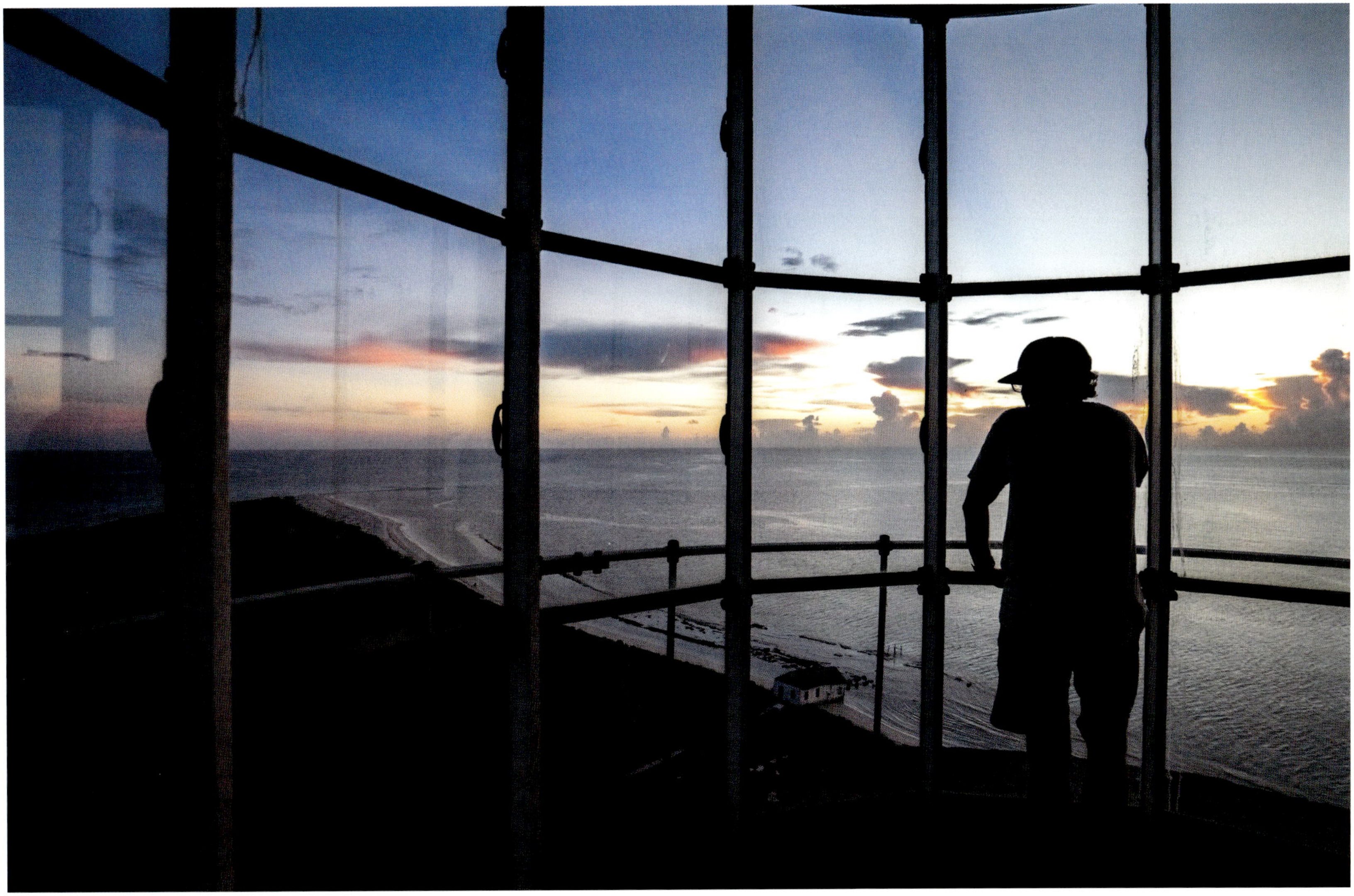

Artist Austin Armstrong, checking out the view from Loggerhead light.

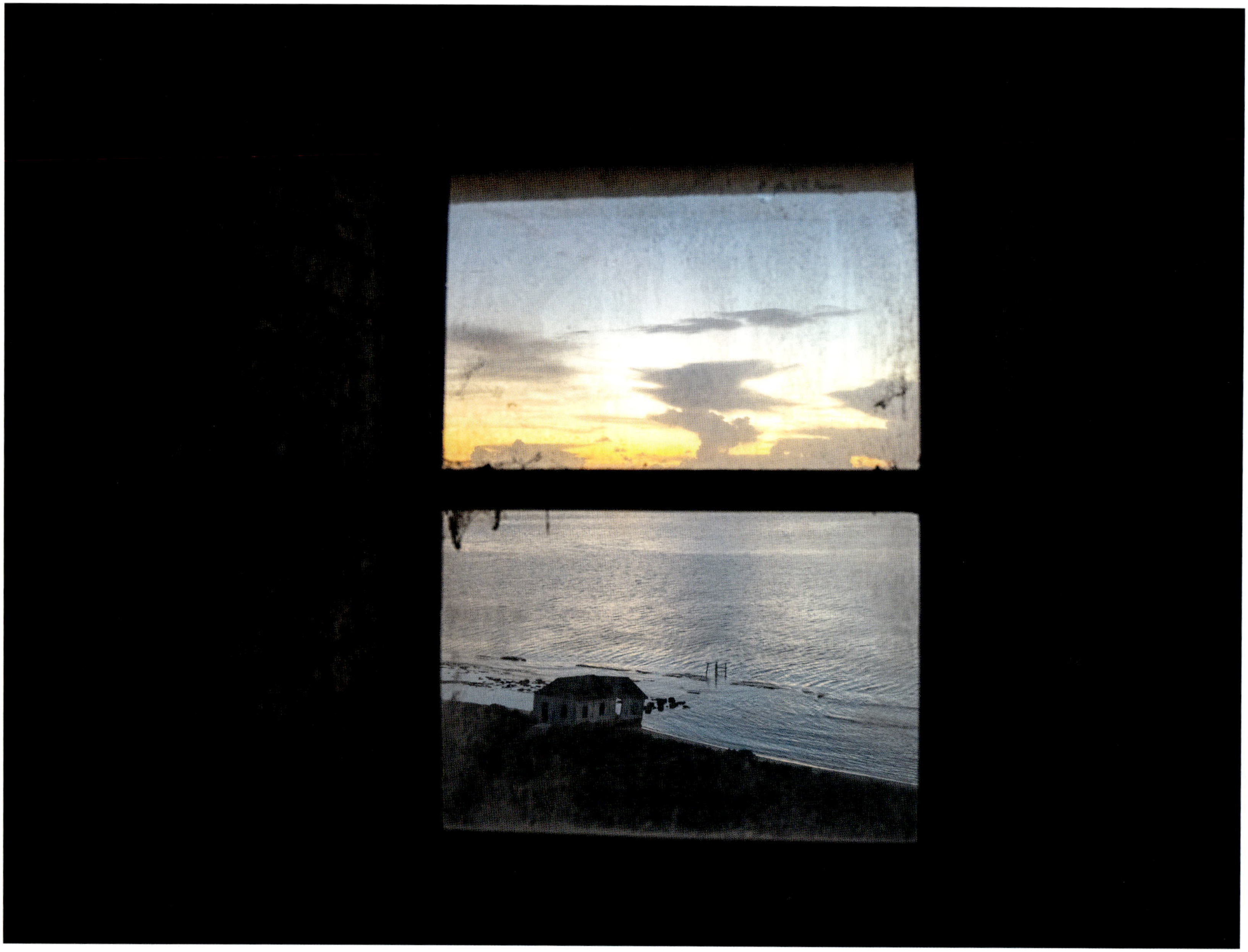

View from Loggerhead Key lighthouse to the old boathouse.

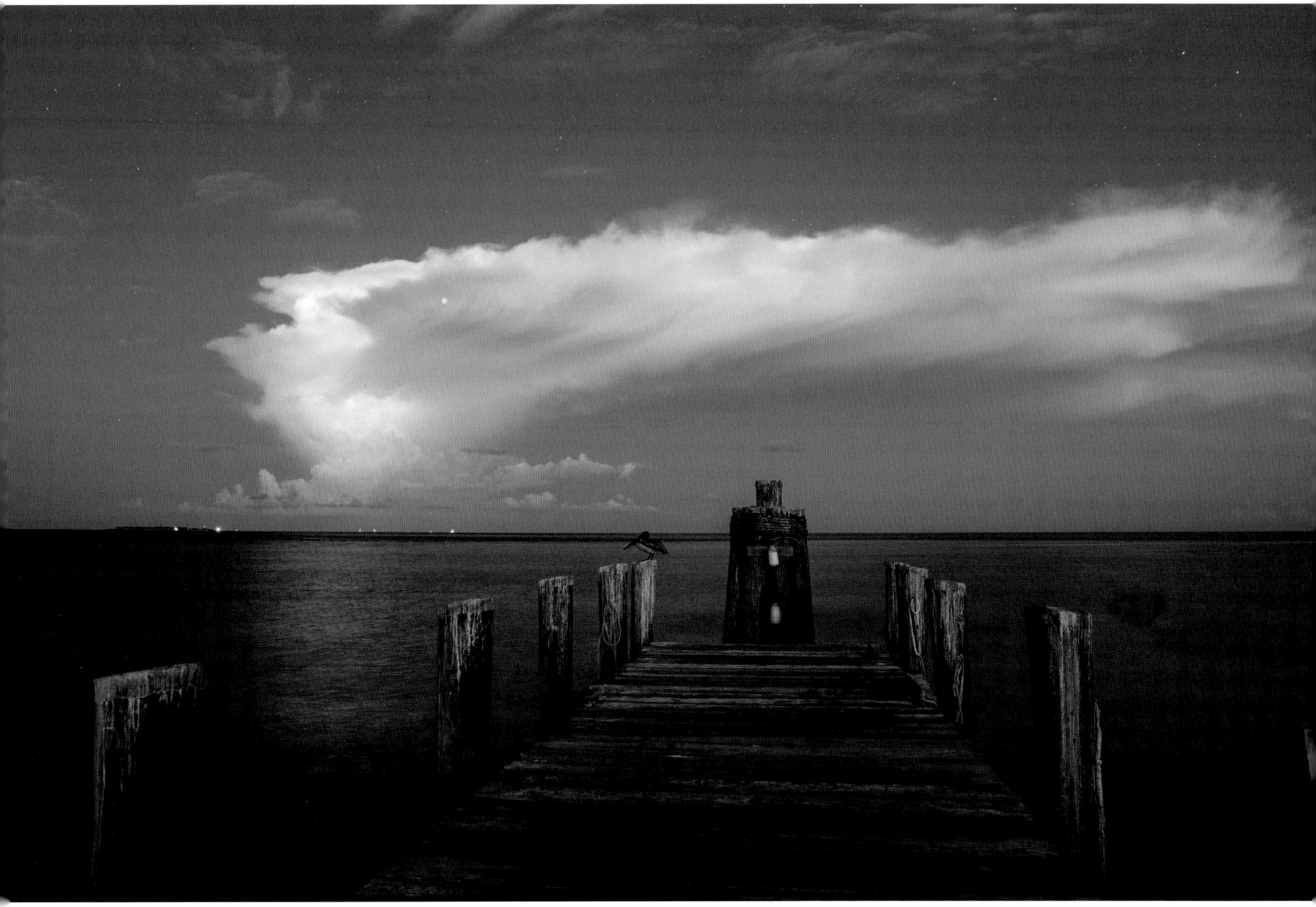

Twilight from the loading dock on Loggerhead Key.
A storm brews in the distance over Garden Key.

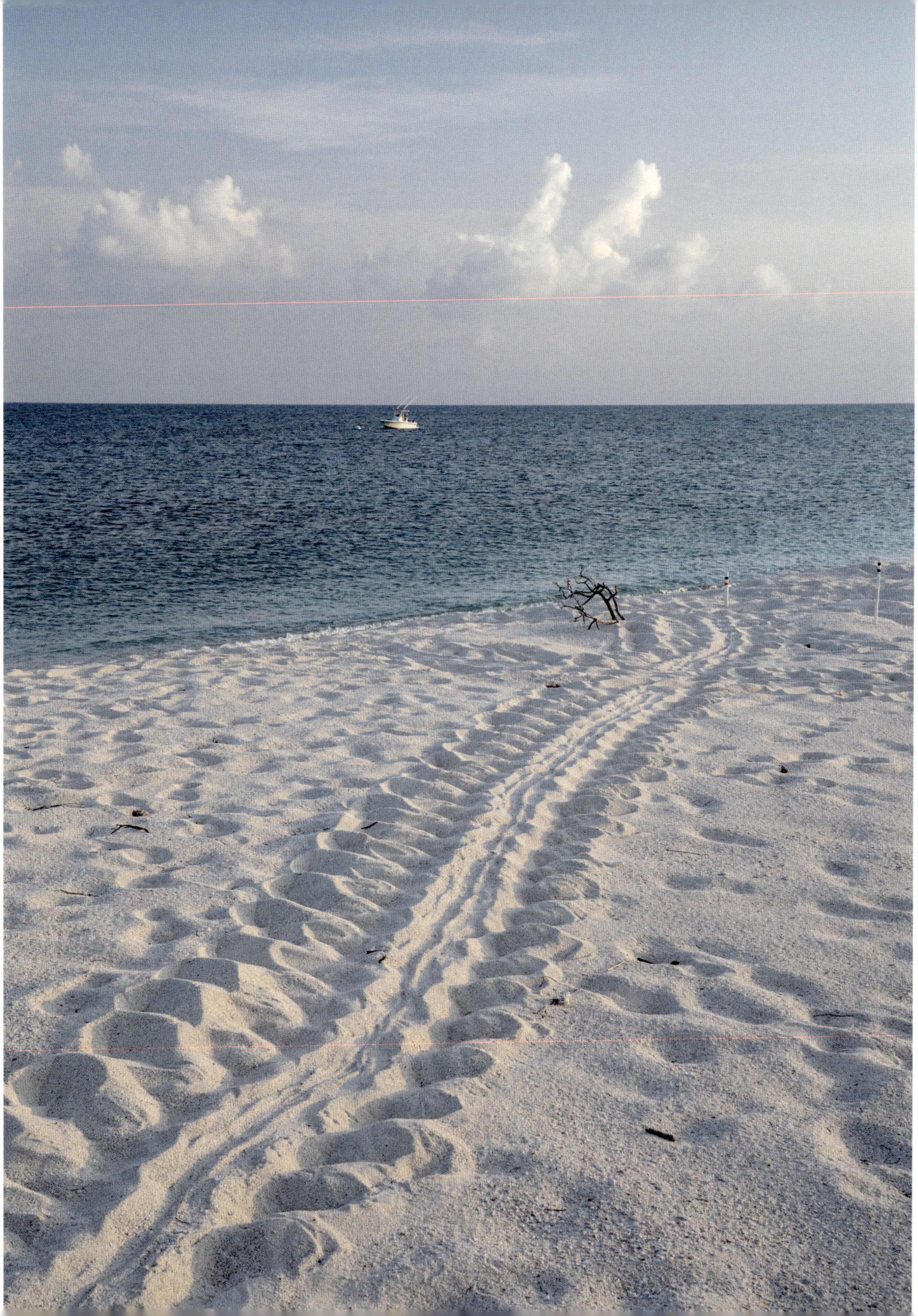

Turtle tracks coming from the ocean. During the nesting season (from March to October on the Keys' Atlantic side and from May to October on the Gulf of Mexico side), female turtles leave the water and drag their bodies up the beach to find a place to dig a nest and lay eggs.

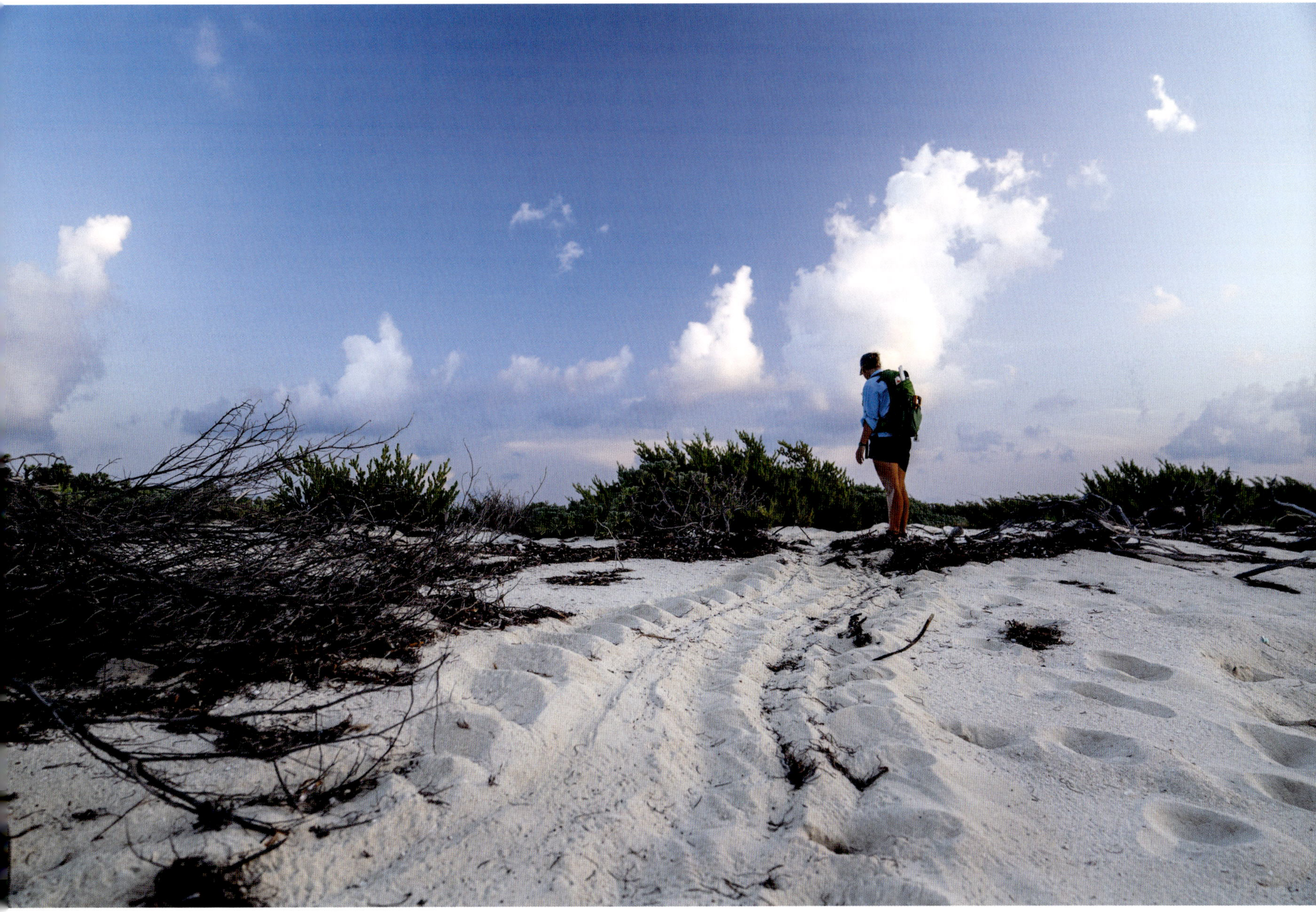

A park intern surveys a recently dug turtle nest.

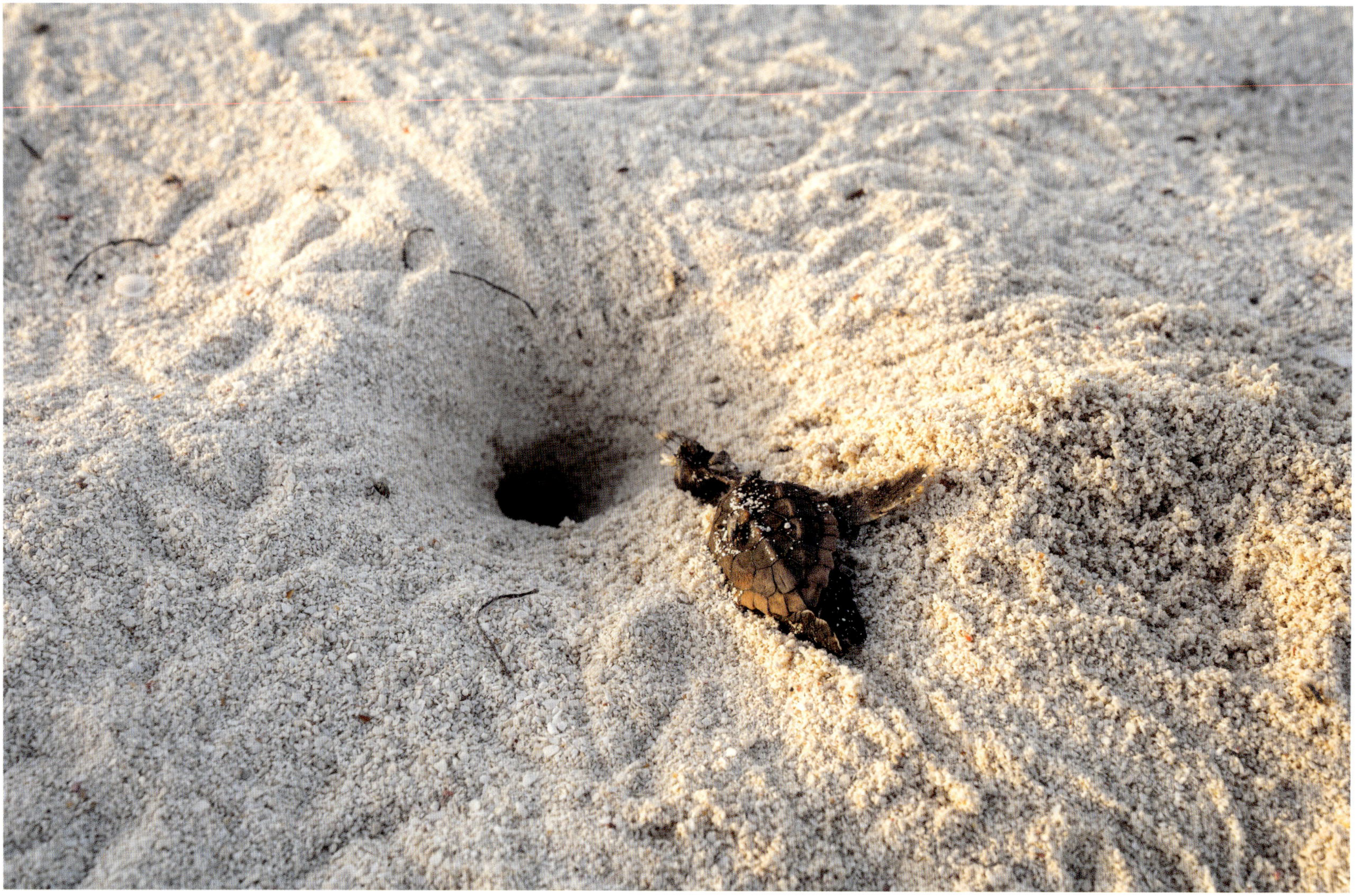

A dead juvenile Loggerhead turtle (*Caretta caretta*), soon to be eaten, lies in the sand just outside the hole of a ghost crab (family Ocypodinae).

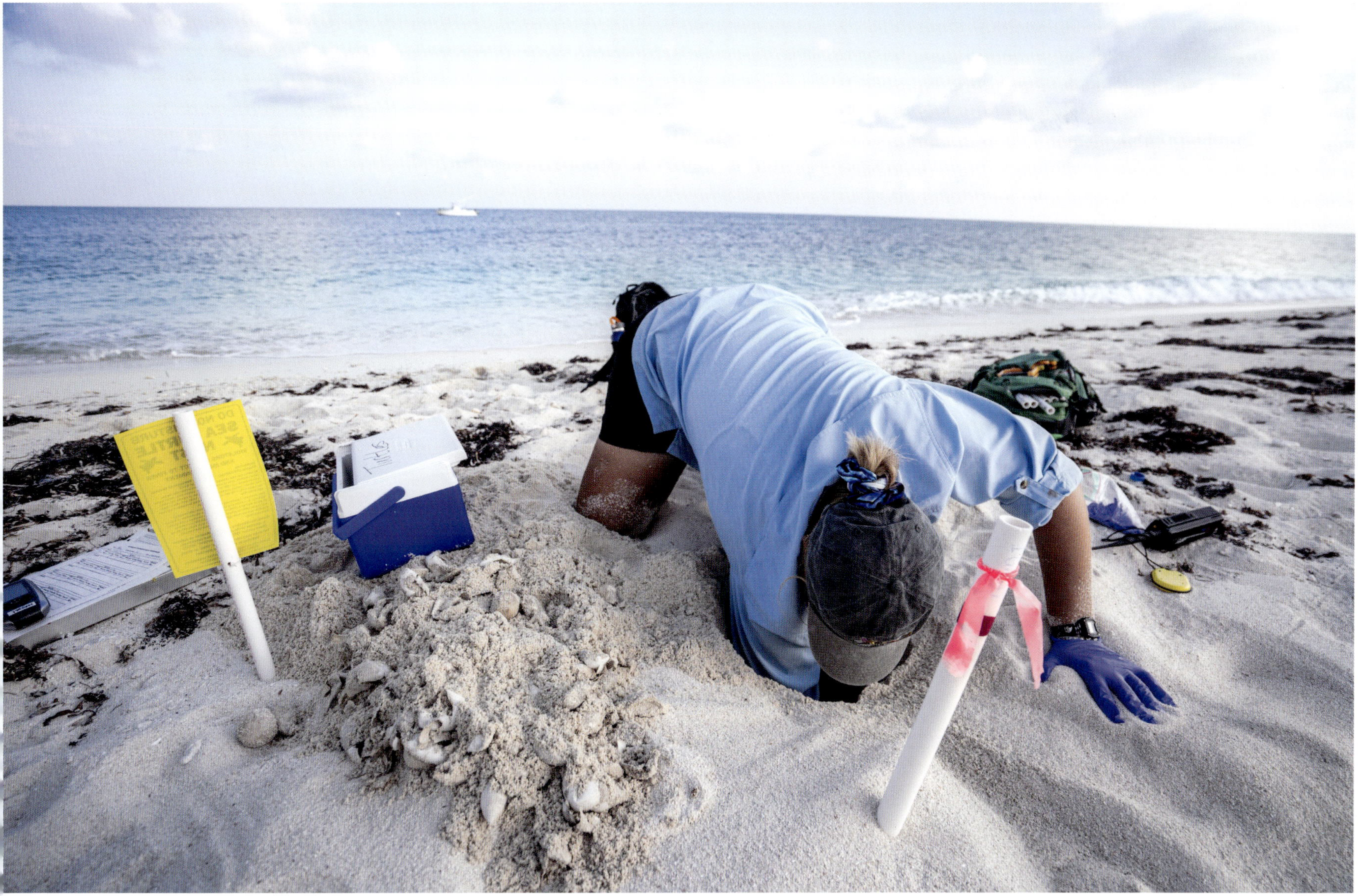

A natural resource intern surveys a turtle nest on Loggerhead Key.

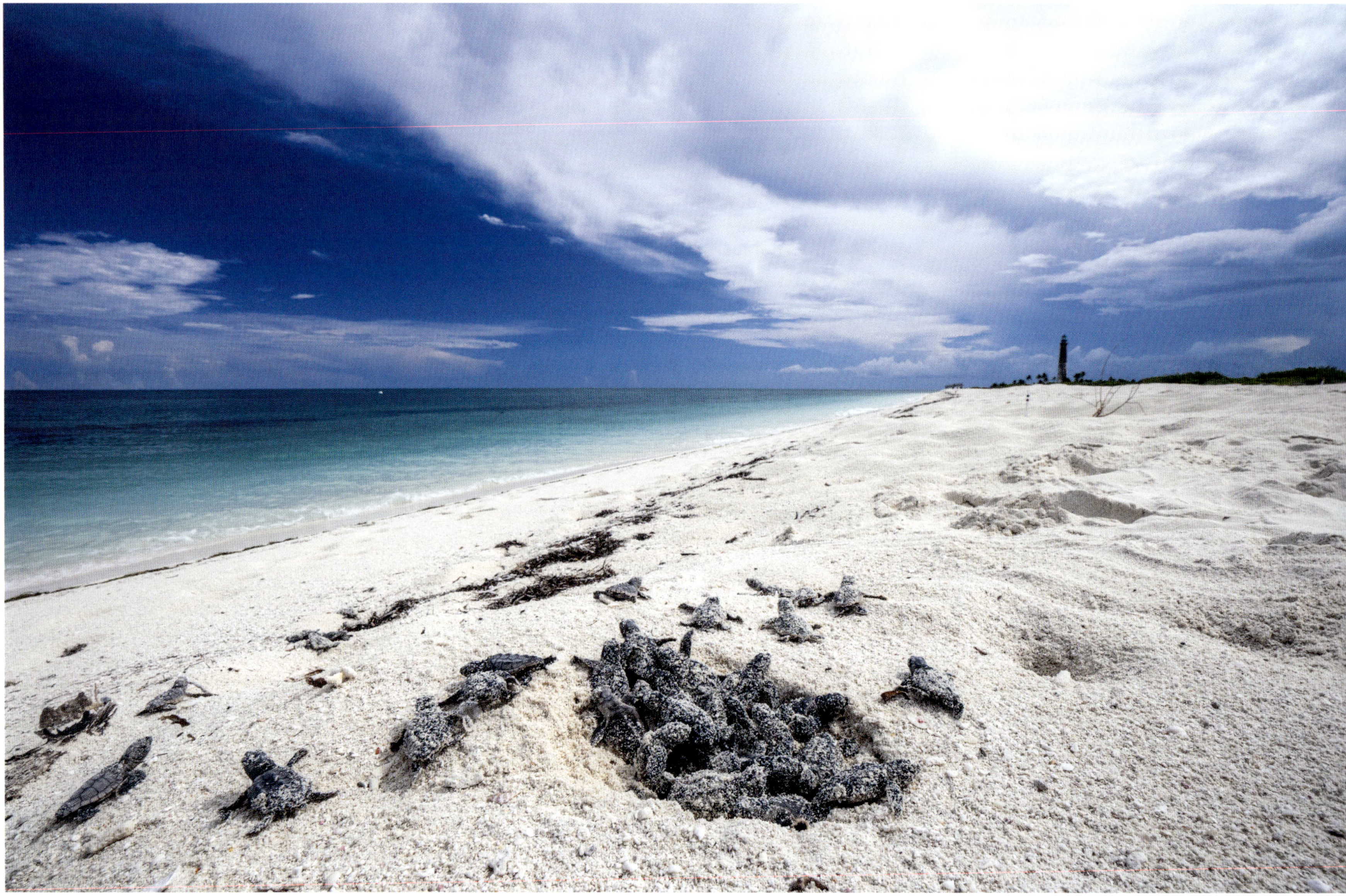

Newly hatched Loggerhead turtles pop-dig out of their nest and race toward the ocean.

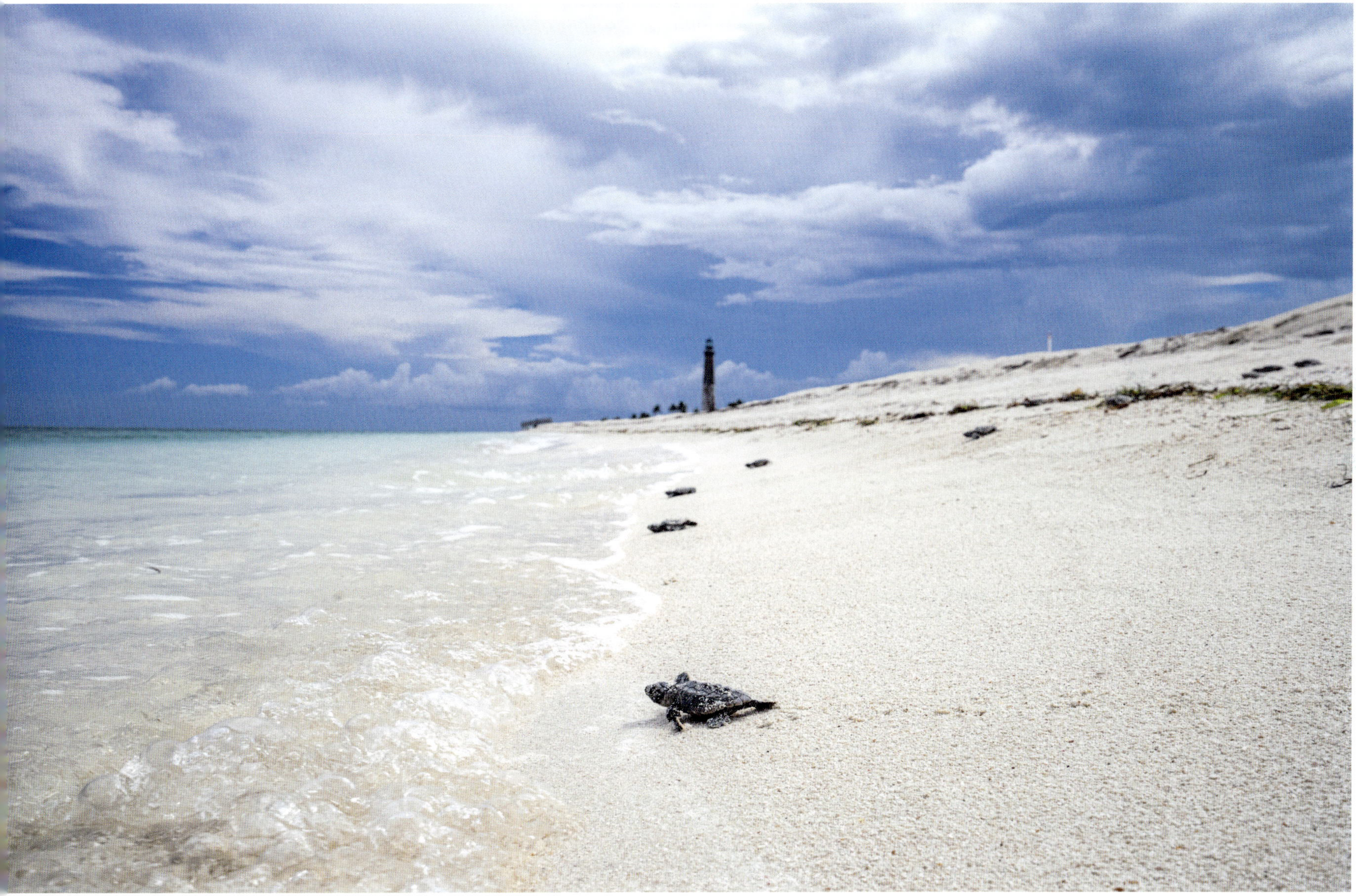

Baby Loggerhead turtles about to embrace
the gulf waters for the first time.

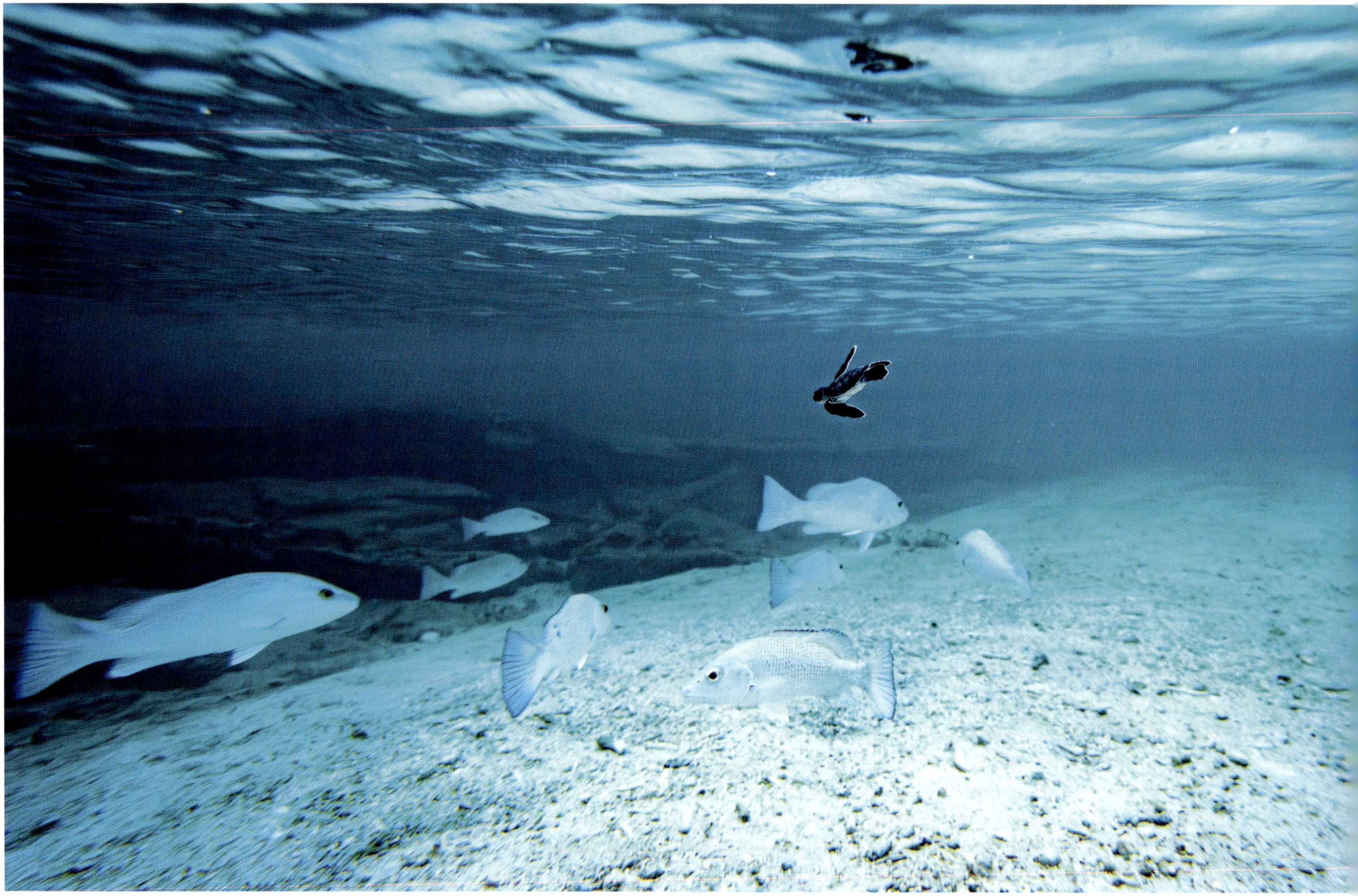

Juvenile green turtles (*Chelonia mydas*) navigate through a school of hungry gray snapper.

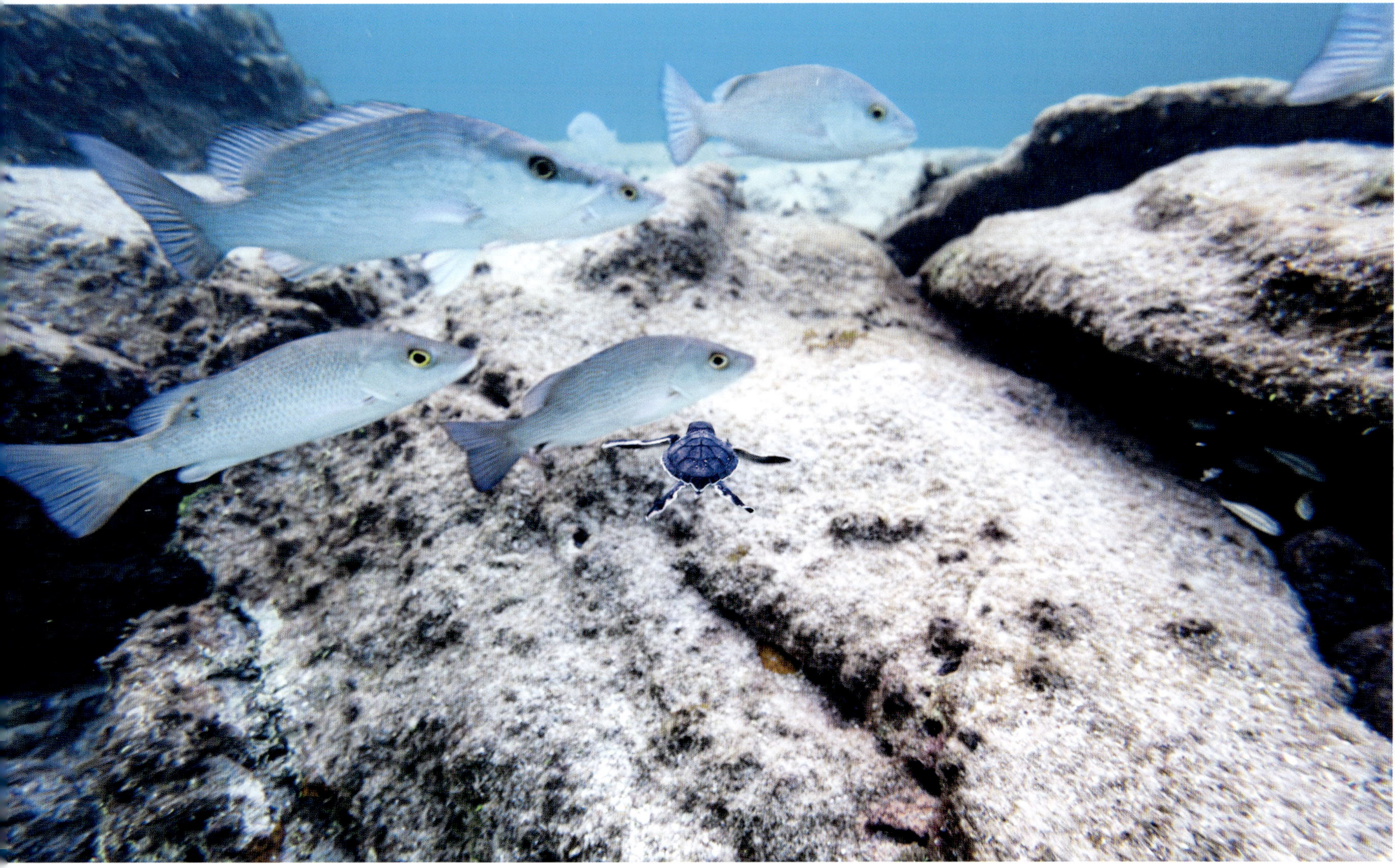

For a green turtle hatchling, the reef holds many dangers.

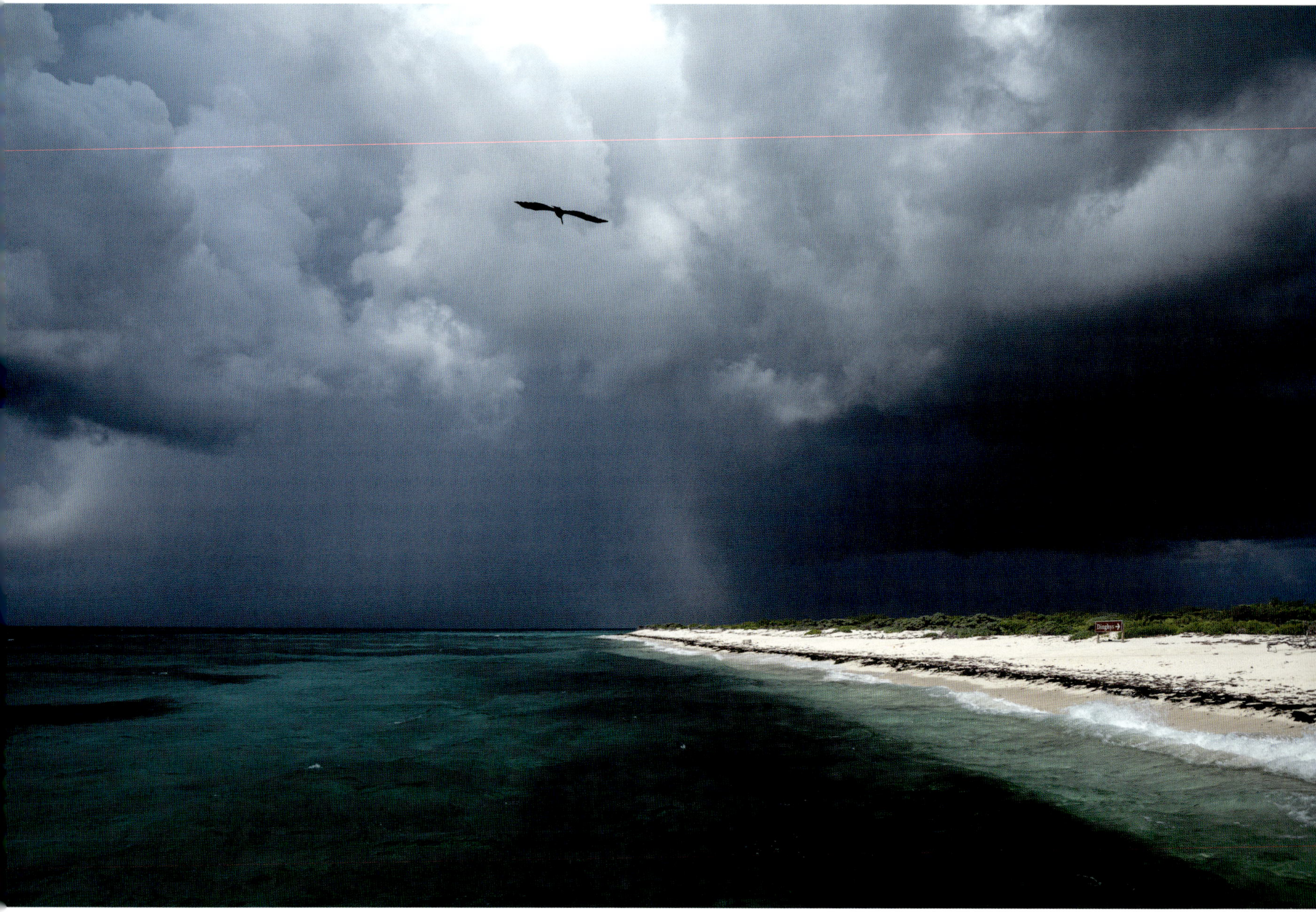

A pelican (*Pelecanus occidentalis*) flies into an oncoming storm.

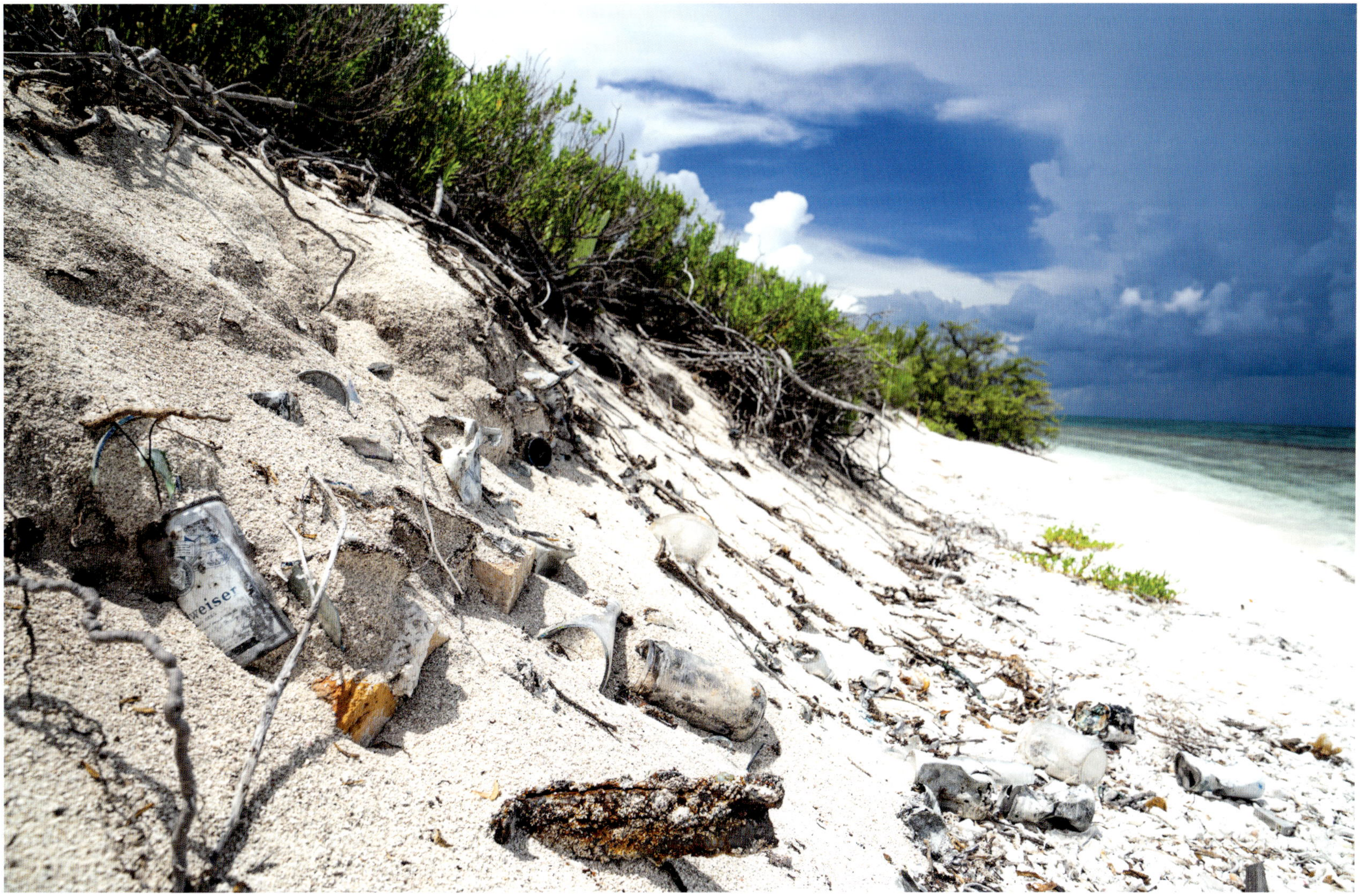

Some decades old, aging trash piles from past island residents are revealed by island erosion.

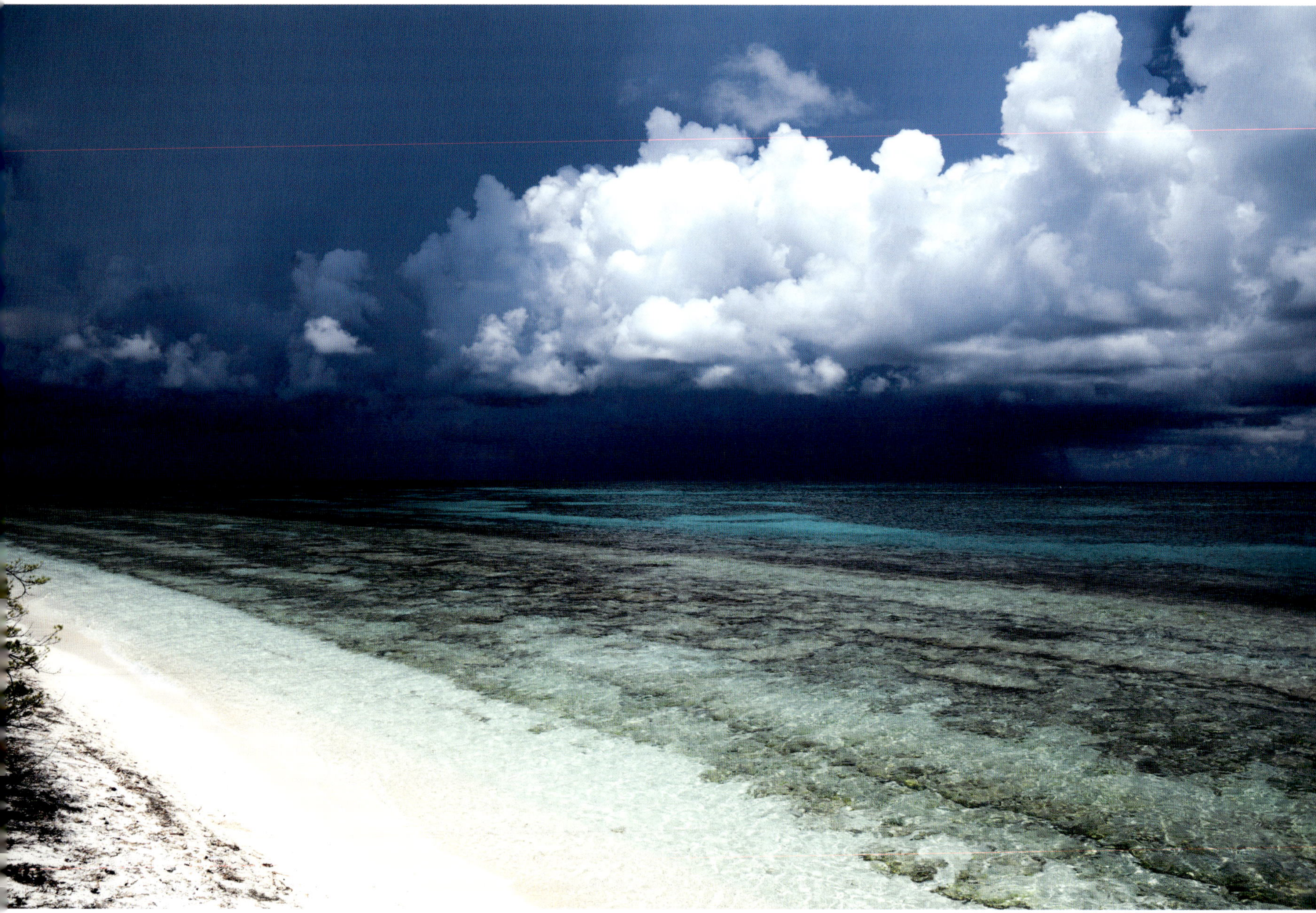

Pockets of sunshine expose the nearshore reef known as Little Africa.

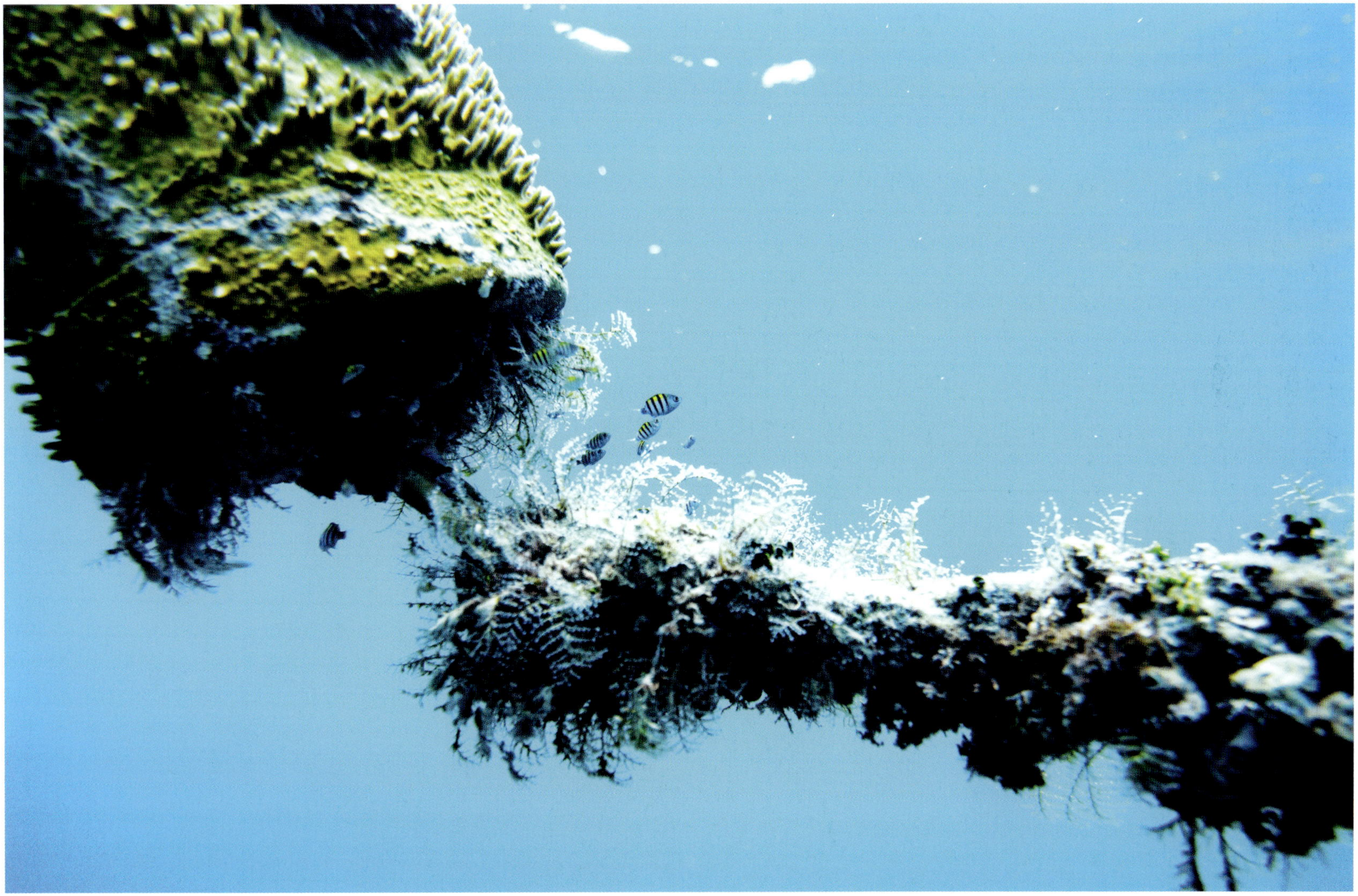

The sergeant major fish (*Abudefduf saxatilis*) is a species of damselfish. Here, a juvenile takes shelter under a coral-crusted swim buoy.

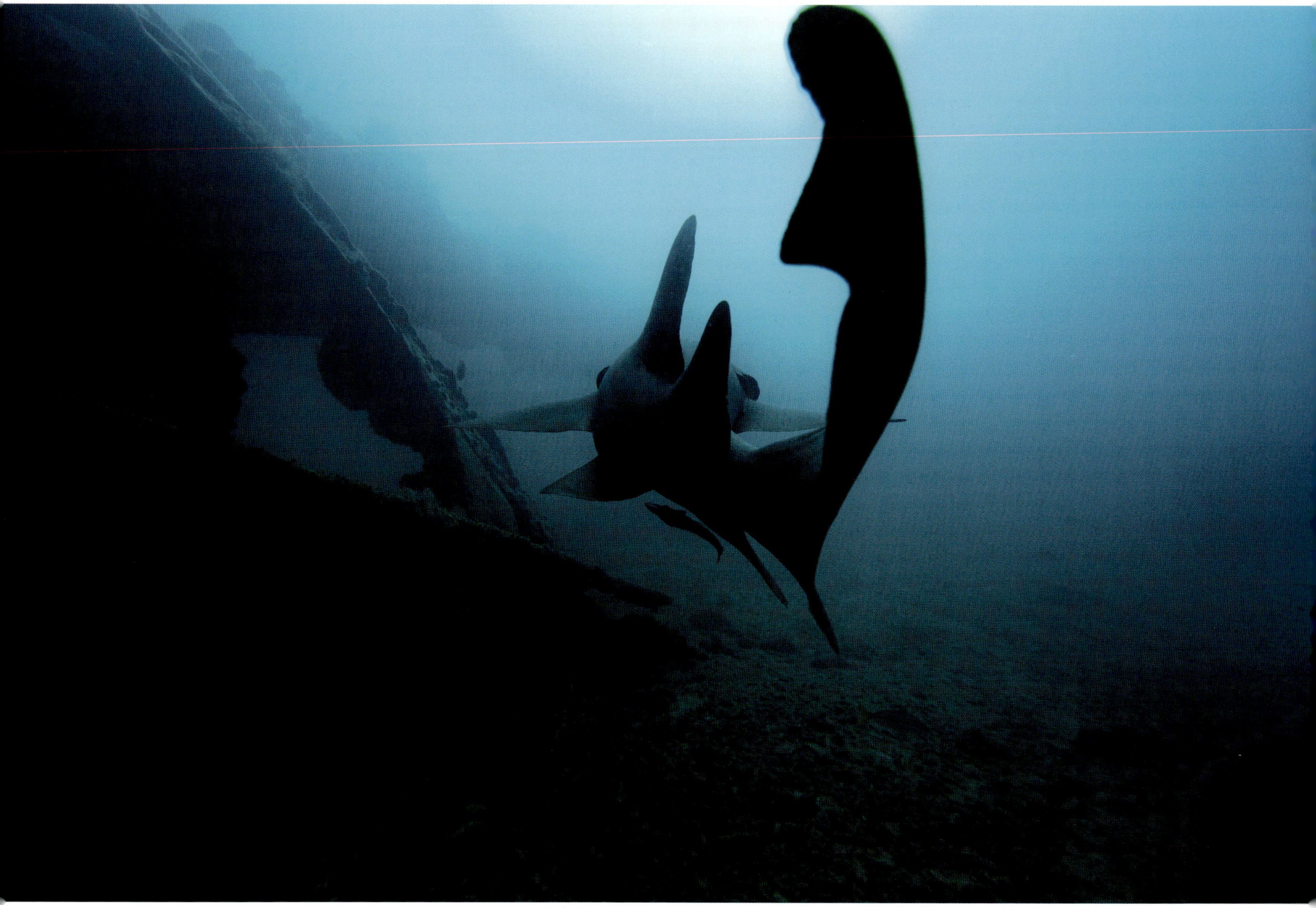

A large nurse shark (*Ginglymostoma cirratum*) swims in the shadow of the Windjammer wreck.

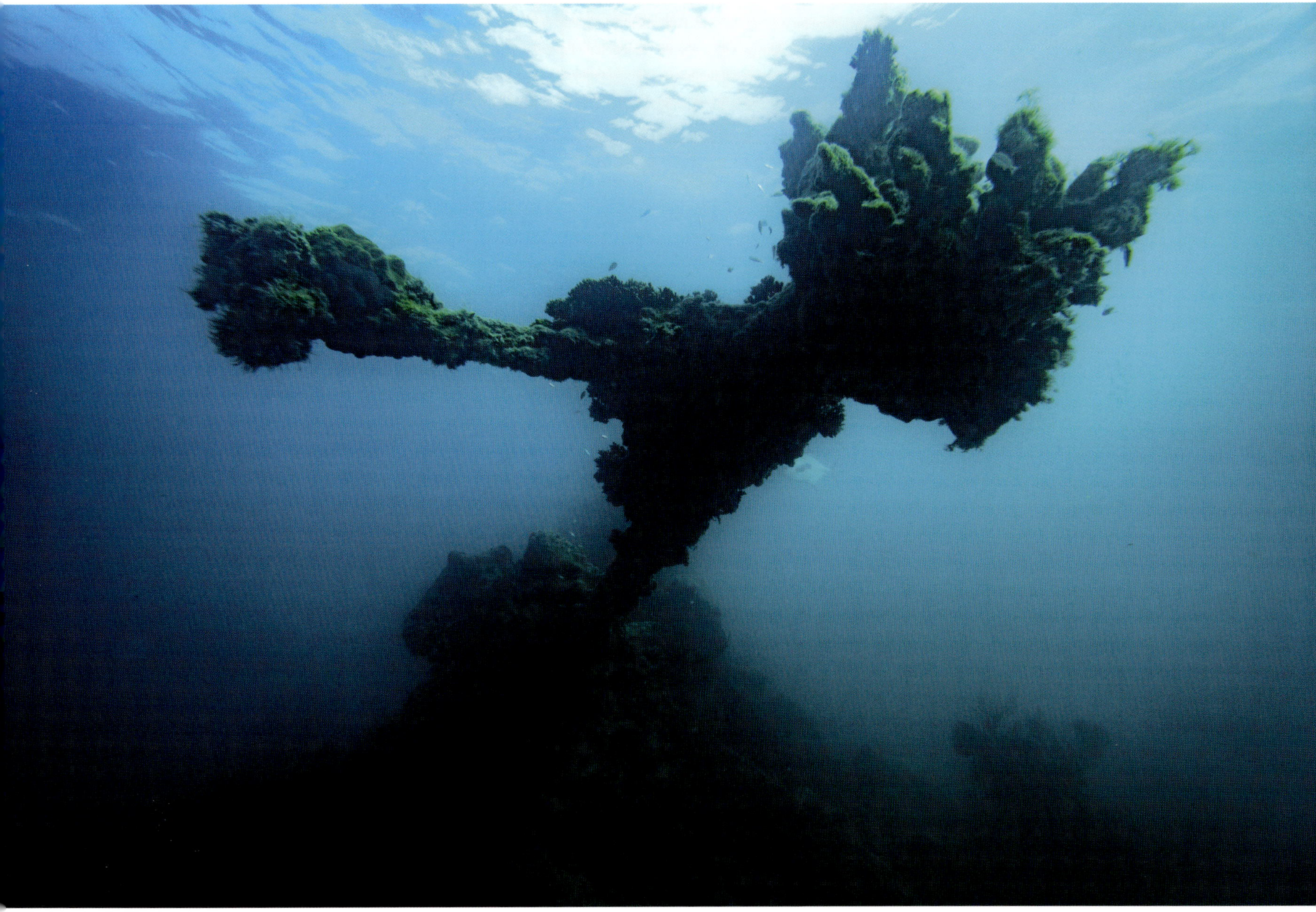

Old mast section from the wrecked *Avanti* at the Windjammer site.

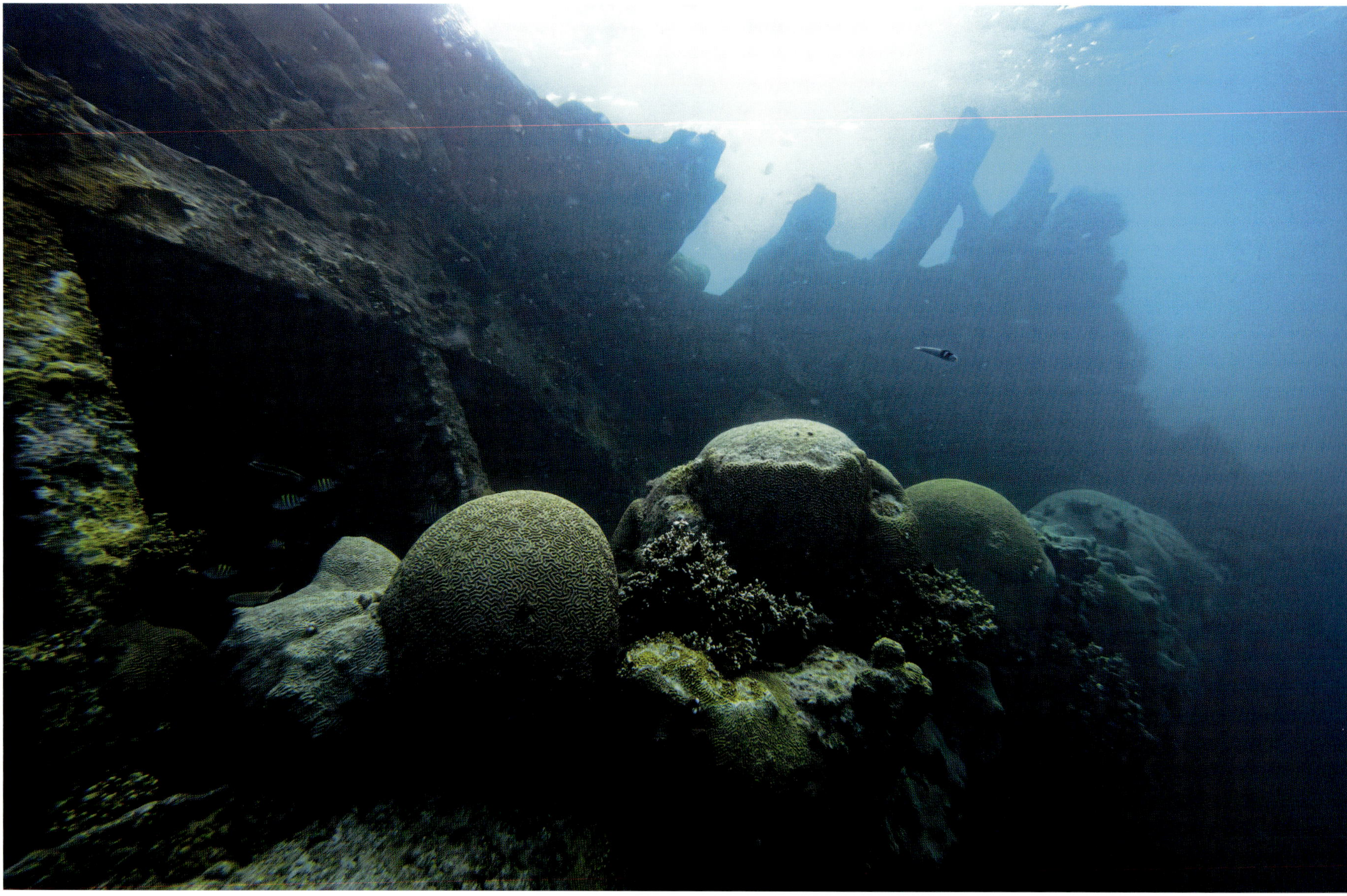

At the Windjammer site, stony coral cover the *Avanti* wreck.

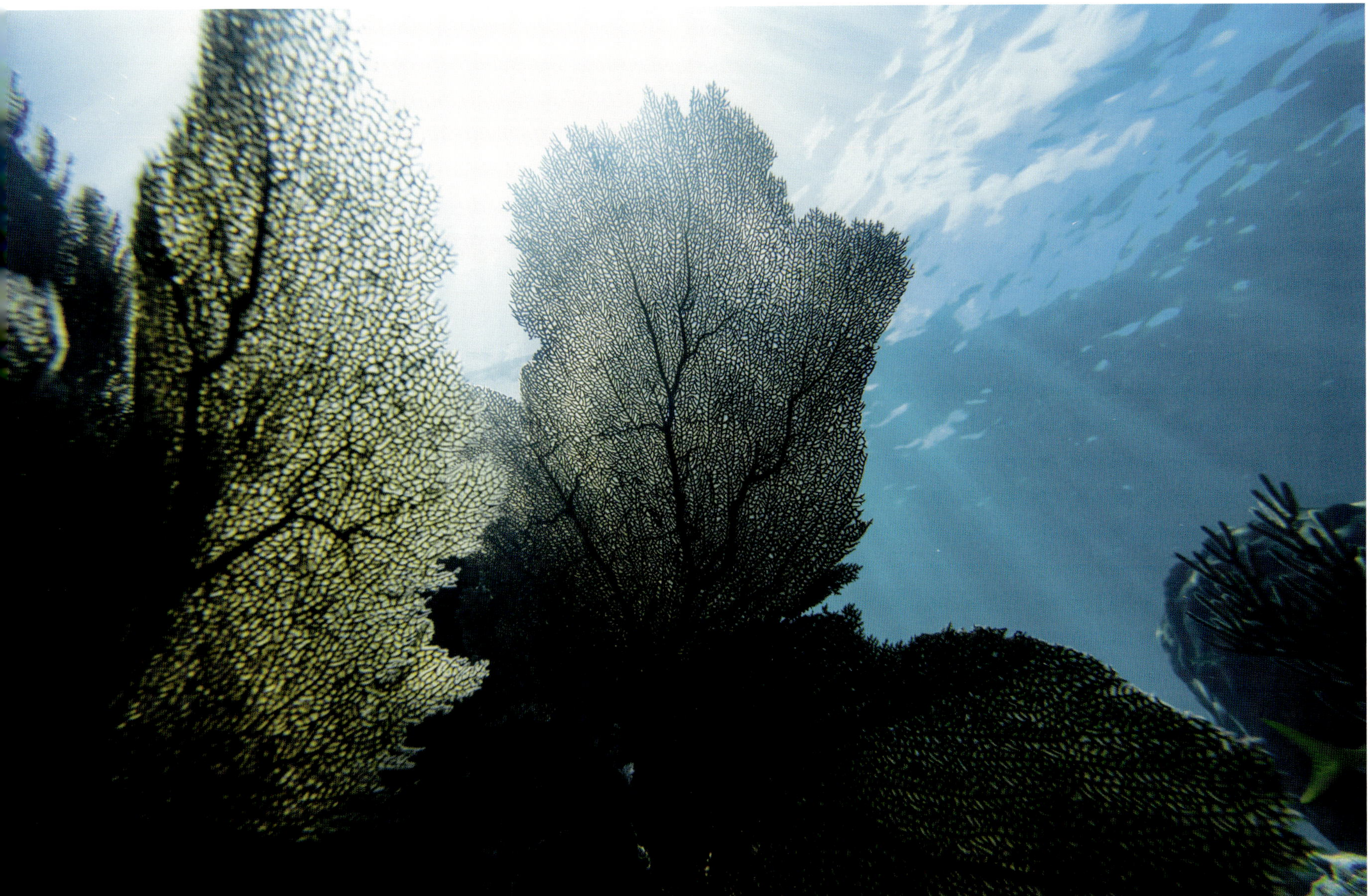

Sea fans in the sunlight.

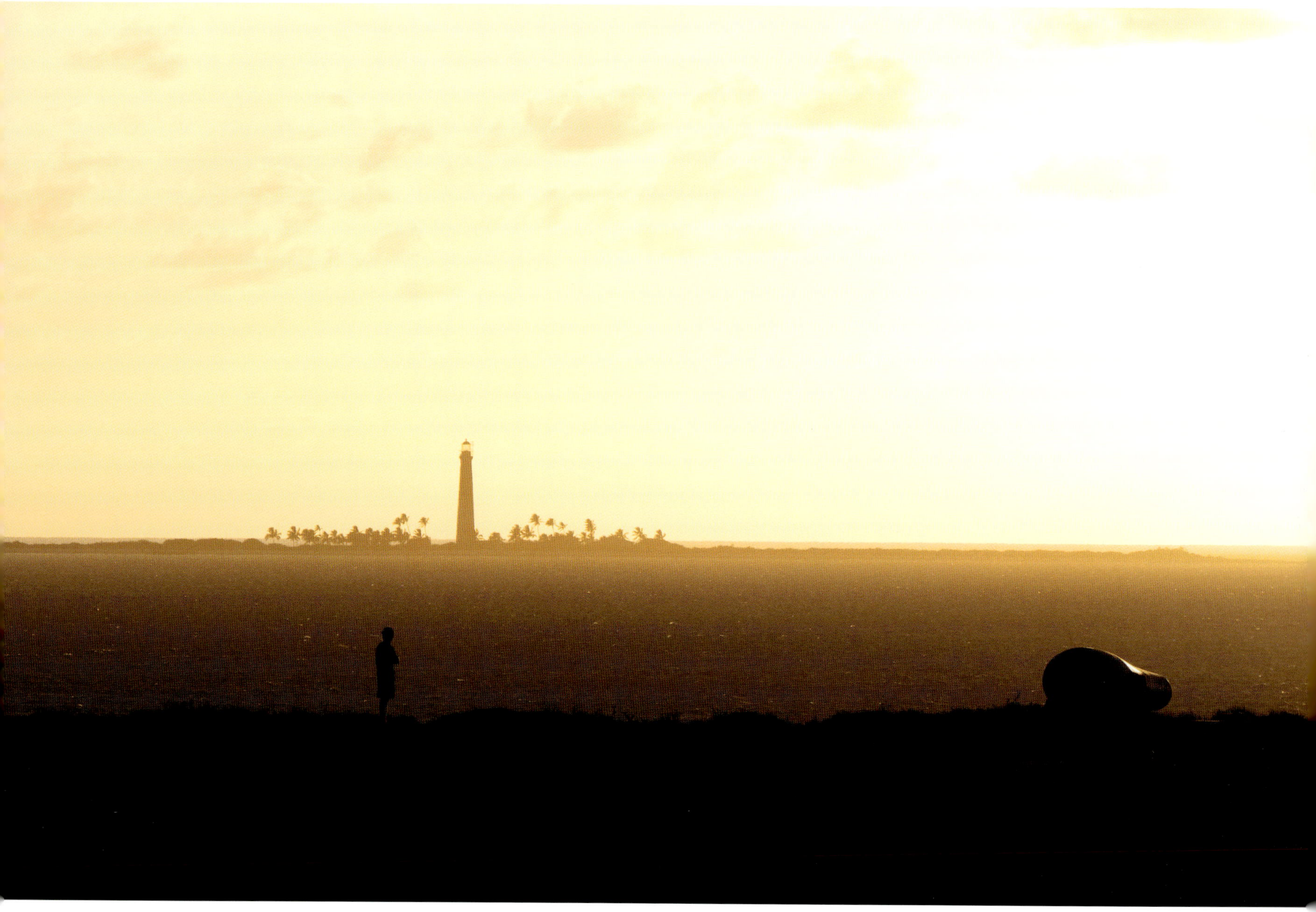

Looking west toward Loggerhead Key from atop Fort Jefferson on Garden Key. It is three miles from one island to the other.

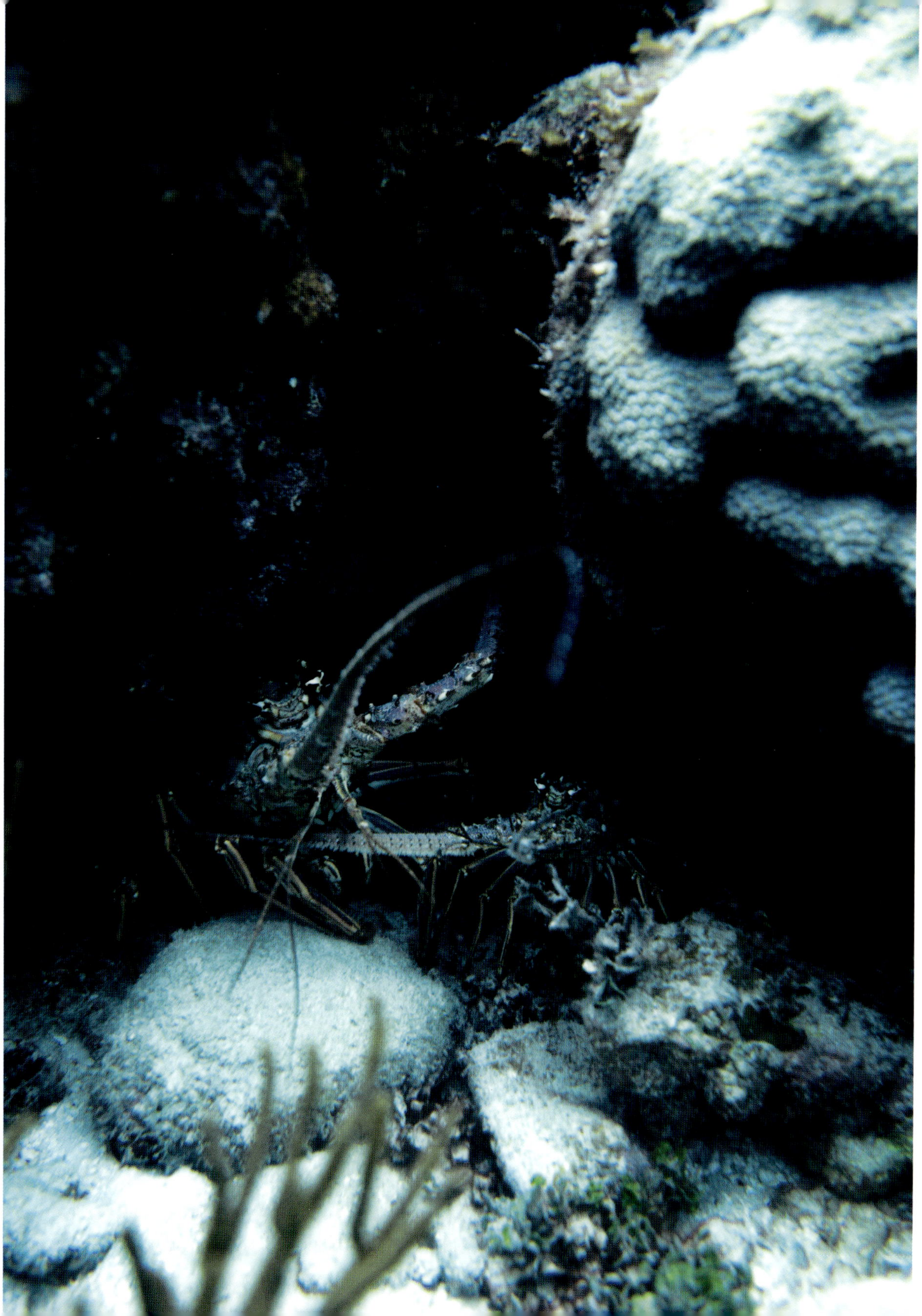

Spiny lobster tucked up in the coral.

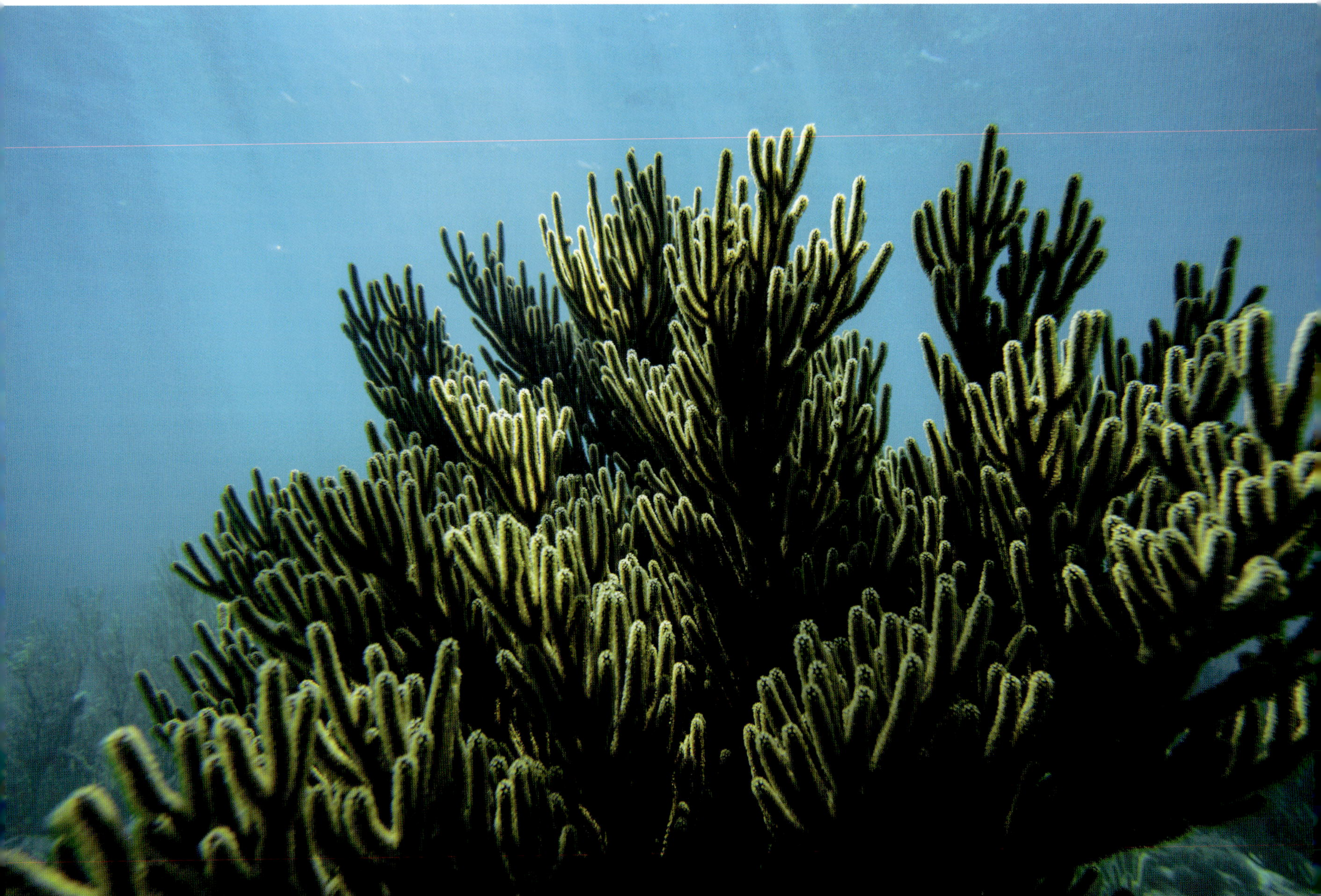

A beautiful soft coral (family Gorgoniidae) in the light.

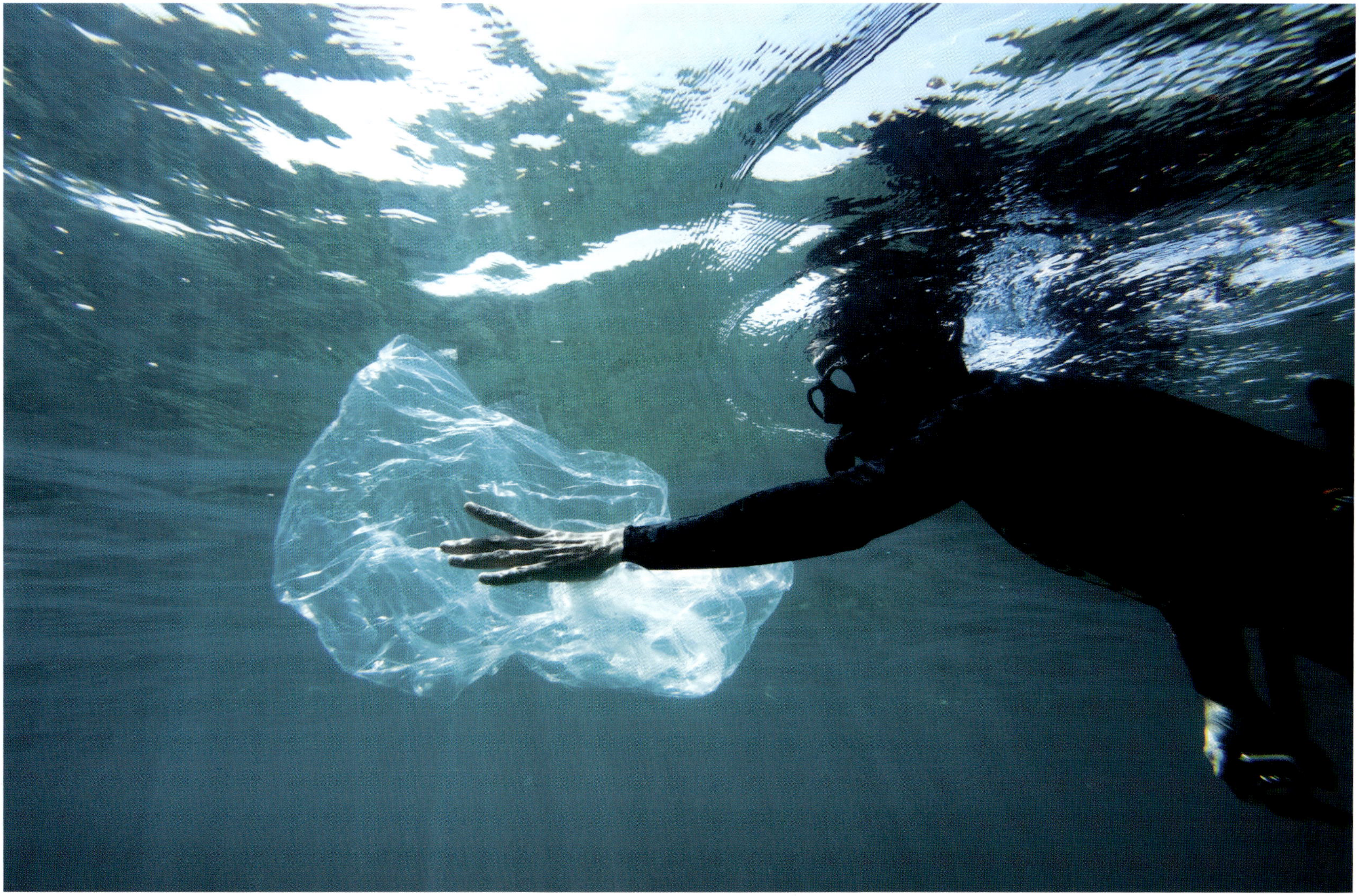

A swimmer grabs trash out of the waters off Loggerhead Key near Little Africa Reef.

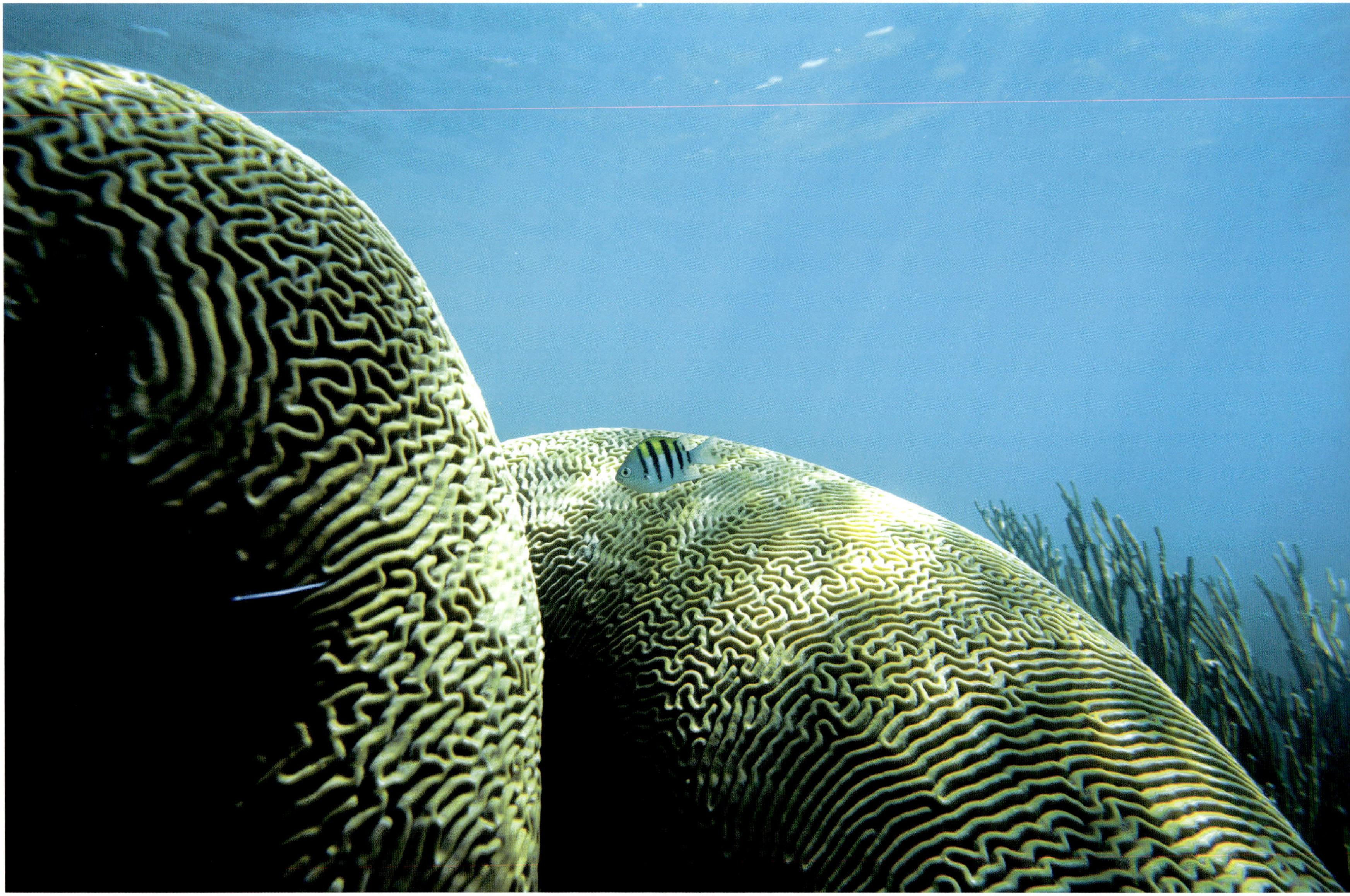

Healthy brain coral on Little Africa Reef.

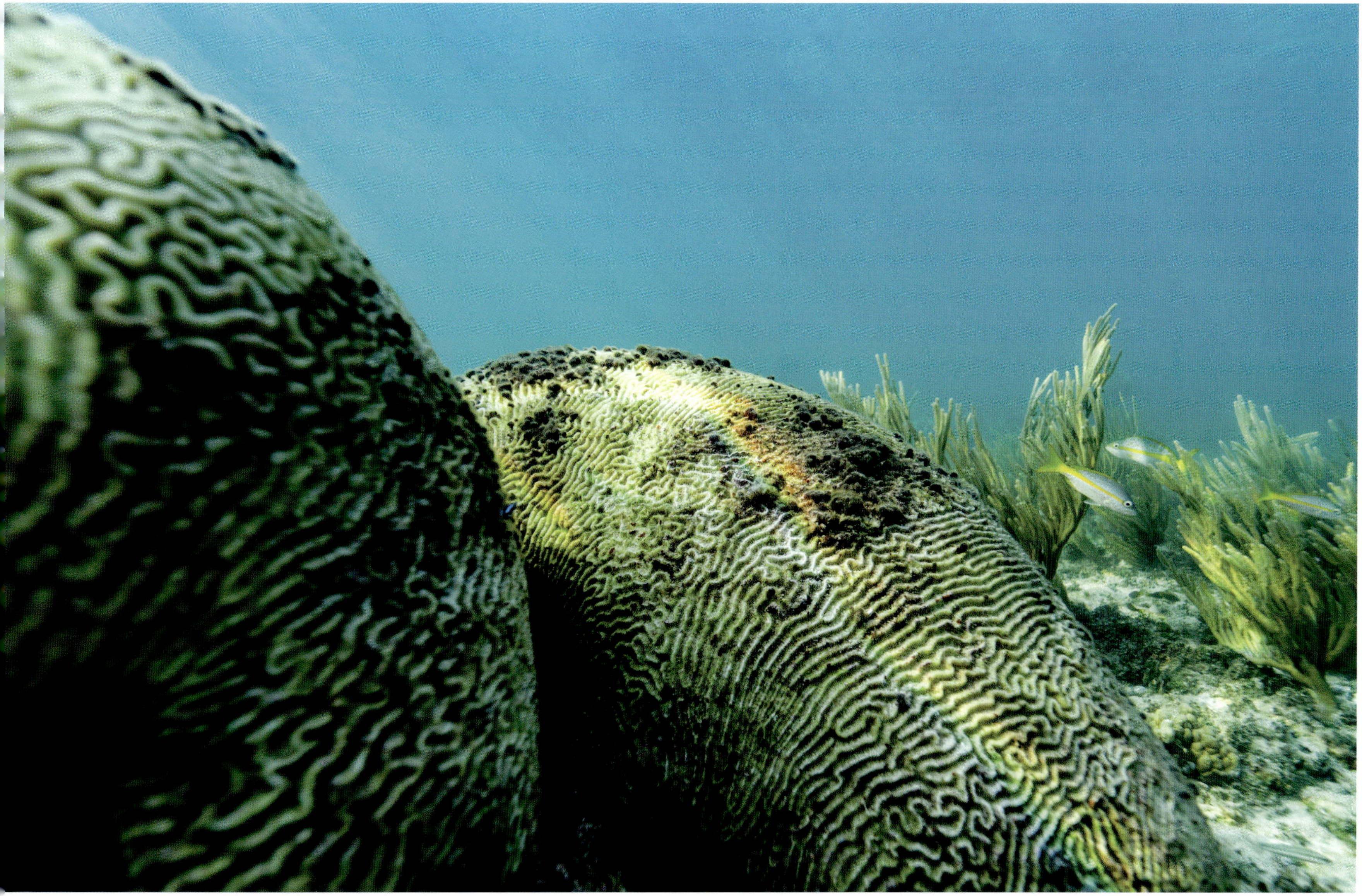

The same coral a year later: dead, due to the highly lethal stony coral tissue loss disease (SCTLD).

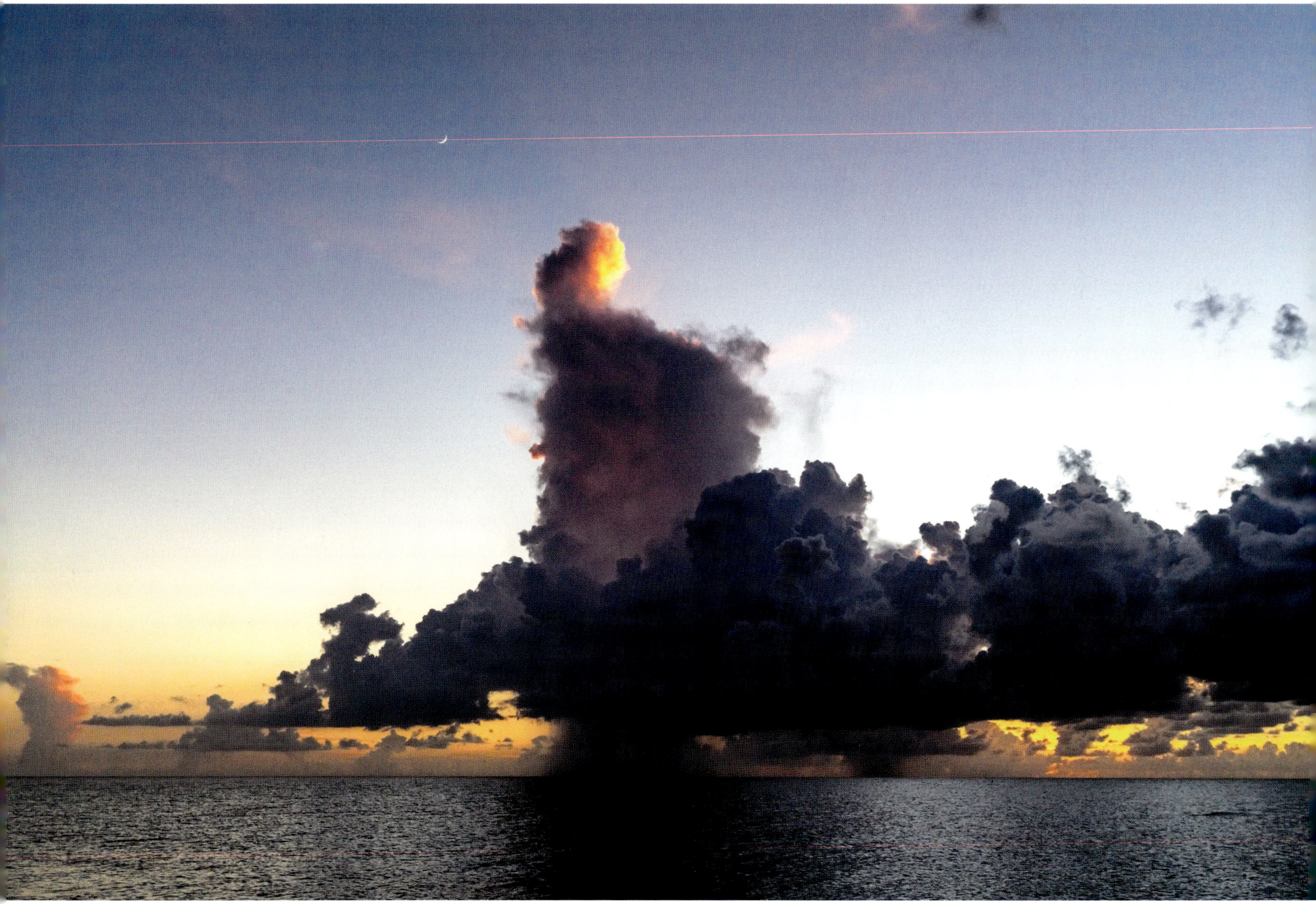

A crescent moon rises above
an evening storm cloud.

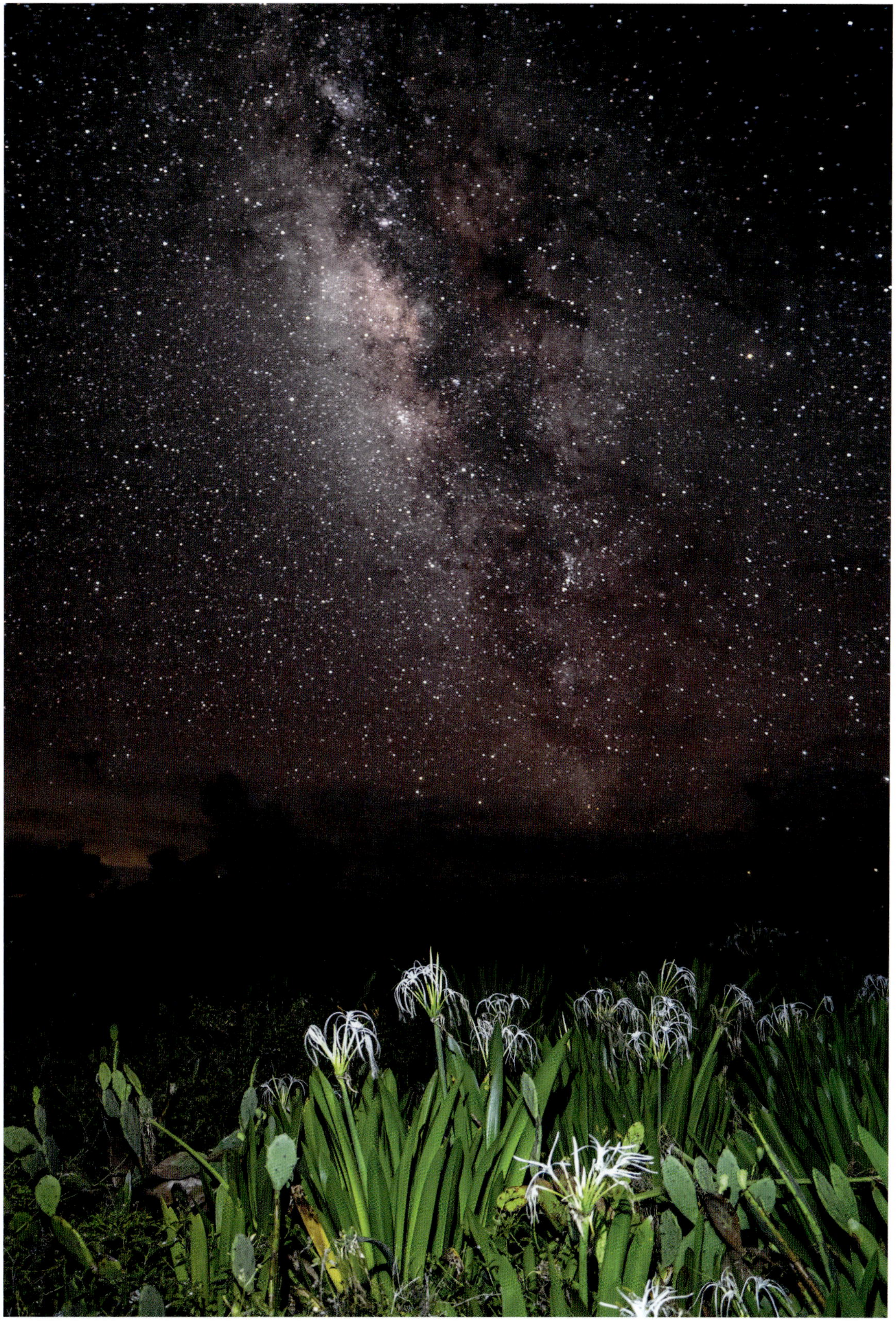

Sea lilies (*Crinum asiaticum*) reach up toward the Milky Way.

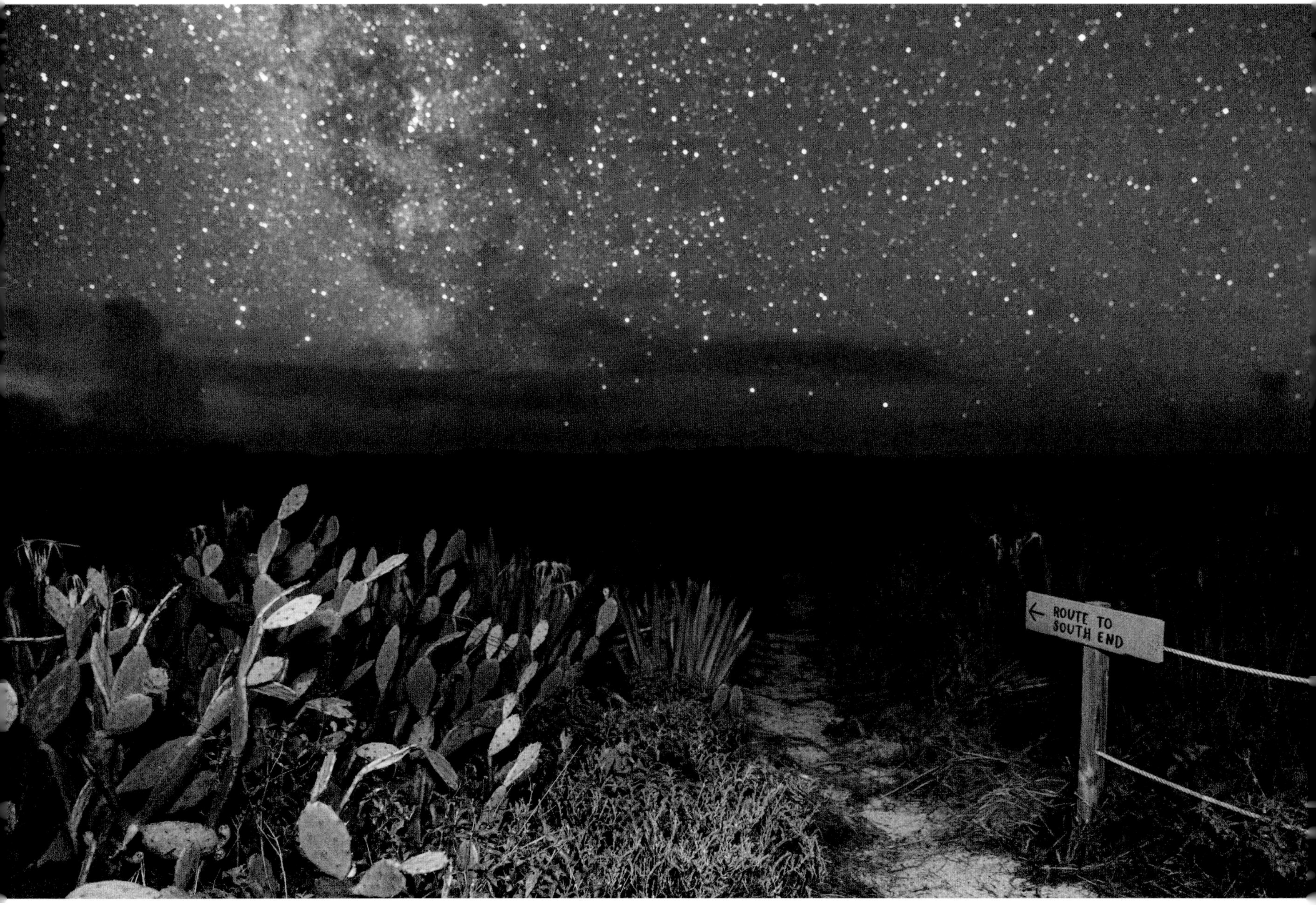

Island trails.

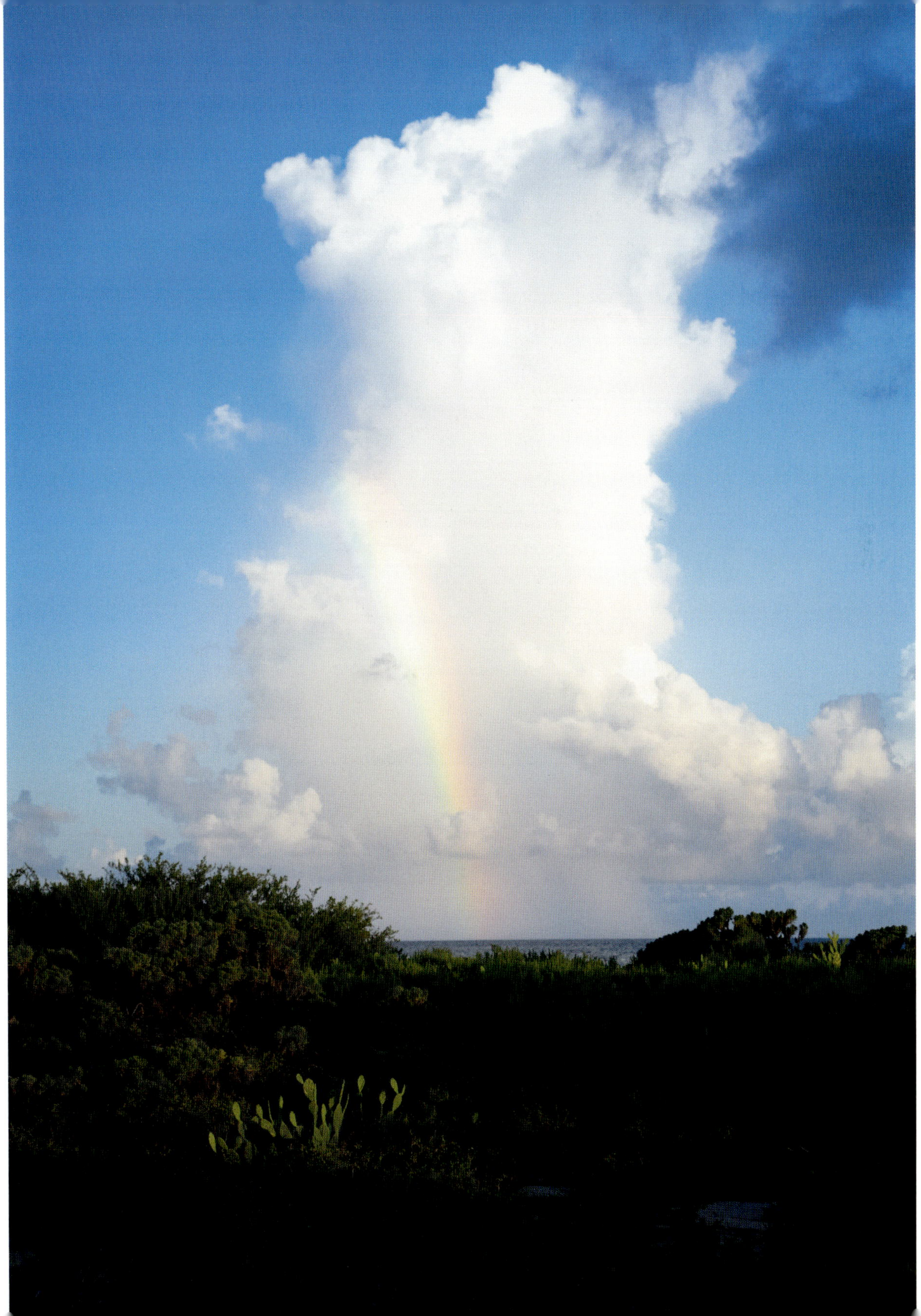

Subtle pastels of Loggerhead Key.

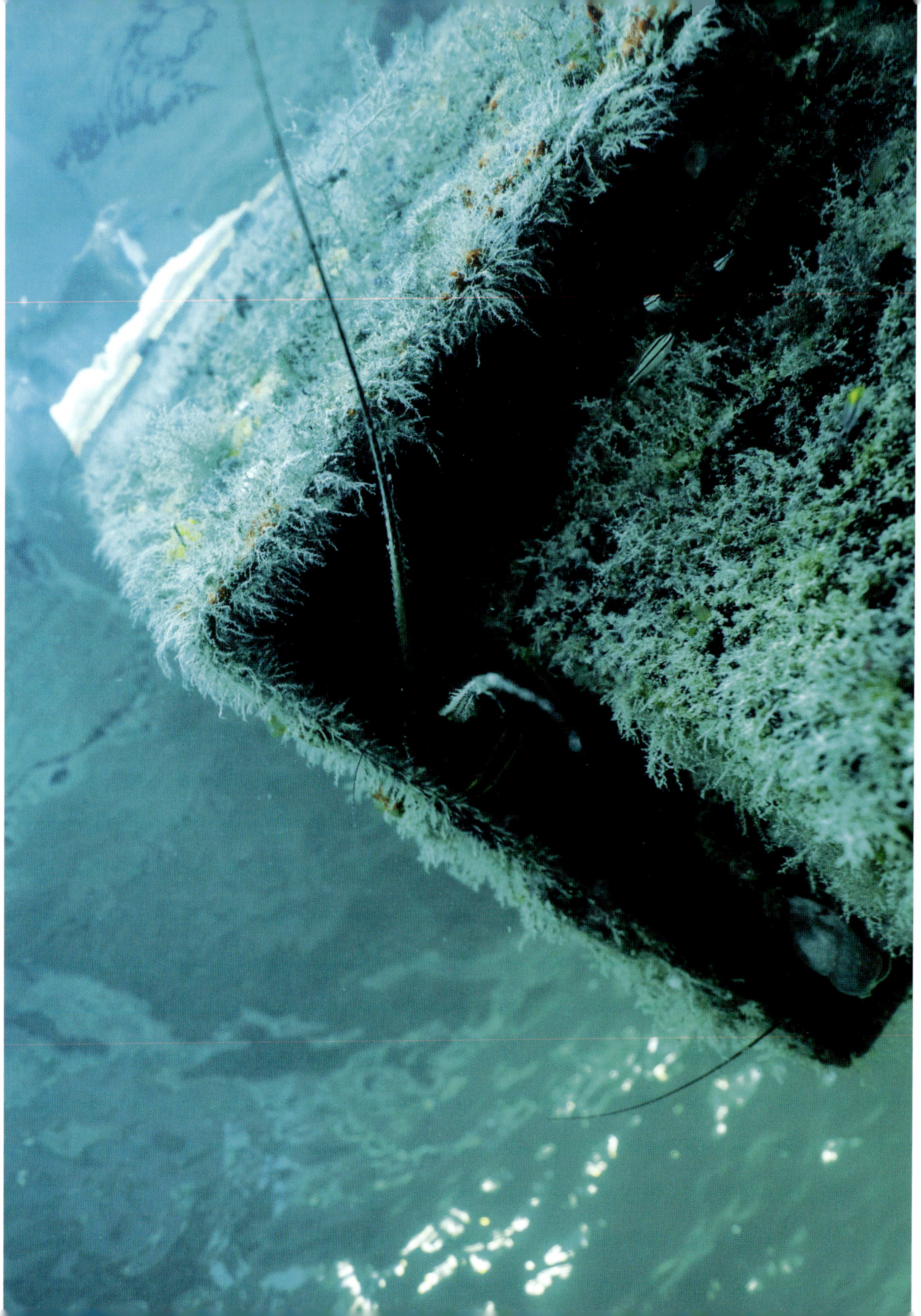

A spiny lobster's antennas stick out from its dock-post hiding spot.

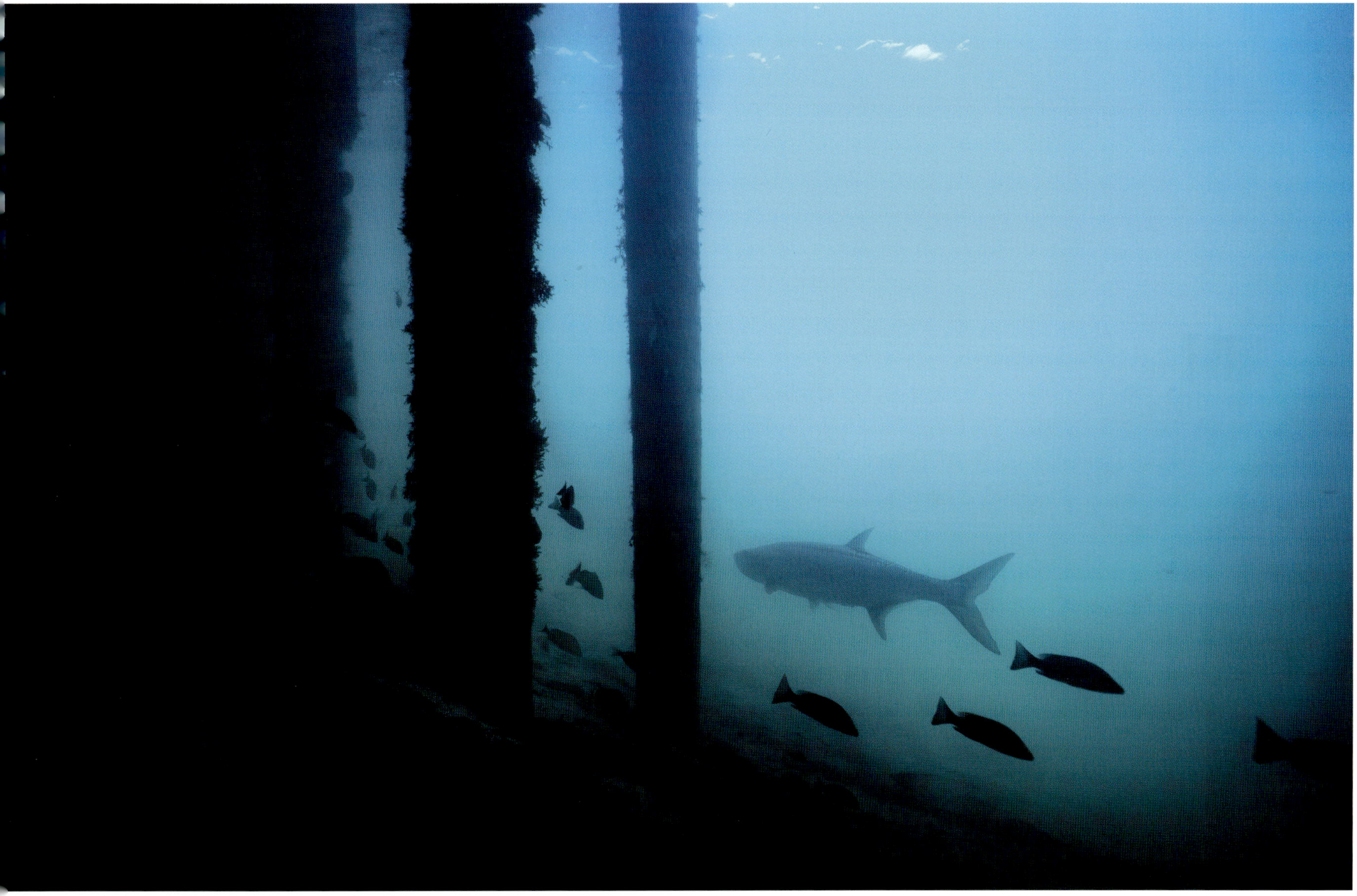

A tarpon swims along the edge of the Garden Key ferry dock.

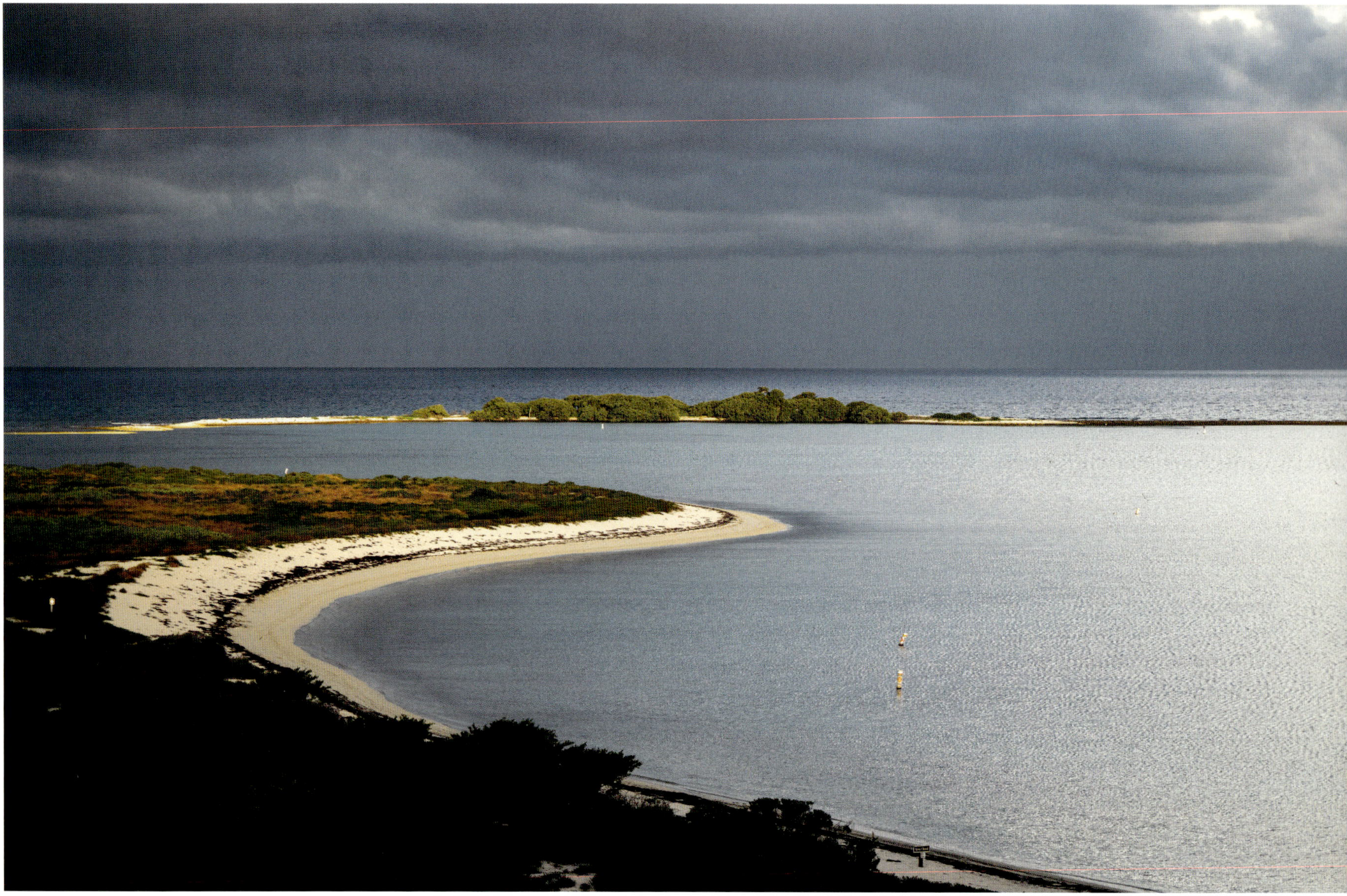

A pocket of sunlight illuminates Bush and Long Keys.

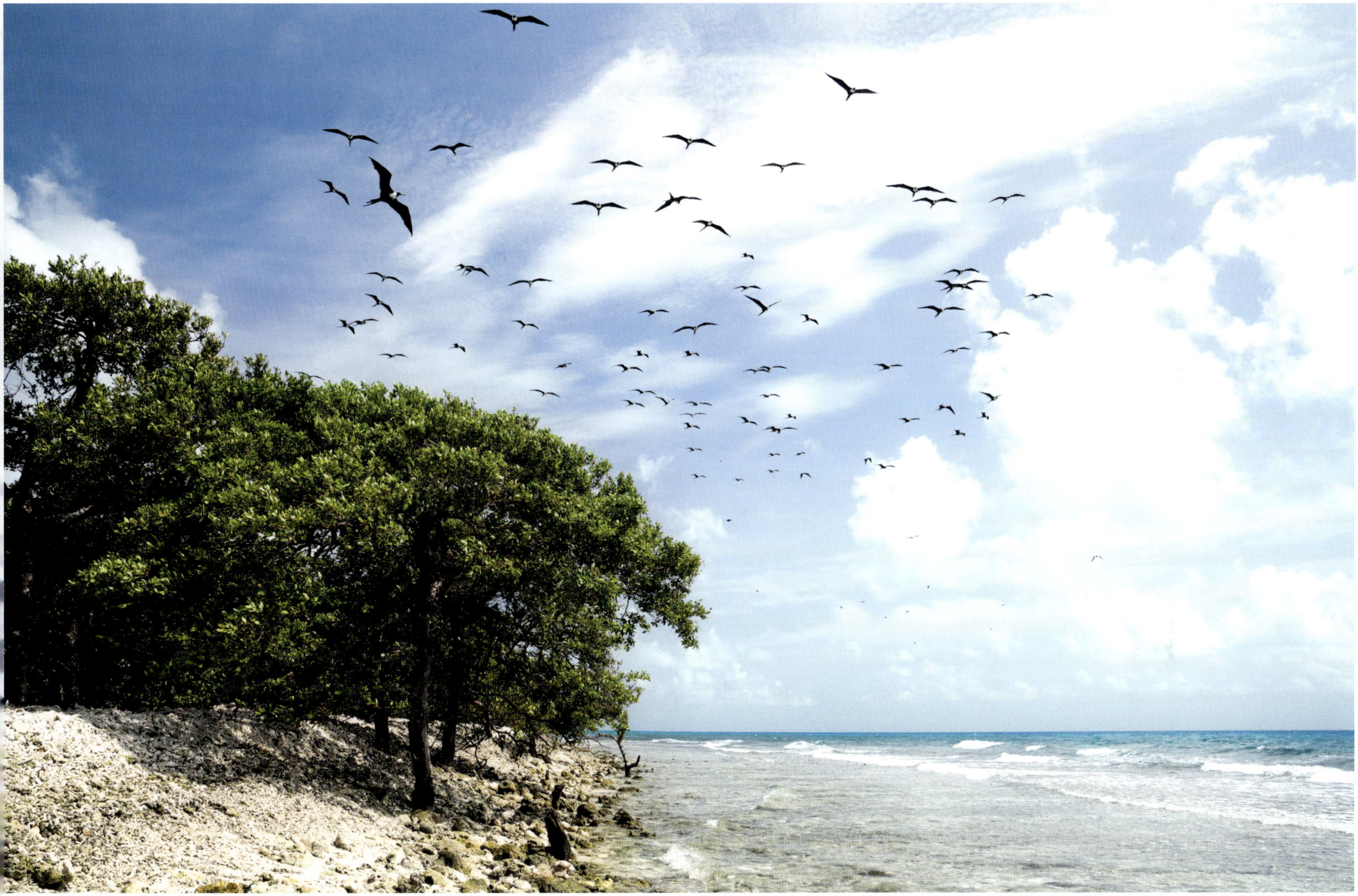

Magnificent frigatebirds (*Fregata magnificens*) fly over Long Key.

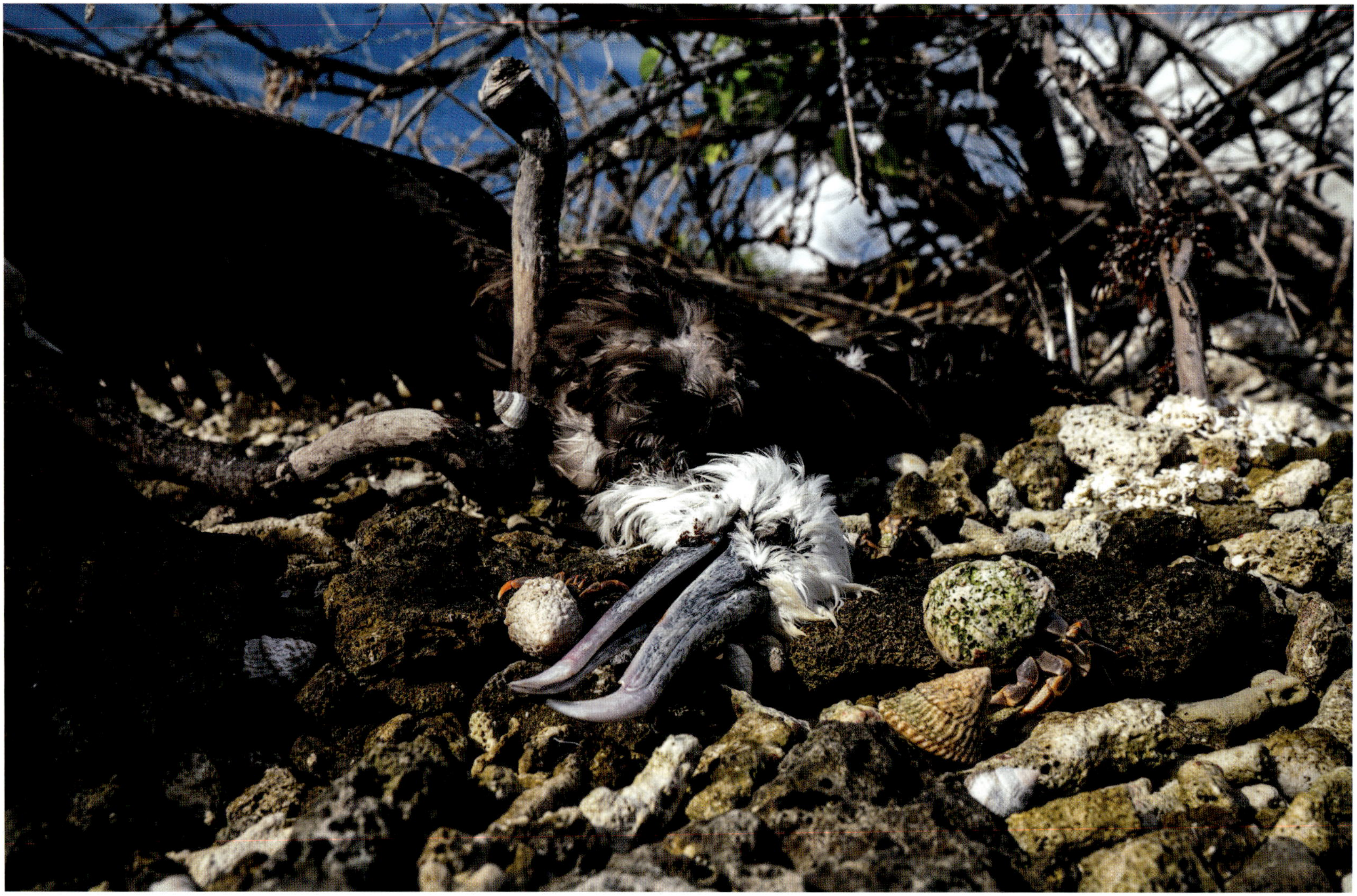

Hermit crabs feast on a recently dead frigatebird.

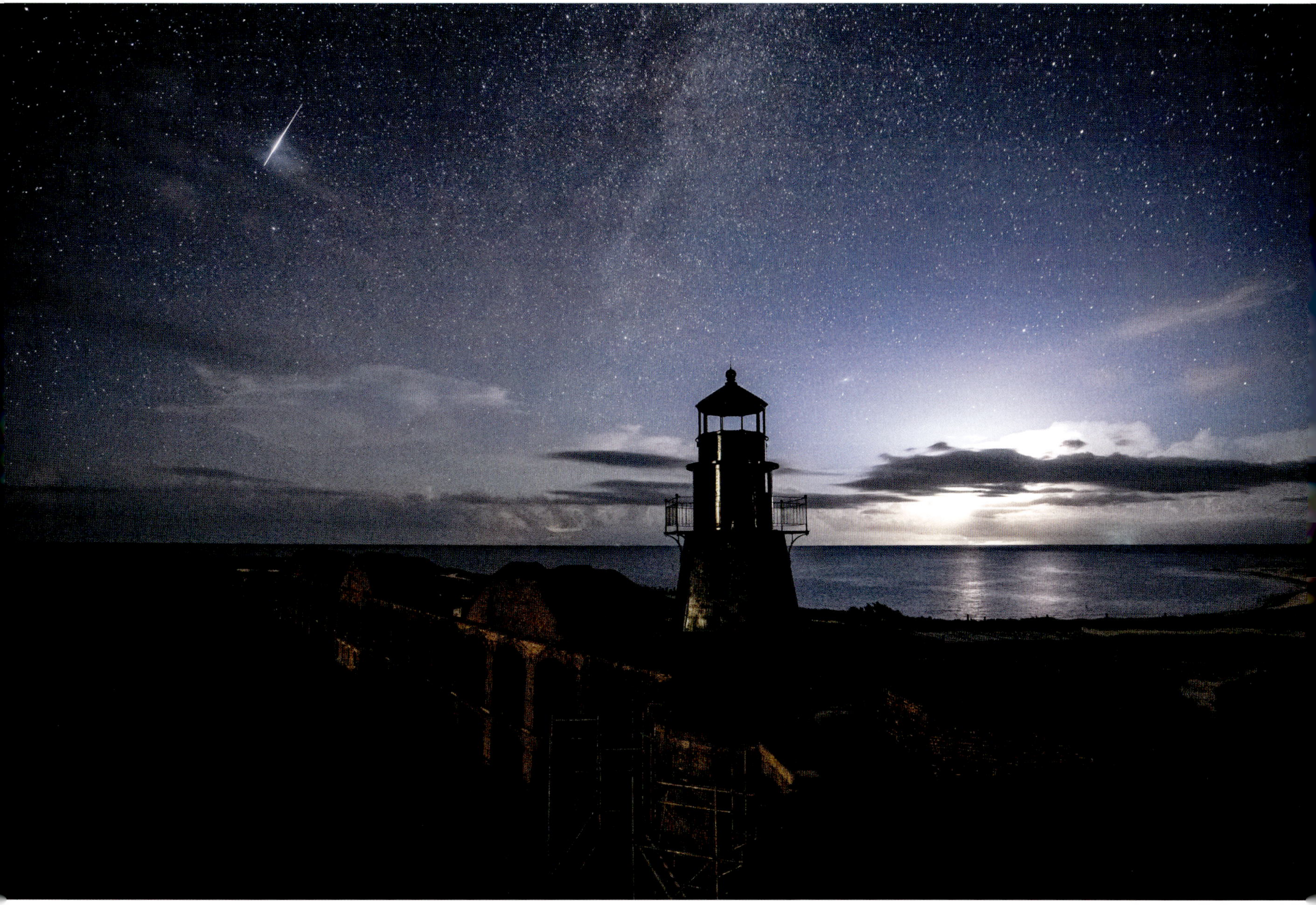

A shooting star leaves a trail over Fort Jefferson.

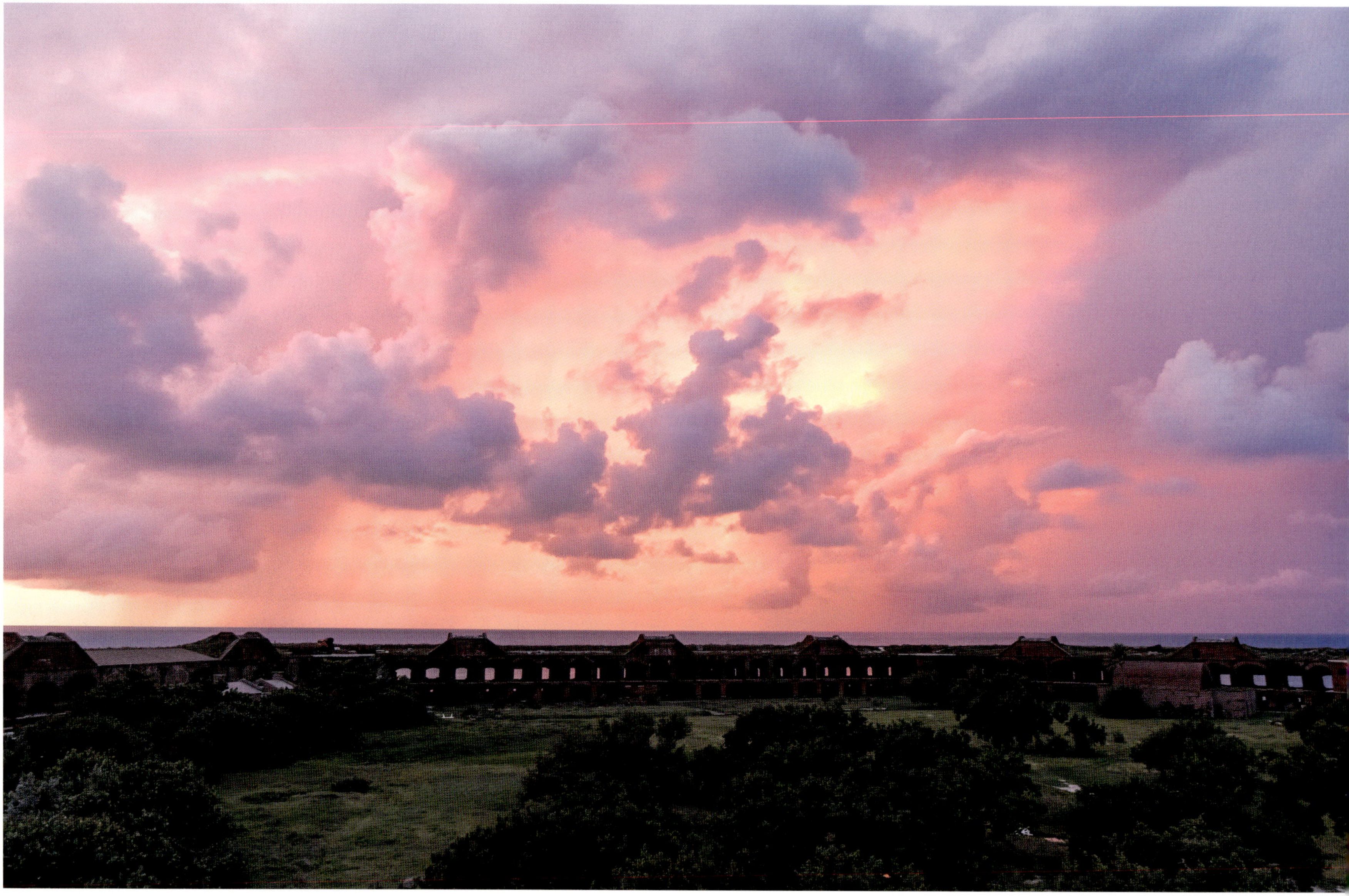

Stormy sunset light over Fort Jefferson.

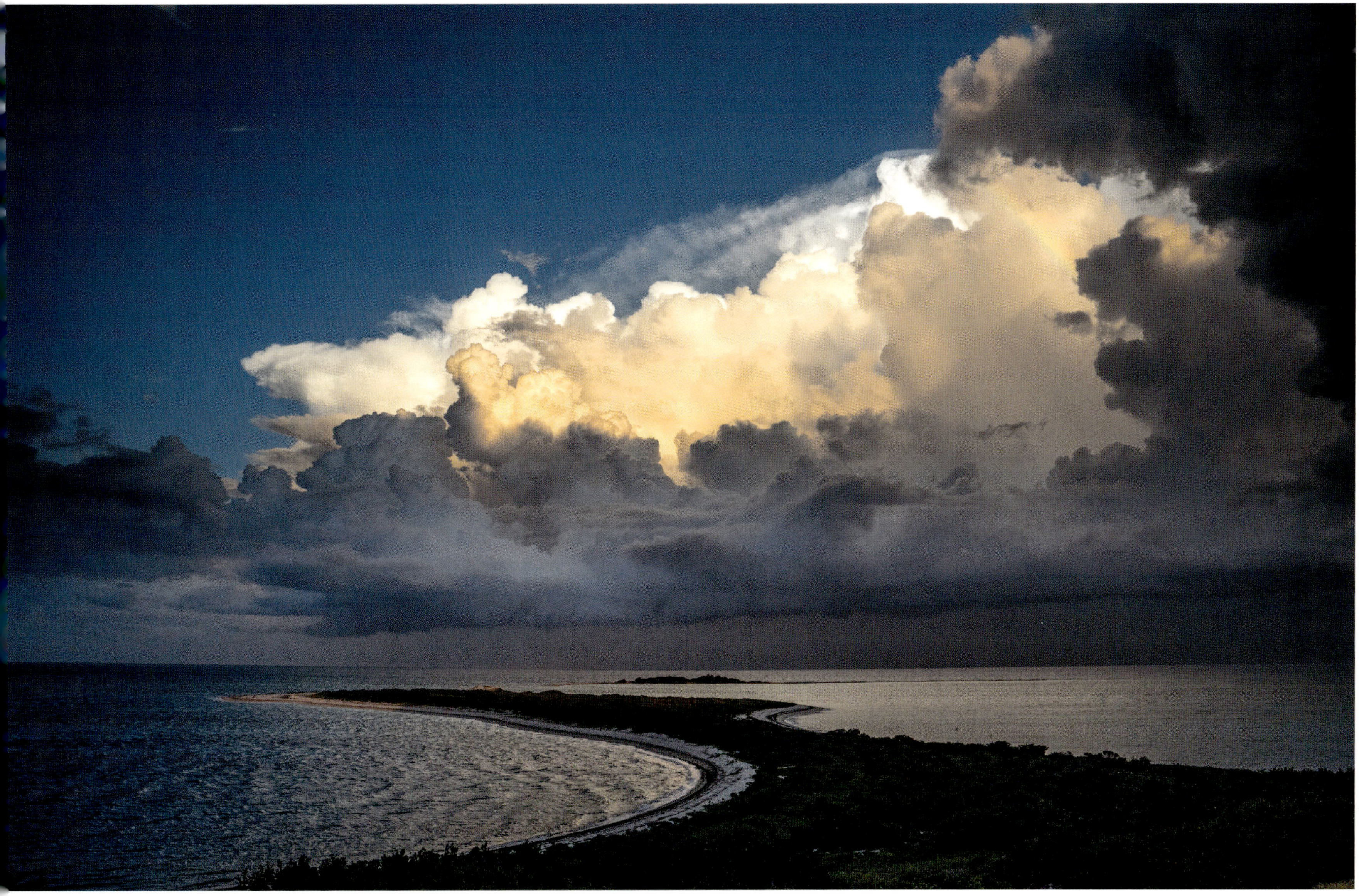

Storm clouds build in the distance off Long Key.

A commercial fishing vessel in Bird Key Harbor awaits a wall of rain.

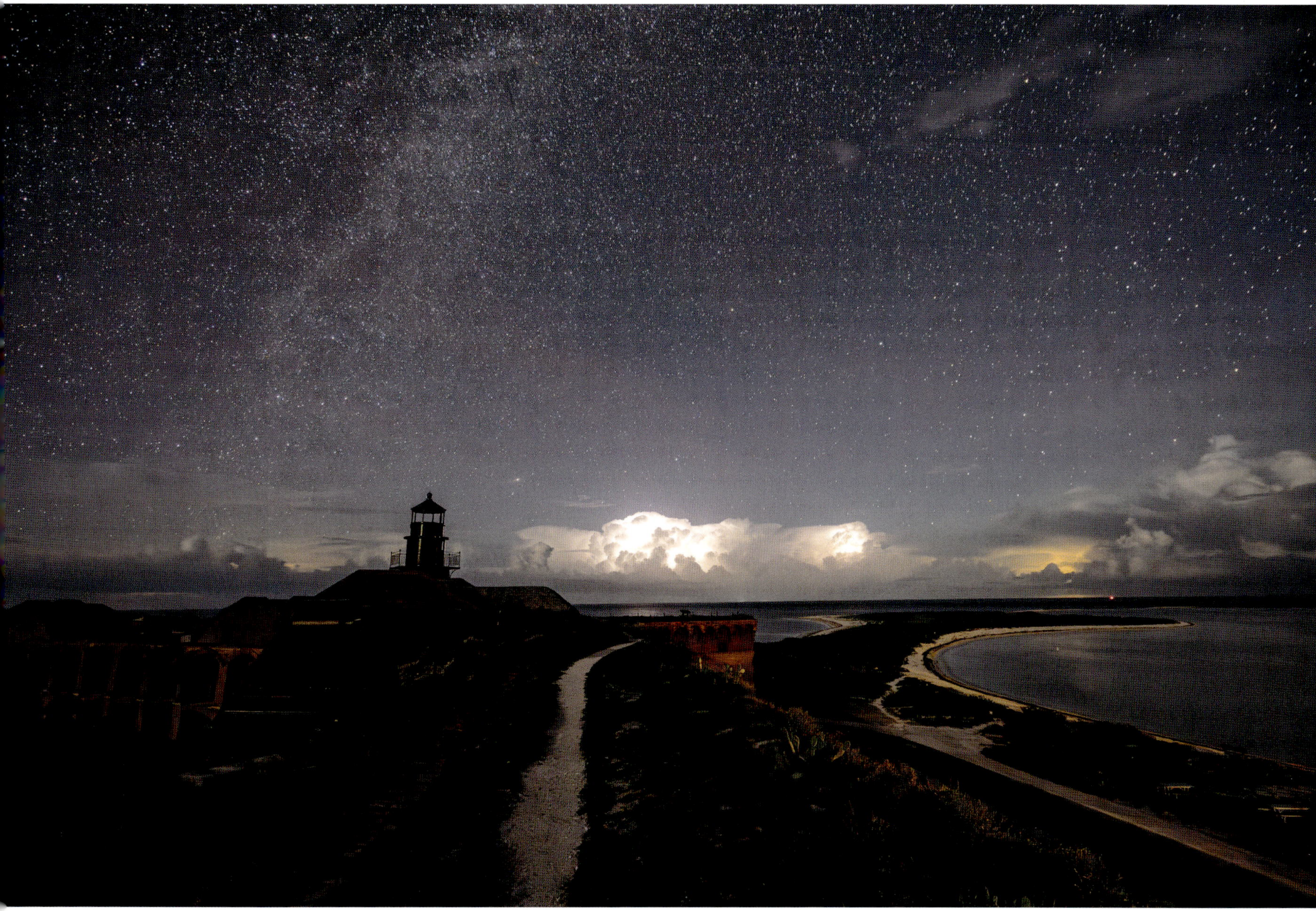

Night sky from the top of Fort Jefferson.

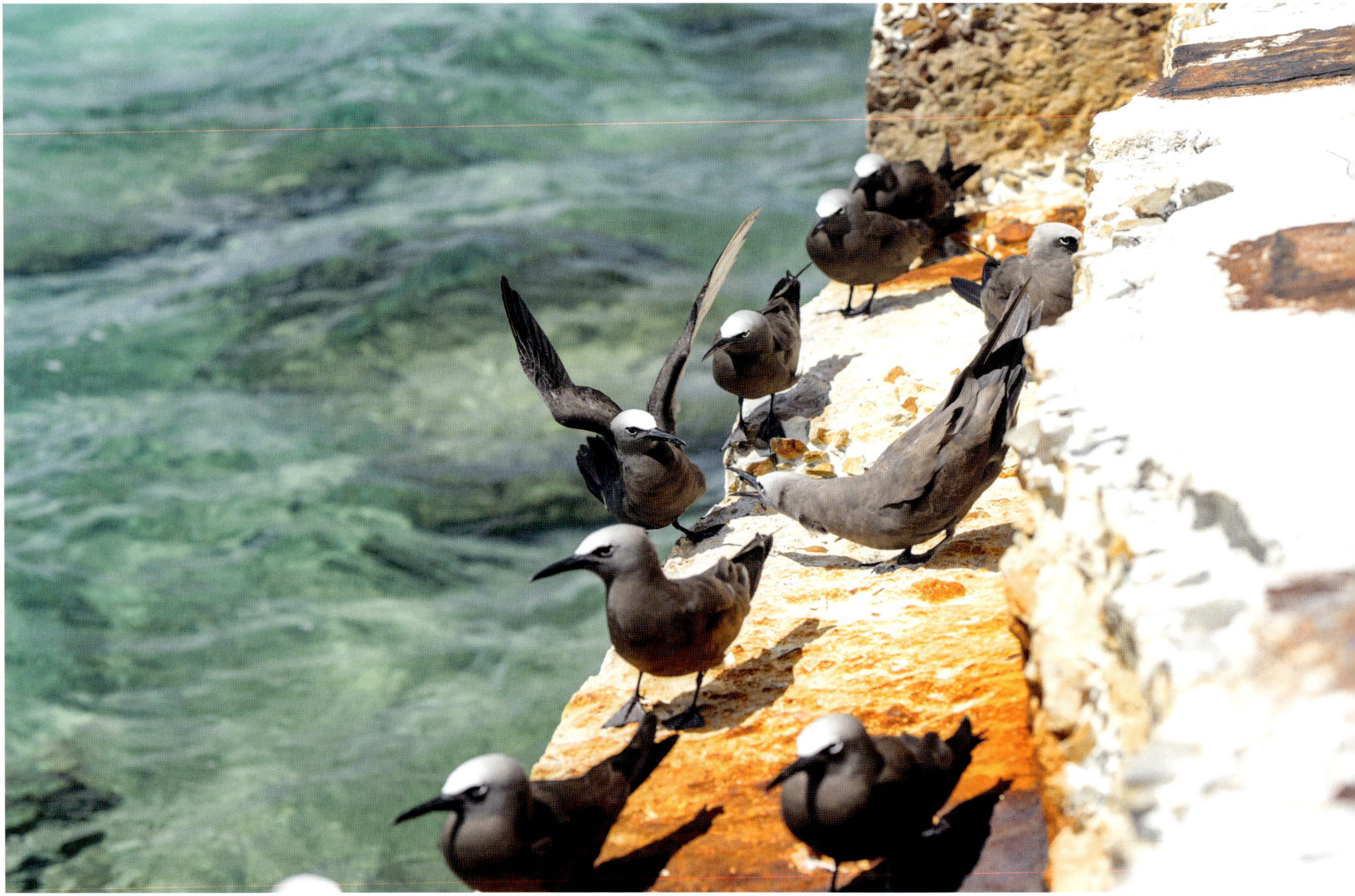

Brown noddies (*Anous stolidus*) quarrel for spots on one of Garden Key's rock ledges.

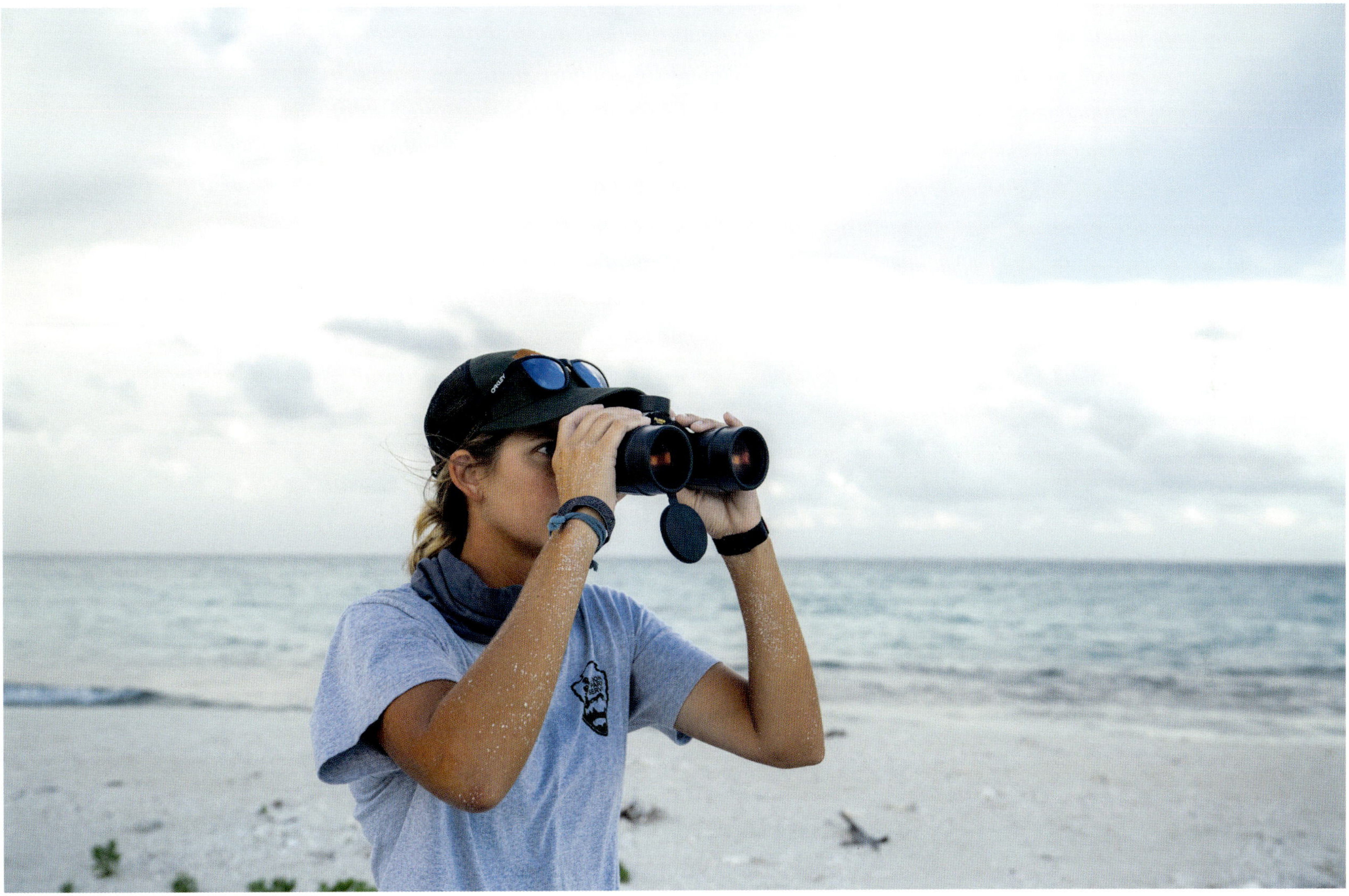

Jess Stuczynski, a staff biologist with the park,
scans the horizon off Bush Key.

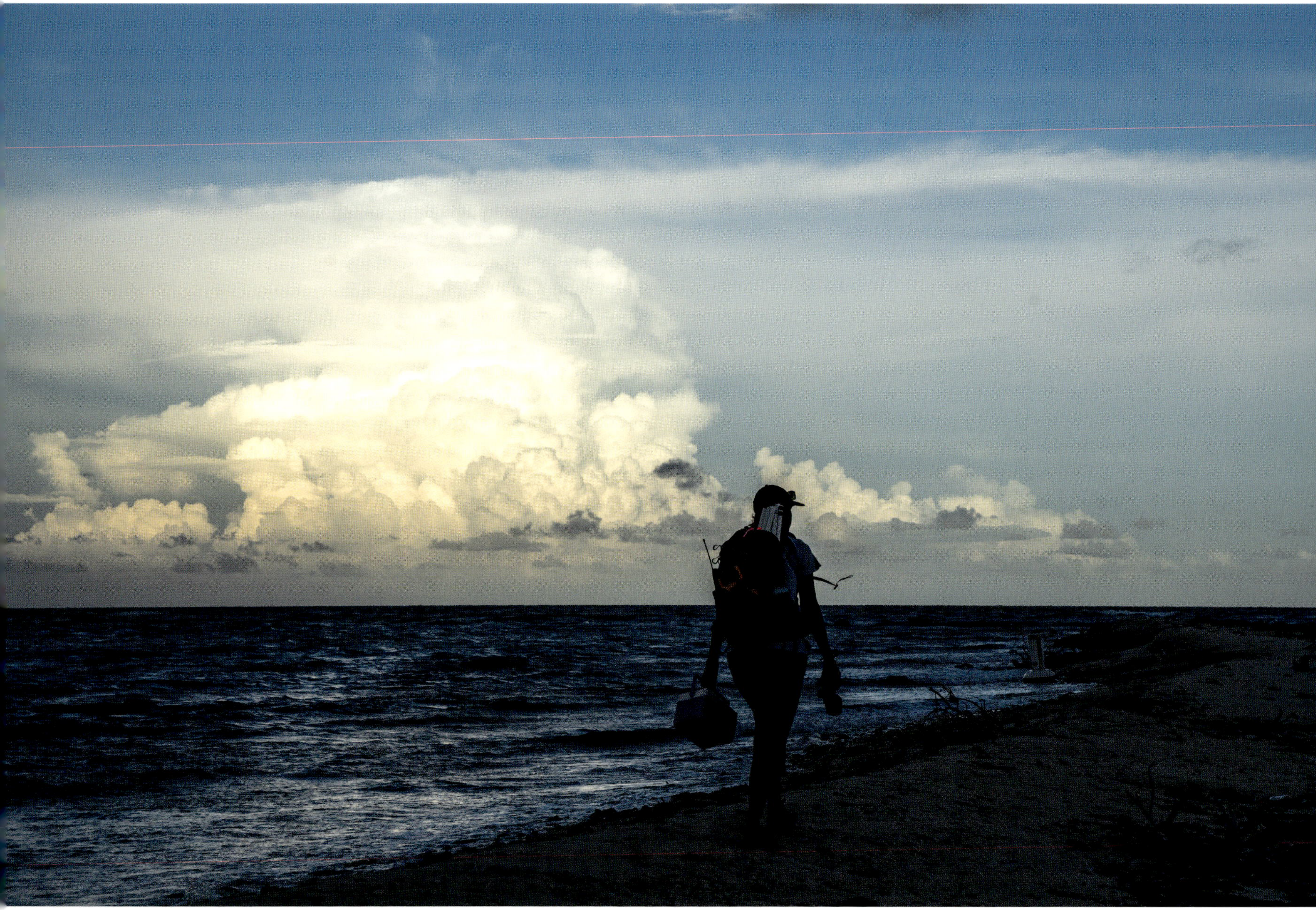

On a bird survey, Jess Stuczynski walks the beach
on a turtle survey.

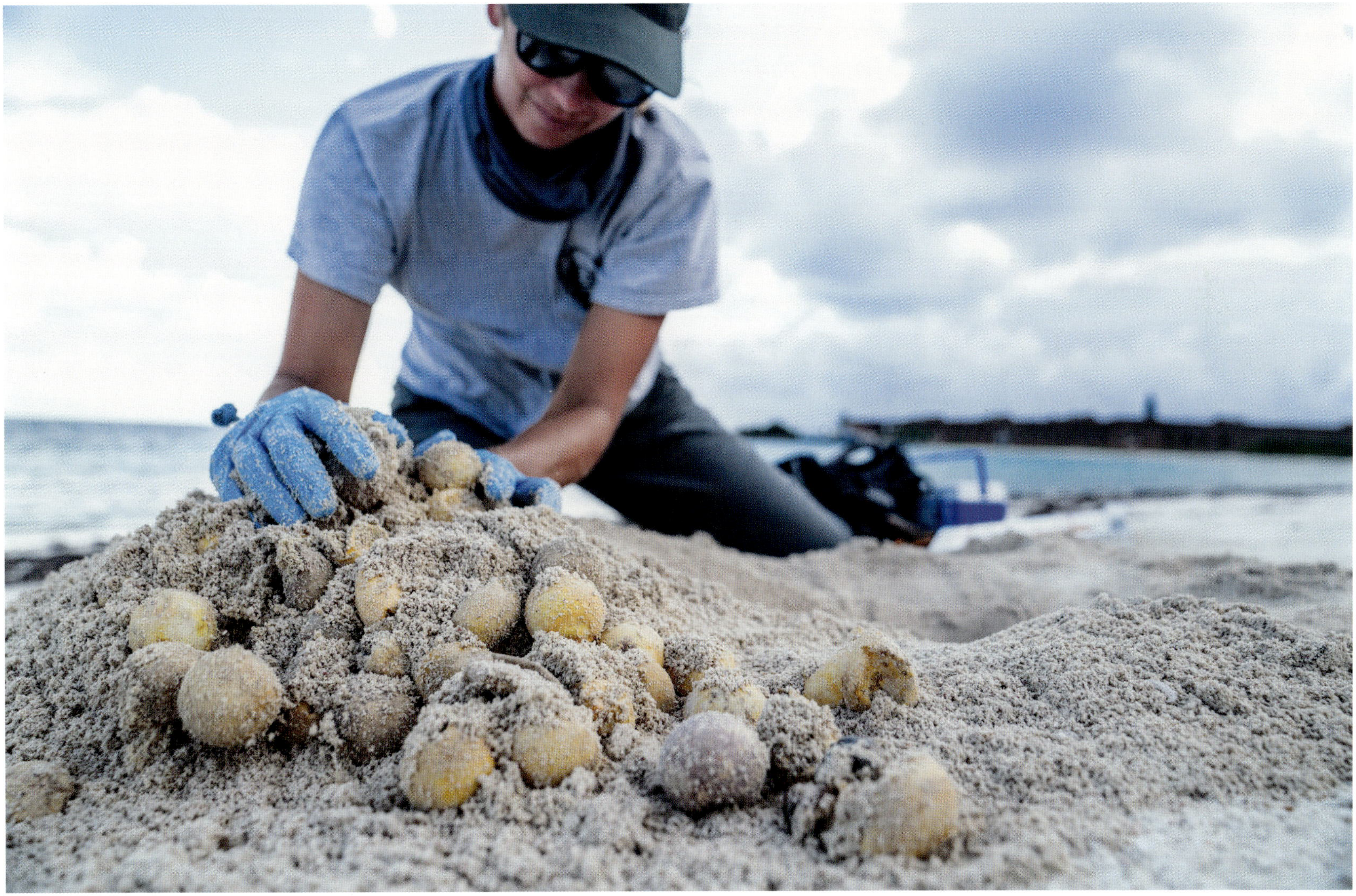

Jess Stuczynski digs out a flooded turtle nest.

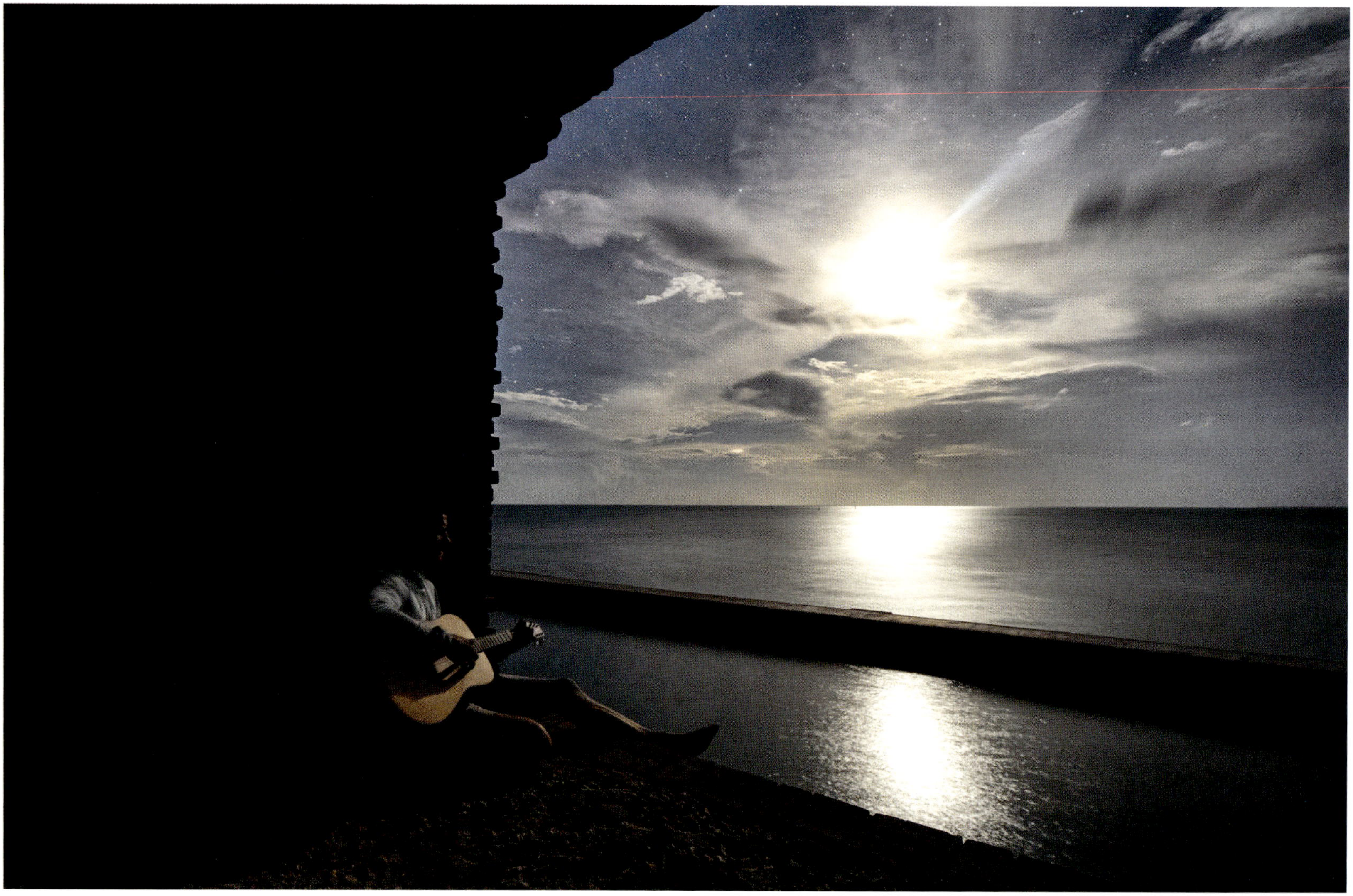

Austin Armstrong plays guitar in the starlight.

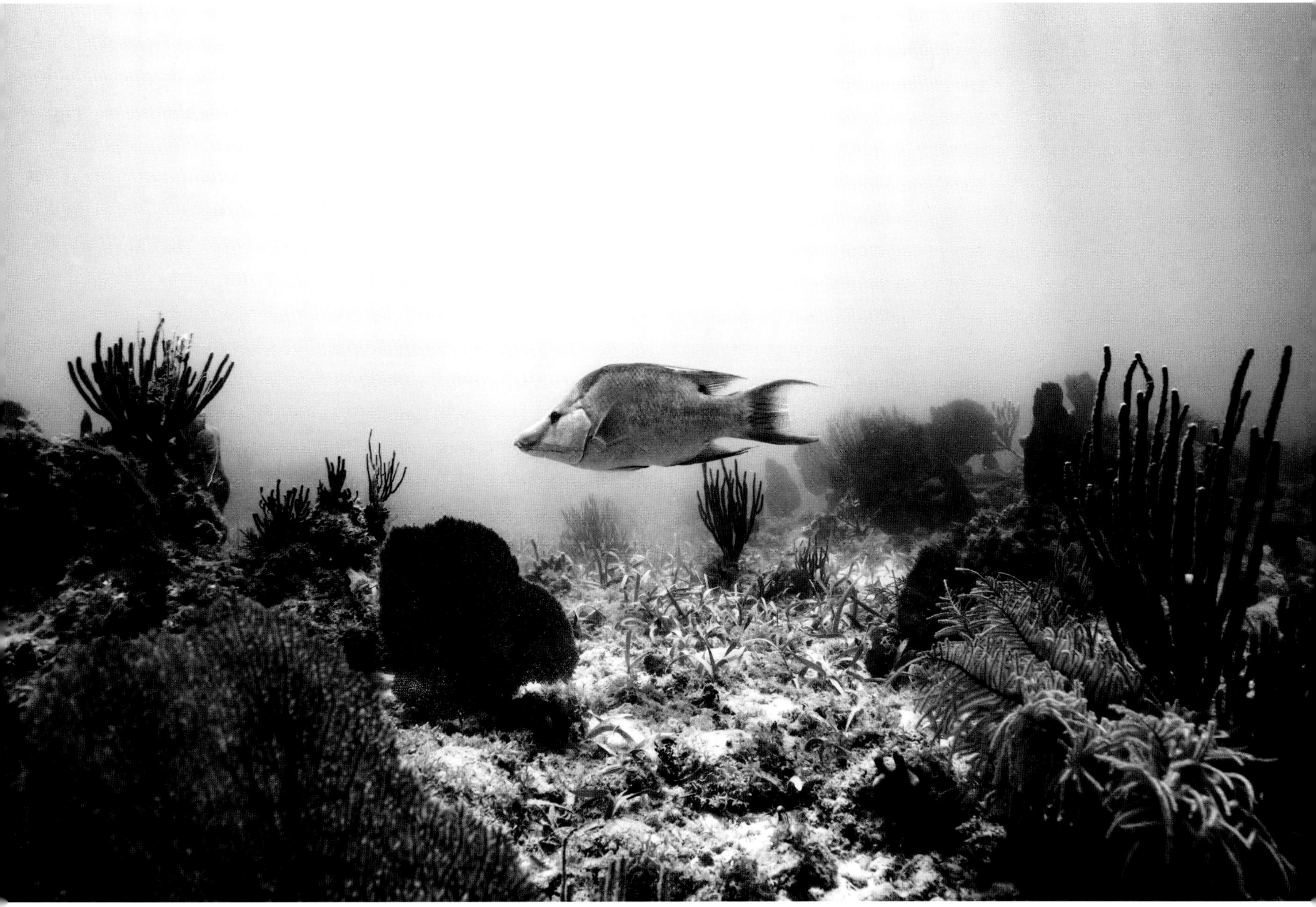

A hogfish swims through sea fans.

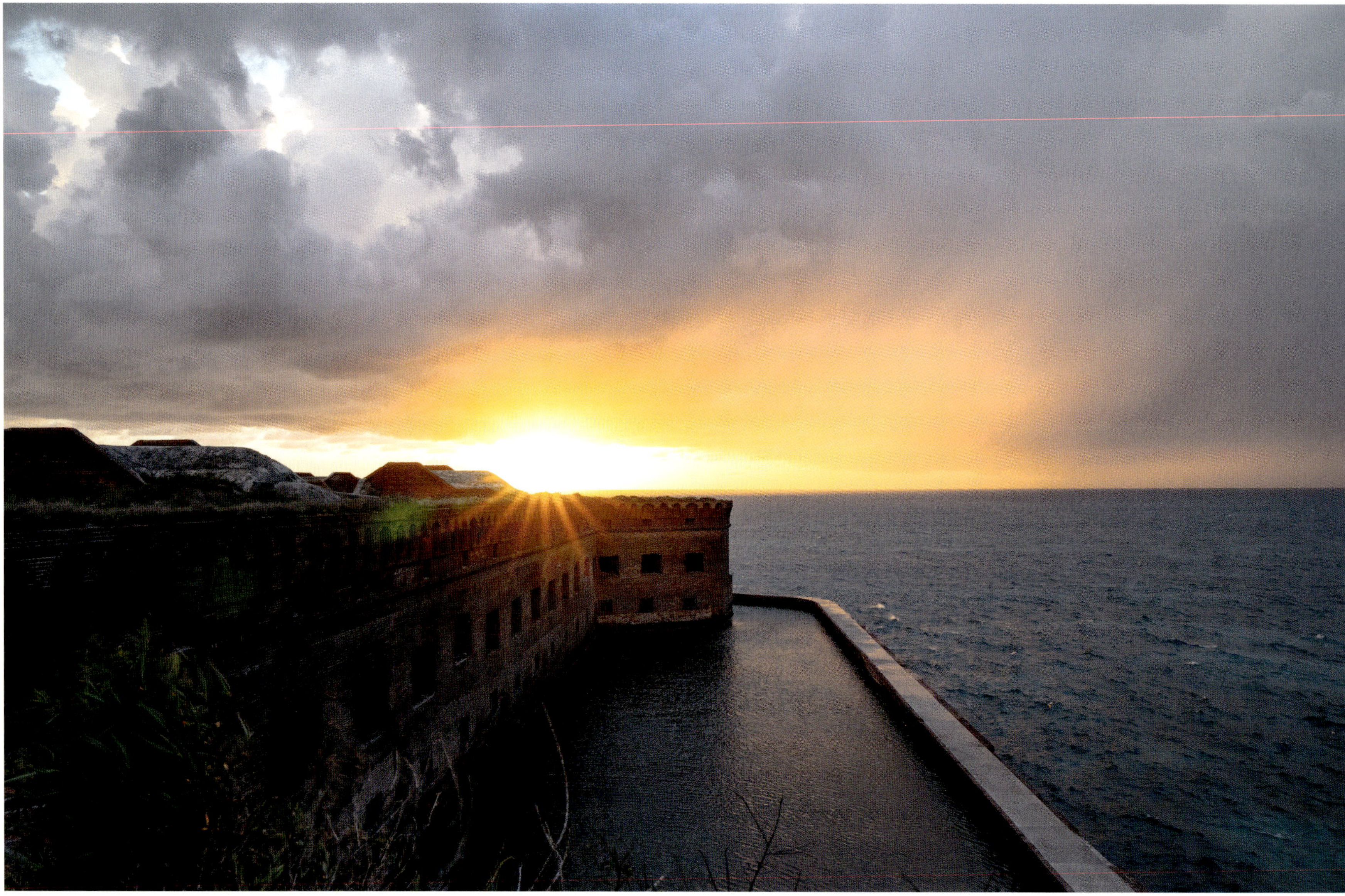

Sunset from one of Fort Jefferson's six bastions.

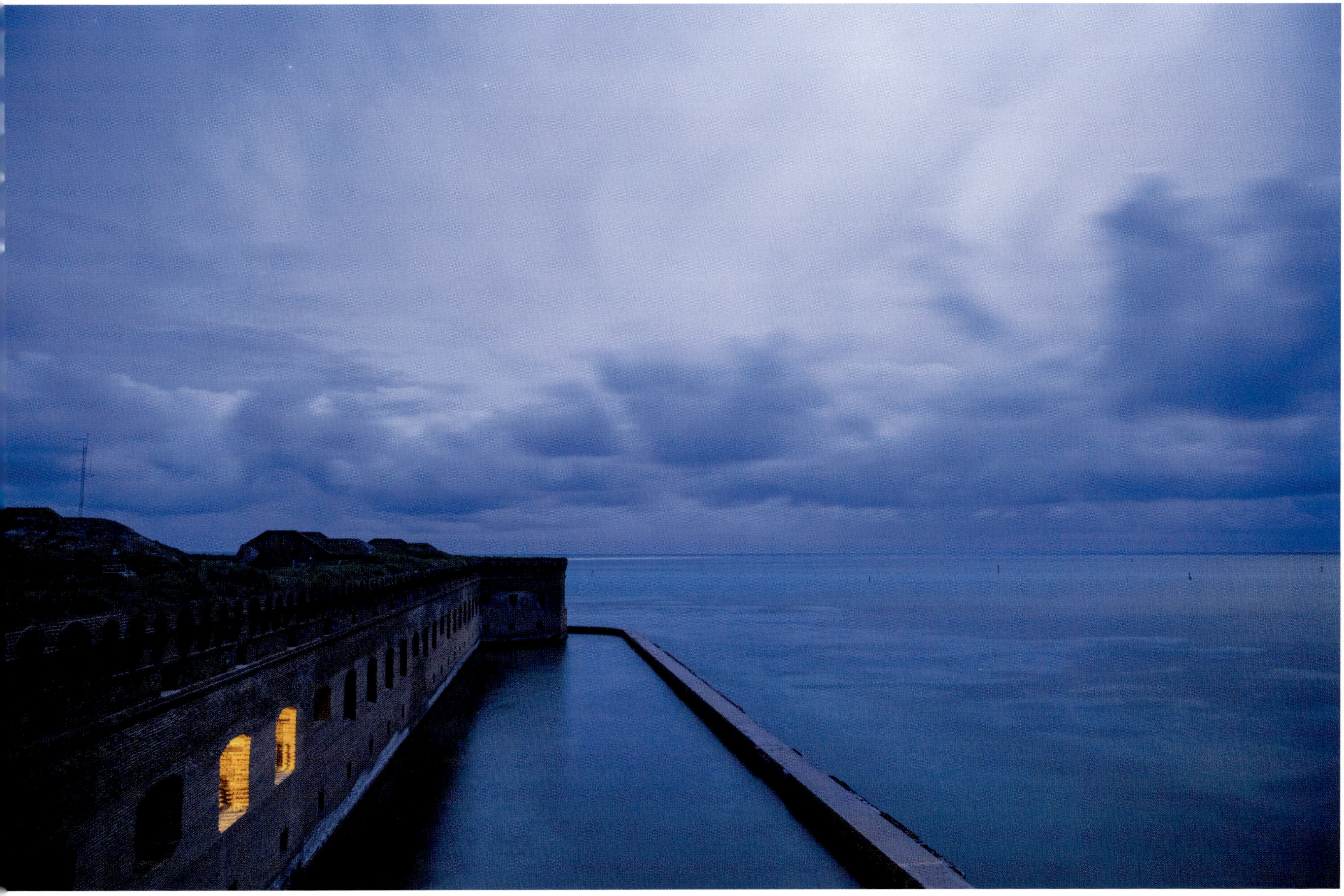

Twilight from a Fort Jefferson bastion.

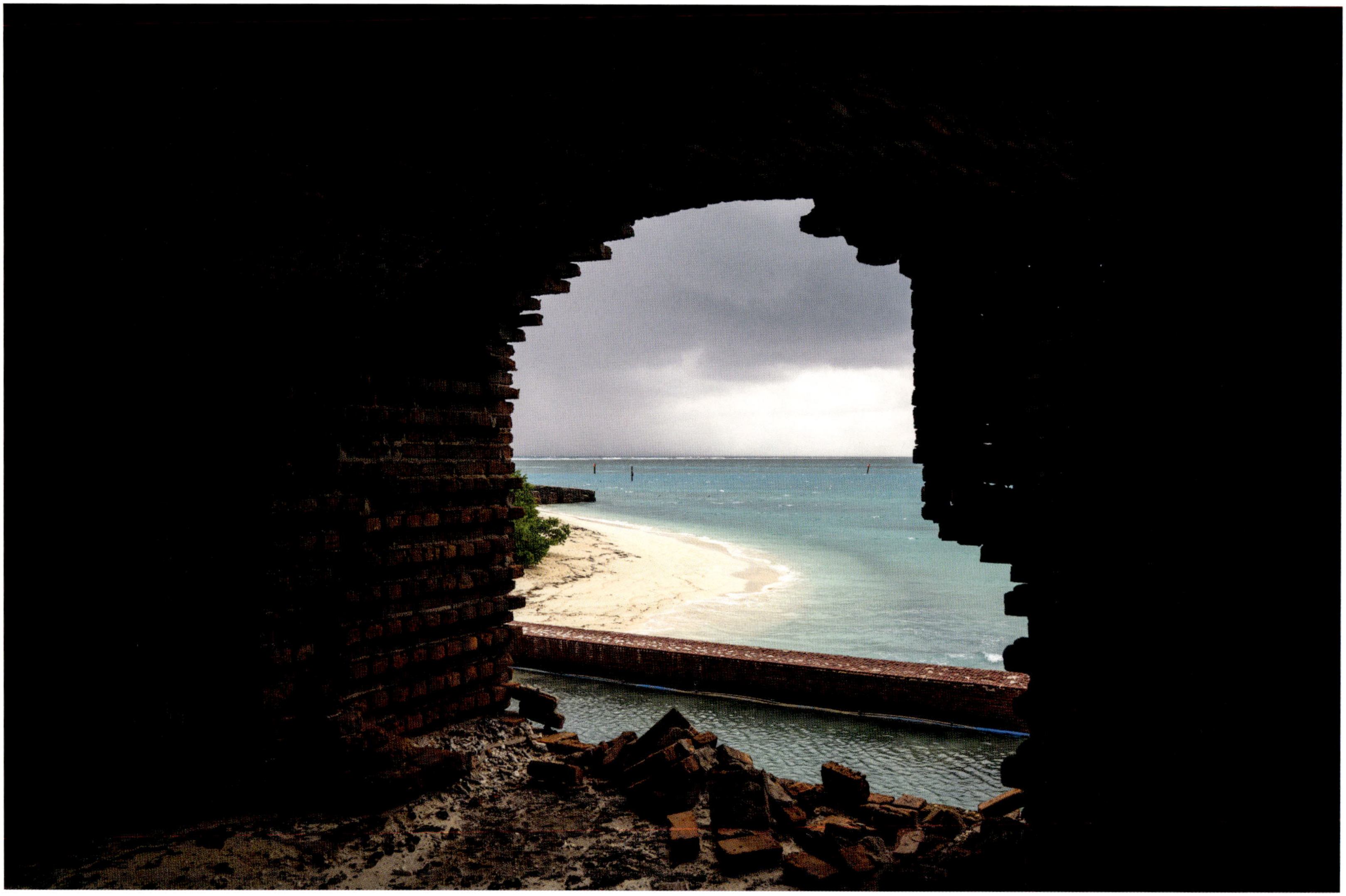

Storm clouds accumulate beyond the fort walls.

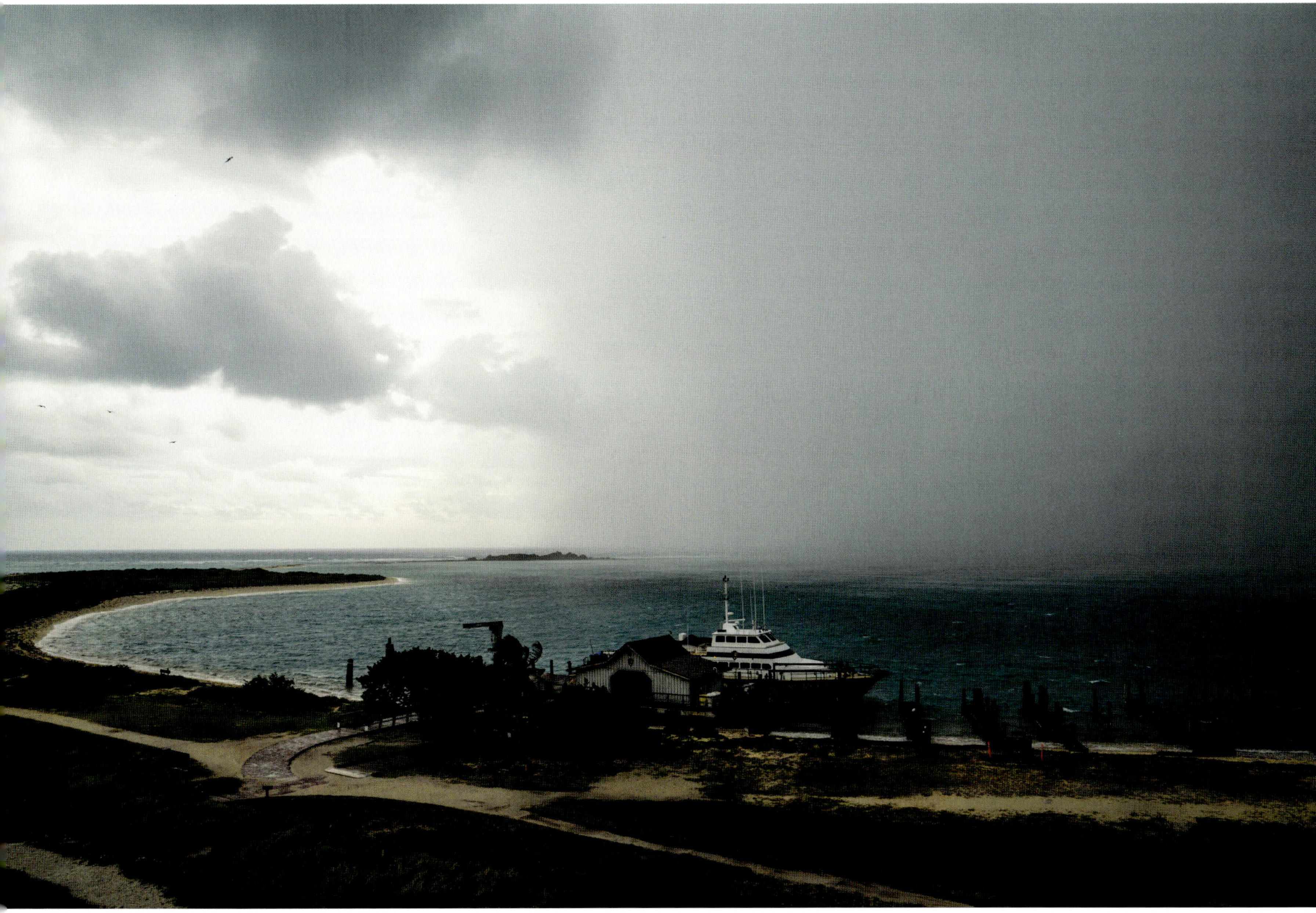

Rain bands make their way toward Fort Jefferson.

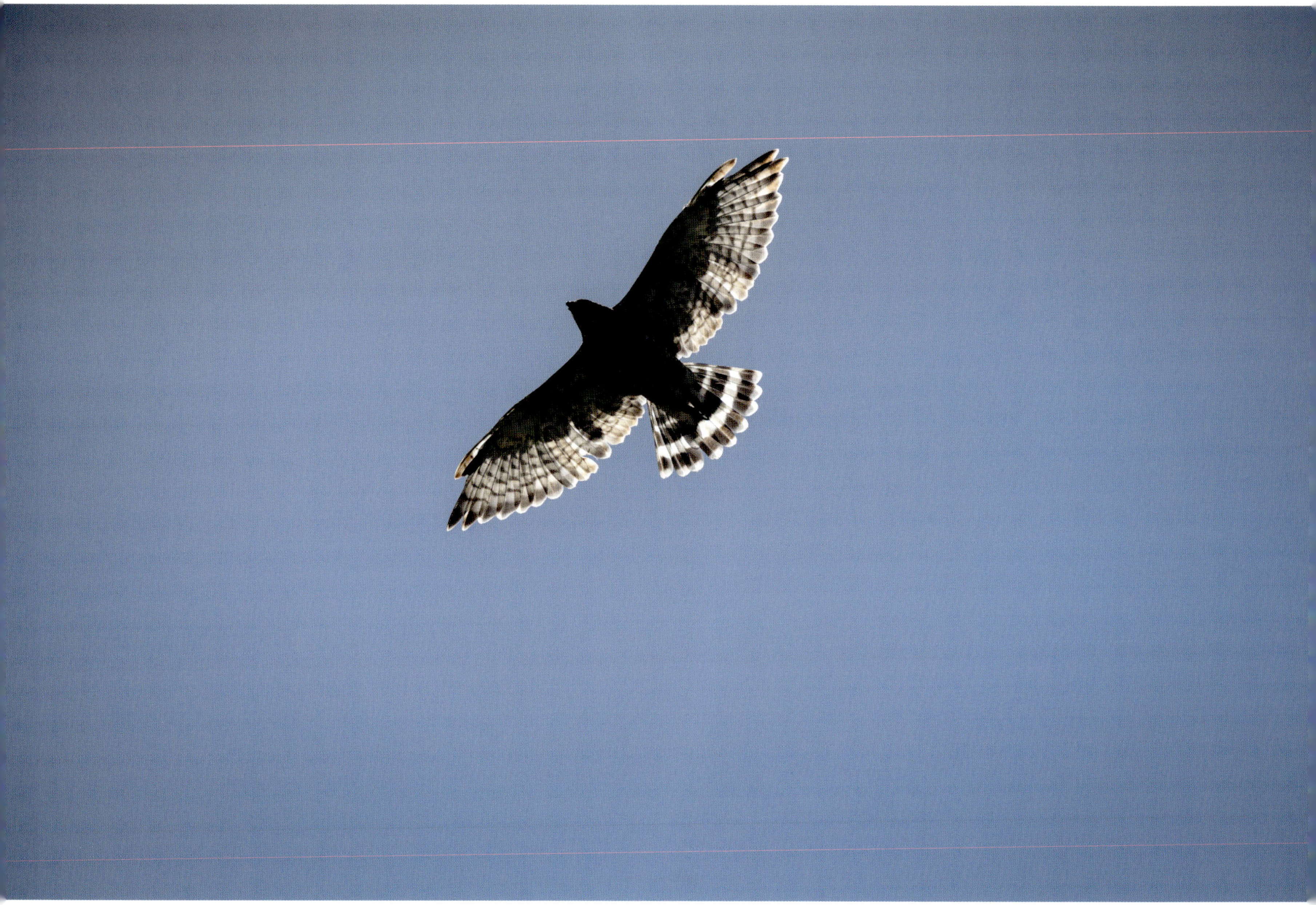

A red-tailed hawk (*Buteo jamaicensis*) flies over Fort Jefferson.

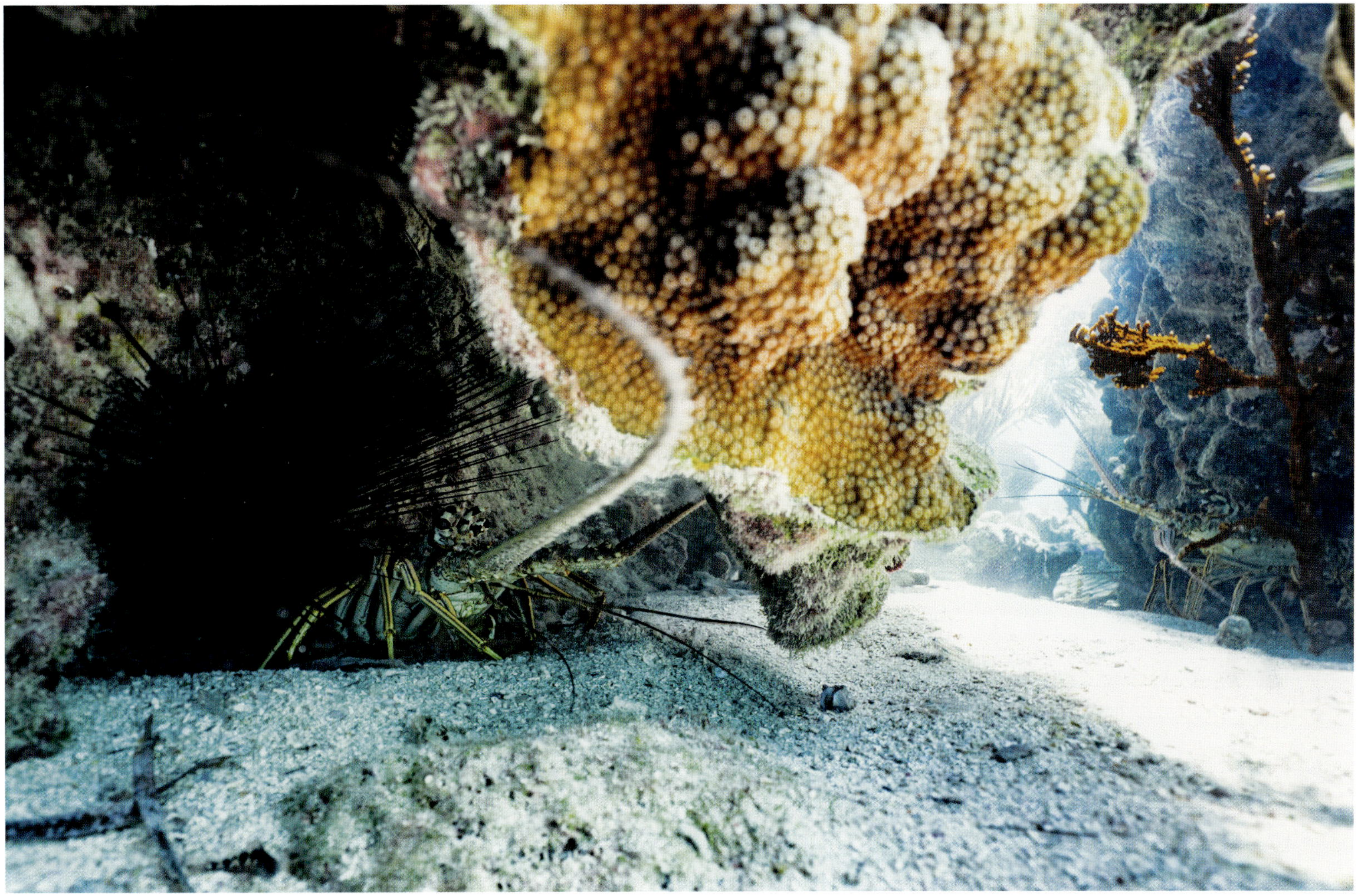

Spiny lobster and long-spine sea urchins (*Diadema antillarum*) share coral cover.

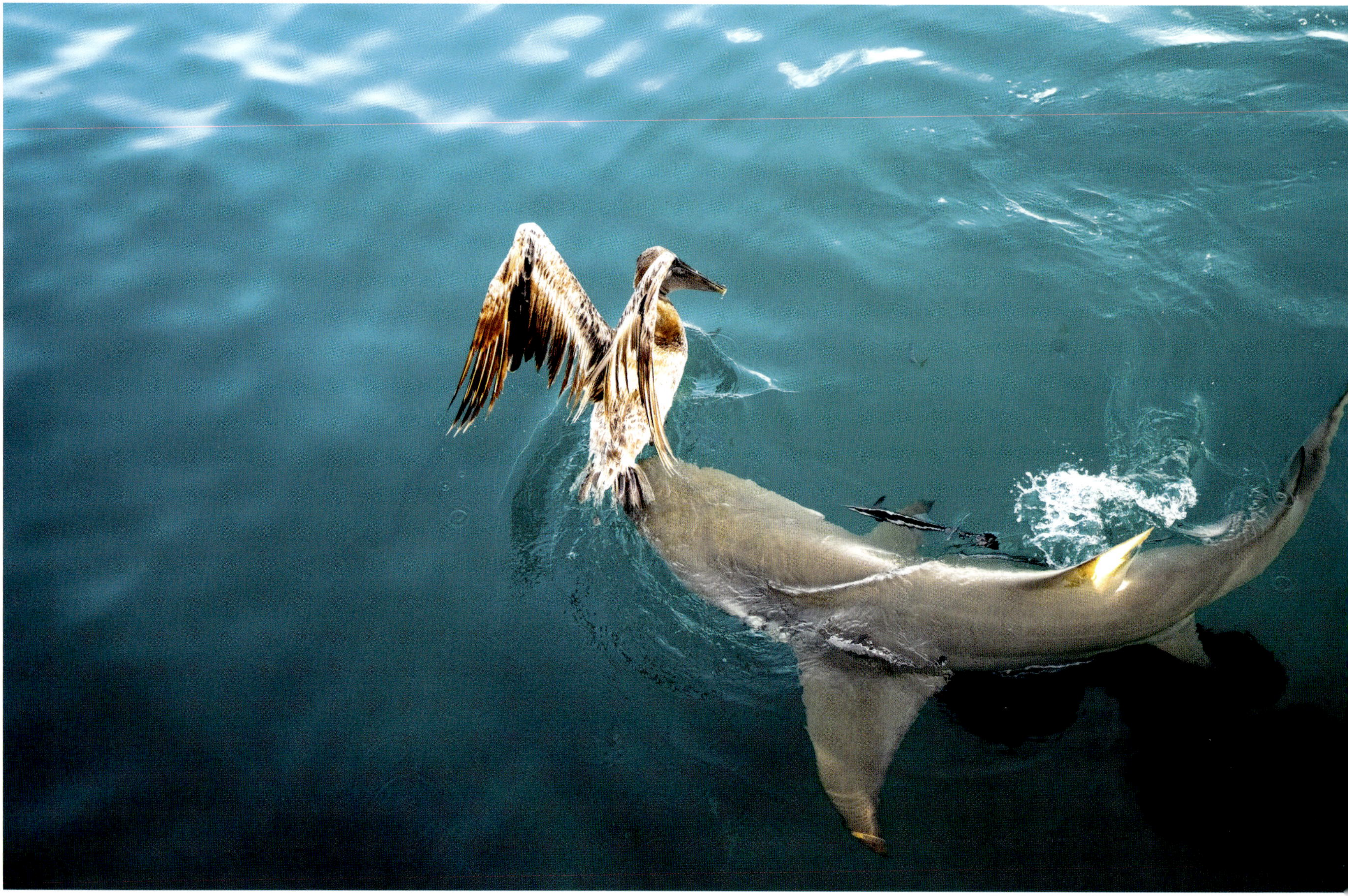

The resident ferry dock lemon shark (*Negaprion brevirostris*) takes a swipe at a pelican off Garden Key.

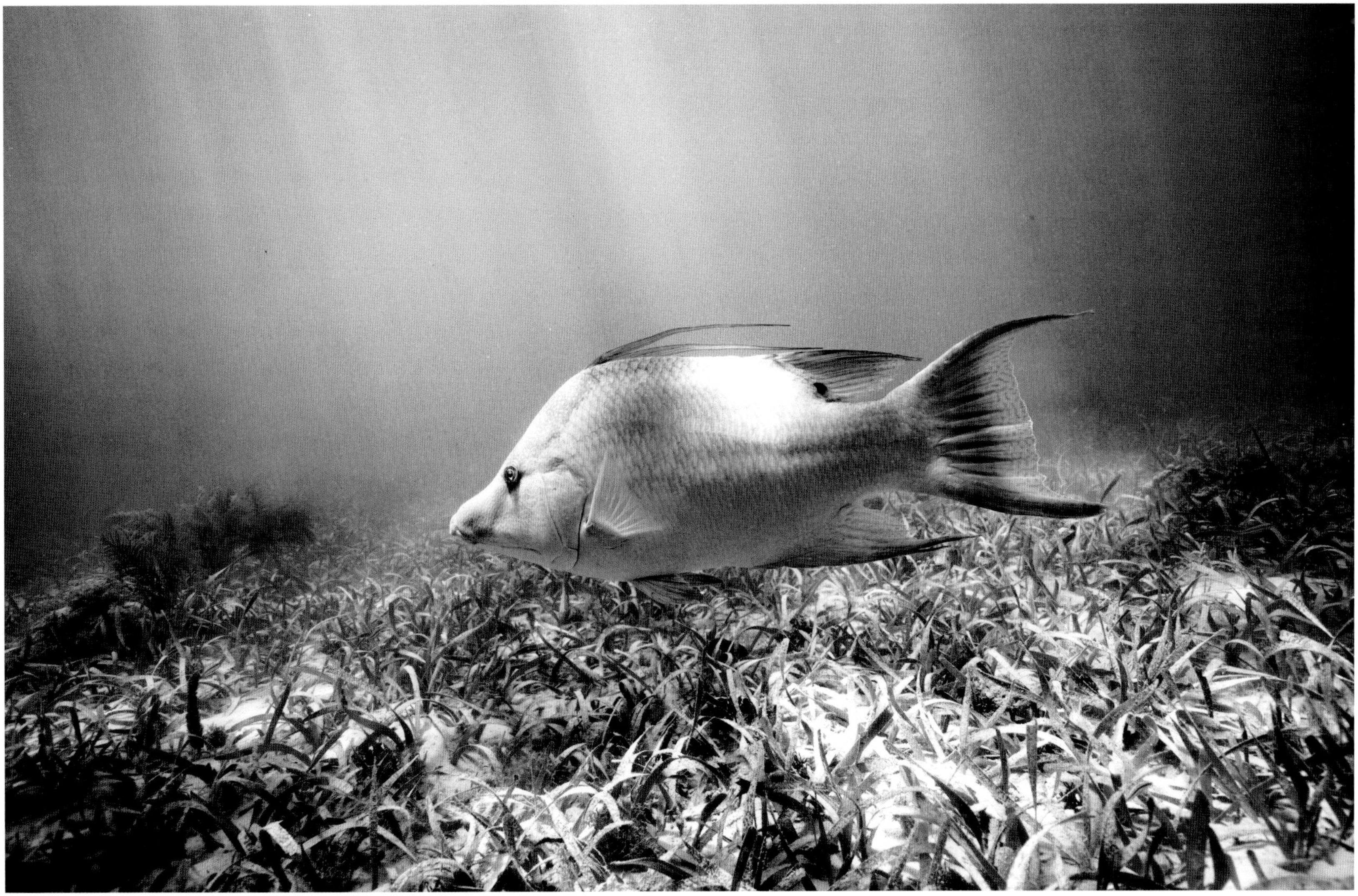

A hogfish in the lush seagrass off Garden Key.

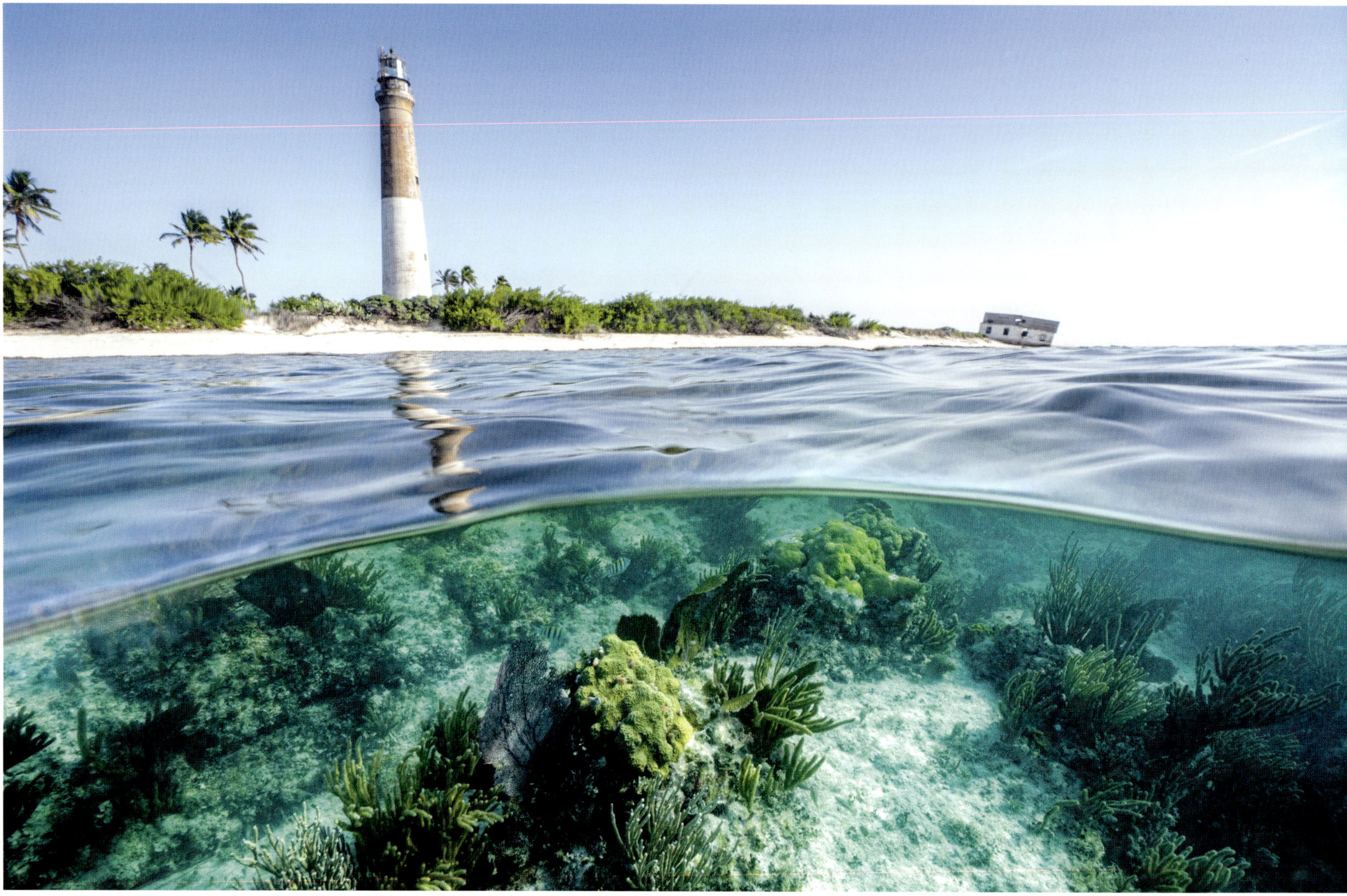

Watery paradise. Little Africa Reef with the old boathouse and light station in sight, west shore of Loggerhead Key.

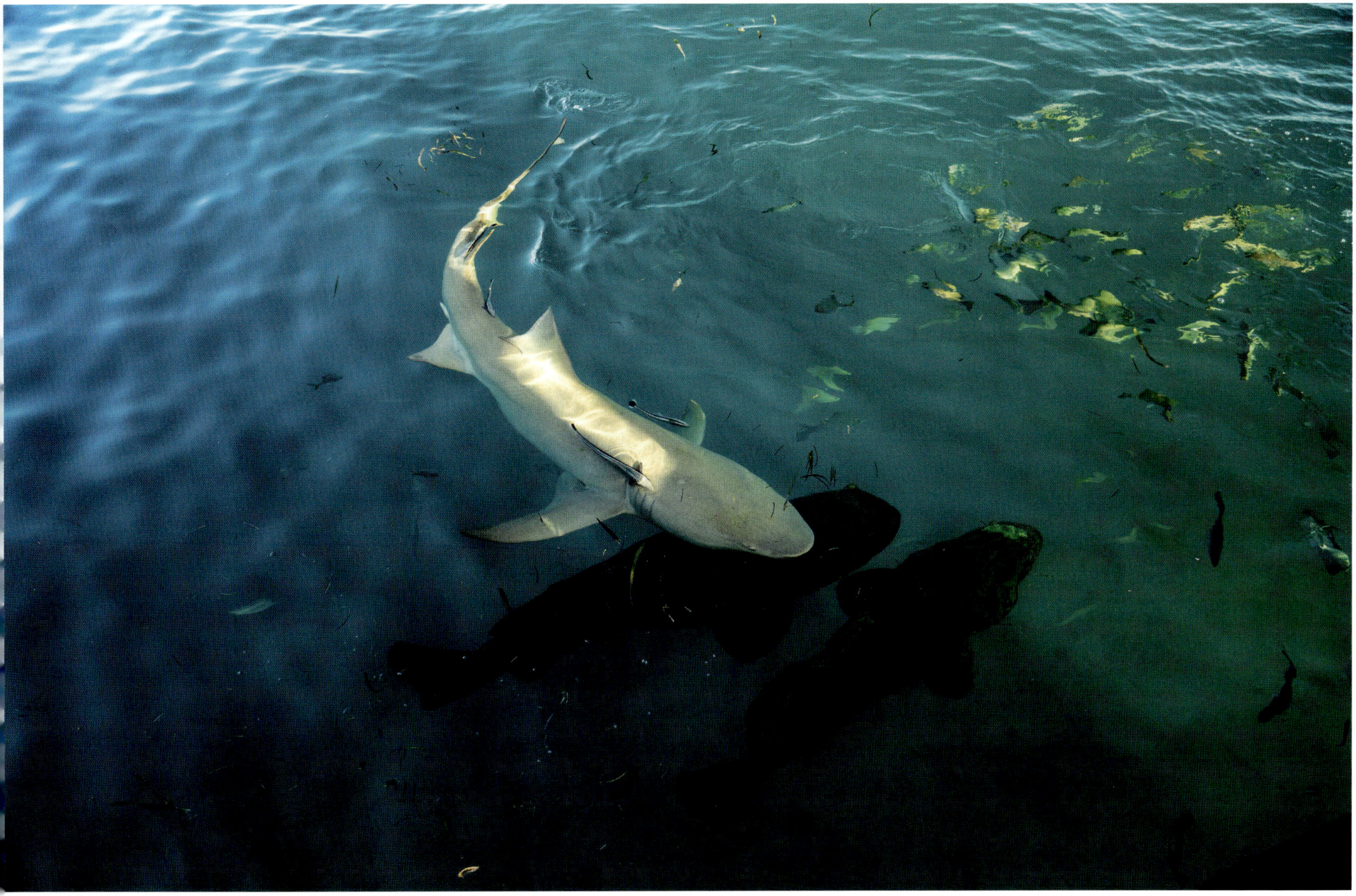

Ferry dock residents: lemon shark, goliath grouper, and mangrove snapper (*Lutjanus griseus*) off Garden Key.

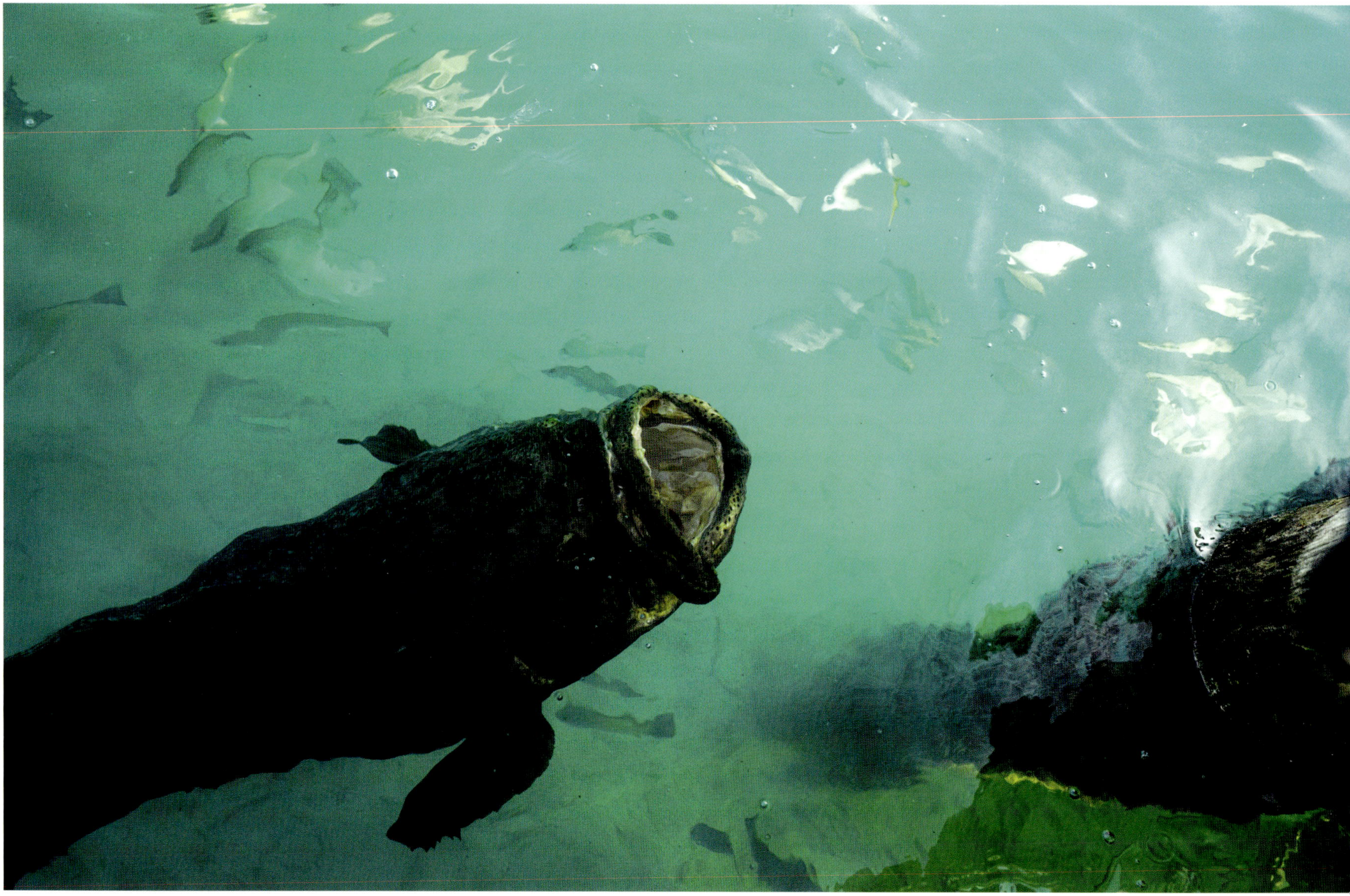

A goliath grouper hoping to get a free meal.

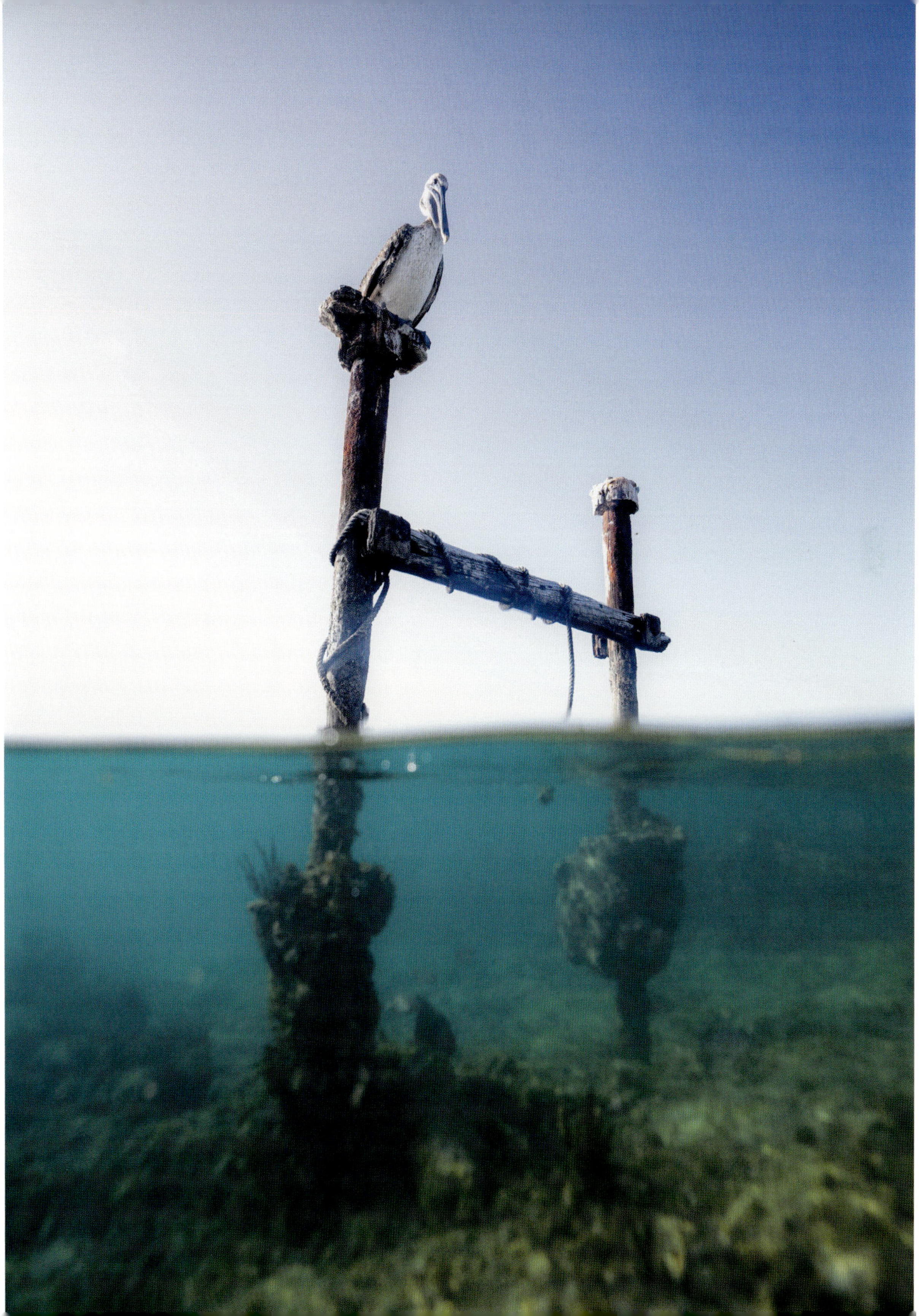

A pelican sits in wait for its next meal.

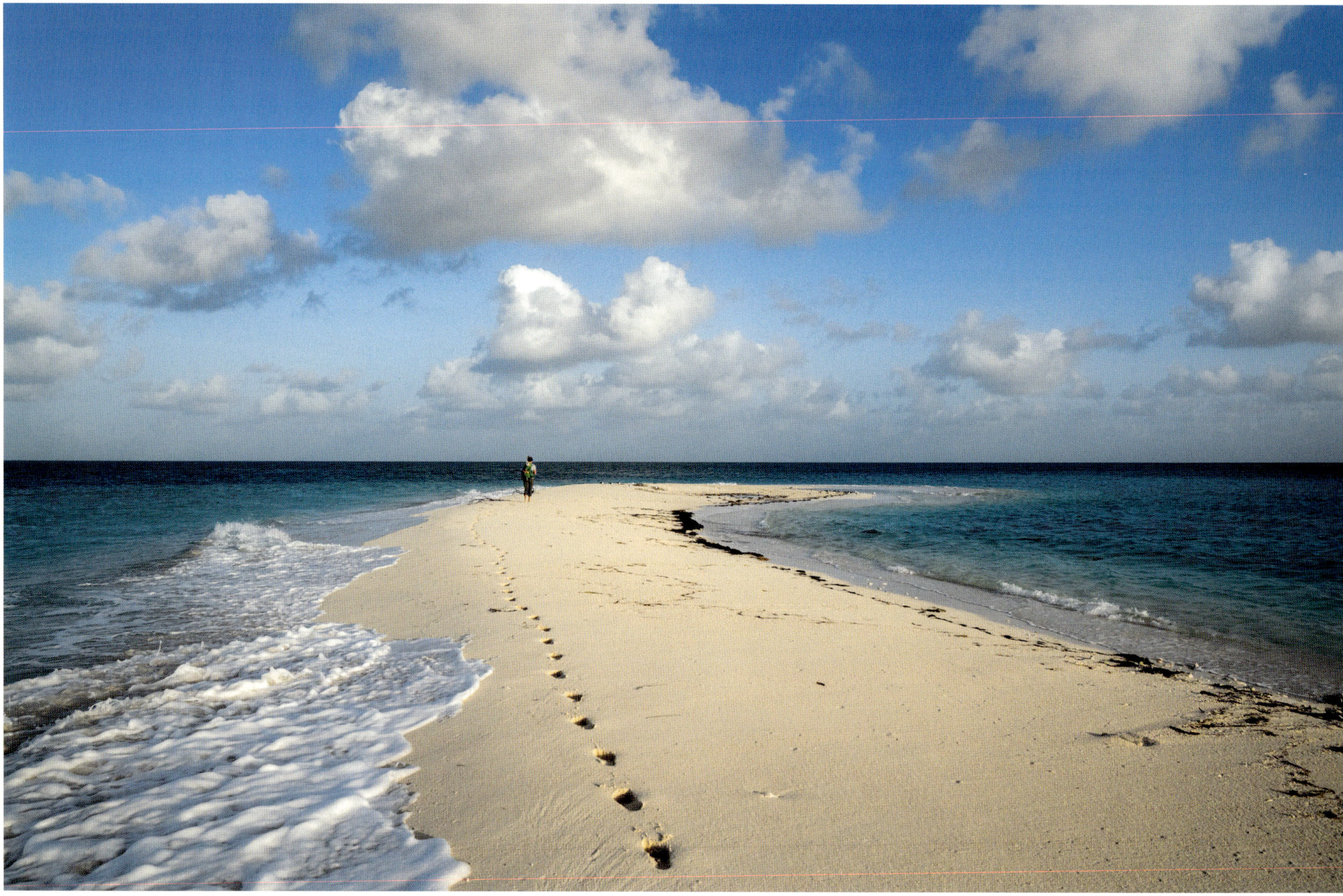

A park employee does bird surveys on a sand point.

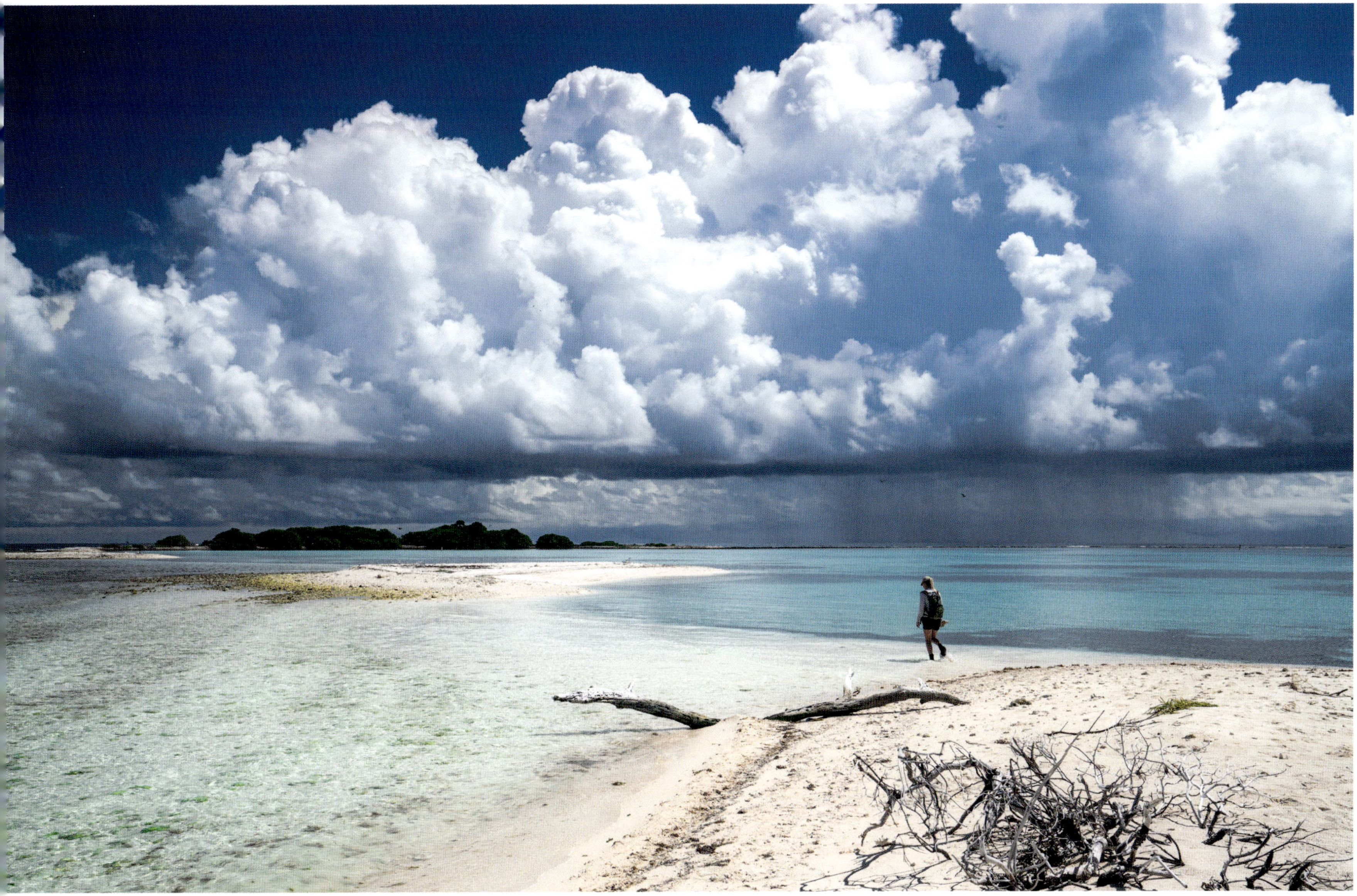

The sandbar between Bush and Long Keys shifts constantly and maintains my favorite park views when open.

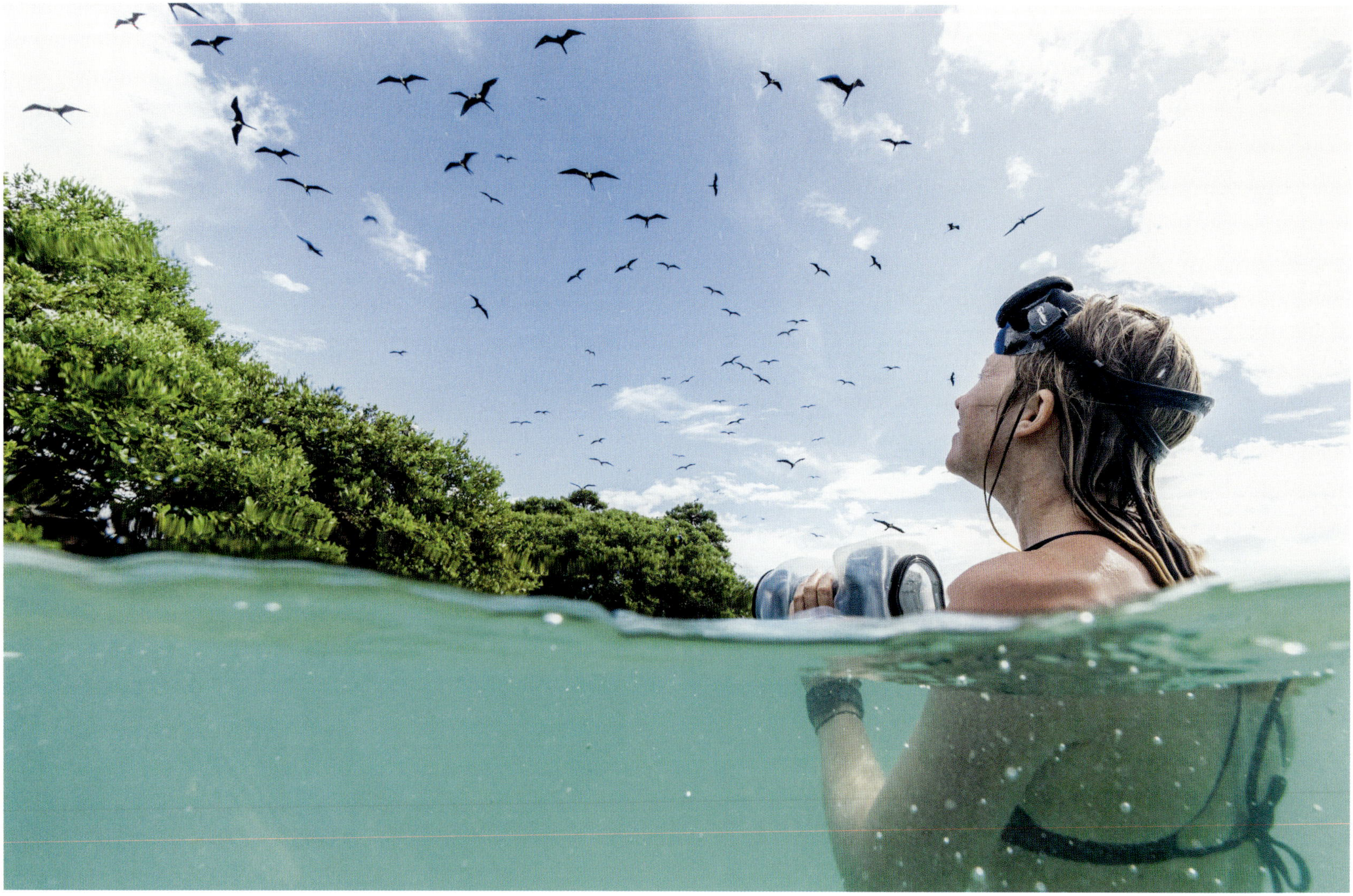

A park volunteer, camera in hand, observes frigatebirds soaring above the black mangroves (*Avicennia germinans*) on Long Key.

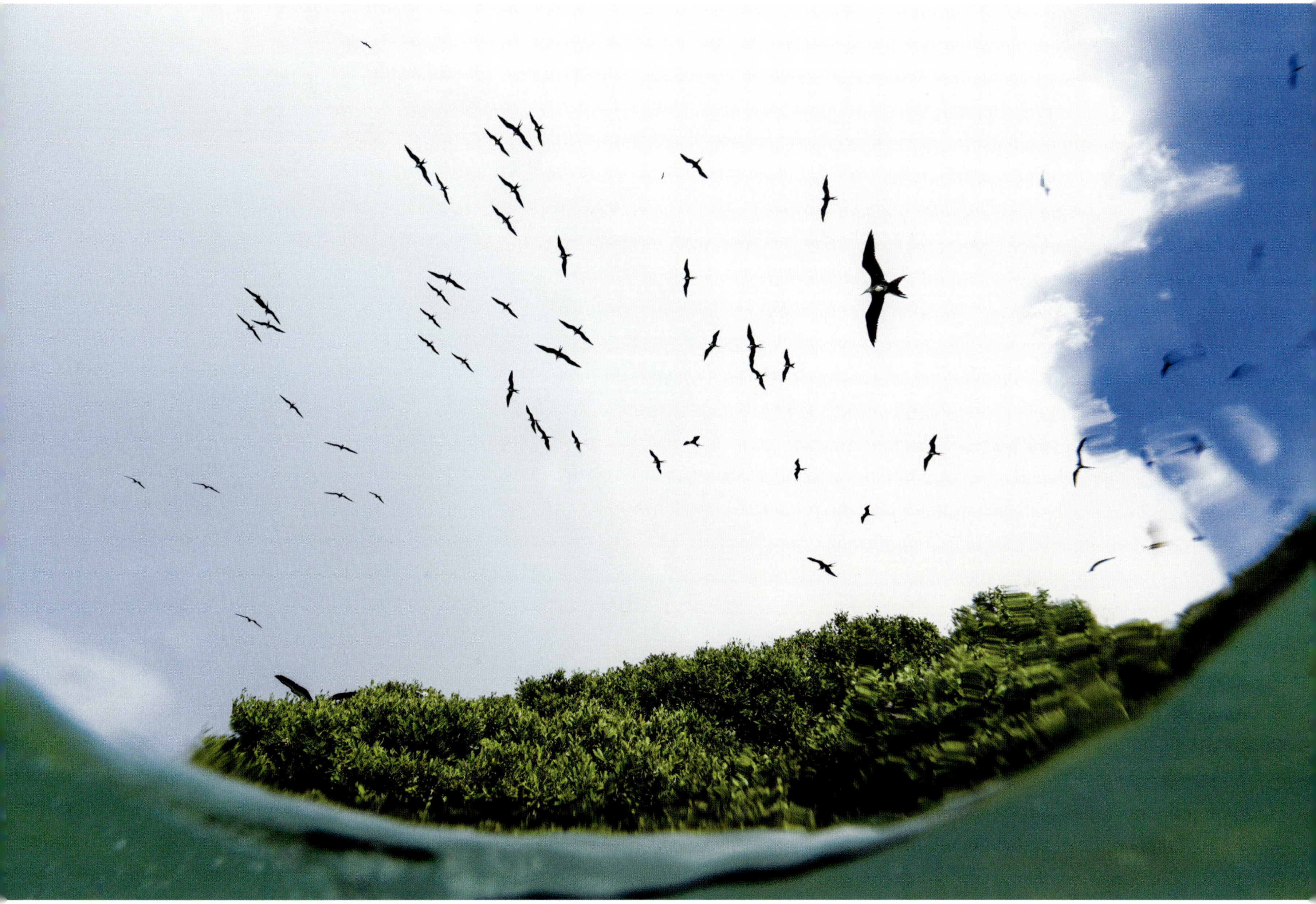

Frigatebirds over Long Key from the water. Before Hurricane Ian, magnificent frigatebirds sought the island's black mangroves as roosting and nesting areas. After Ian's destruction of the mangroves in 2022, the frigatebirds sought new breeding grounds. Happily, the birds have now returned to Long Key to breed.

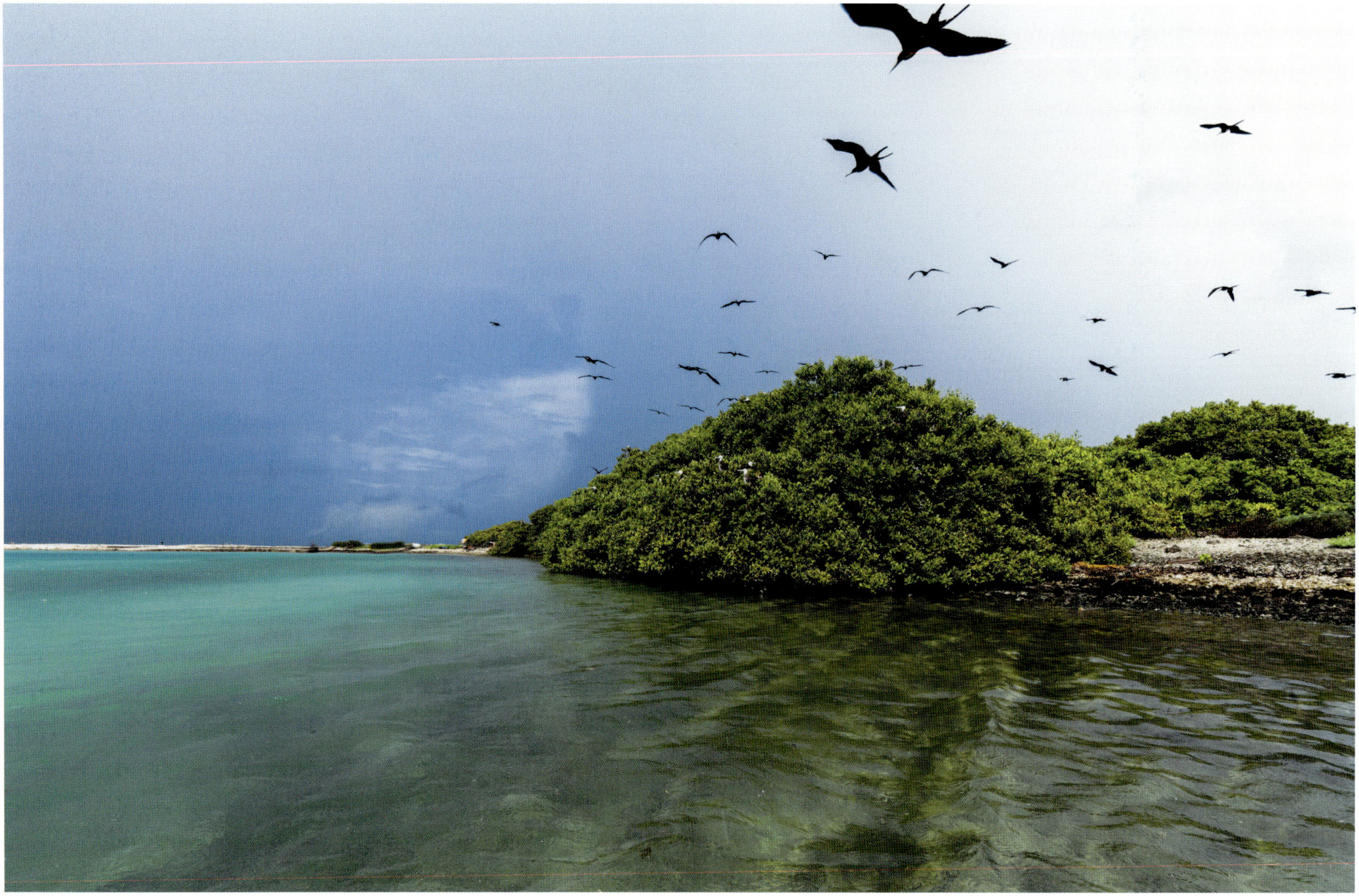

Home to about one hundred nesting pairs, Long Key is the only breeding colony of this angular seabird in the United States.

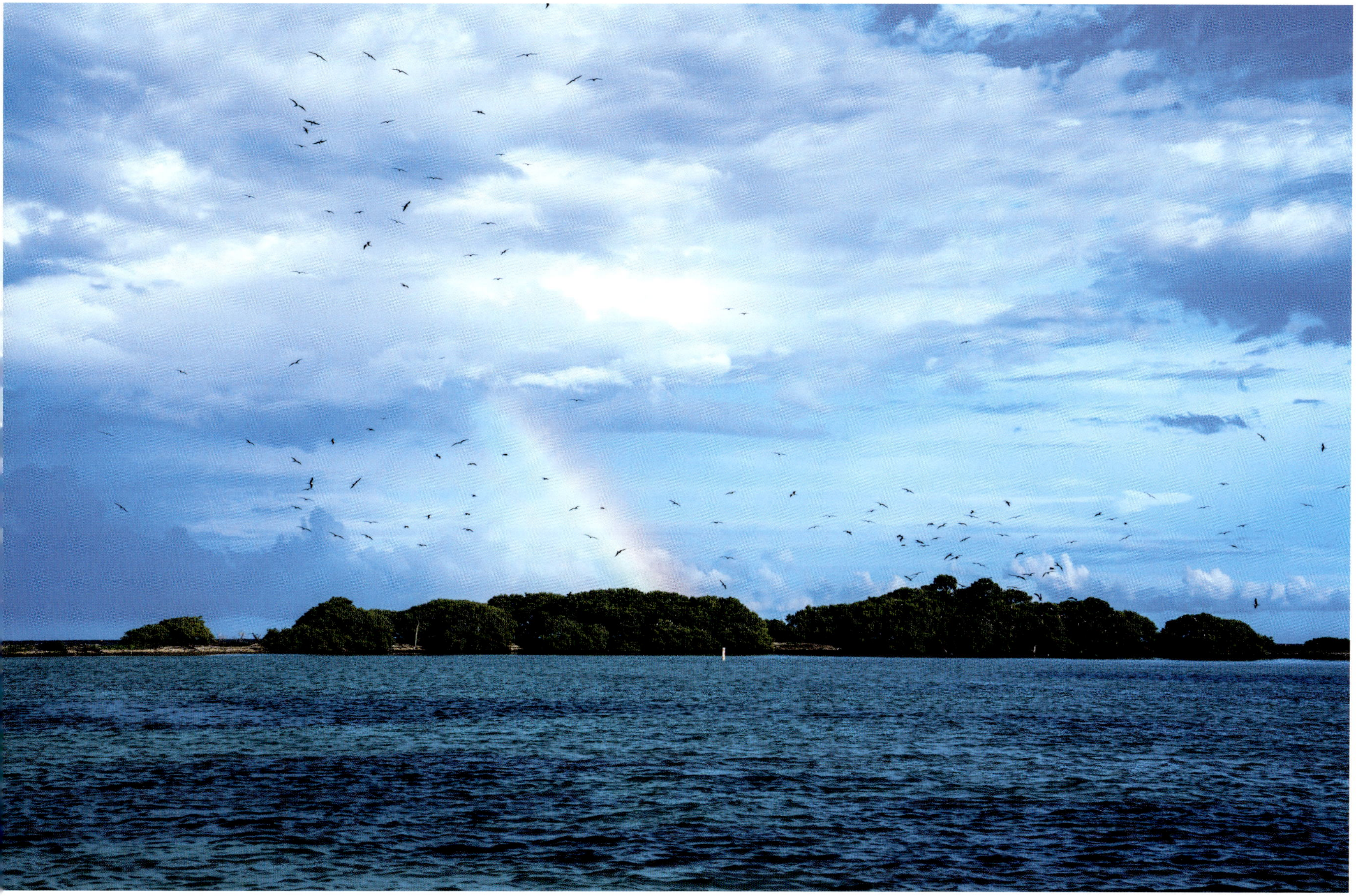

Long Key, pre-Hurricane Ian.

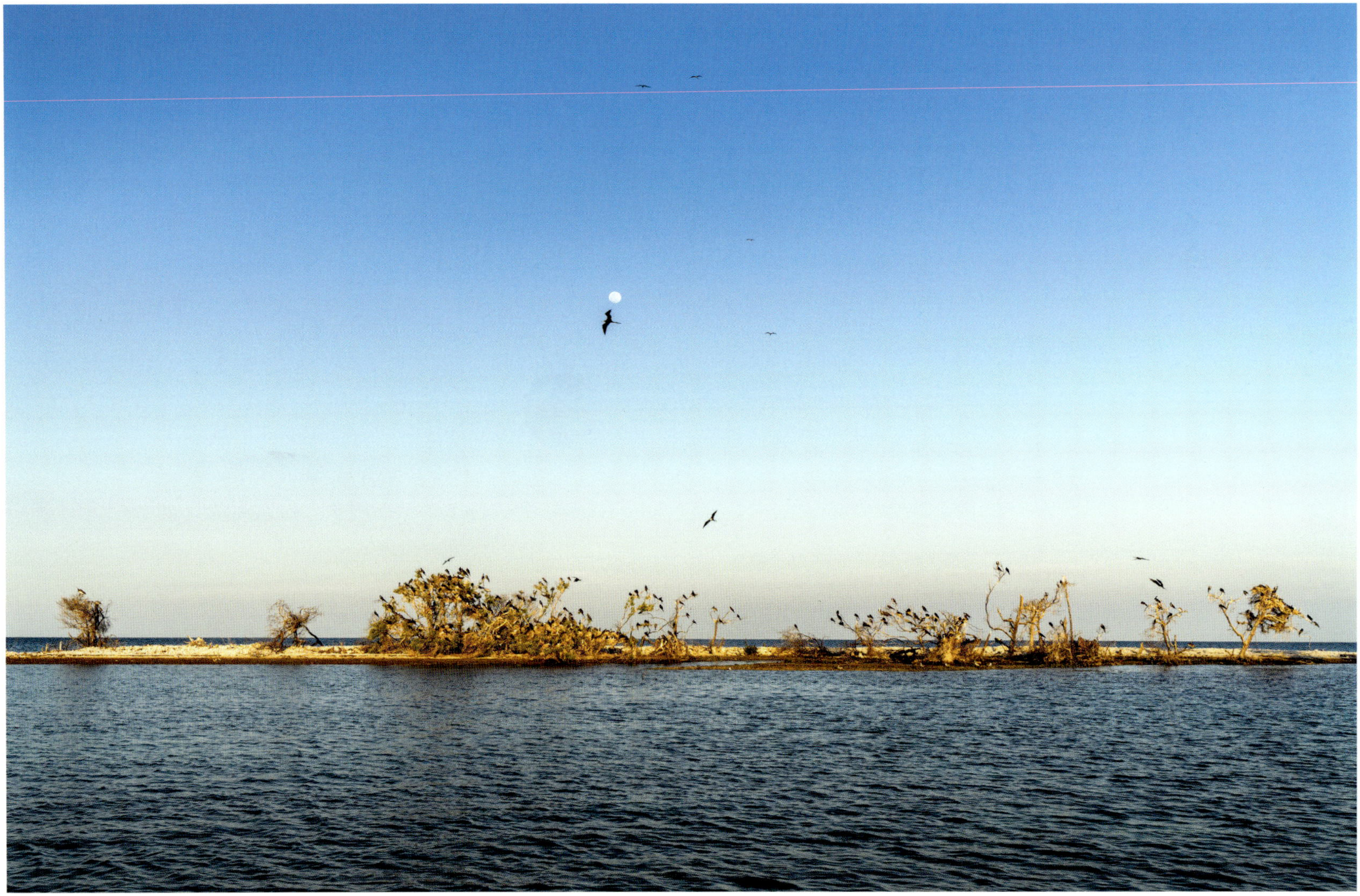

Long Key, post-Hurricane Ian.

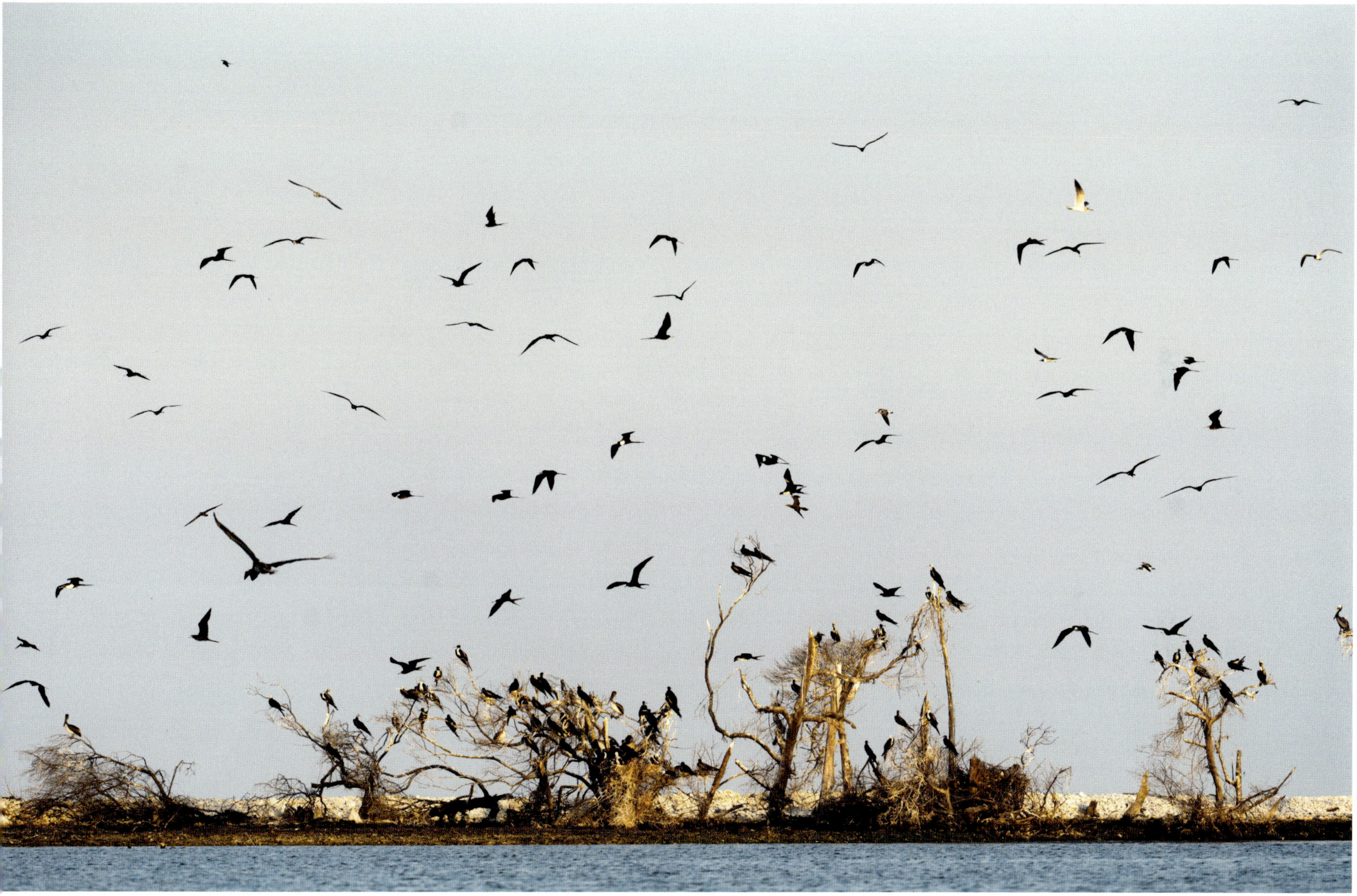

Long Key, magnificent frigatebird colony.

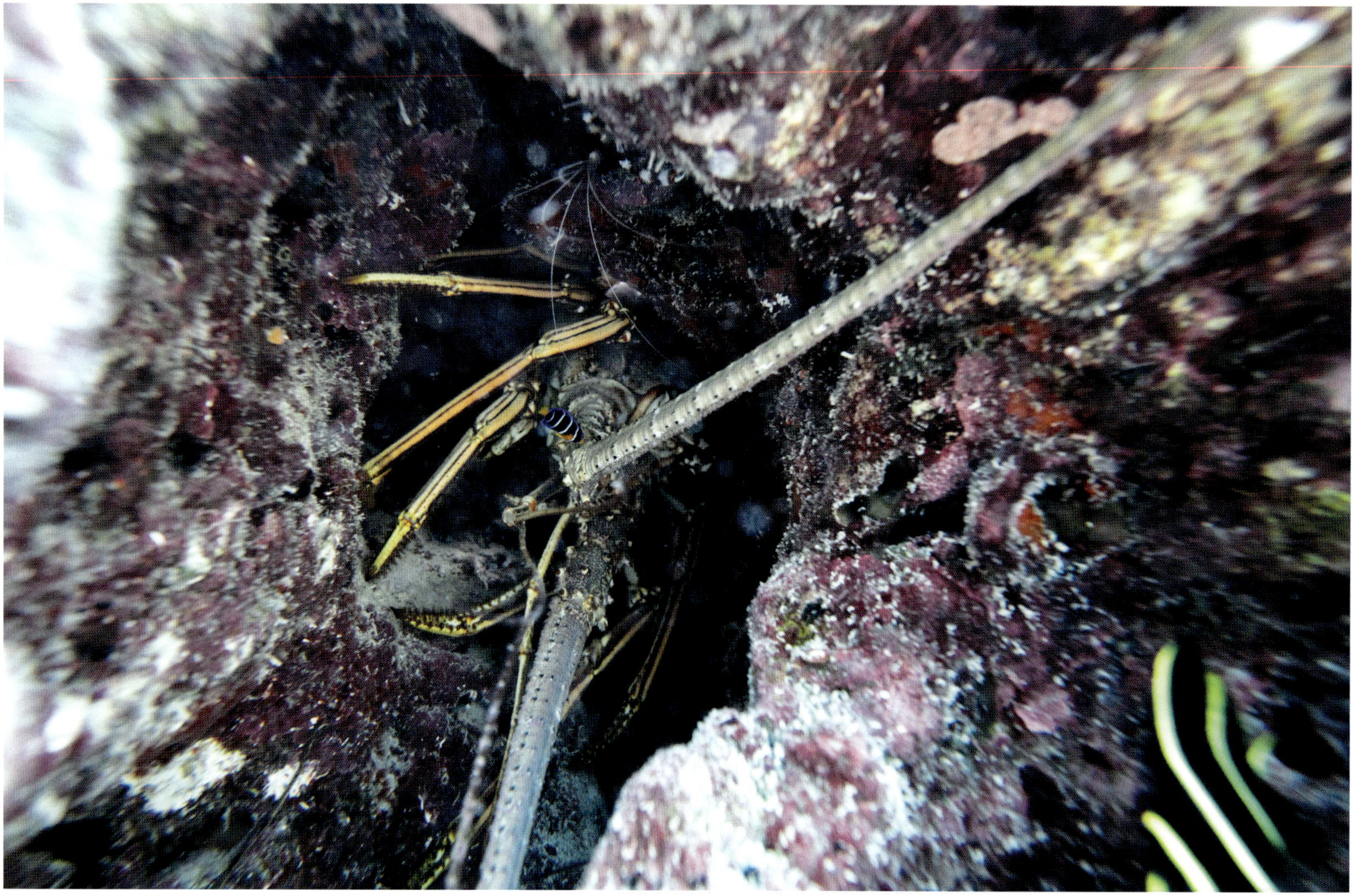

Spiny lobster and juvenile queen angelfish (*Holacanthus ciliaris*).

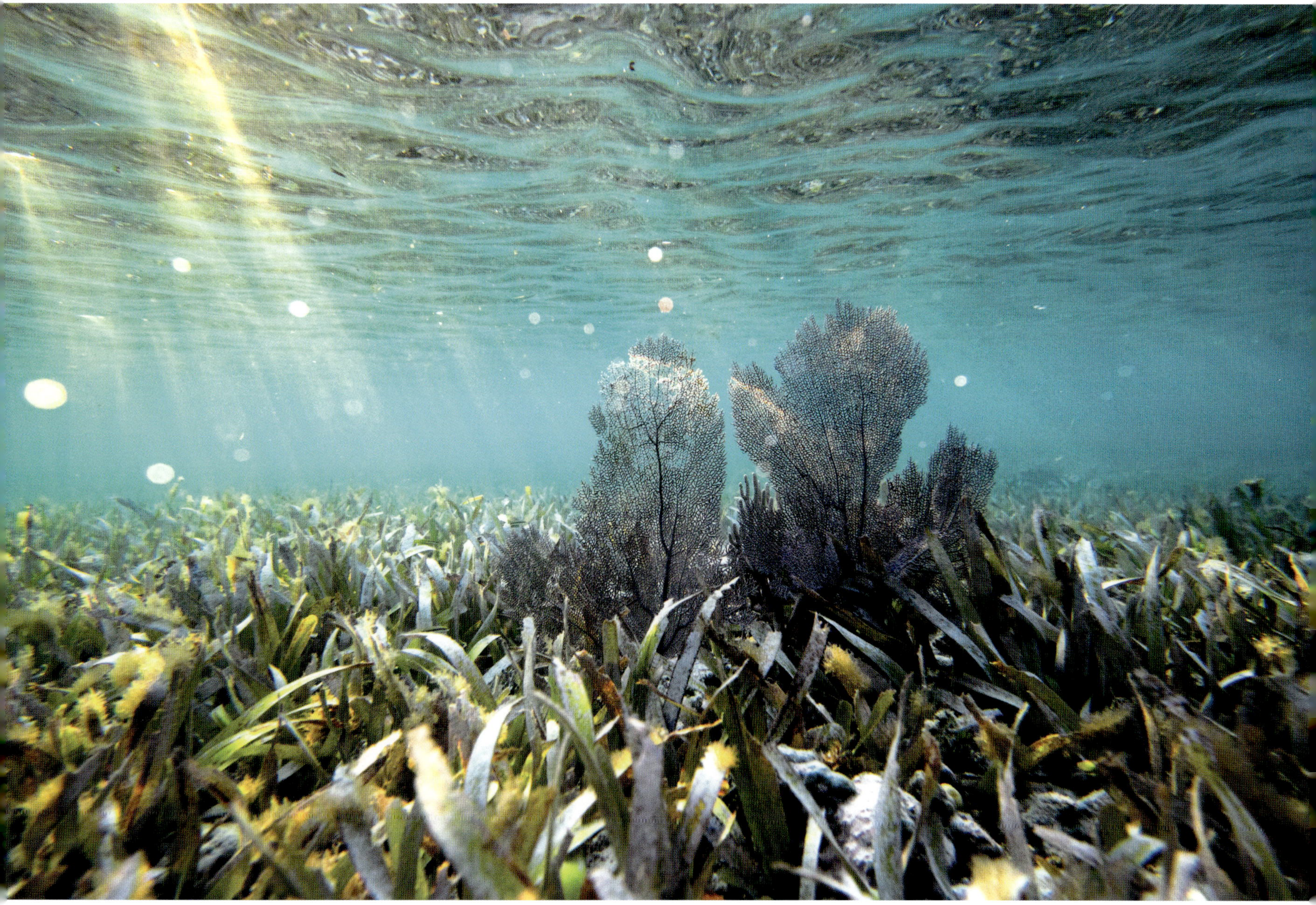
Sea fan in the seagrass.

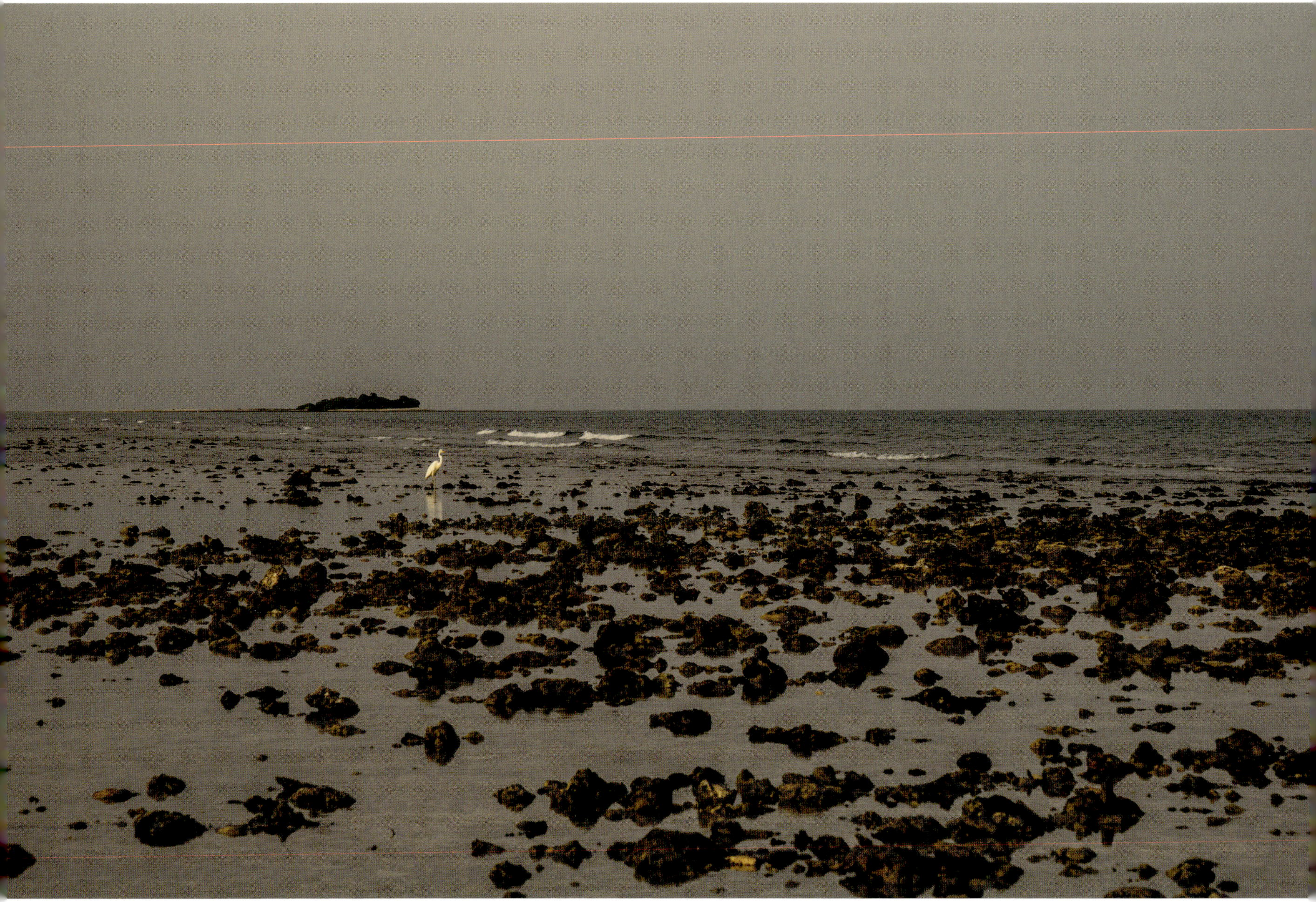

A great egret wades the Bird Key shoal at sunset.

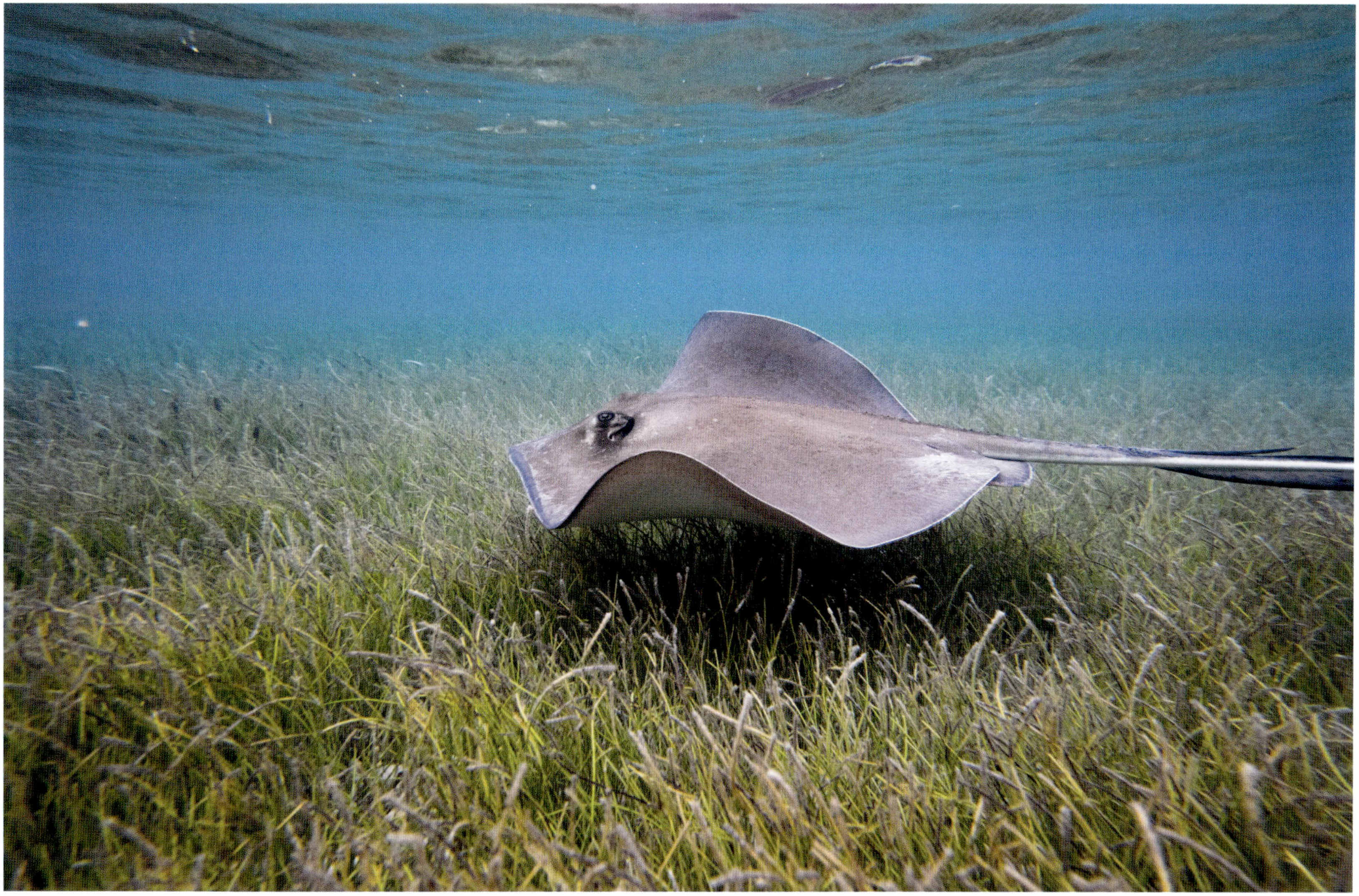

Southern gray stingray (*Hypanus americanus*) off Bird Key.

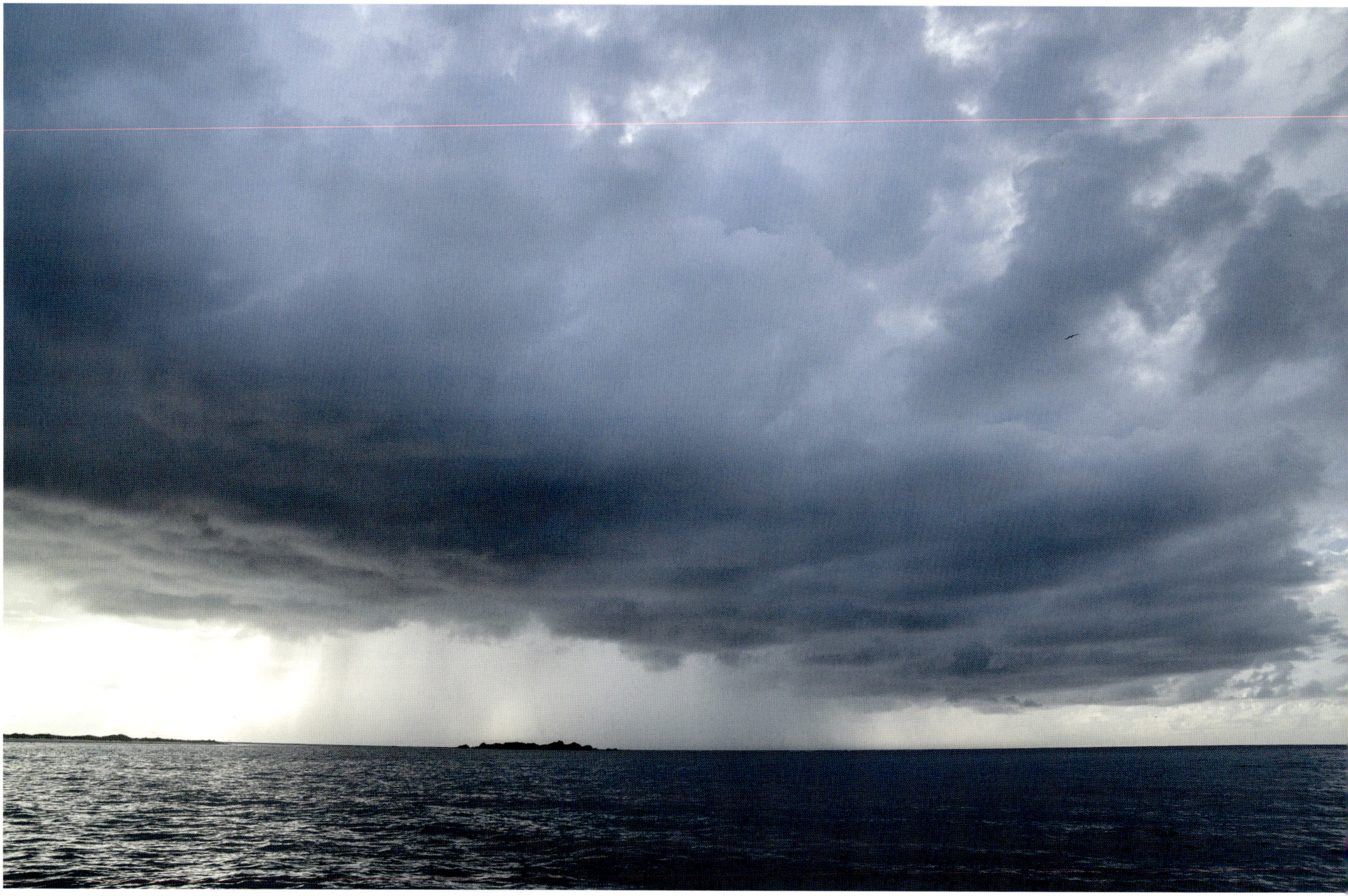

A summer squall passes by Long Key.

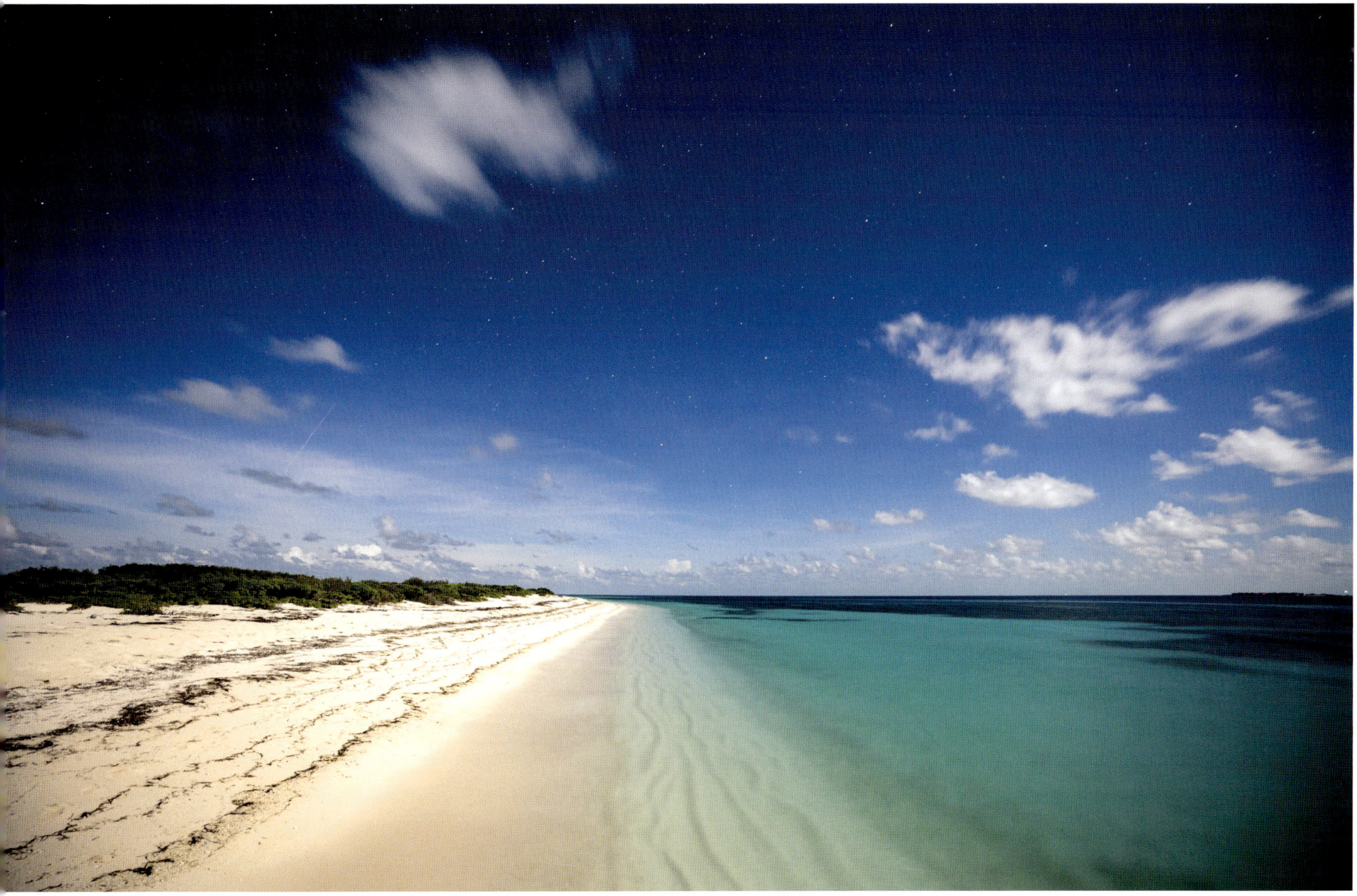

A long-exposure photograph captures Loggerhead Beach under bright moonlight.

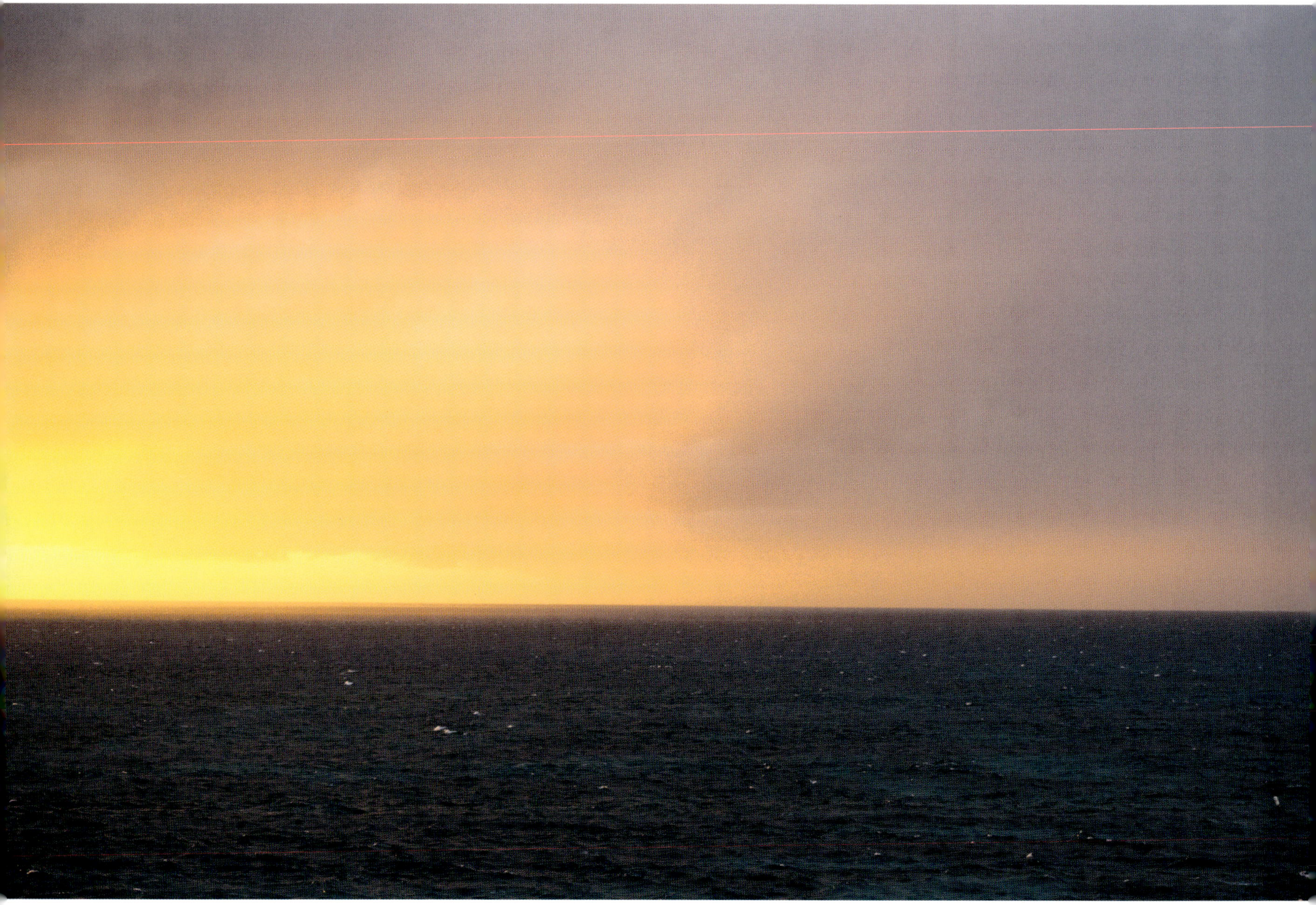

Rain bands are illuminated by the setting sun.

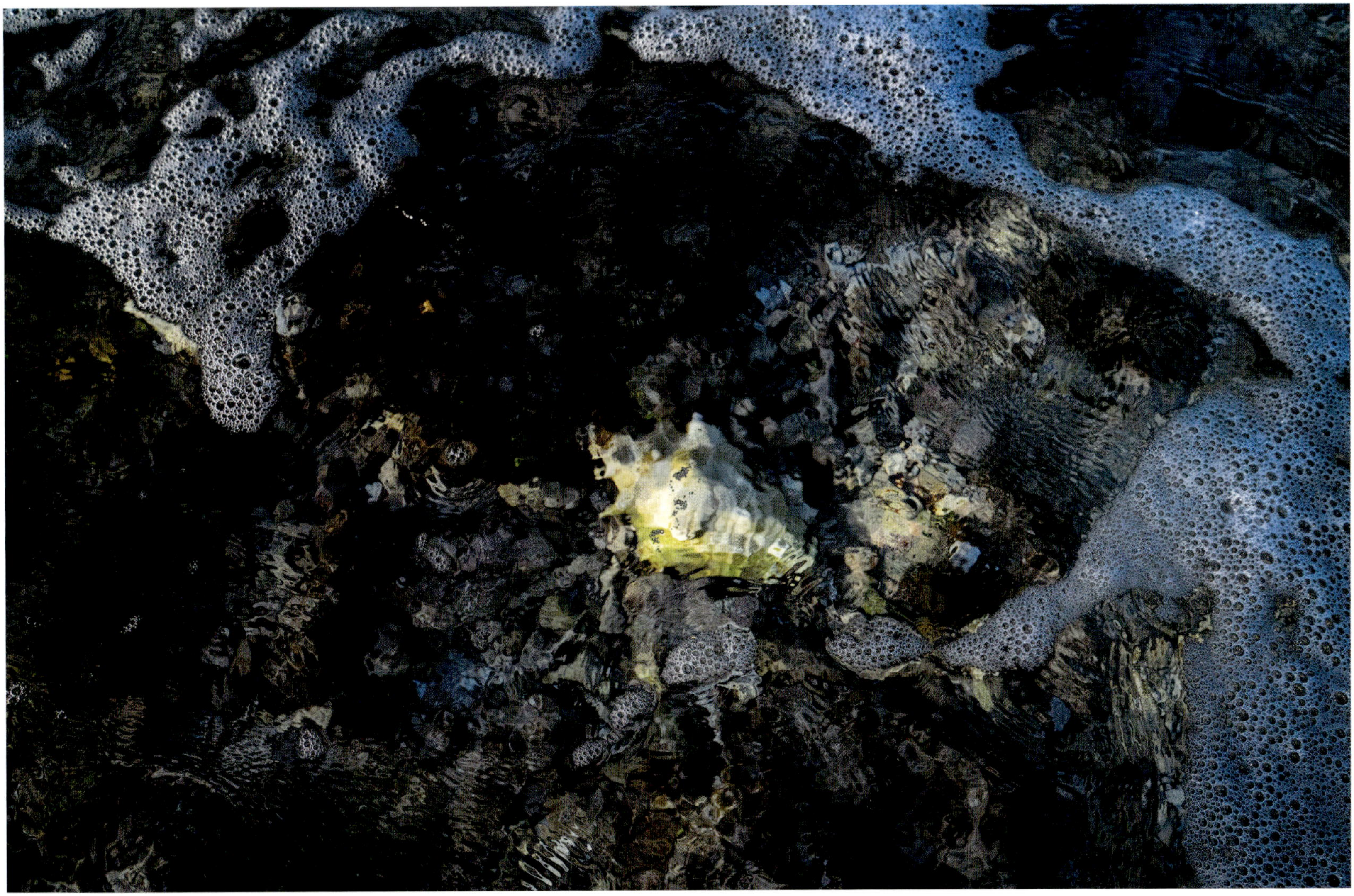

Queen conch (*Strombus gigas*) in the shallows off Bird Key.

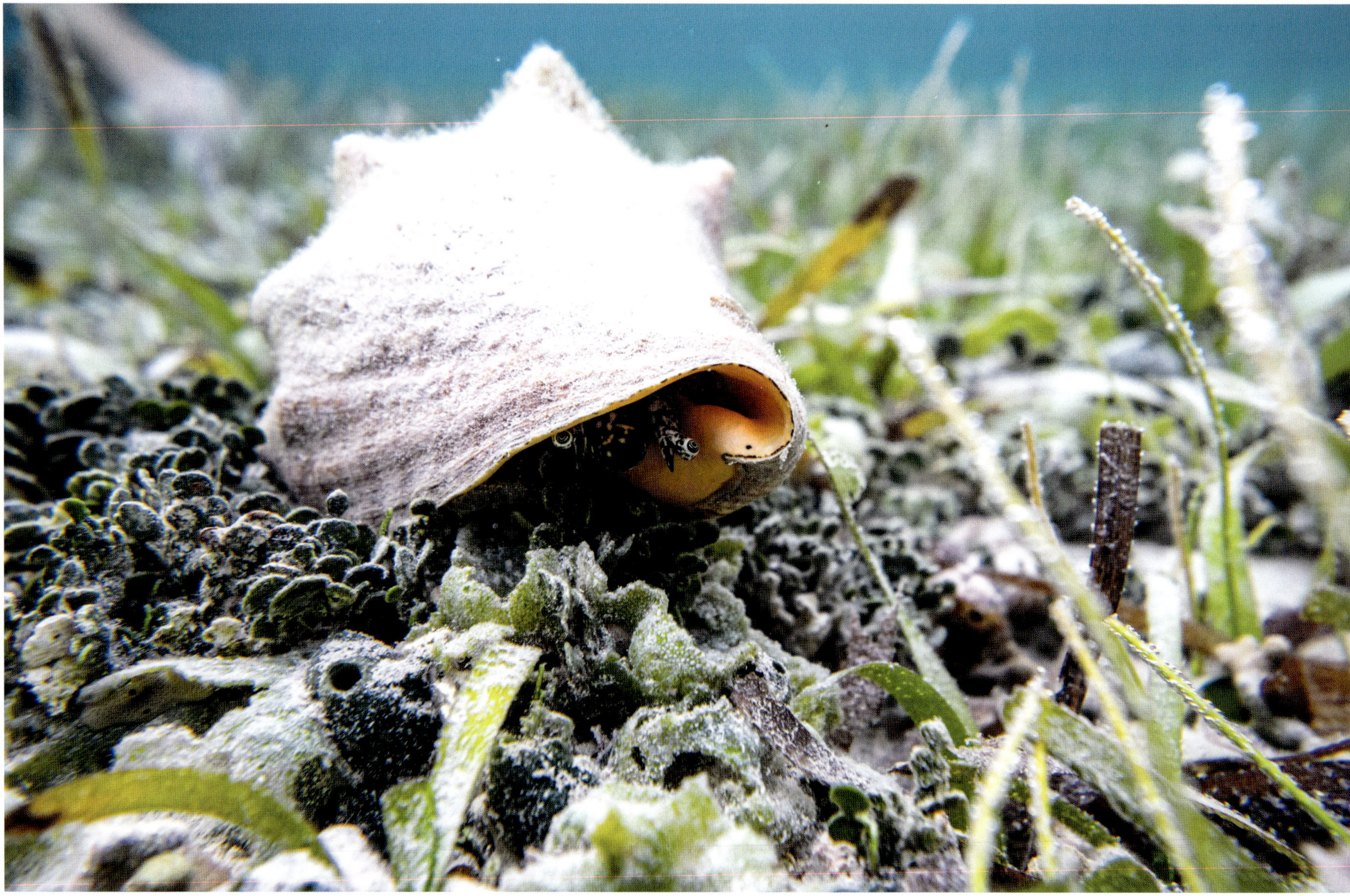

Curious queen conch.

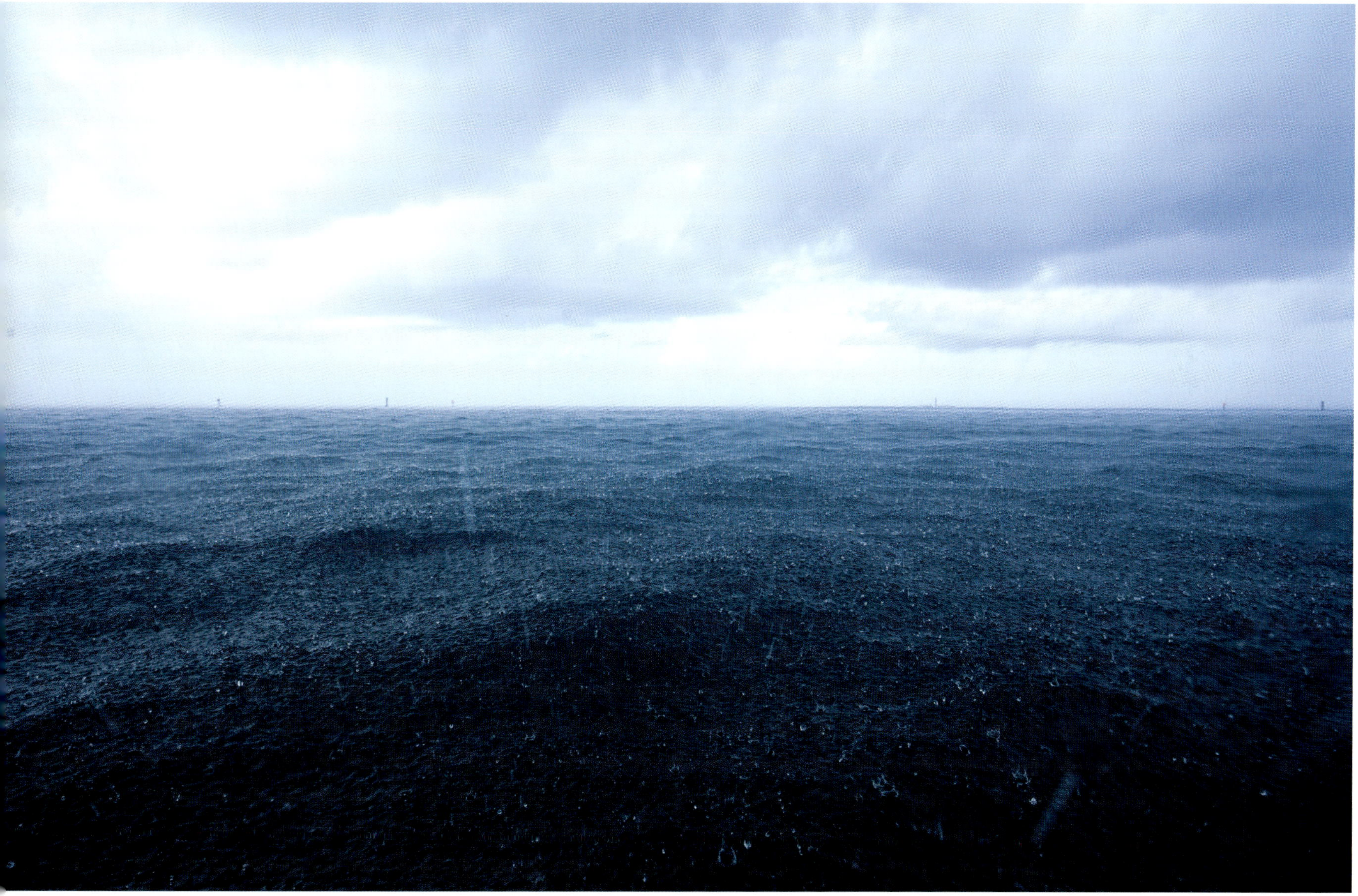

Morning showers off Garden Key.

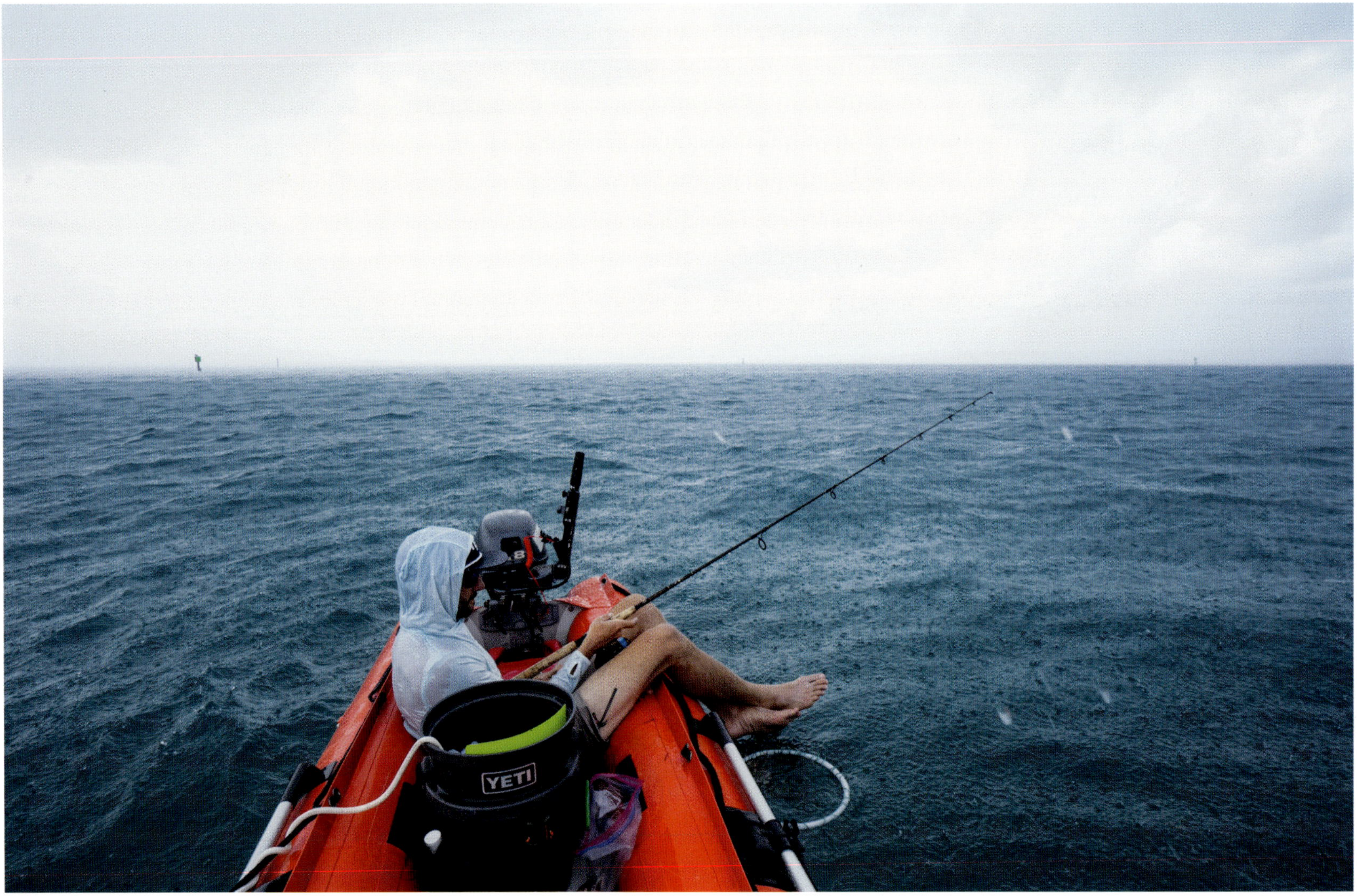

Austin Armstrong fishes for dinner from the dinghy we relied on during our artist residency. Rain or shine, we were out there.

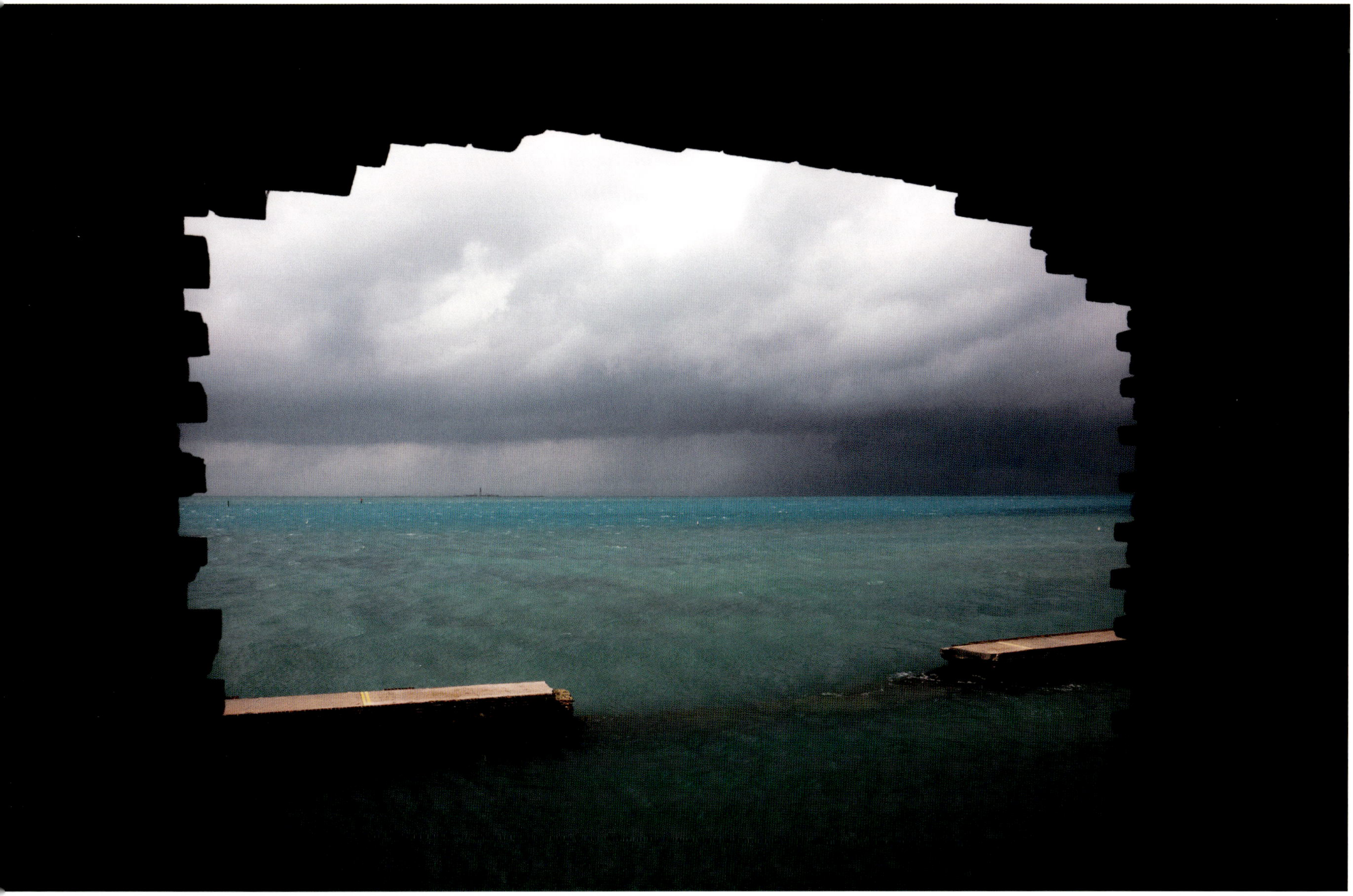

Storm squalls as seen from inside Fort Jefferson's walls.

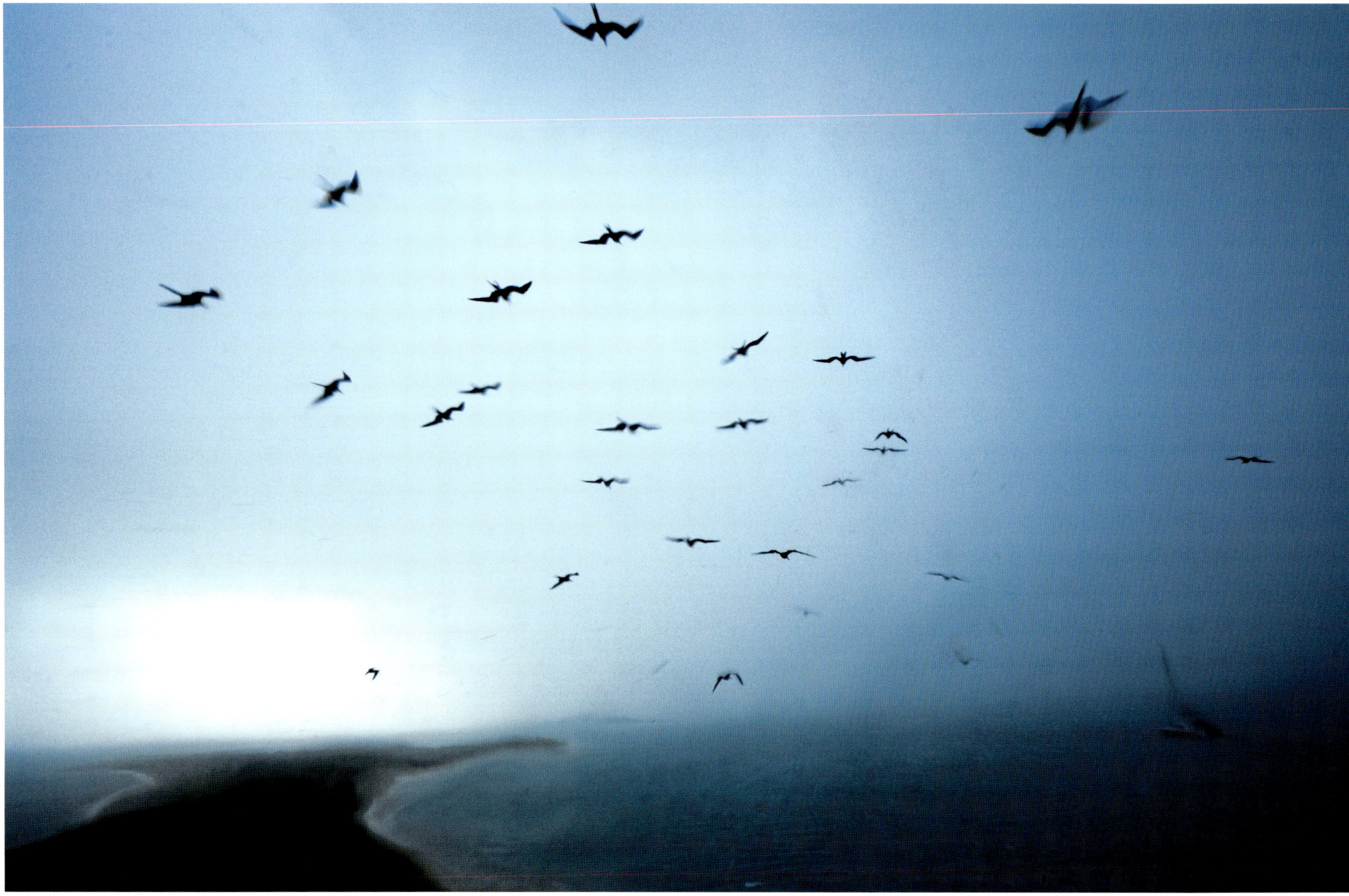

On windy days, the frigatebirds often move as one with the gusts. On this particular day, they favored Fort Jefferson's southernmost bastion.

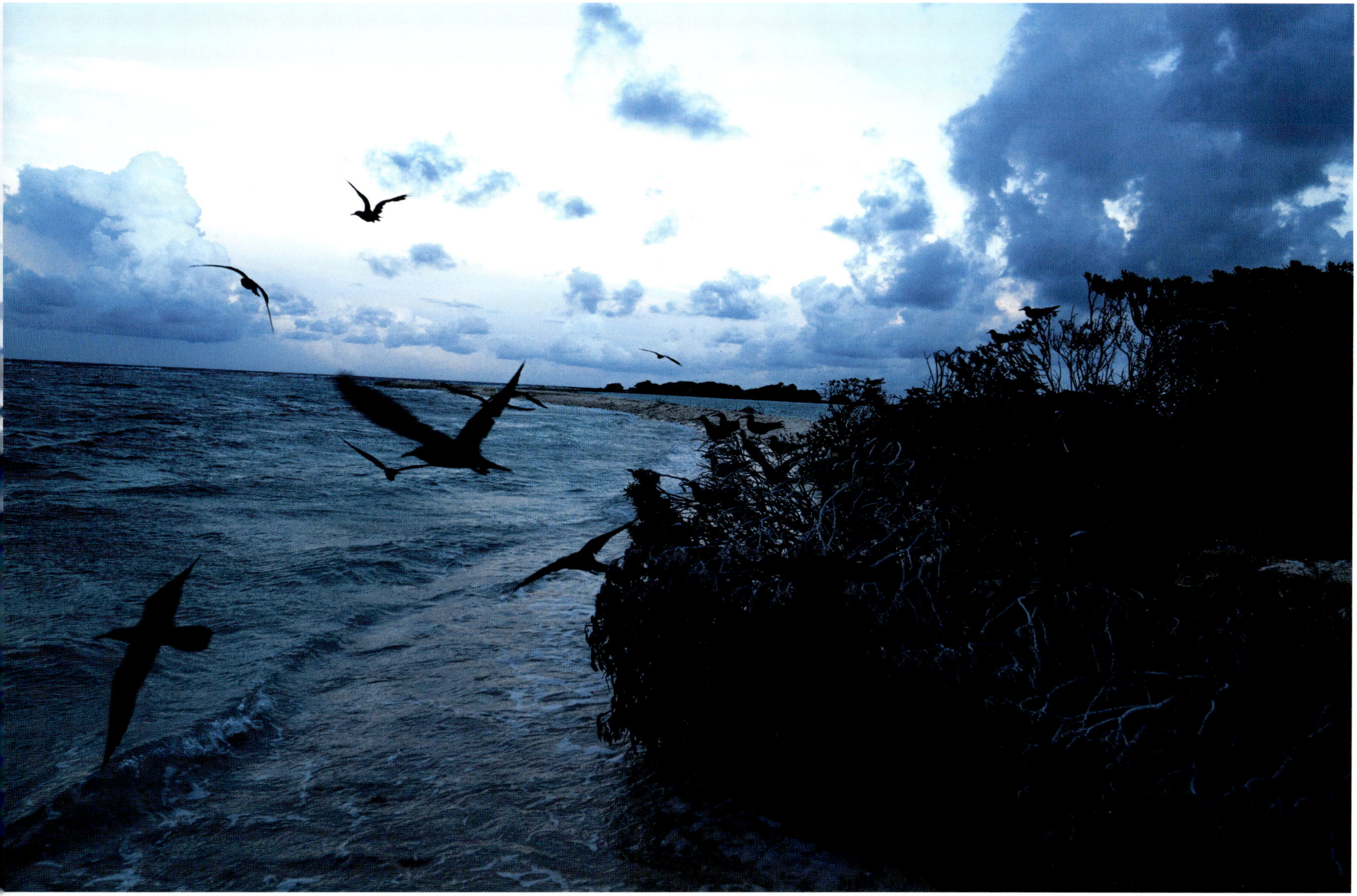

Brown noddies taking flight at dusk off Bush Key.

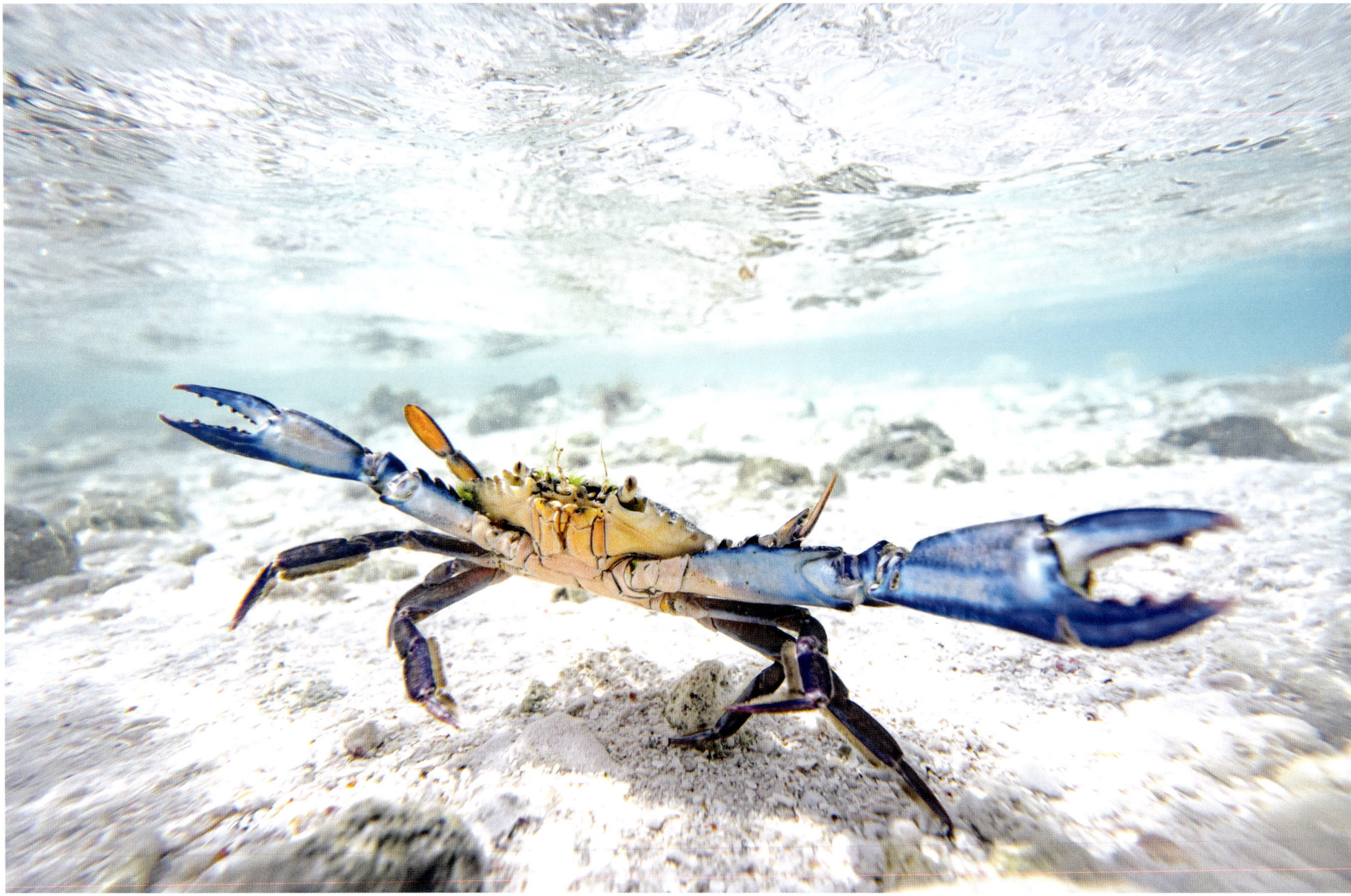

In shallows off the sandbar between Bush and Long Keys, a blue crab (*Callinectes sapidus*) attempts to fend me off.

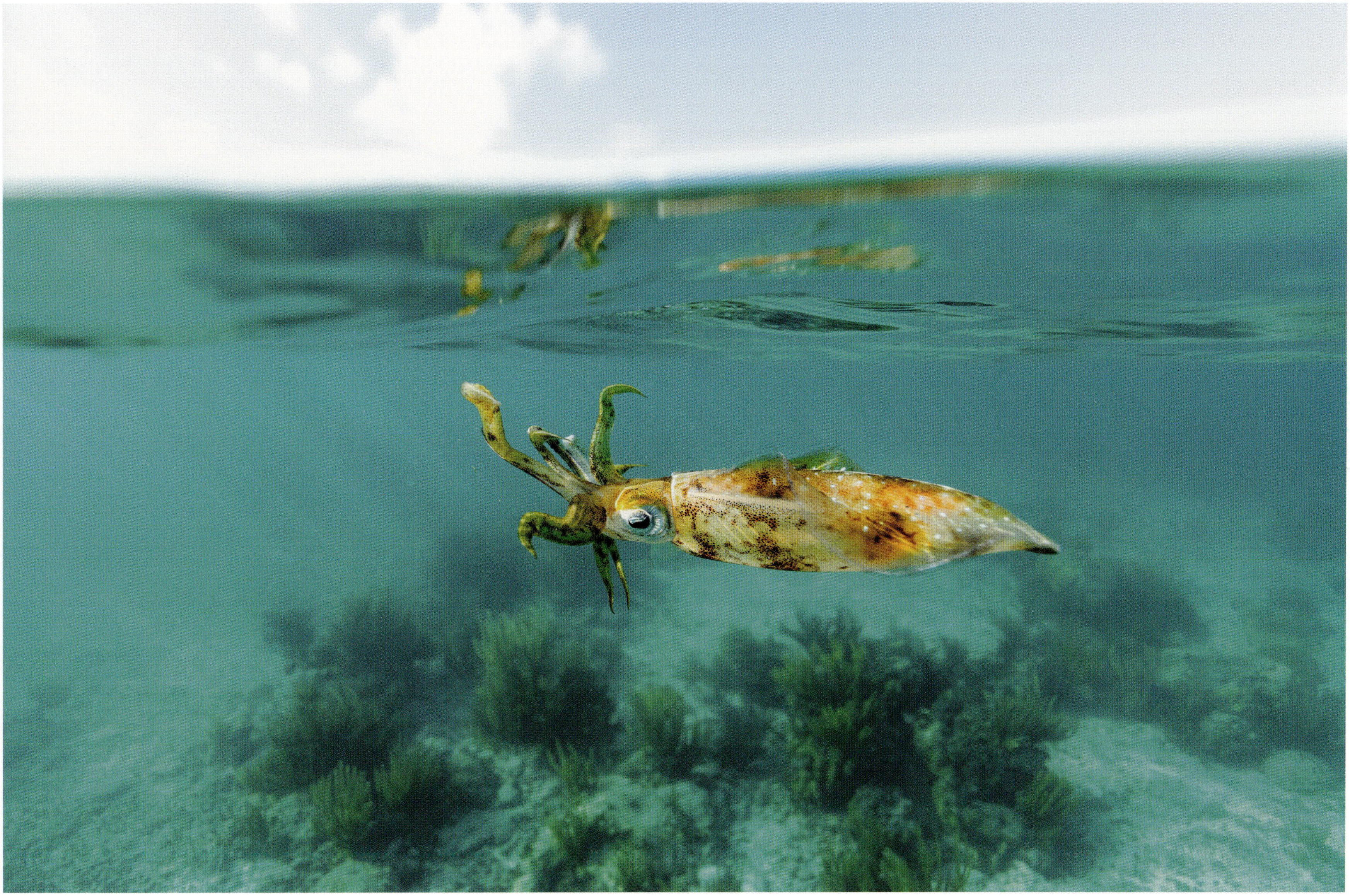

A Caribbean reef squid (*Sepioteuthis sepioidea*) poses for a photo. The reflection in my camera's dome port attracted this beautiful creature to come investigate.

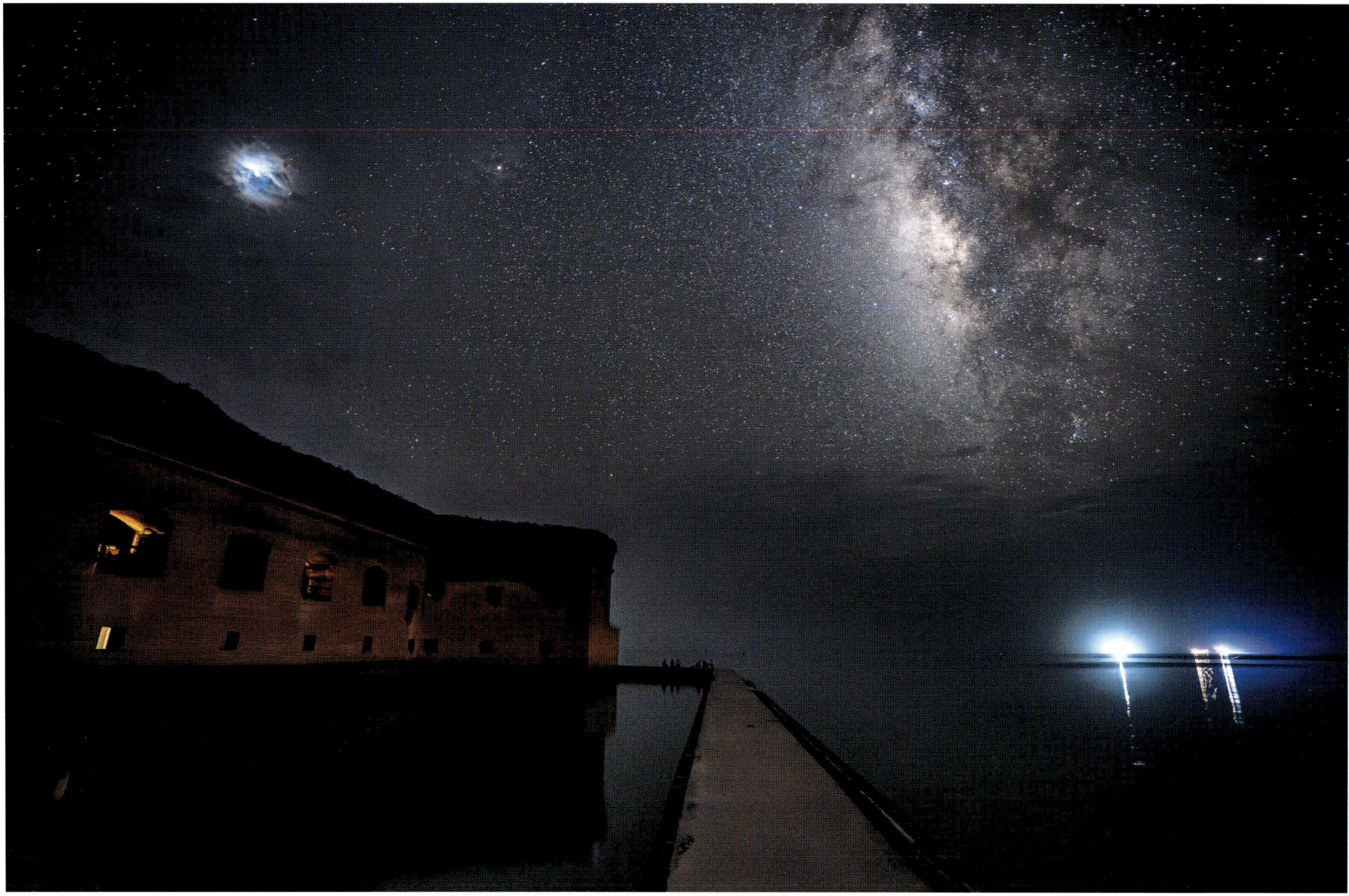

The Milky Way as viewed from Fort Jefferson's moat wall.

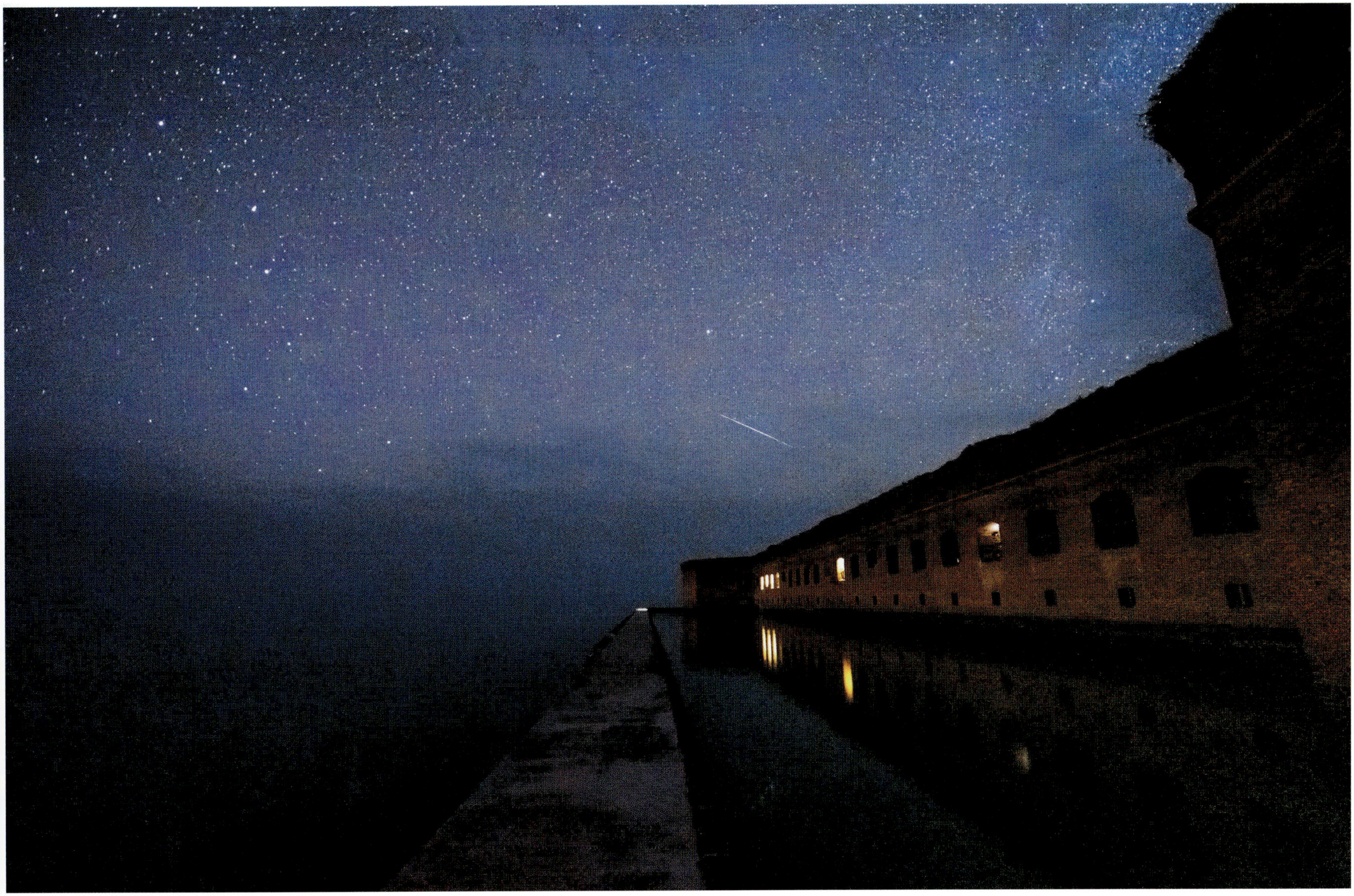

A shooting star glimmers in the distance as I walk the moat wall at night.

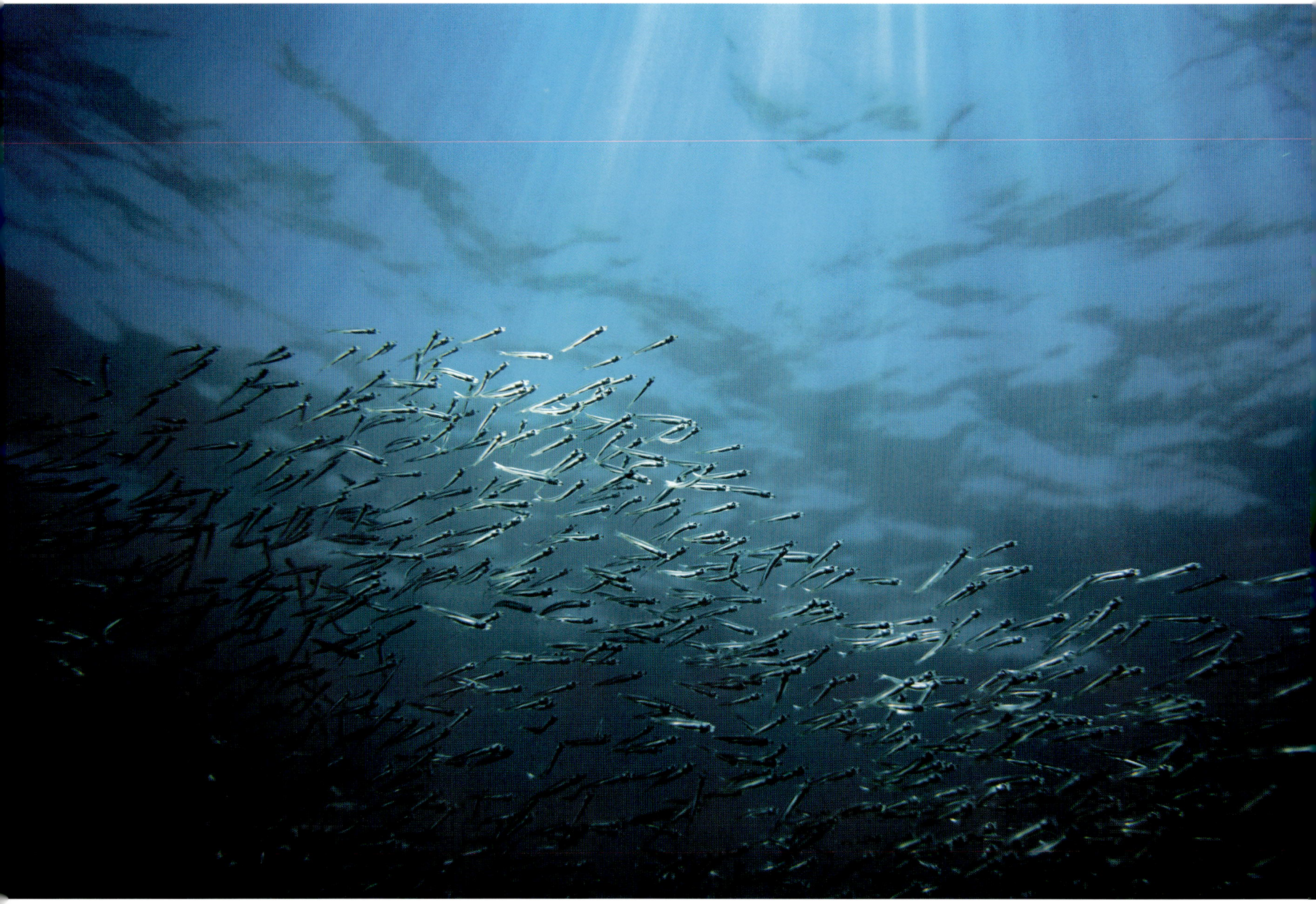

A school of silversides (genus *Atherina*) shimmers in the sunlight.

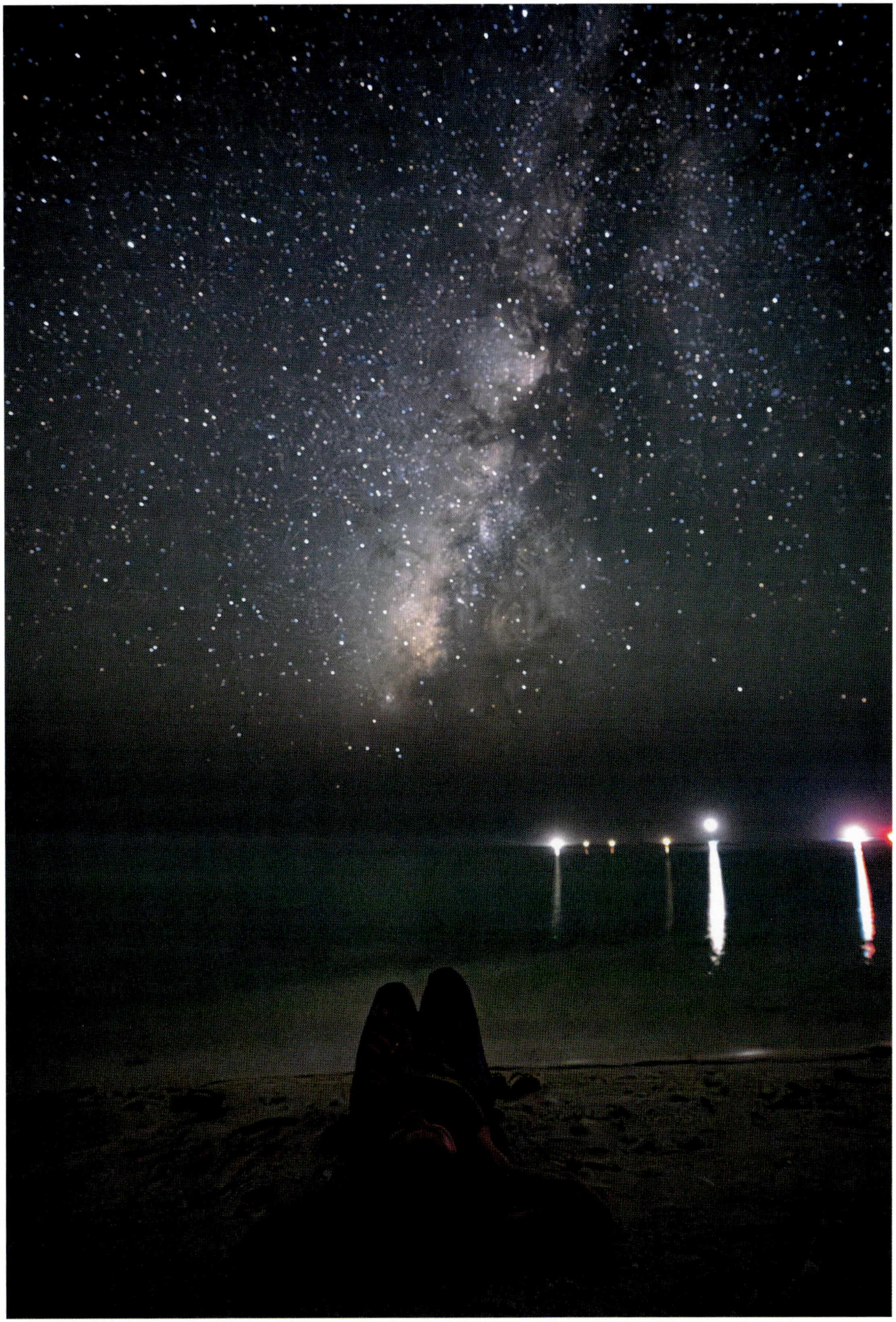

There's no better place to take in the Milky Way than in the Dry Tortugas.

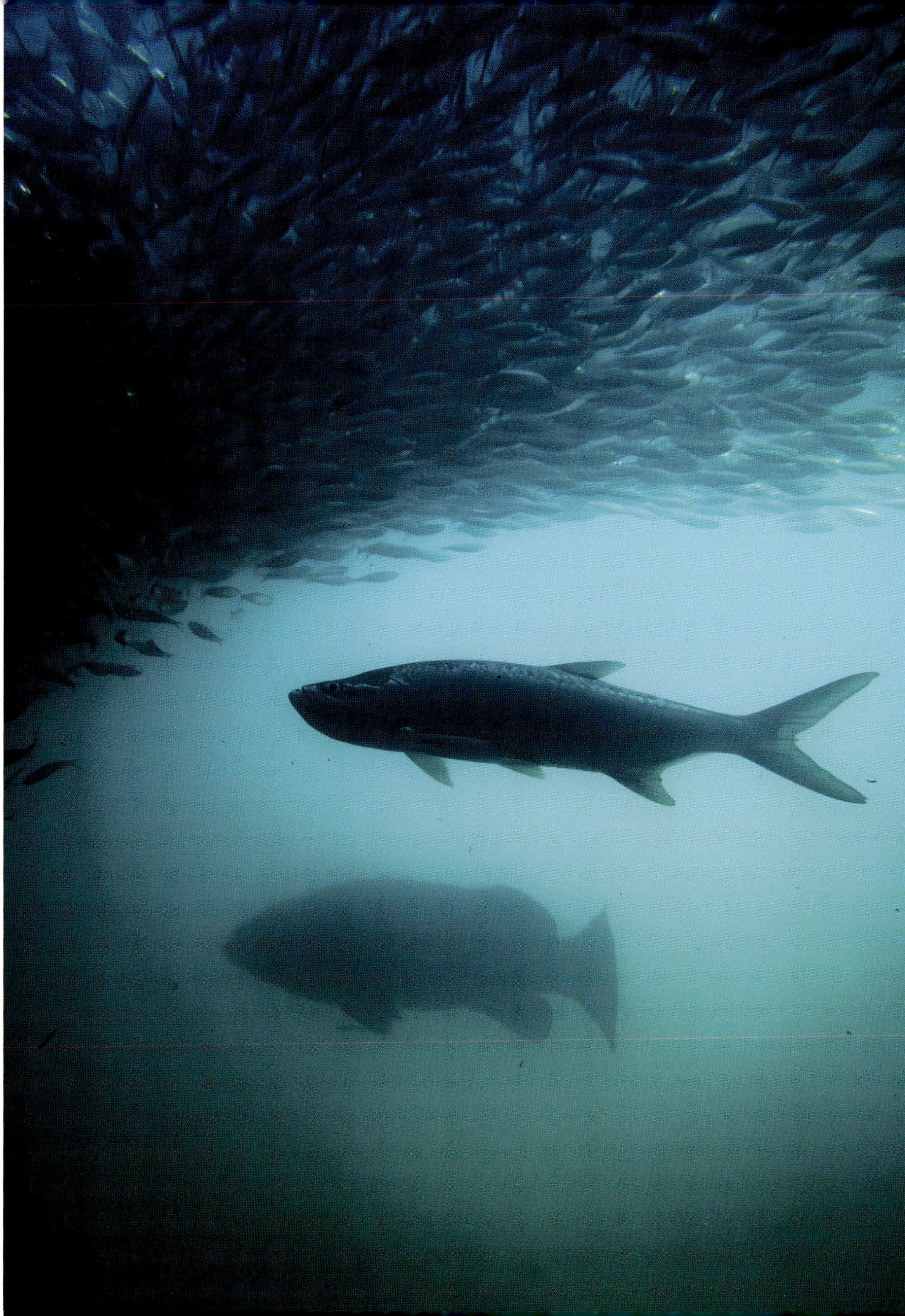

A tarpon and goliath grouper swim beneath a giant school of pilchards (*Harengula jaguana*).

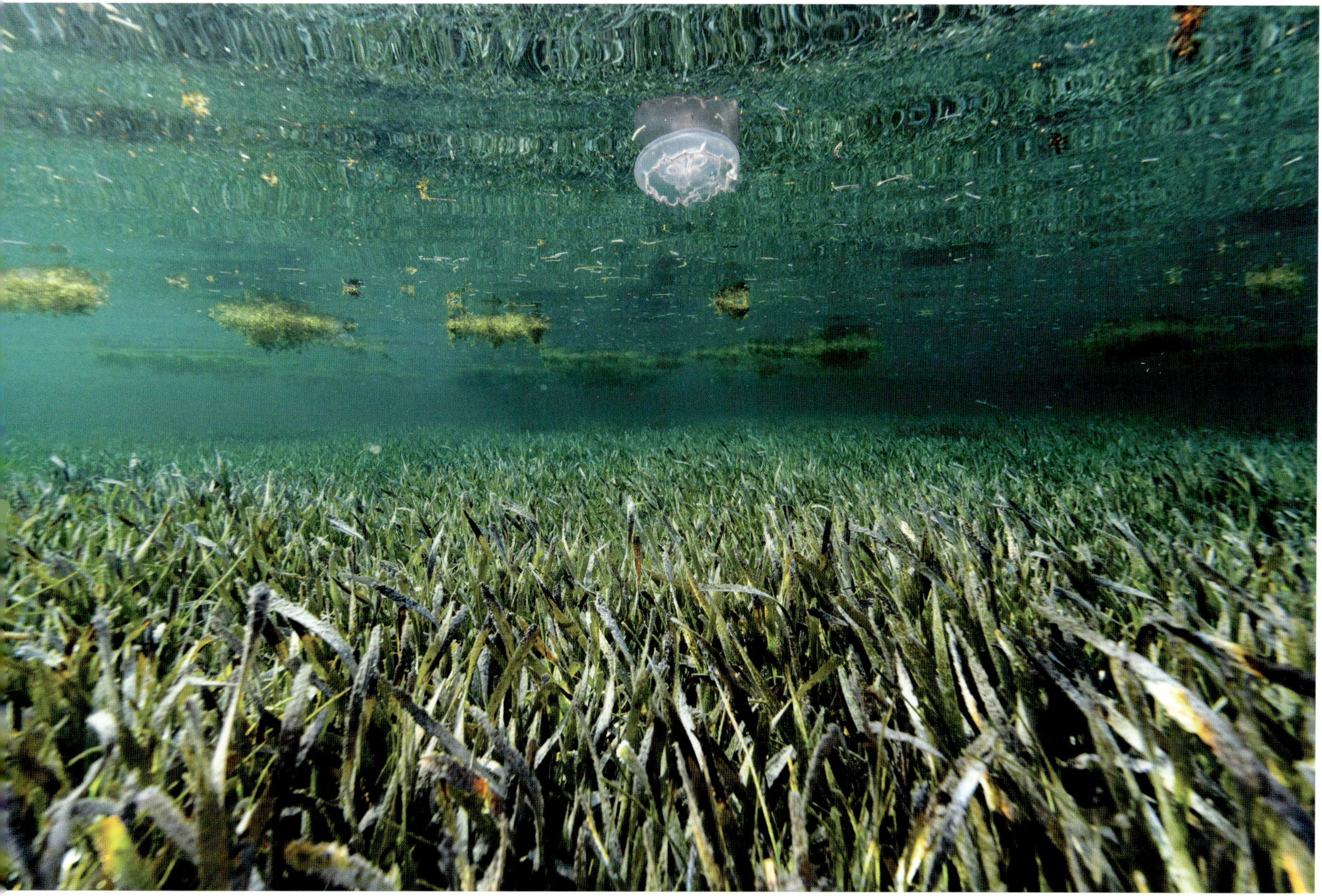

A moon jellyfish (*Aurelia aurita*) drifts across the seagrass flats of Garden Key.

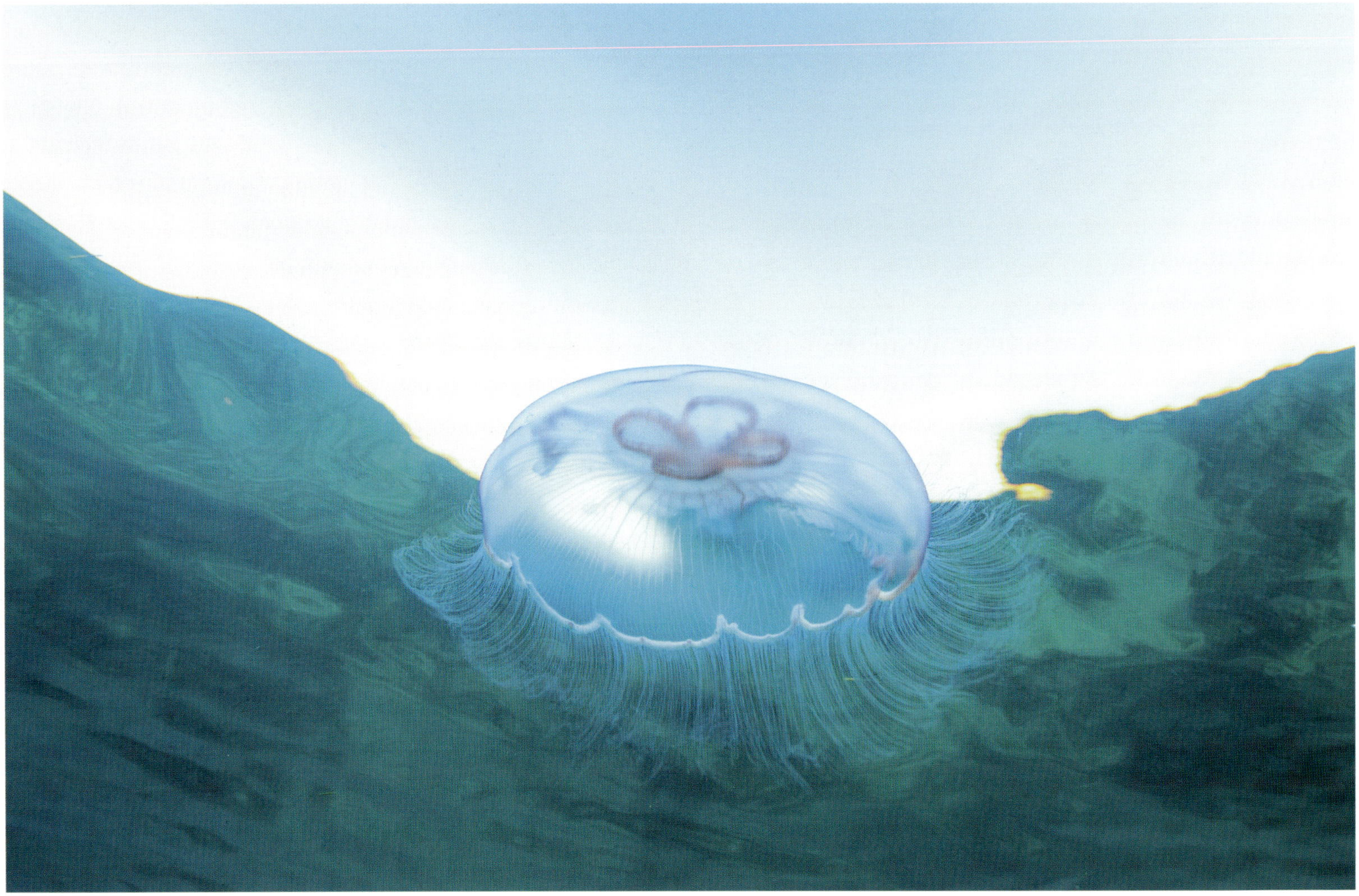

A moon jellyfish absorbs the last light of day.

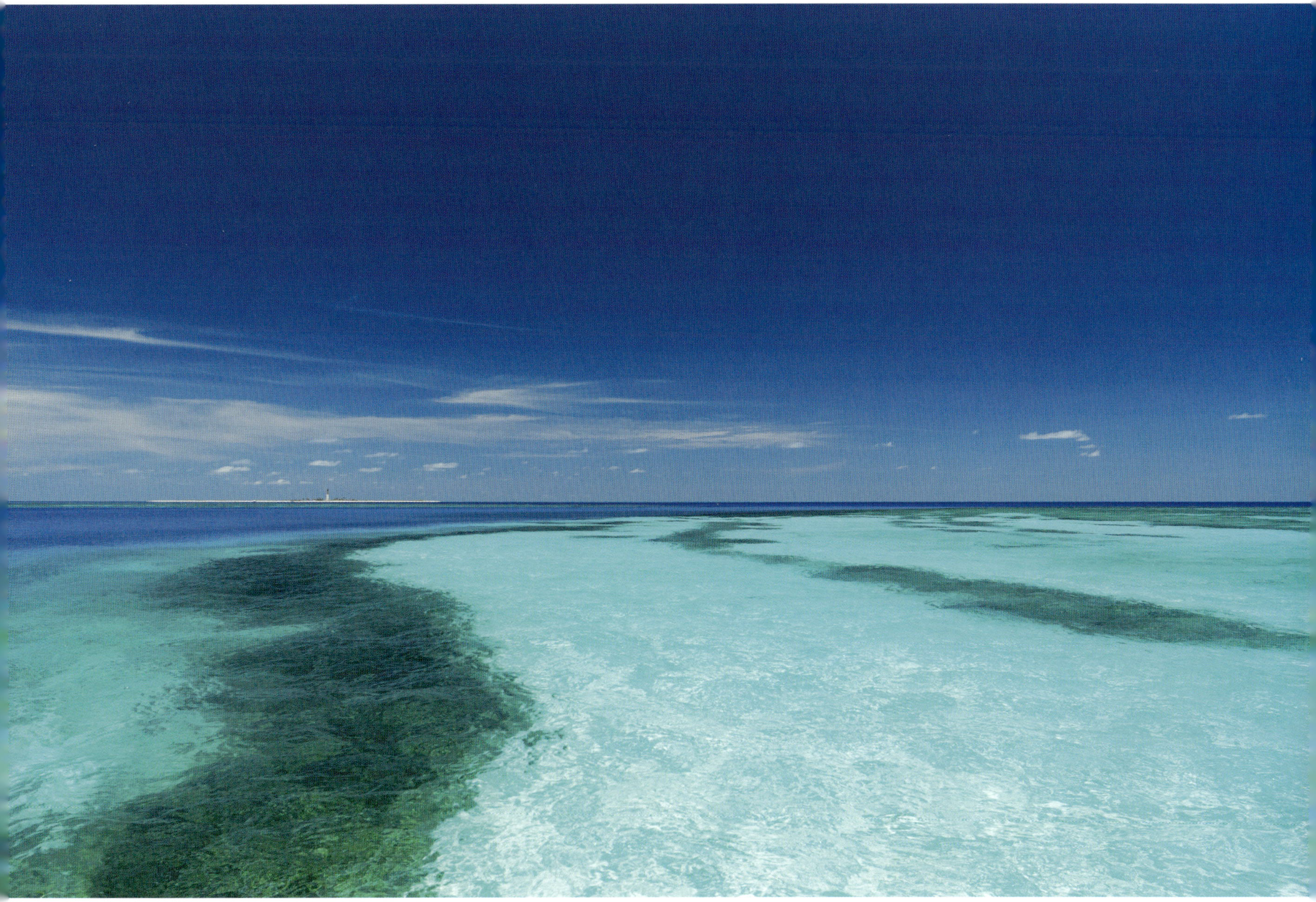

The water surrounding Fort Jefferson can provide the most mesmerizing color schemes.

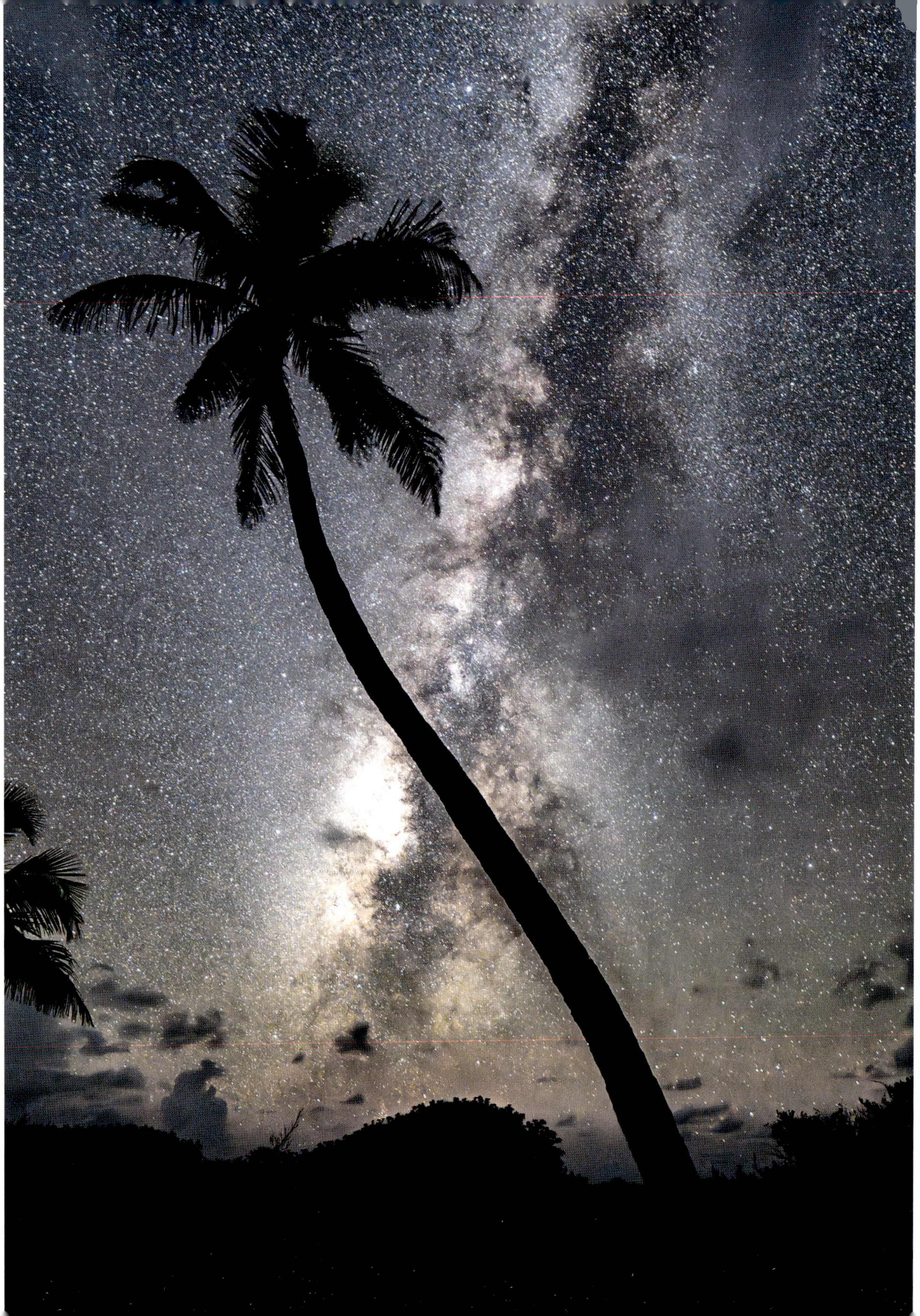

A palm tree caresses the Milky Way on Loggerhead Key.

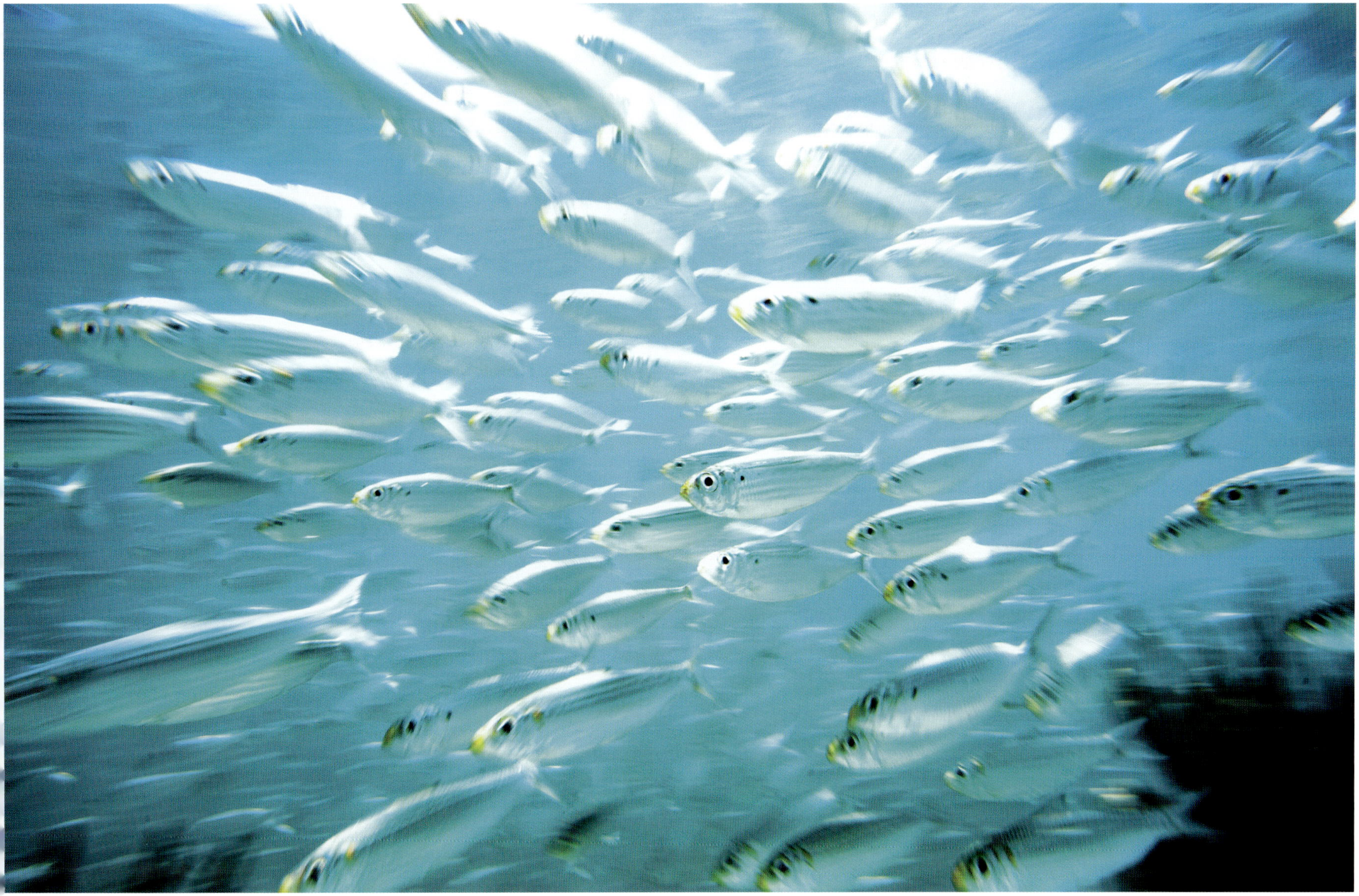

Giant schools of pilchards, some in the thousands, often can be seen in the waters surrounding Garden Key.

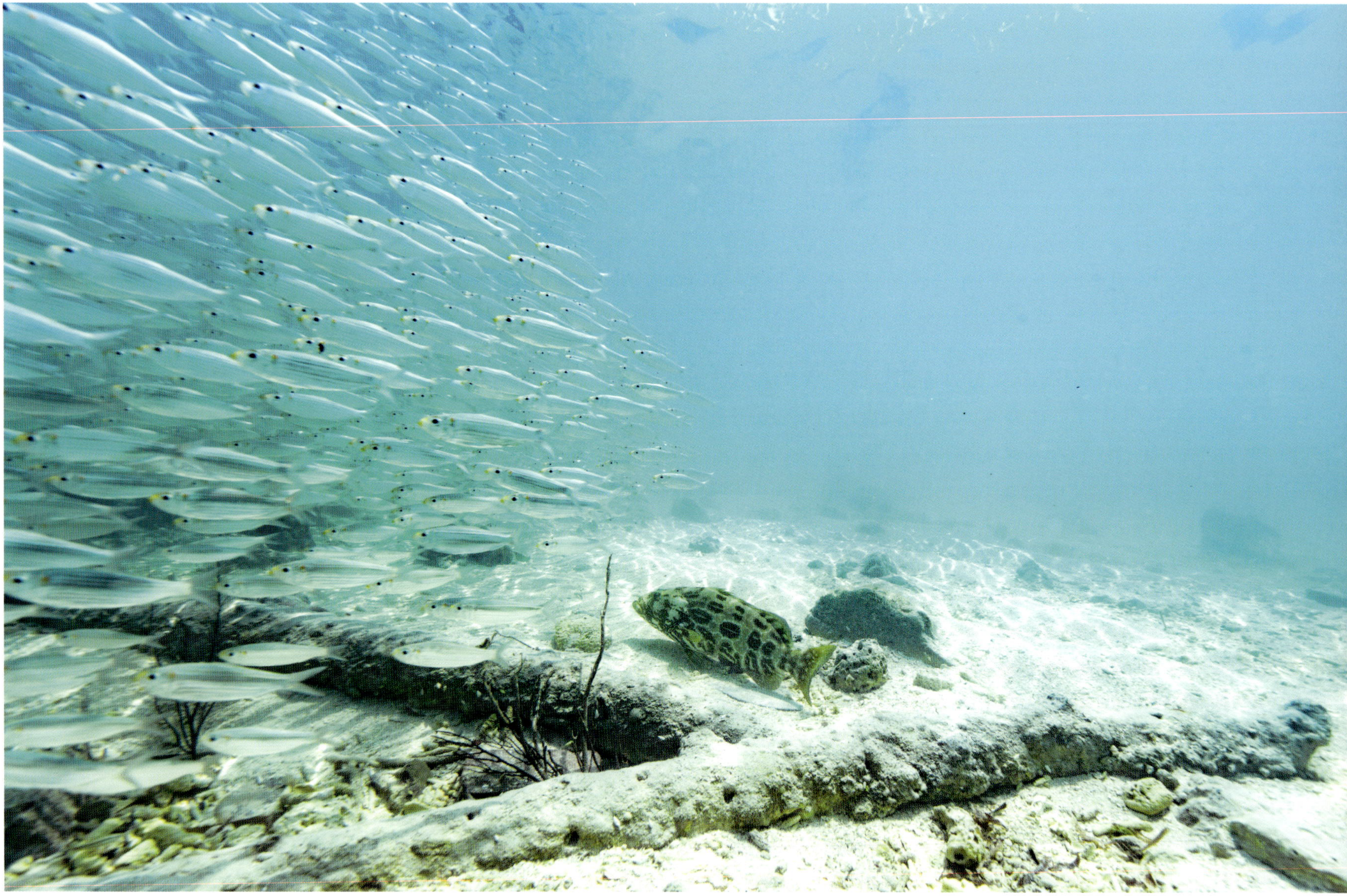

A black grouper corrals a school of pilchards in the shallow waters off Garden Key.

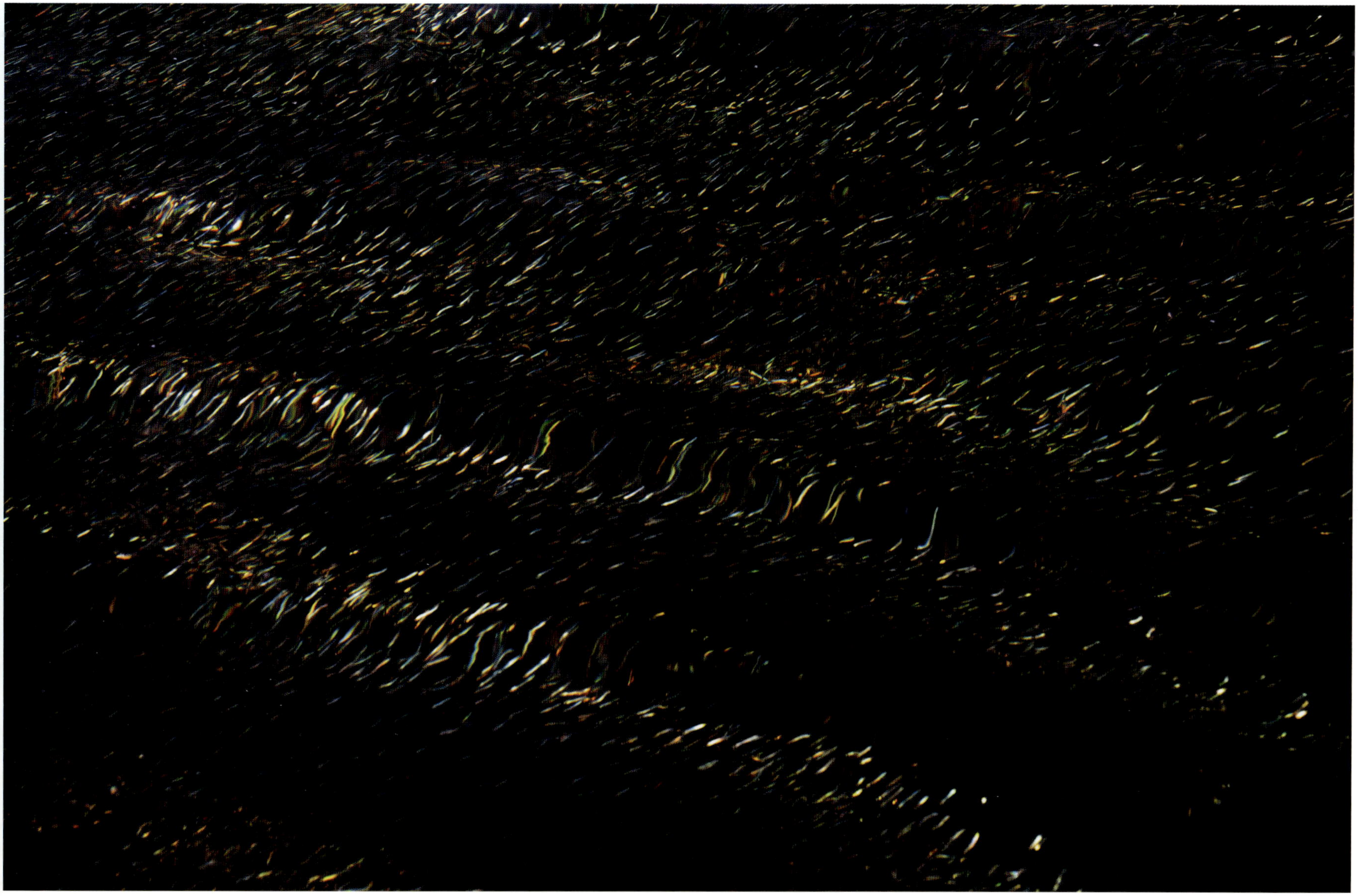

A school of silversides reflects sunset's light in shallow waters.

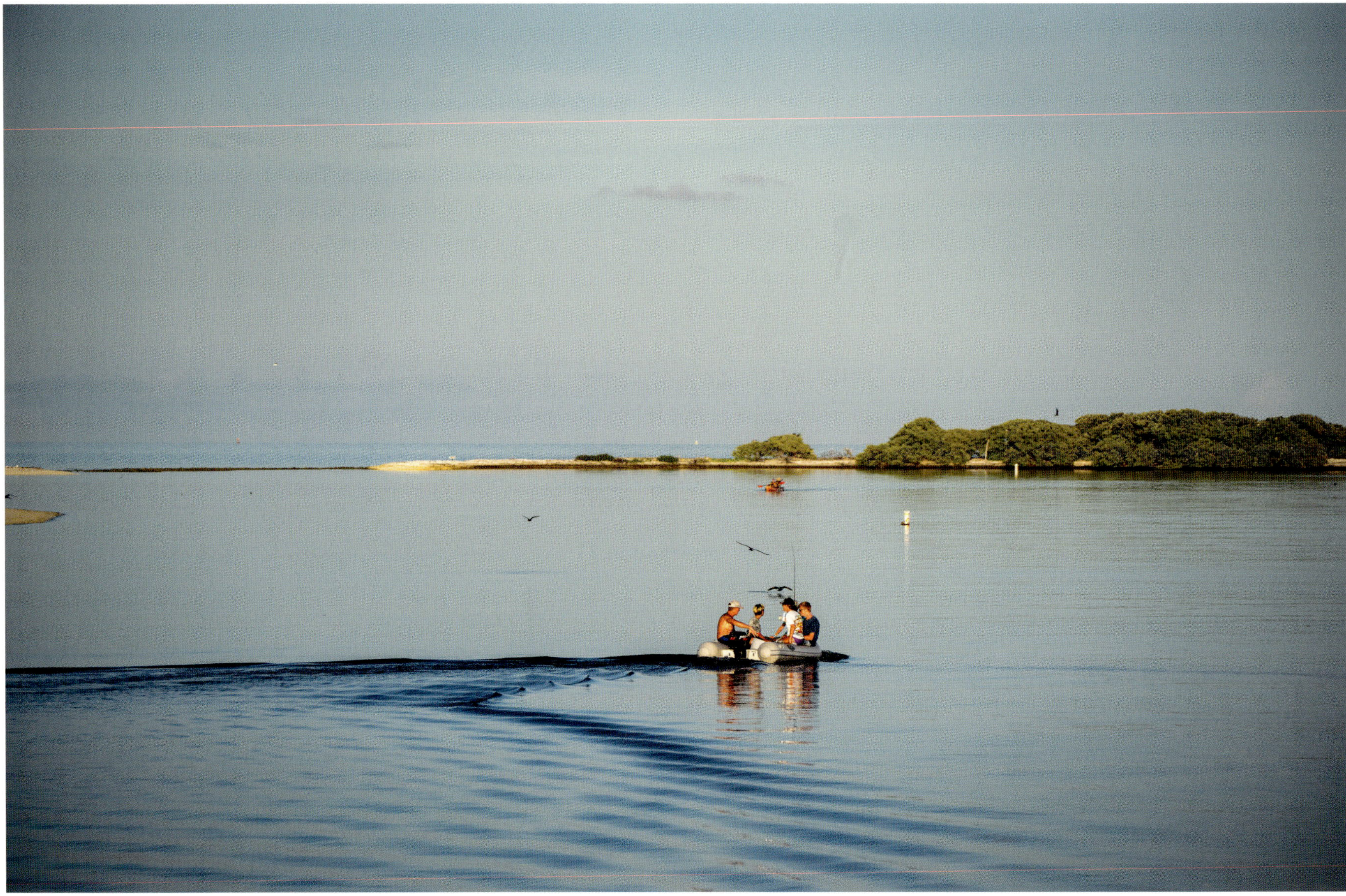

A family takes their dinghy back to the anchorage
on the southern side of Garden Key.

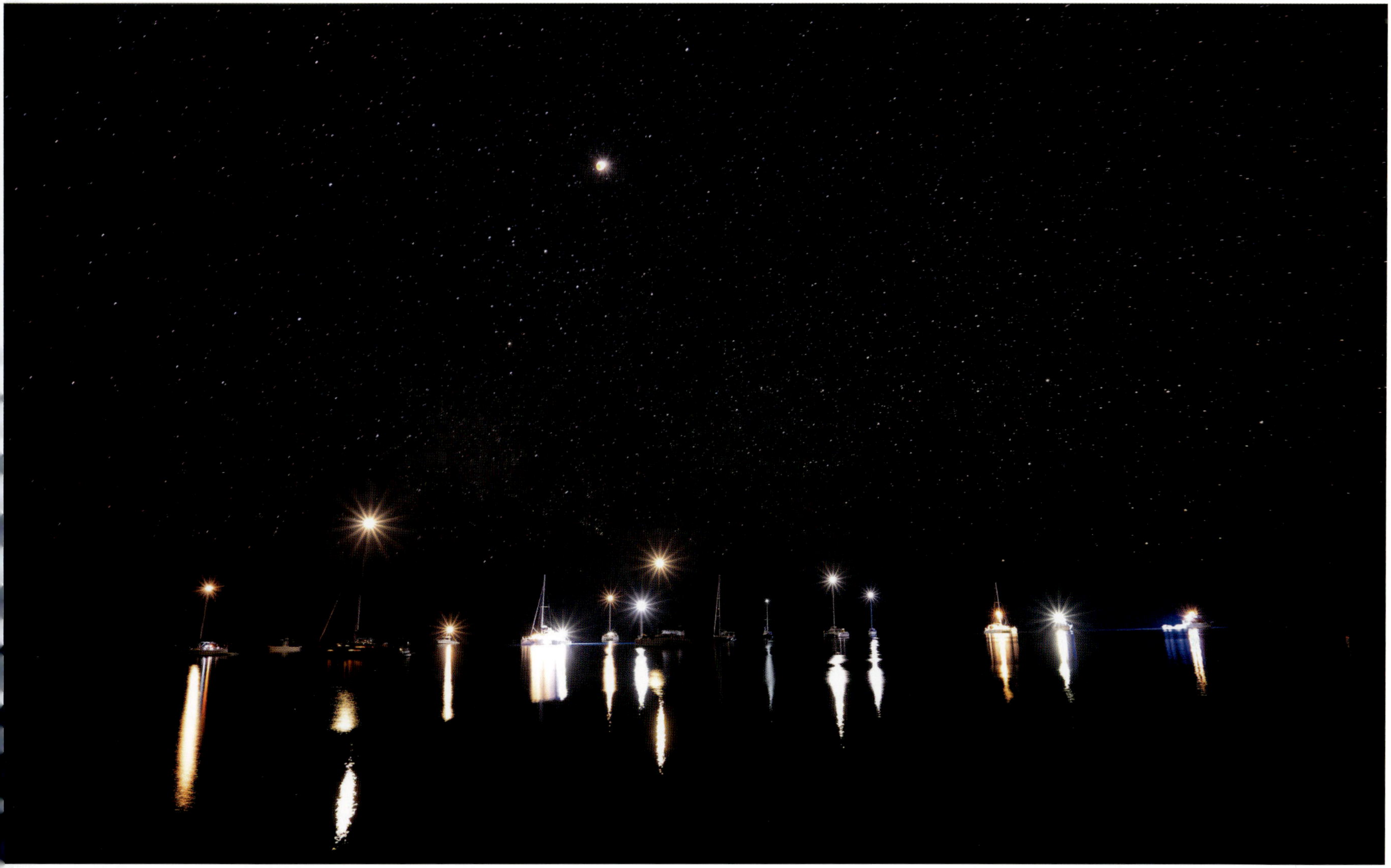

A lunar eclipse shields the moonlight just enough for stars to pop out over the anchorage.

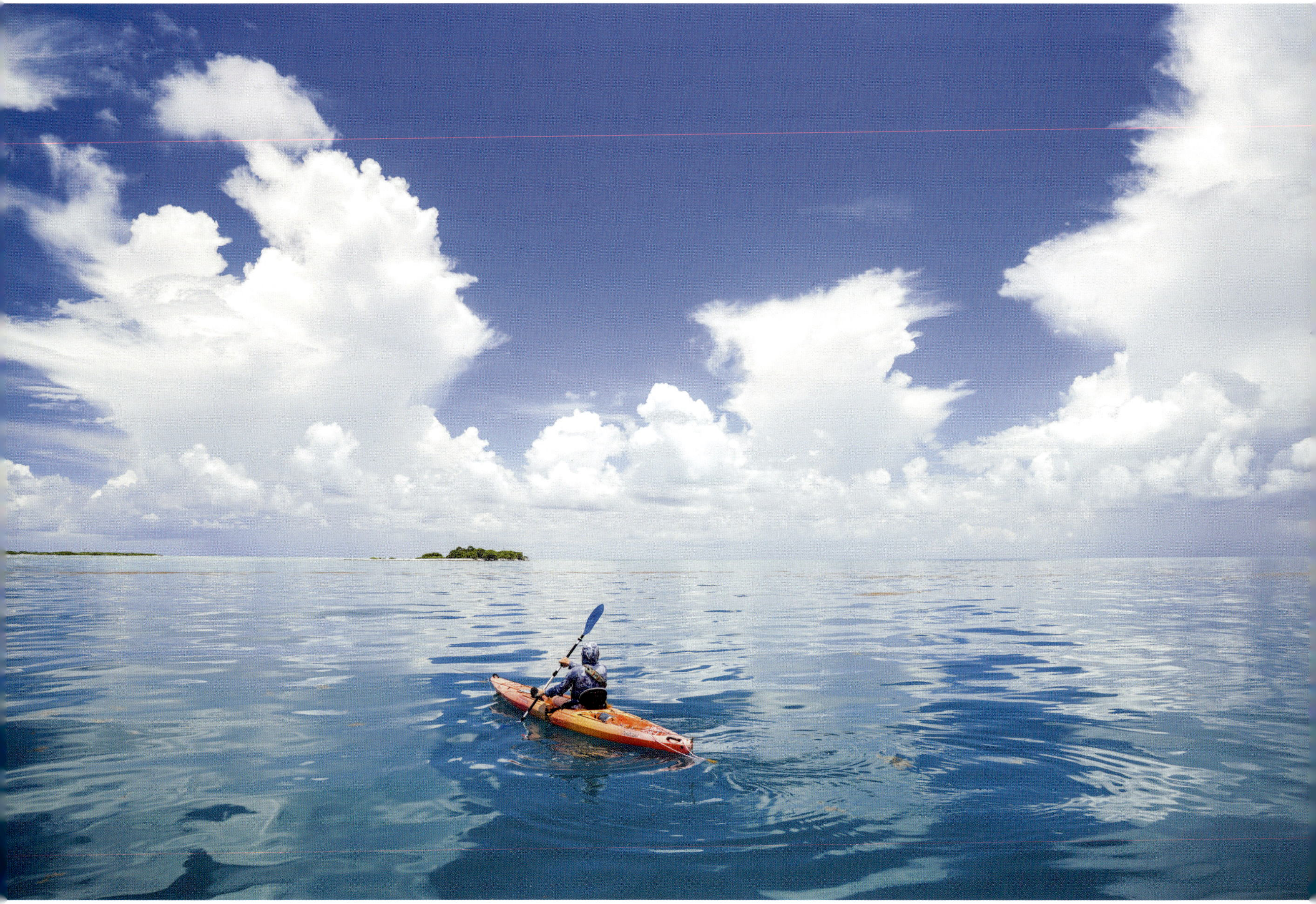

A kayaker enjoys a picture-perfect day in the Dry Tortugas.

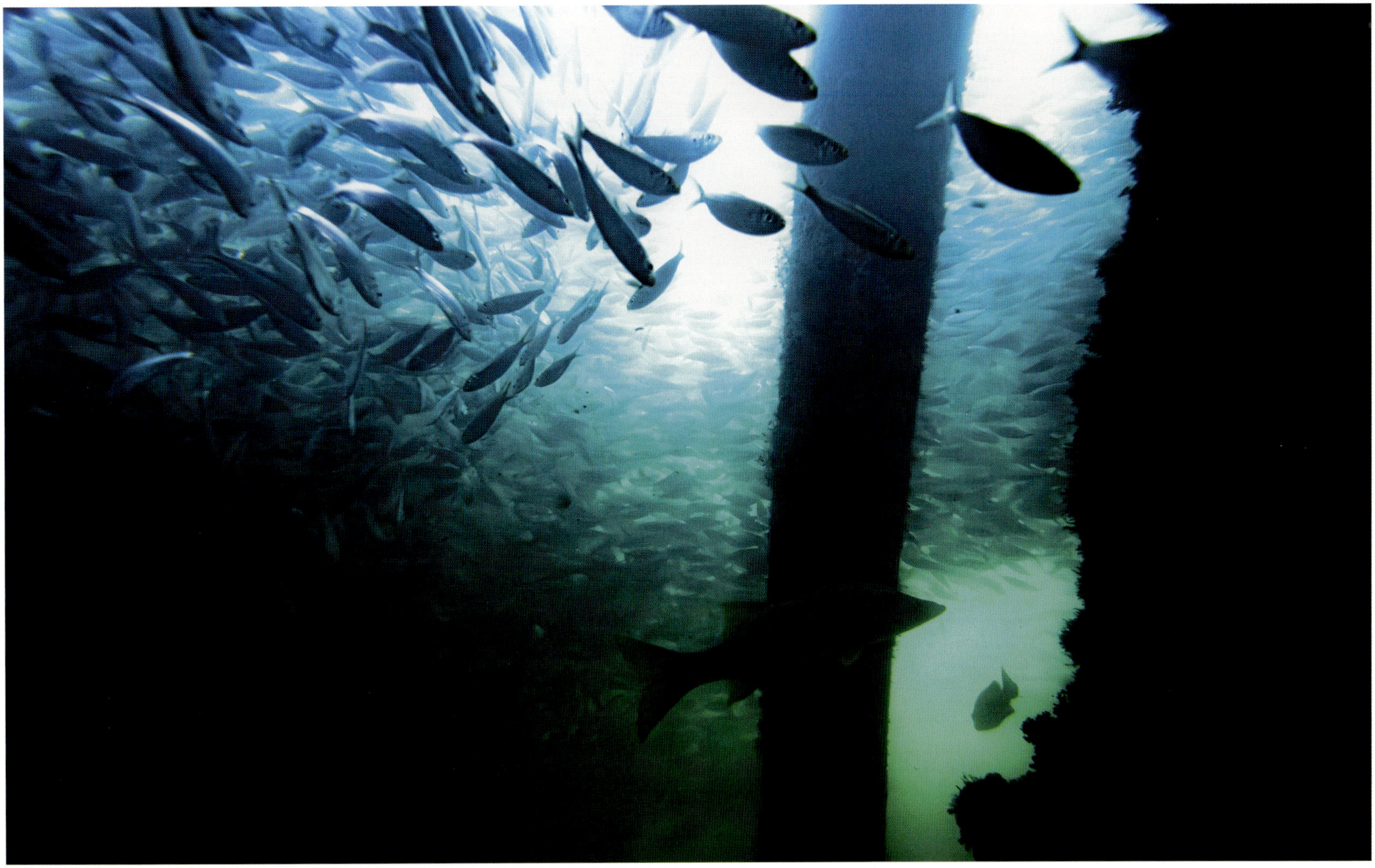

The Garden Key ferry dock often hosts an incredible abundance of life on temperate days. Shown here are a snook (genus *Centropomus*) and pilchards.

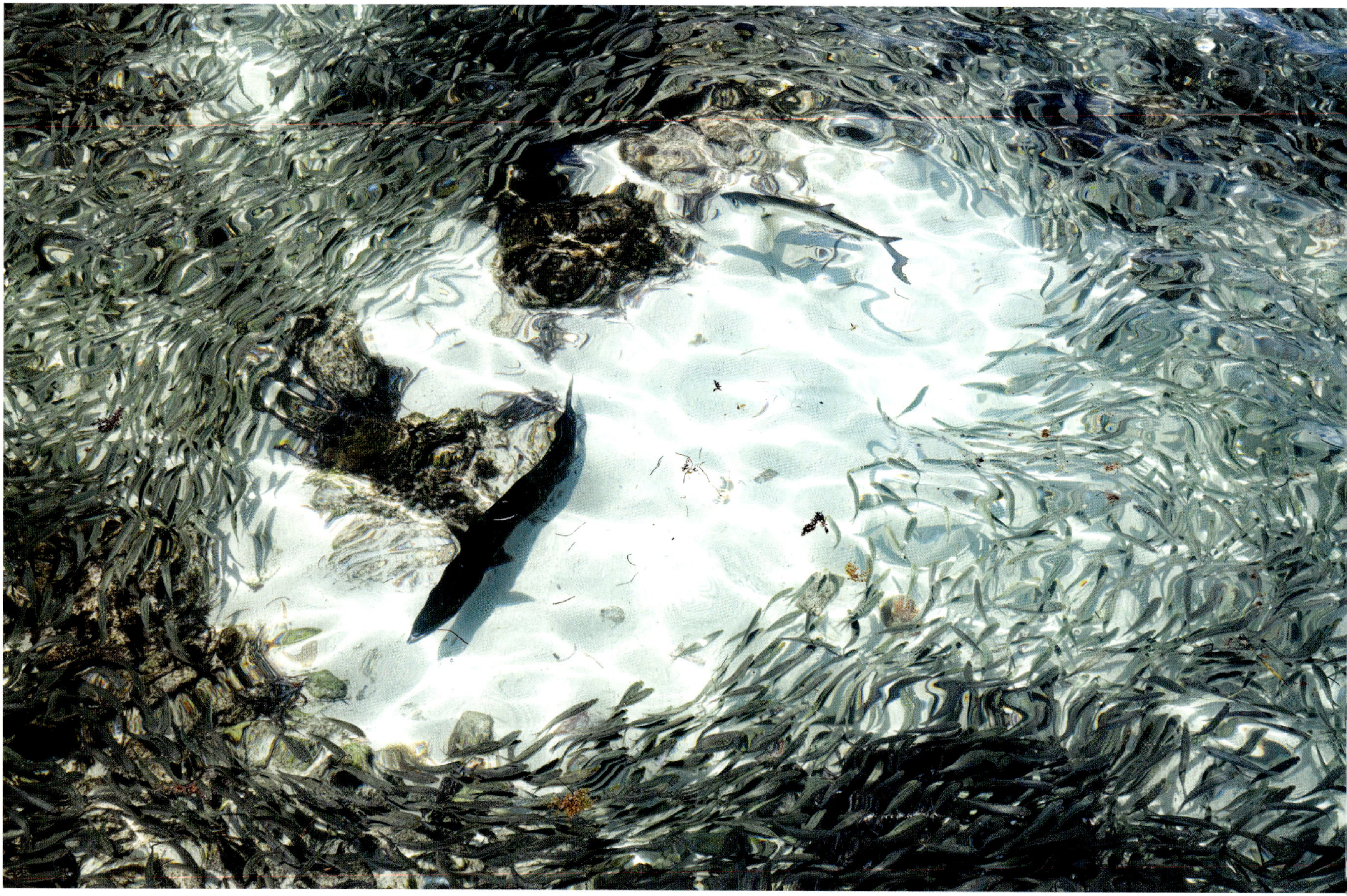

Barracuda and tarpon find themselves surrounded by thousands of pilchards.

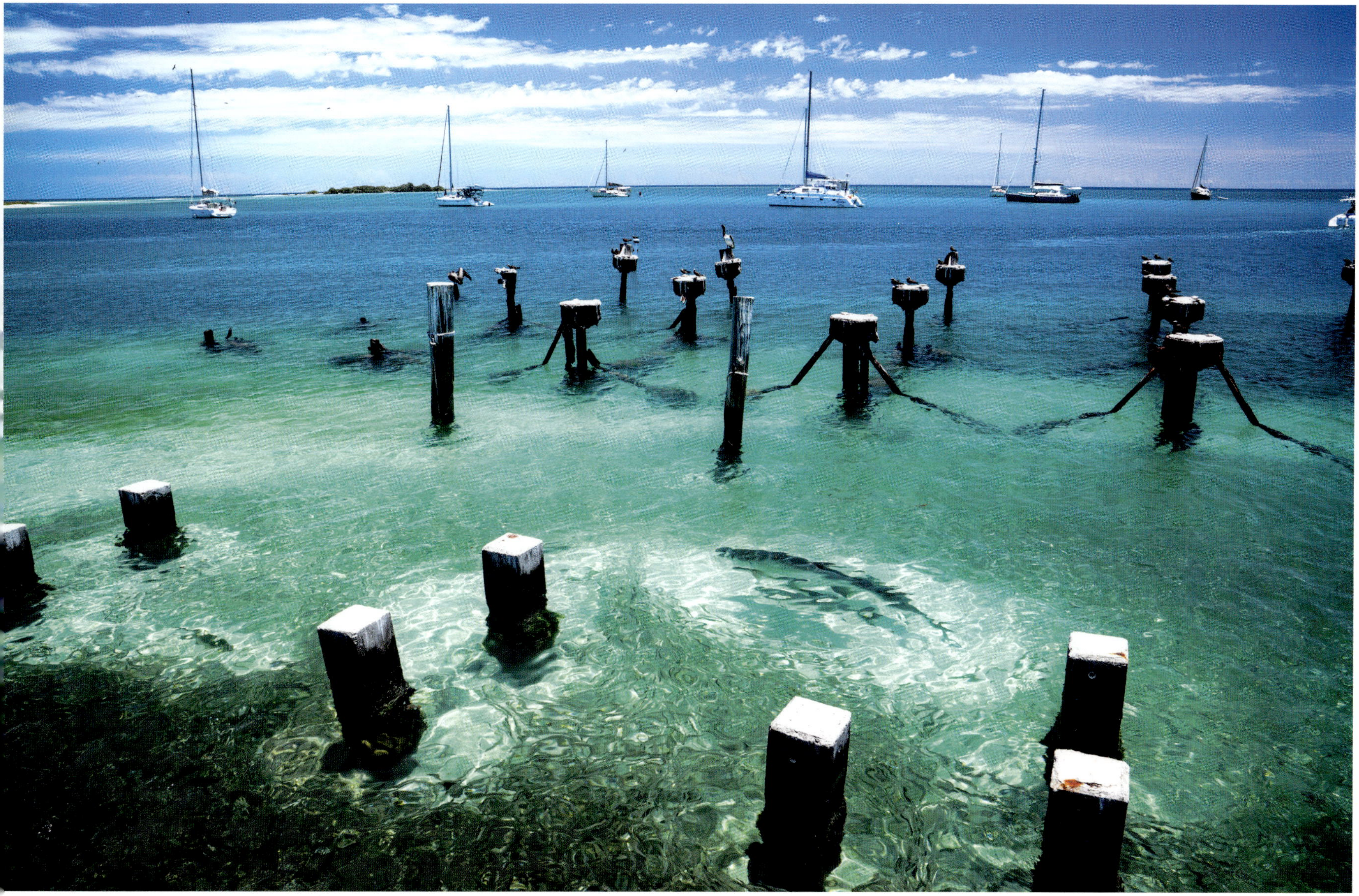

A school of tarpon navigates the coal docks in search of a meal. Located on the south and north sides of Garden Key, coal warehouses and docks, now ruined, were built at Fort Jefferson in 1898 to serve as supply and loading stations for battleships.

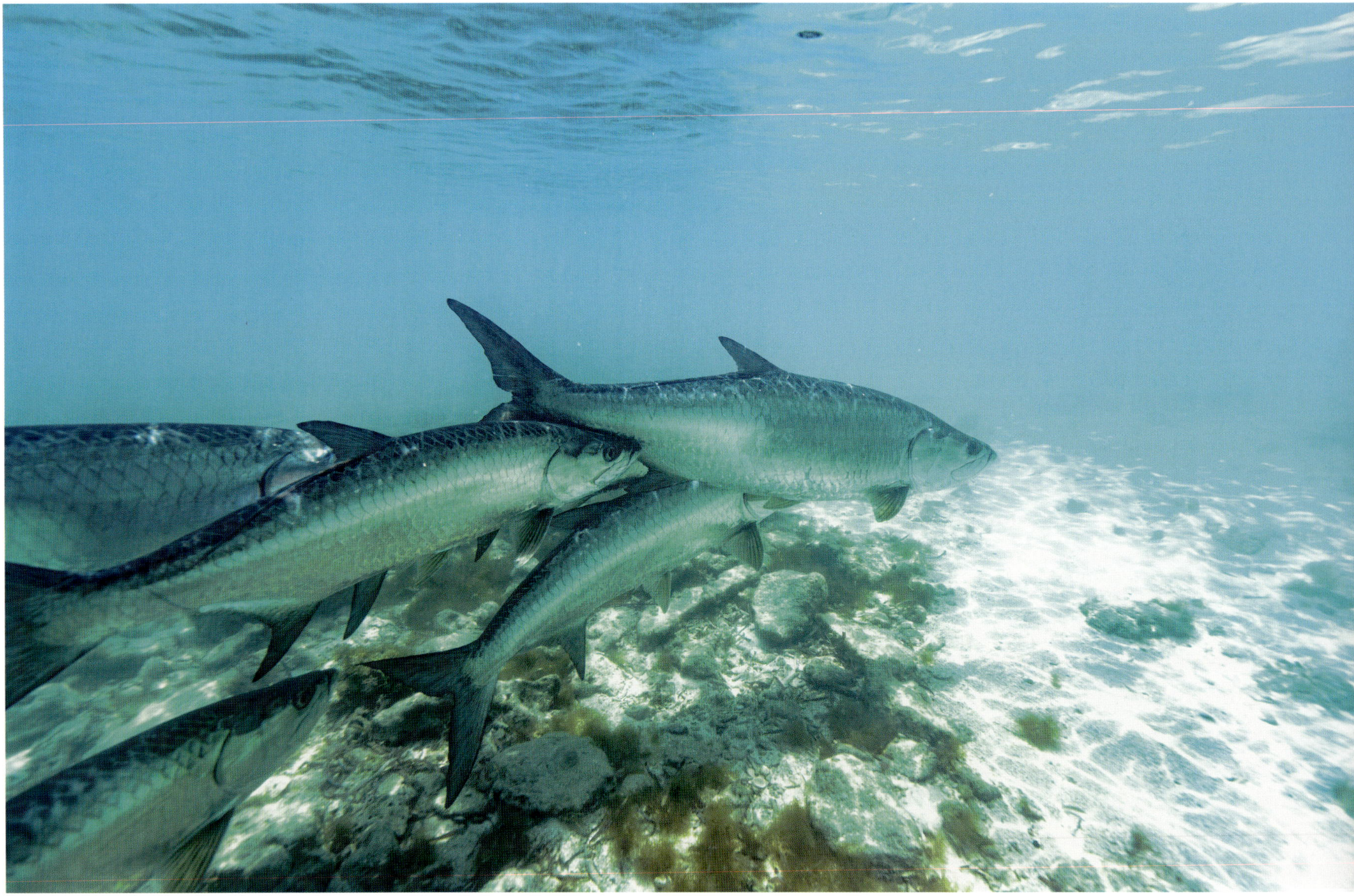

A school of giant tarpon swims the shallows off Garden Key.

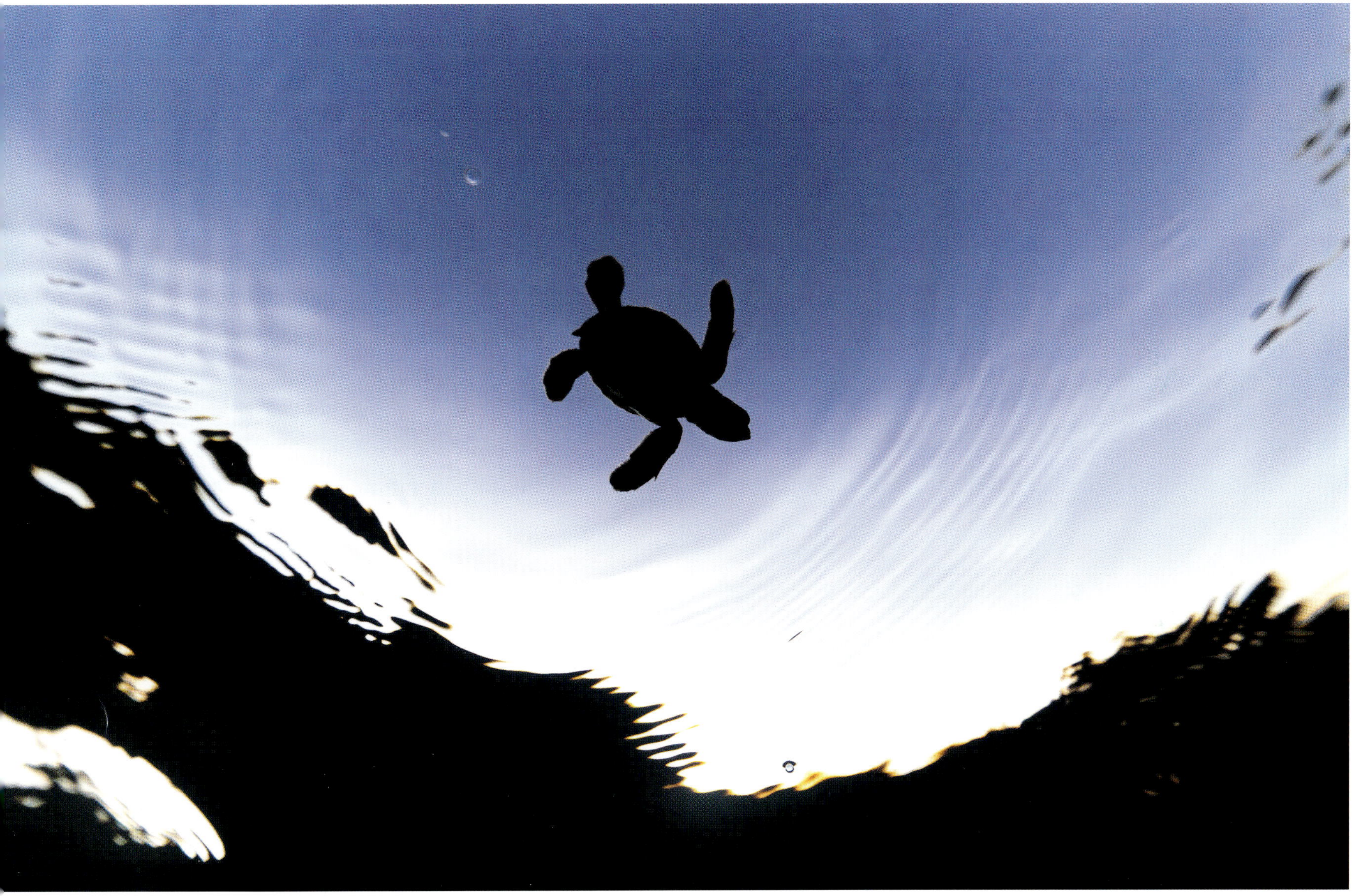

A newly hatched green turtle embarks on the journey of life, lucky enough to start under the oncoming darkness of night.

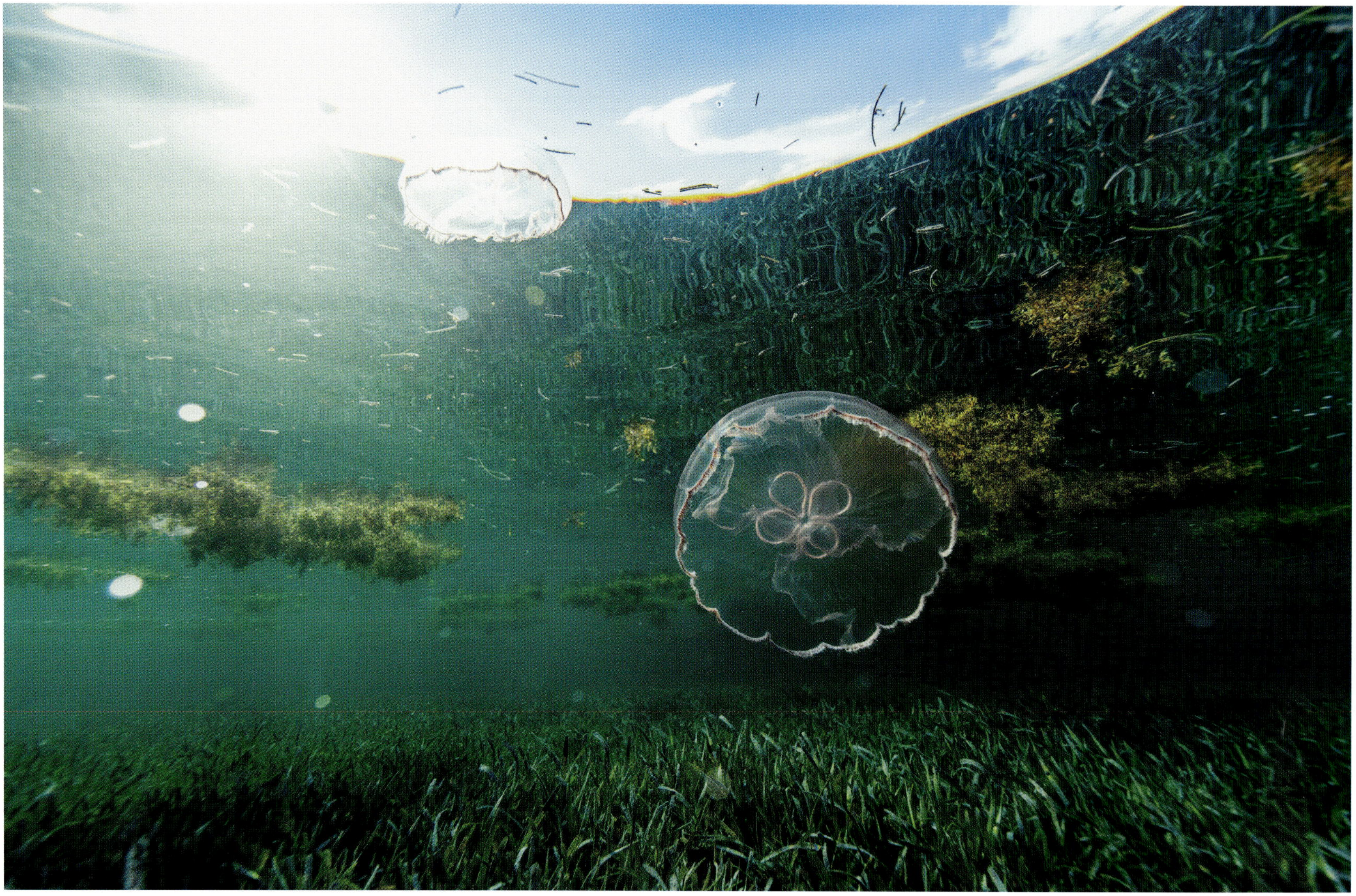

Moon jellyfish drift with the tides across the seagrass flats off Garden Key.

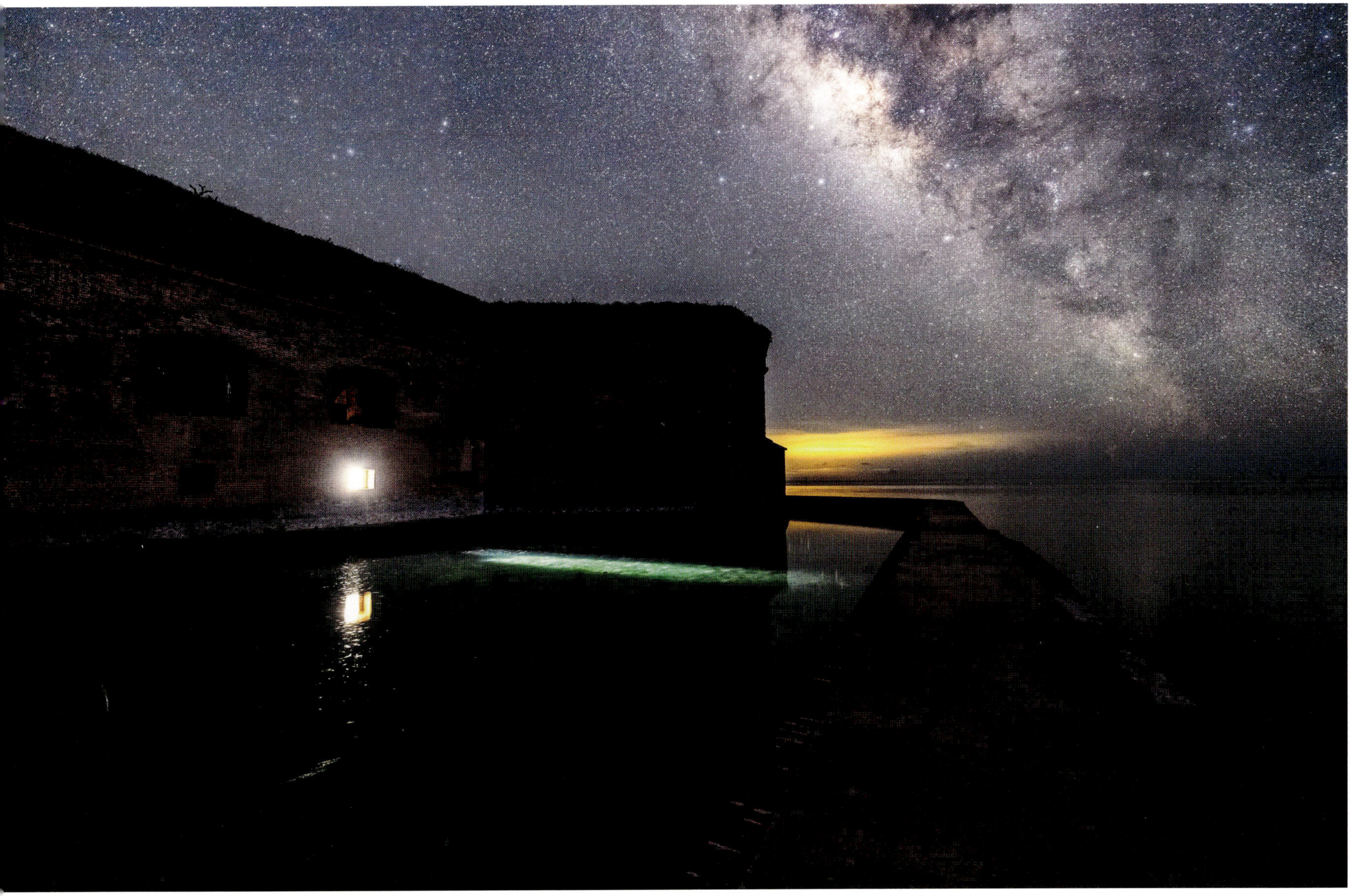

The Milky Way and Fort Jefferson from the moat wall.

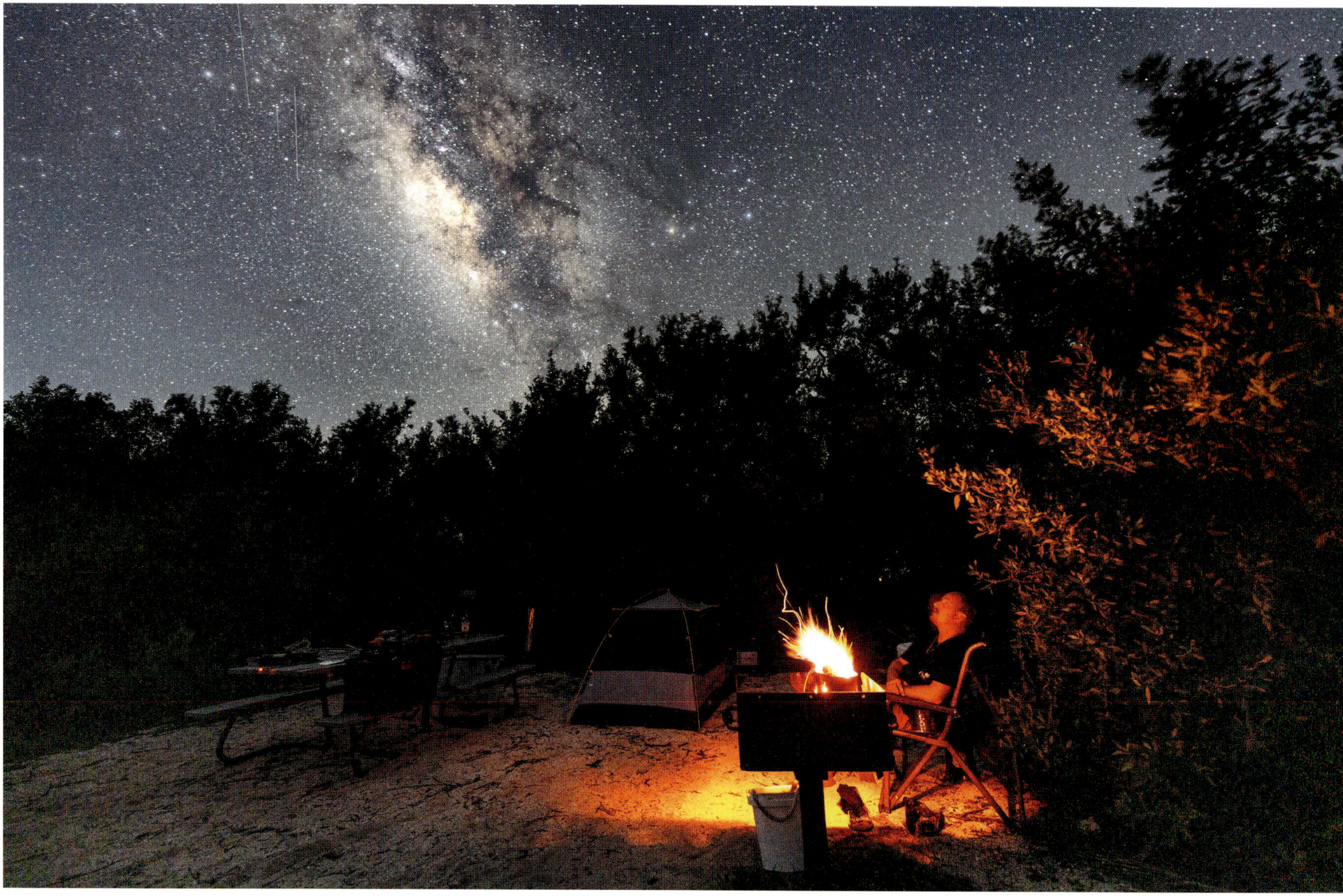

A camper takes in the stars while waiting for the grill to heat up.

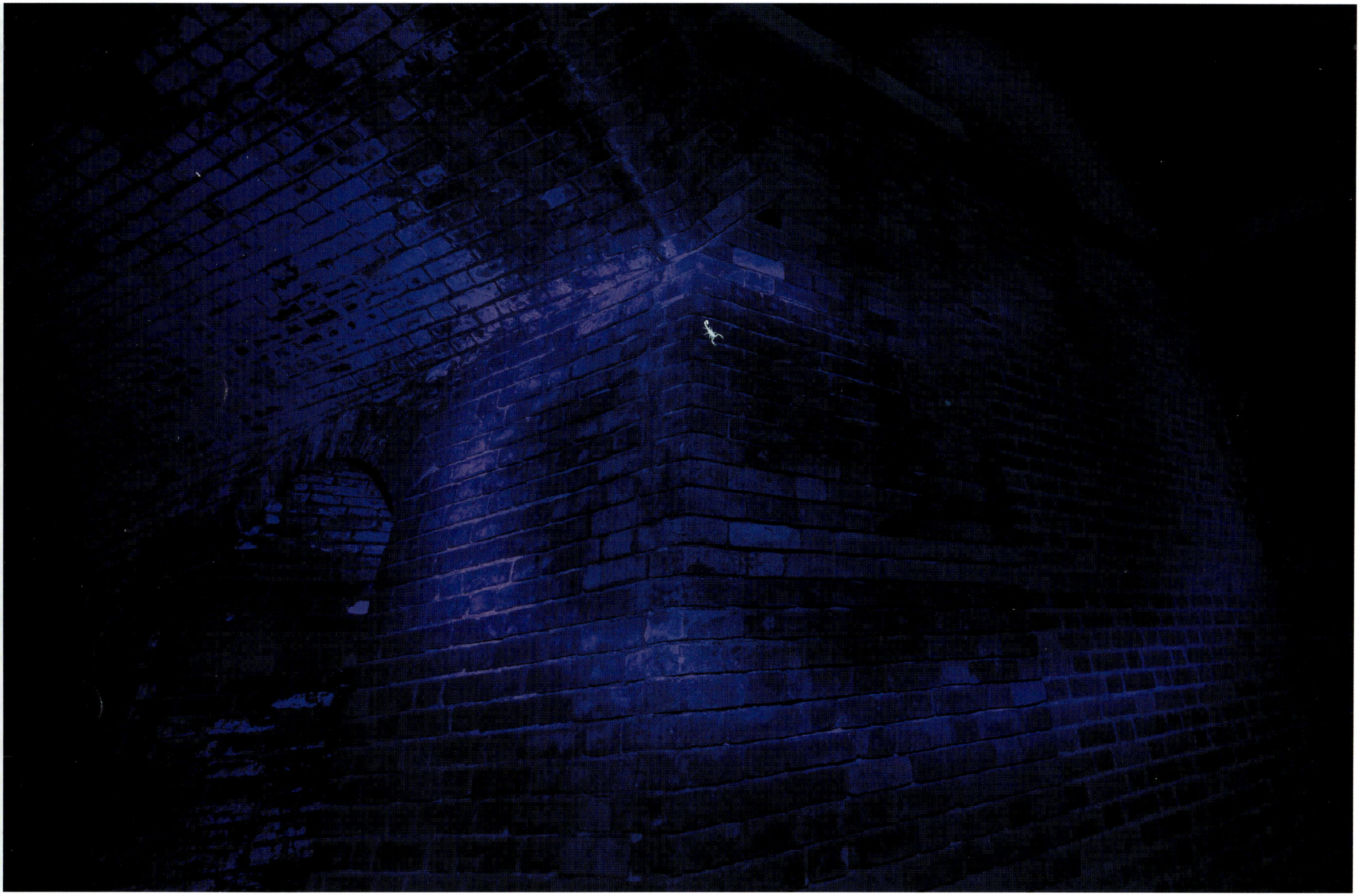

A scorpion illuminated by ultraviolet light searches Fort Jefferson's walls for its next meal.

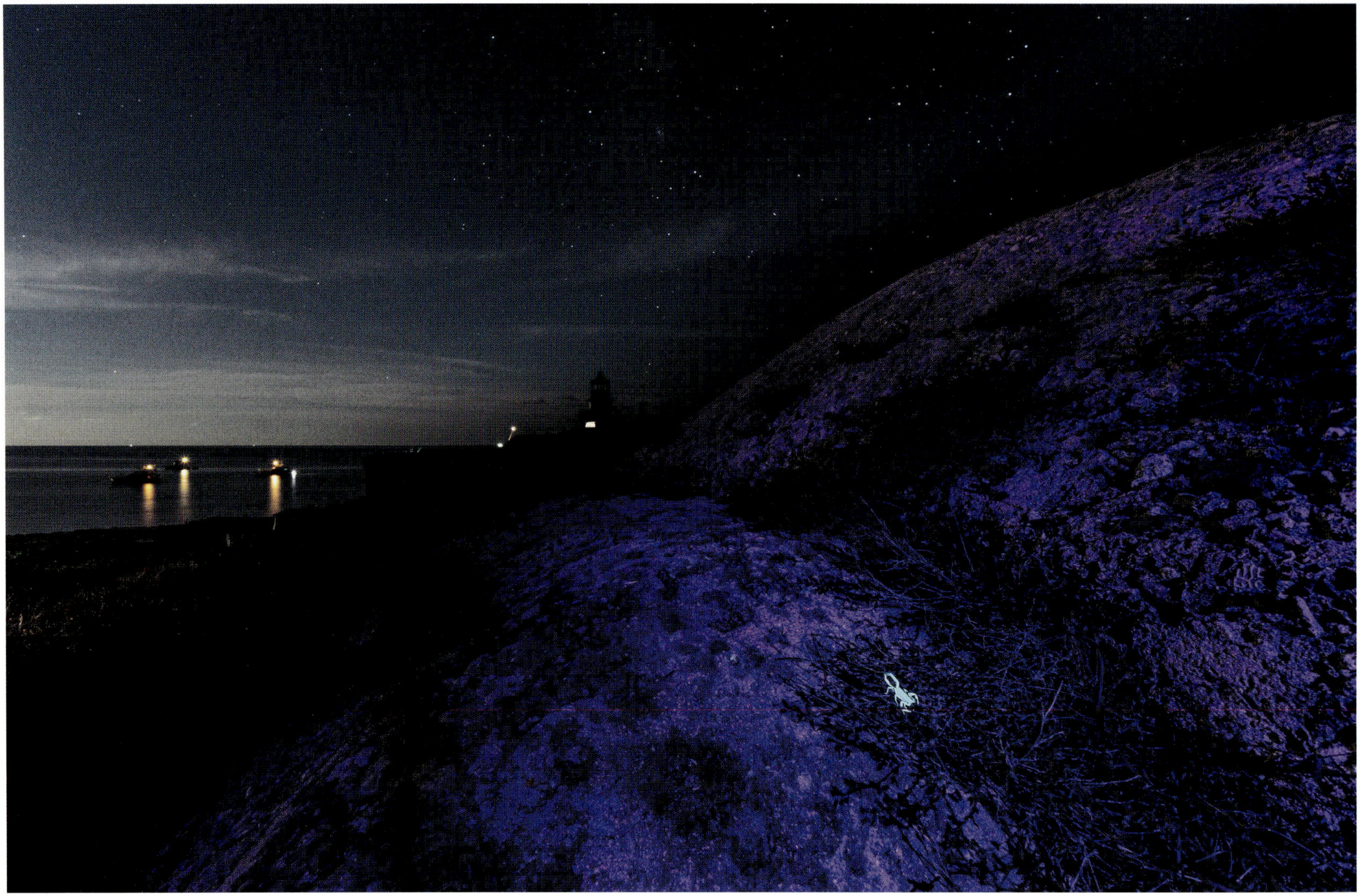

A scorpion illuminated by UV light enjoys a bug snack under the stars.

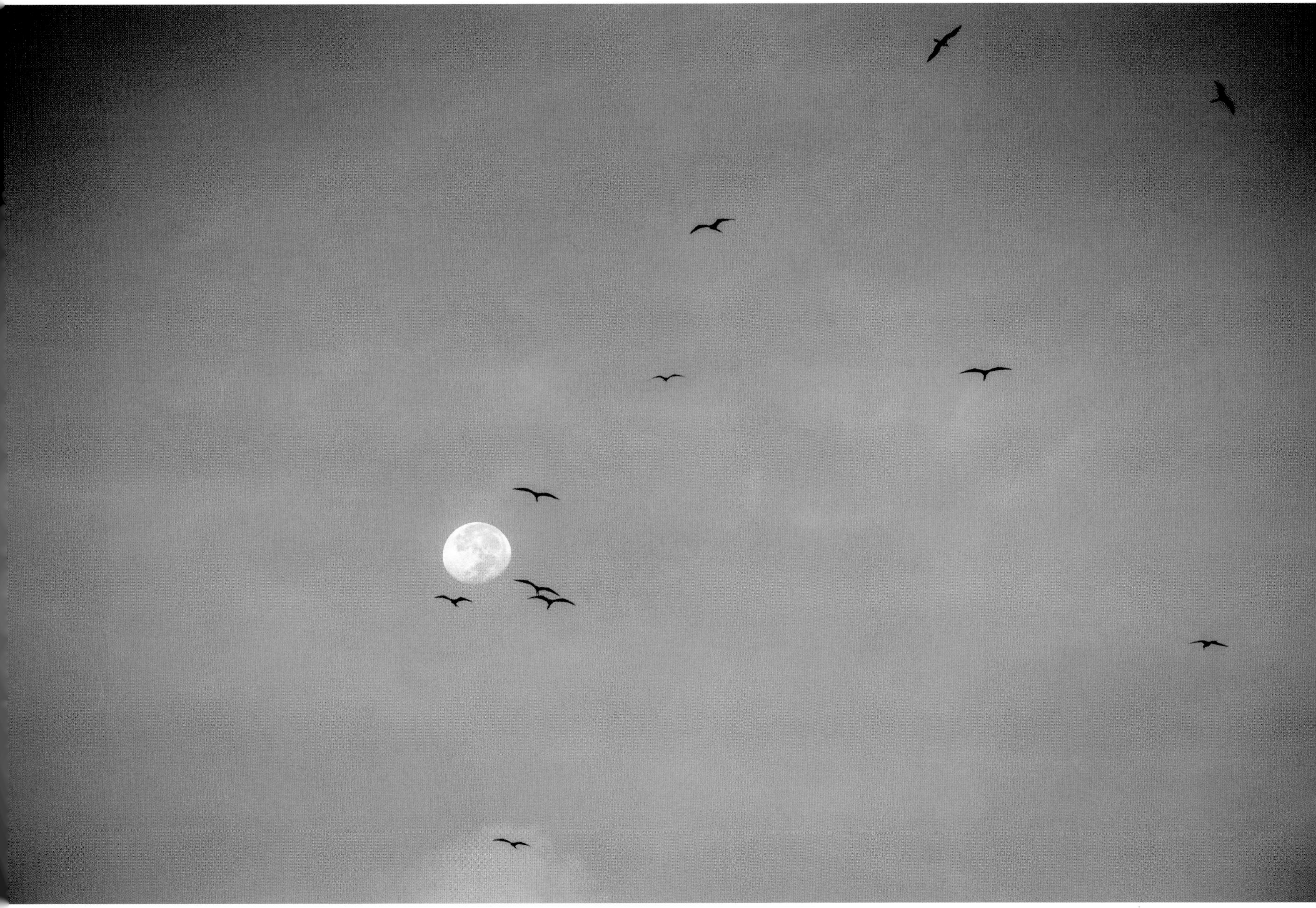

Frigatebirds under the full moon.

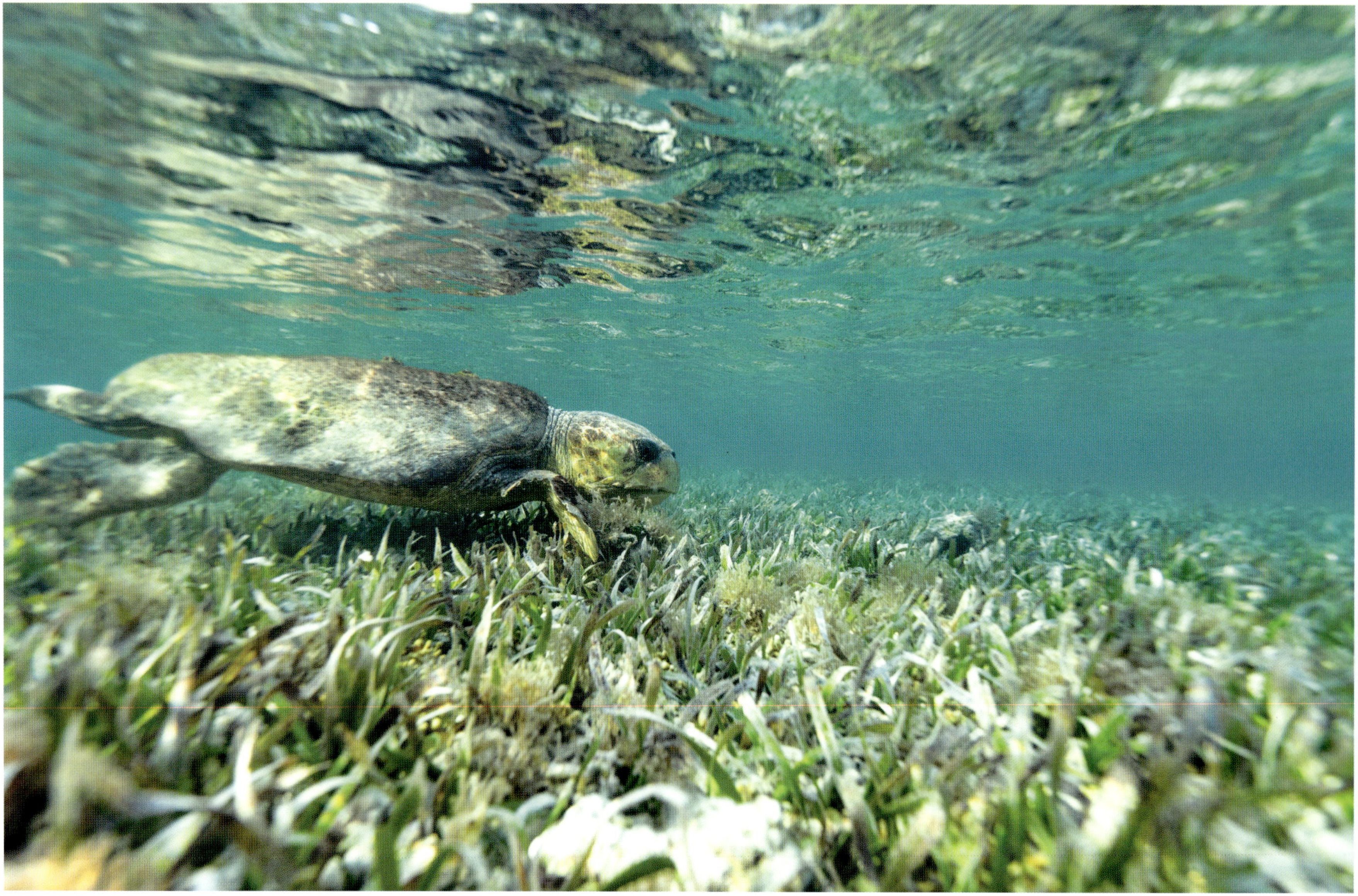

An old Loggerhead turtle searches shallow seagrass flats in search of fresh conch.

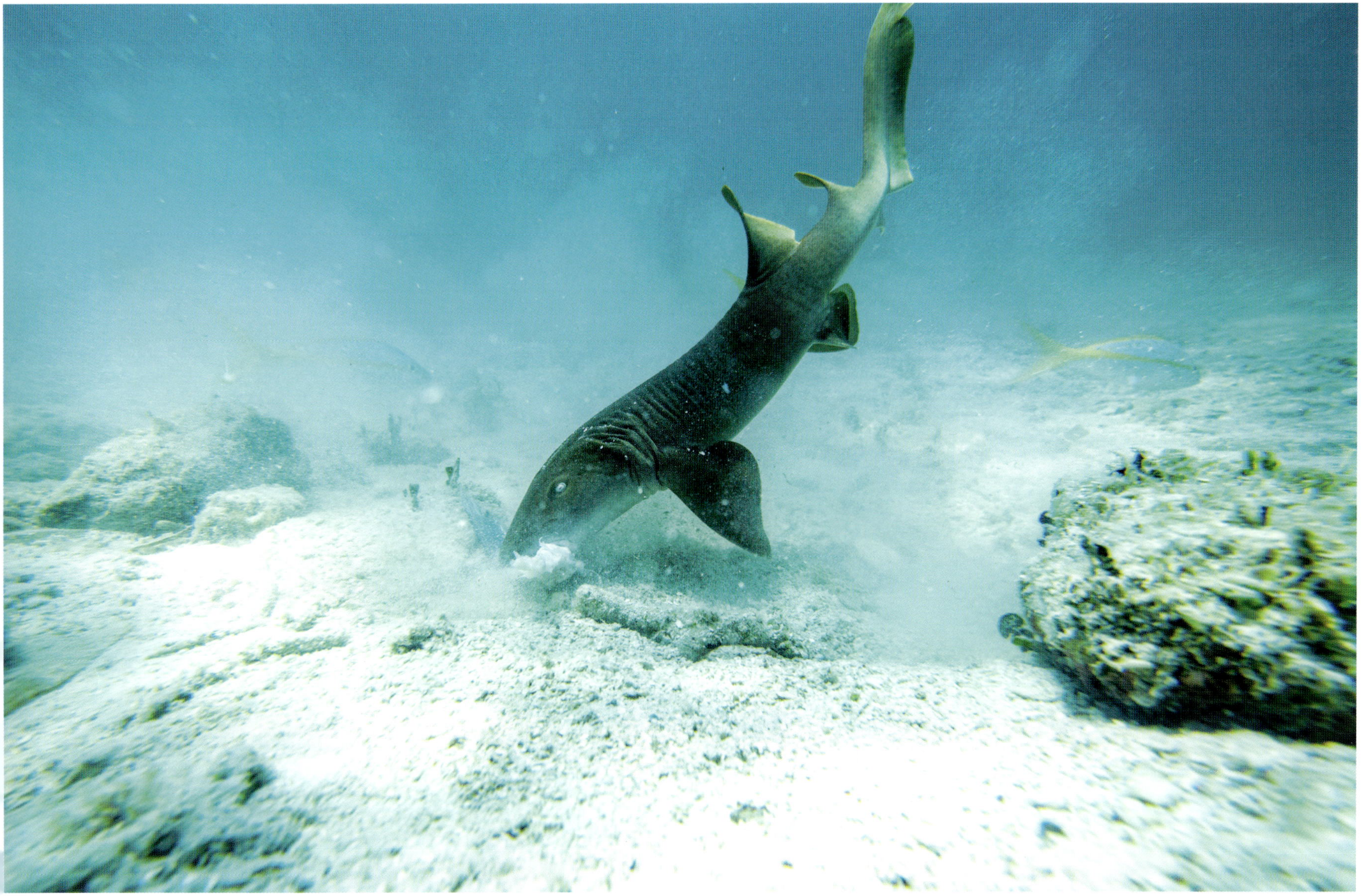

A juvenile nurse shark finds a meal.

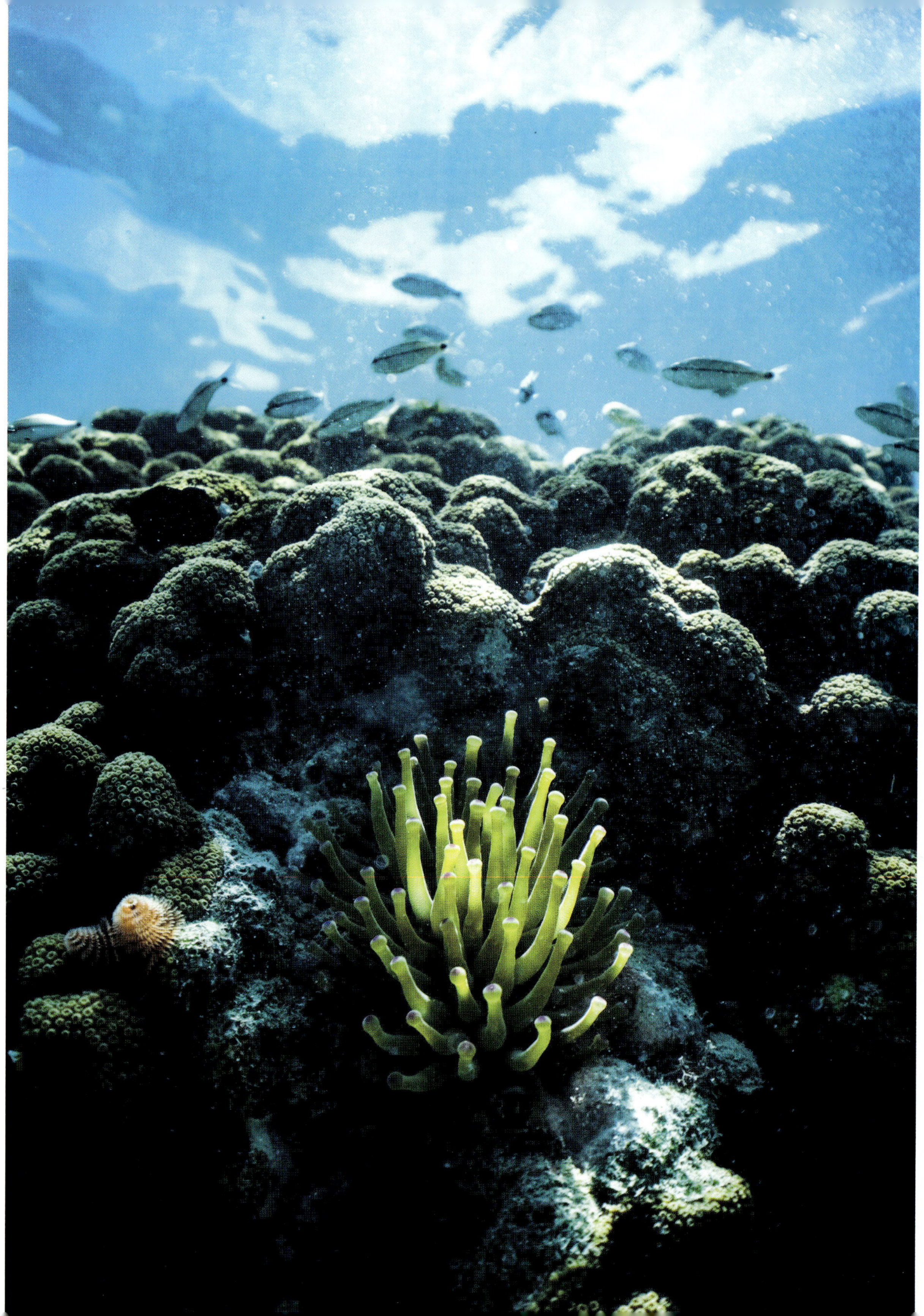

A pink-tipped anemone (*Condylactis gigantea*) reaches up toward the sunlight.

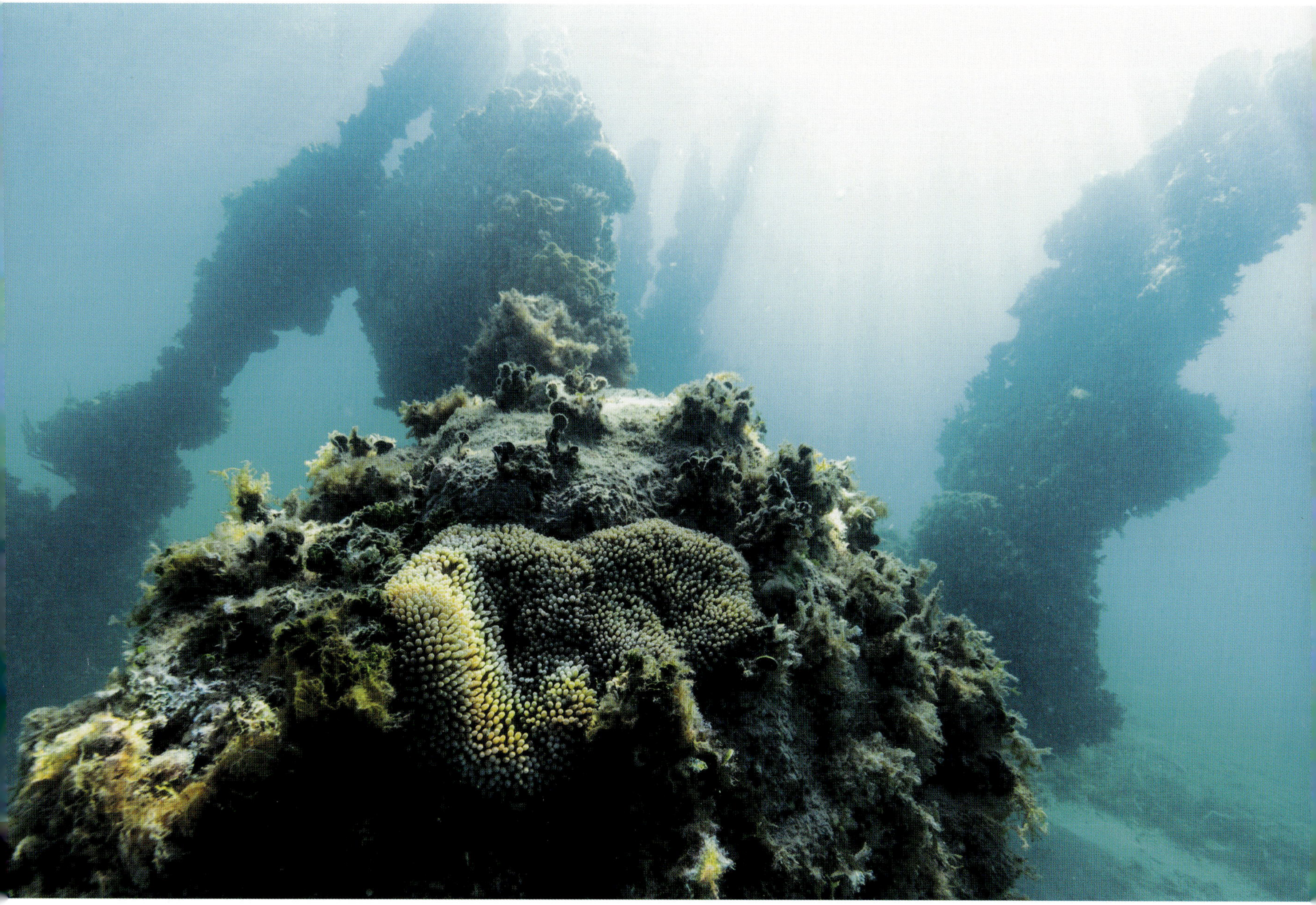

Sea anemones among the sunken piers of Garden Key's southern coal docks.

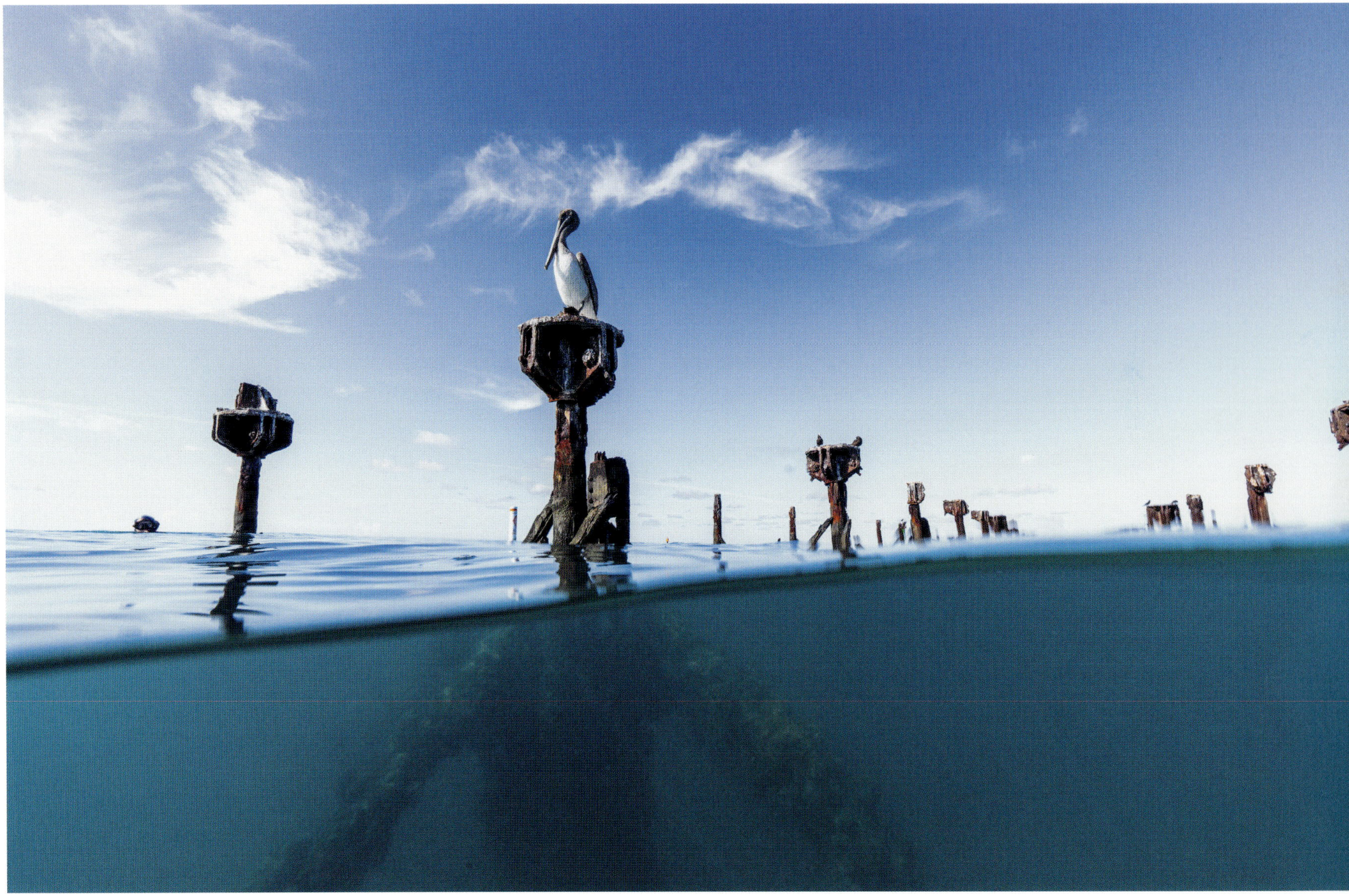

A pelican finds a nice spot to rest on one of the southern coal docks' piers.

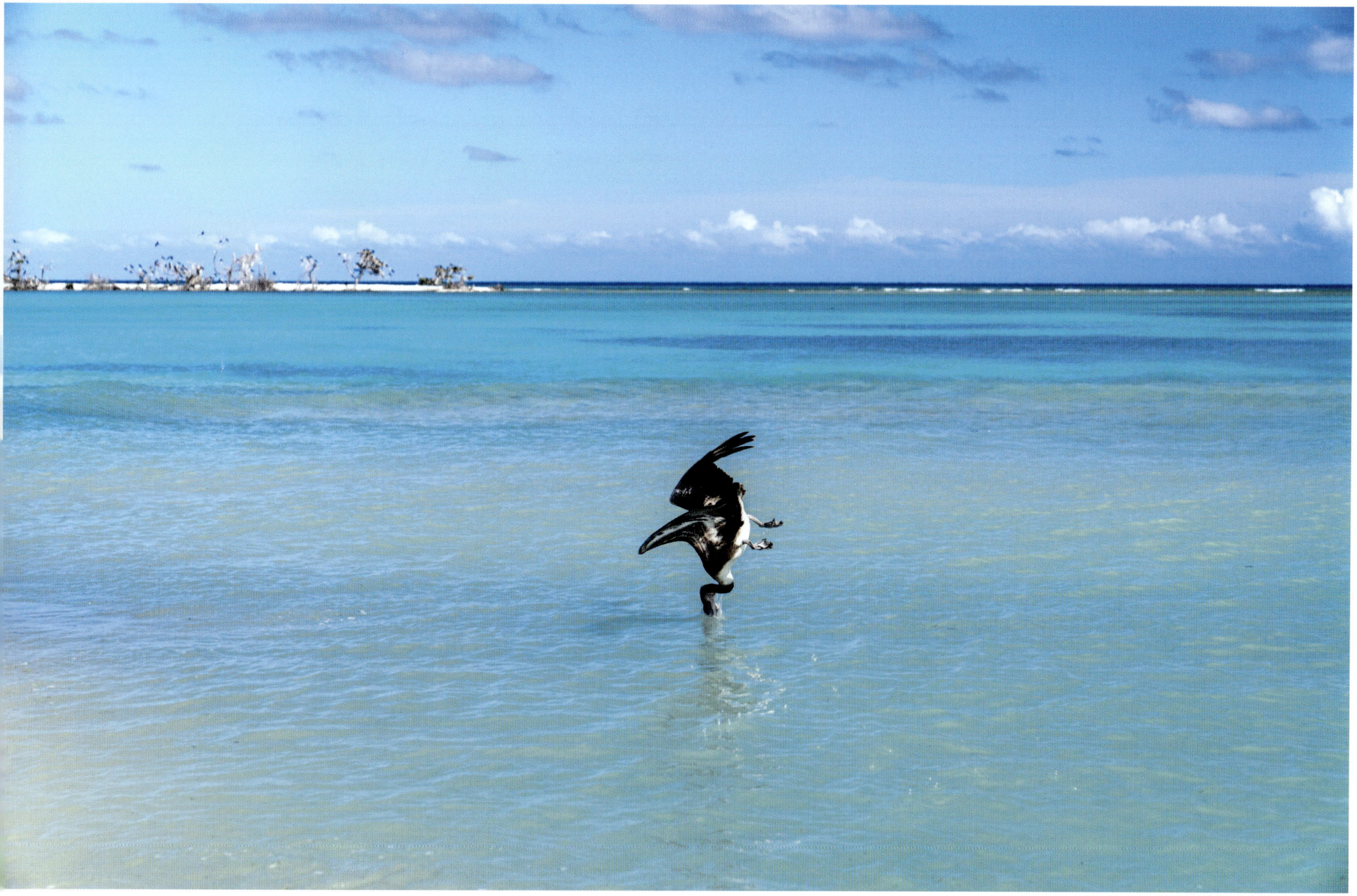

A pelican dives for bait.

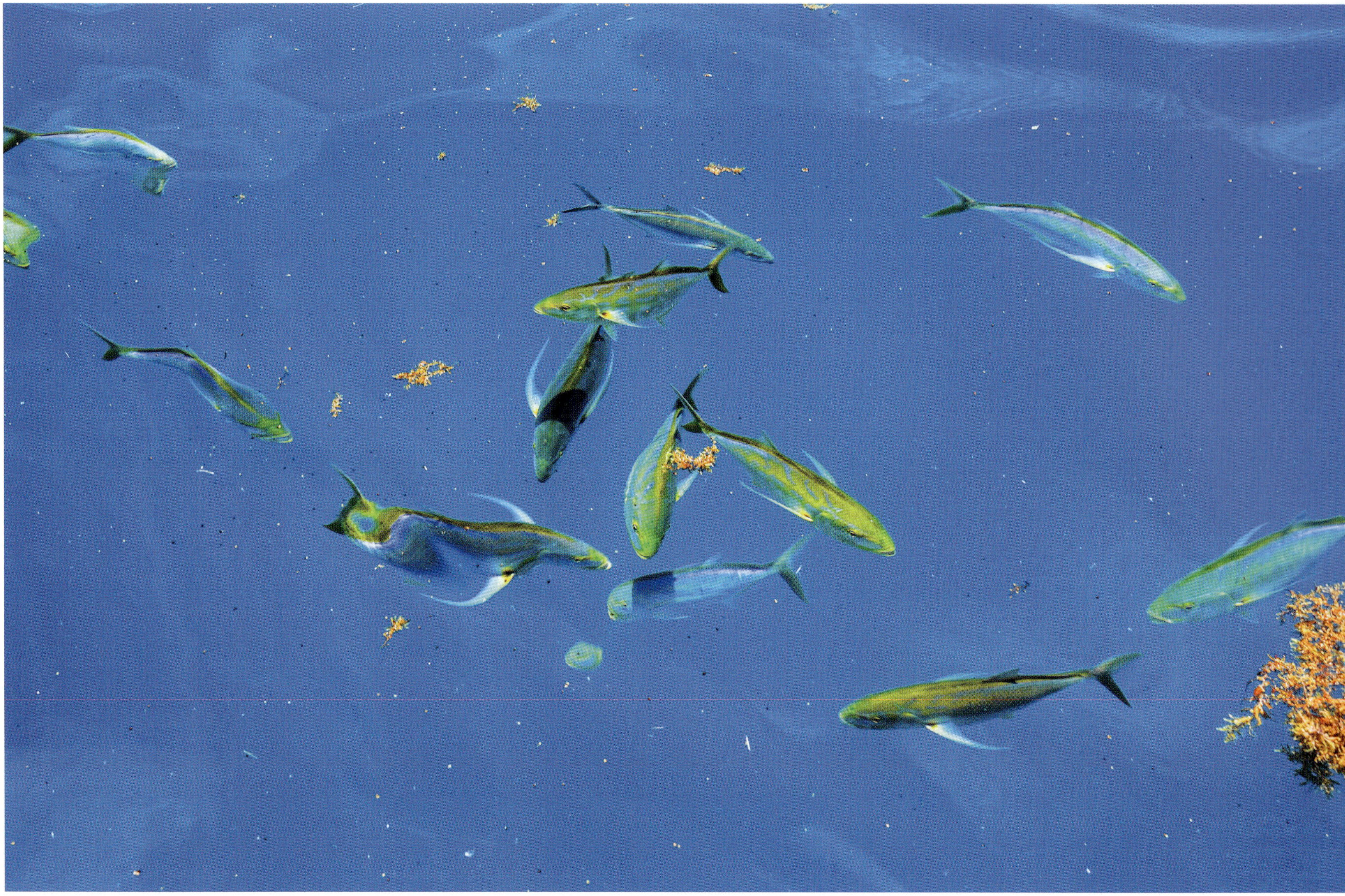

Just off Long Key, a school of yellow jack (*Carangoides bartholomaei*) patrols the sargassum patches for food.

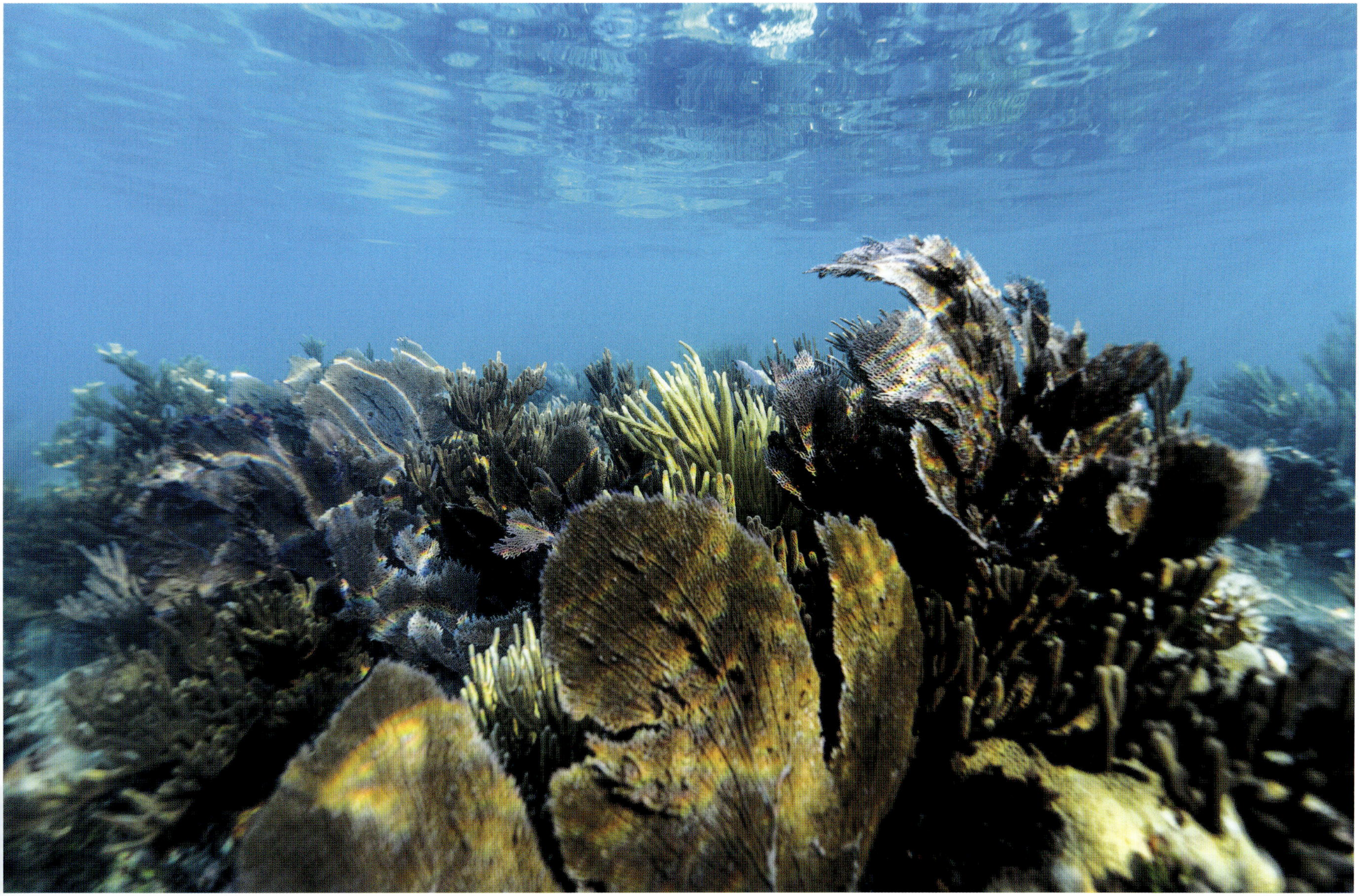

Soft corals off Loggerhead Key bask in late-afternoon light.

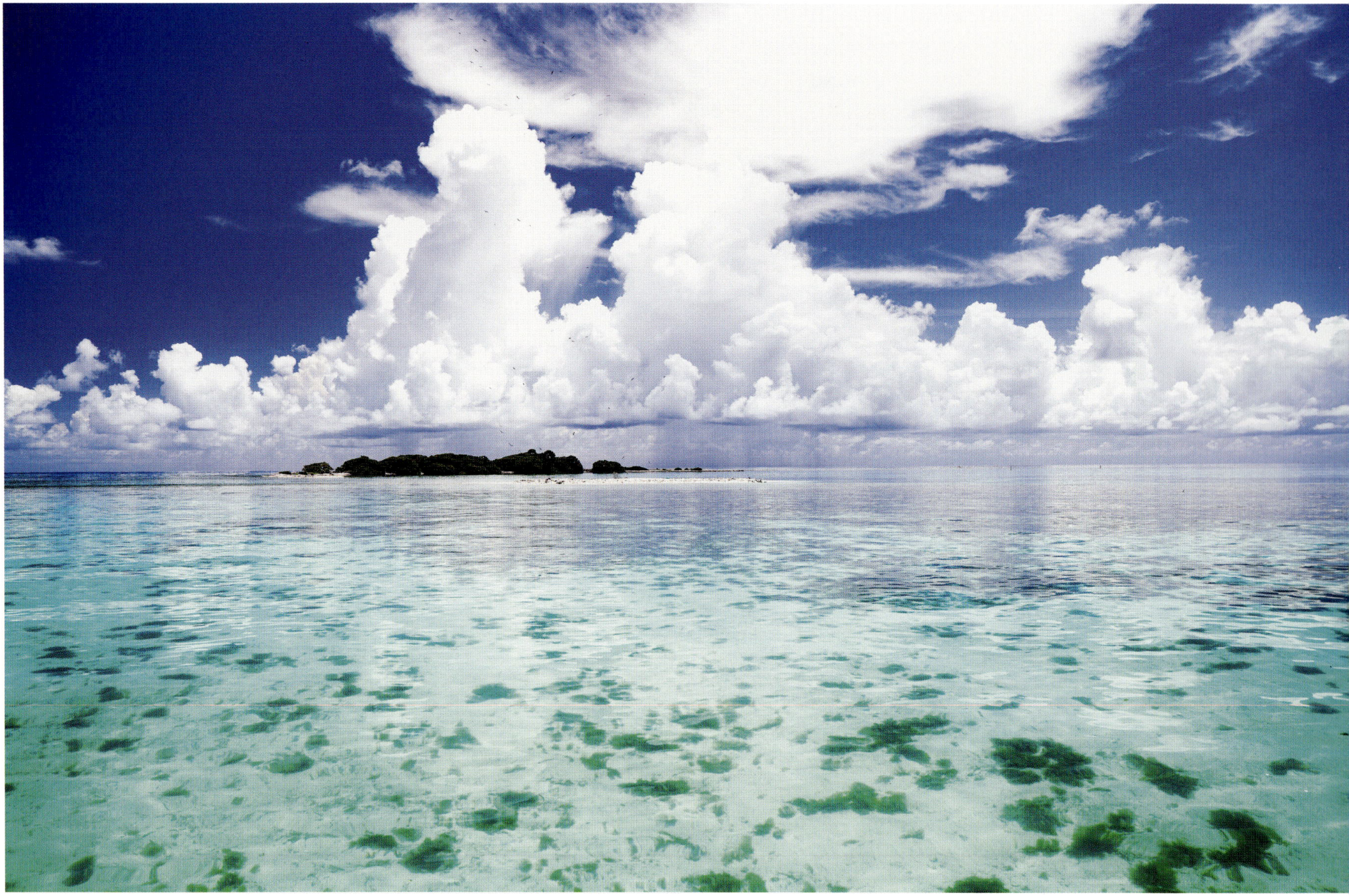

Long Key sandbar.

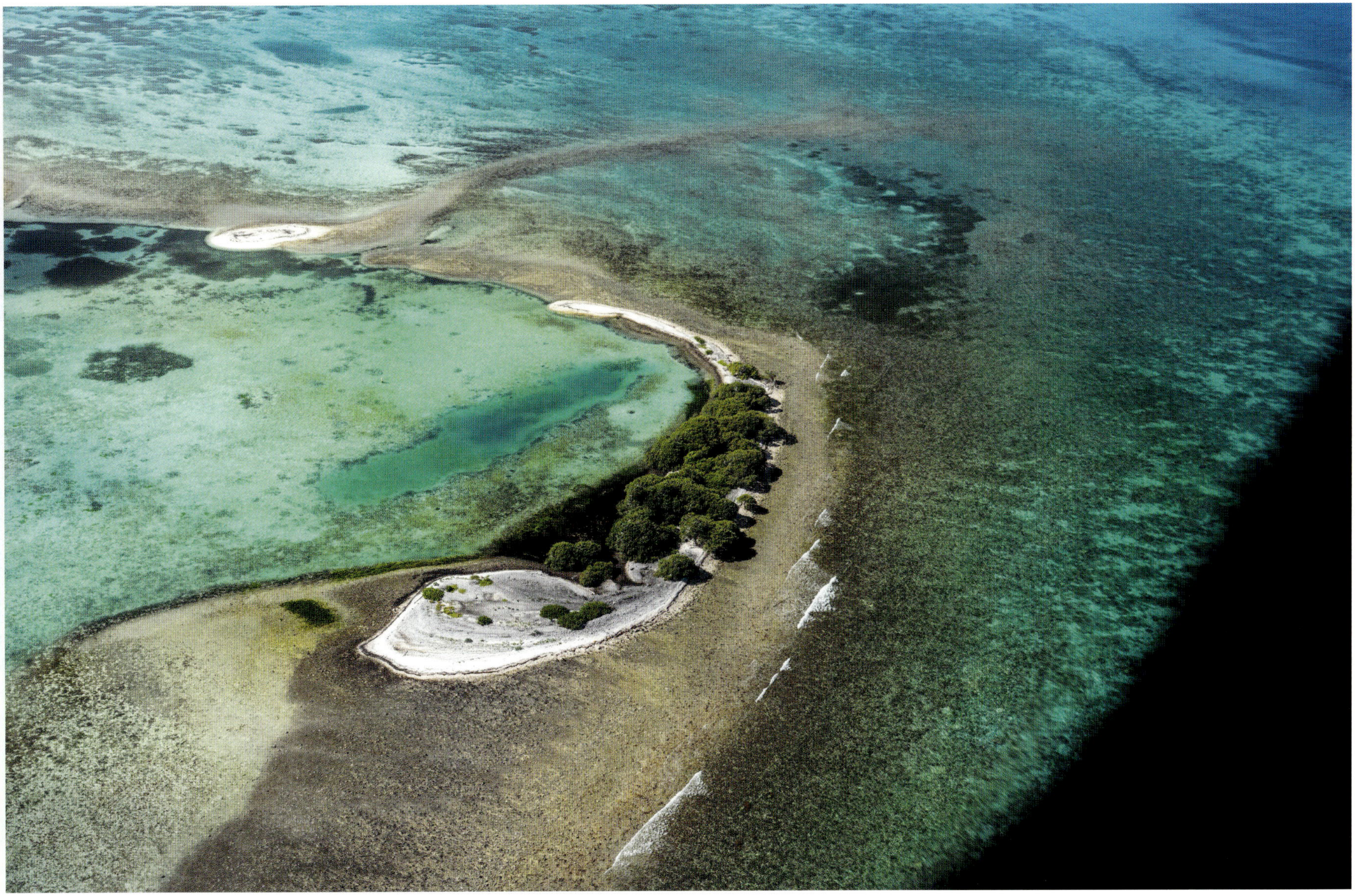

Long Key from the air.

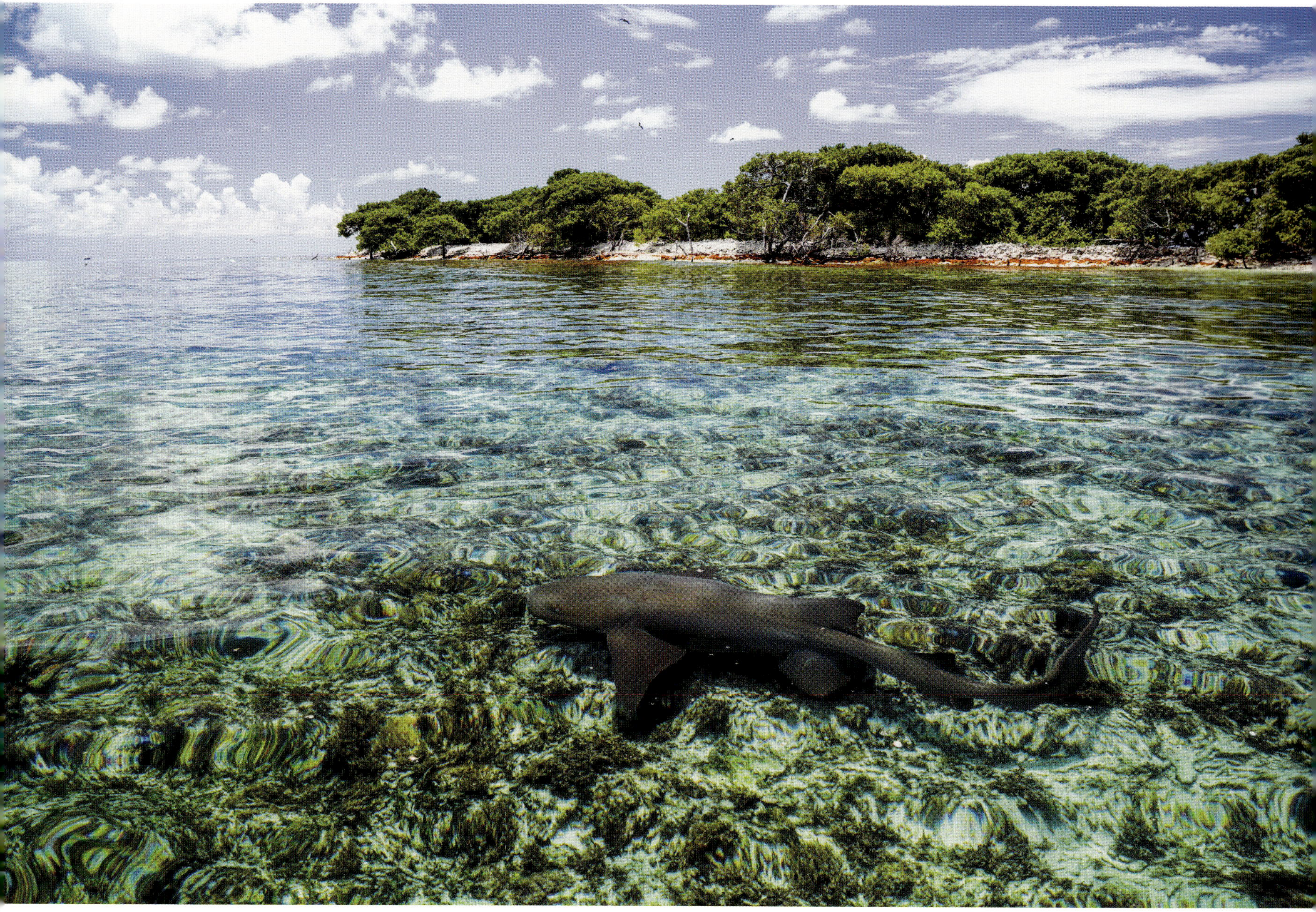

A nurse shark swims in the shallows off Long Key.

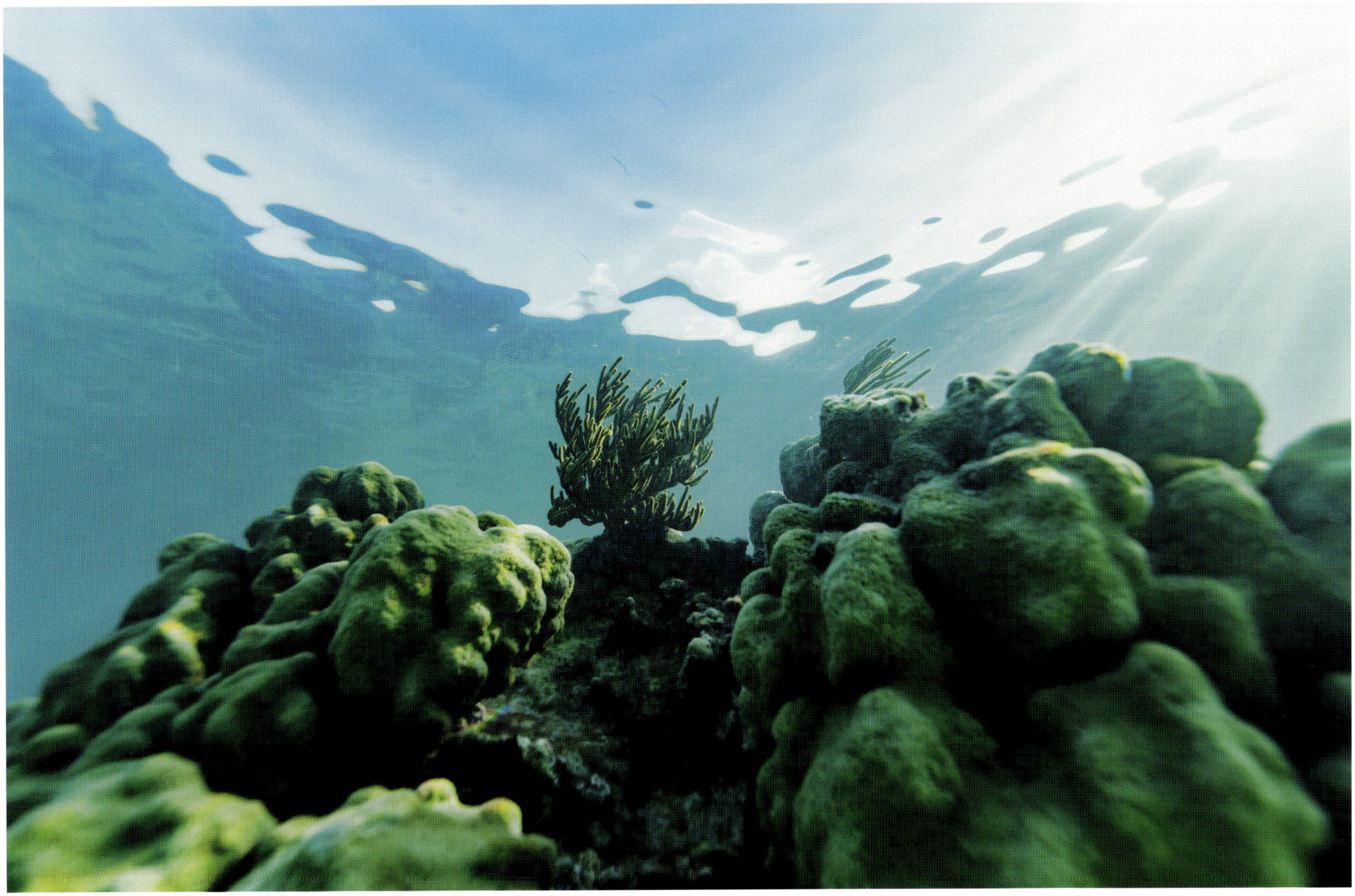

Star coral and a gorgonian cluster along Little Africa Reef off Loggerhead Key.

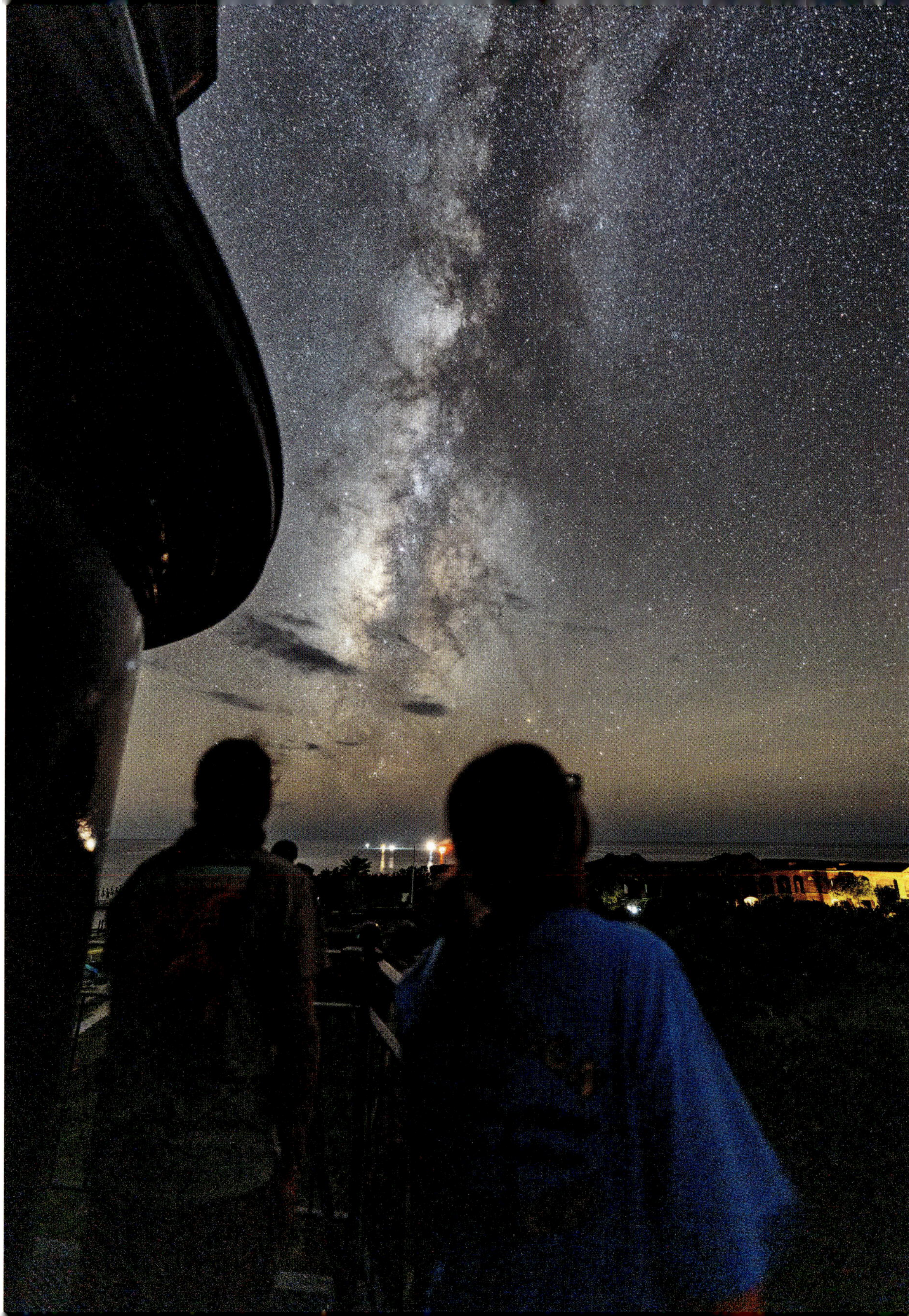

Stargazers take in the Milky Way from the top of the Fort Jefferson lighthouse.

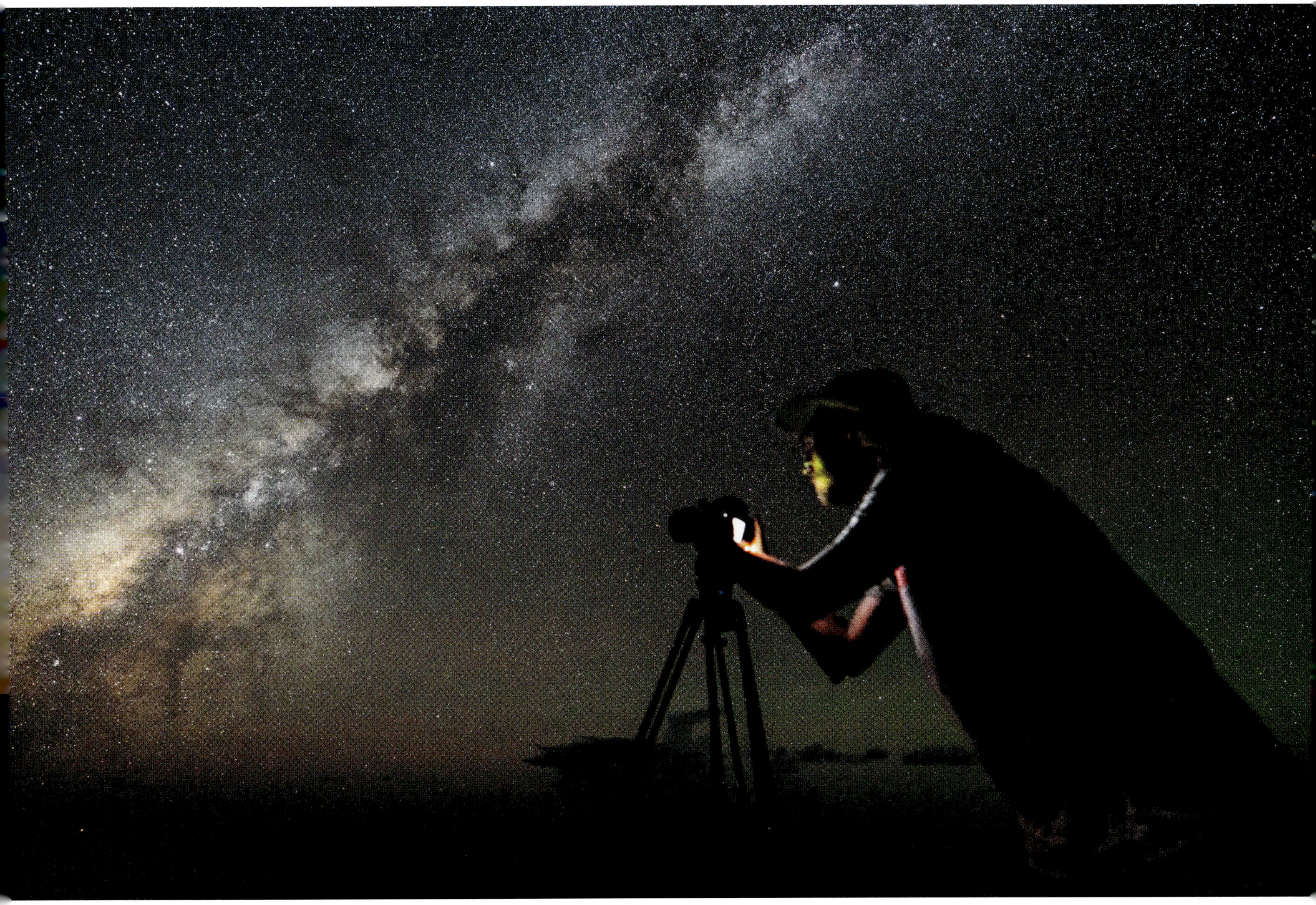

A photographer captures the night sky.

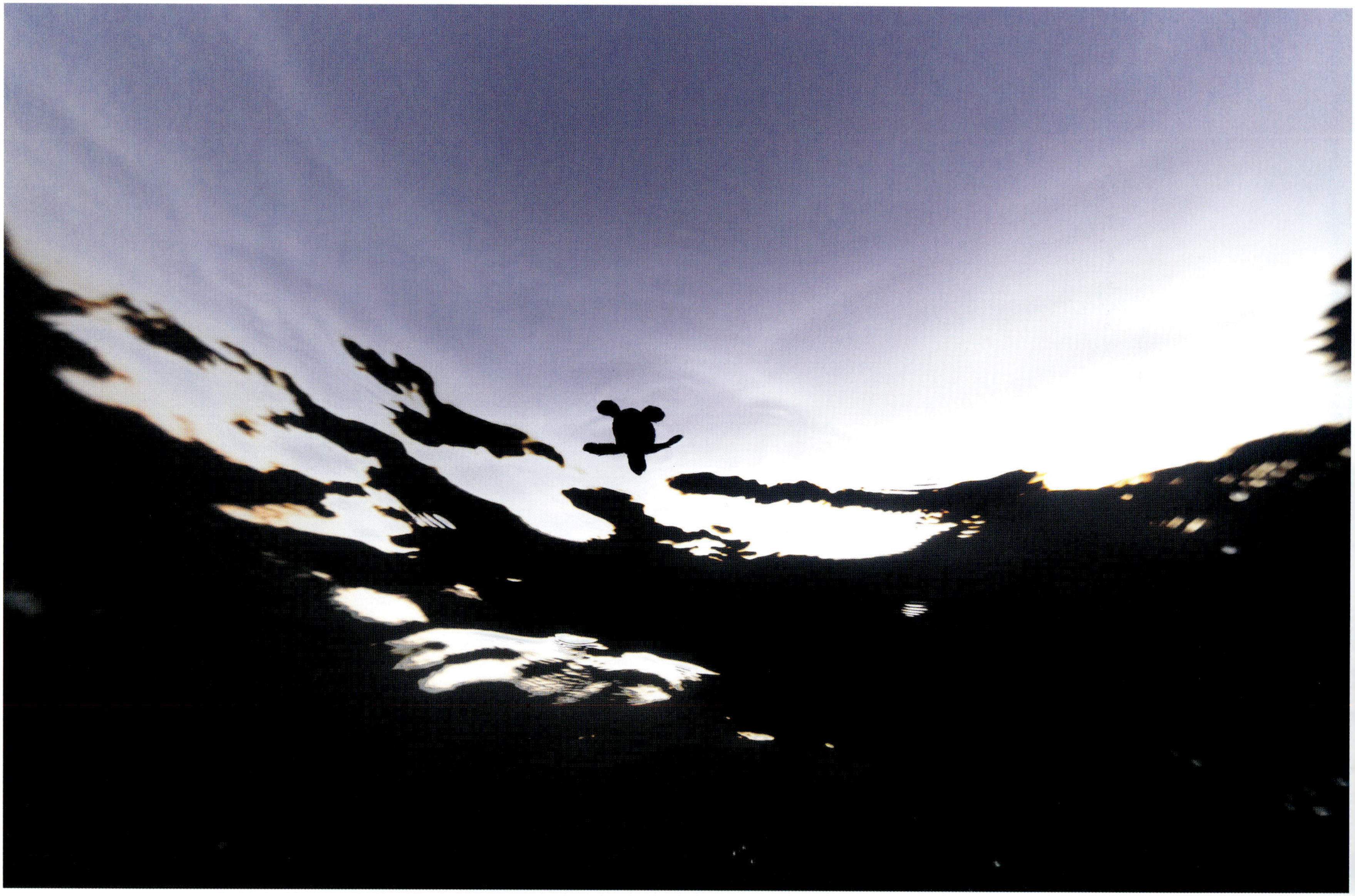

A juvenile sea turtle blends in with the silhouettes of the night.

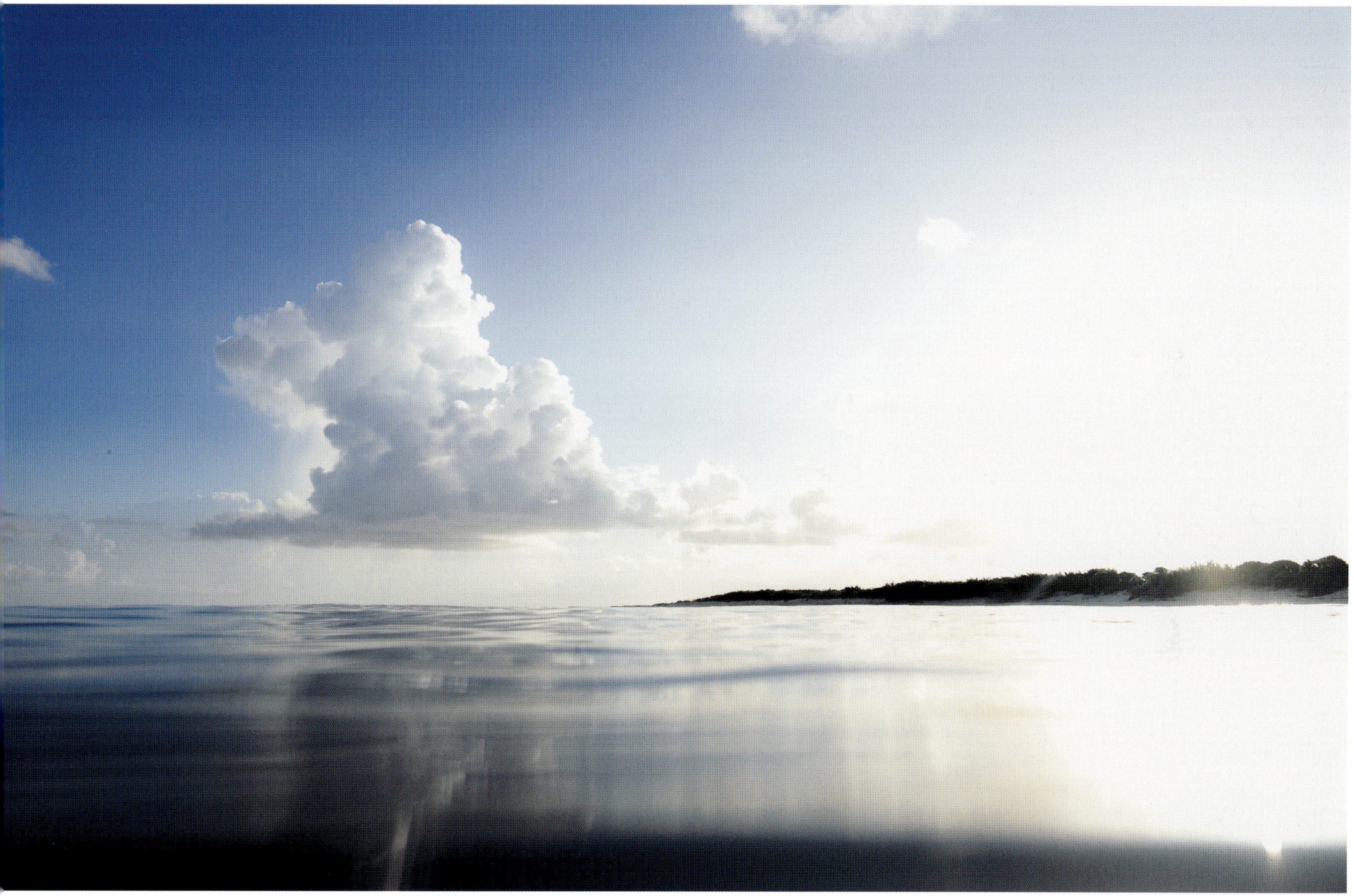

Glassy seascape as seen from Little Africa Reef behind Loggerhead Key.

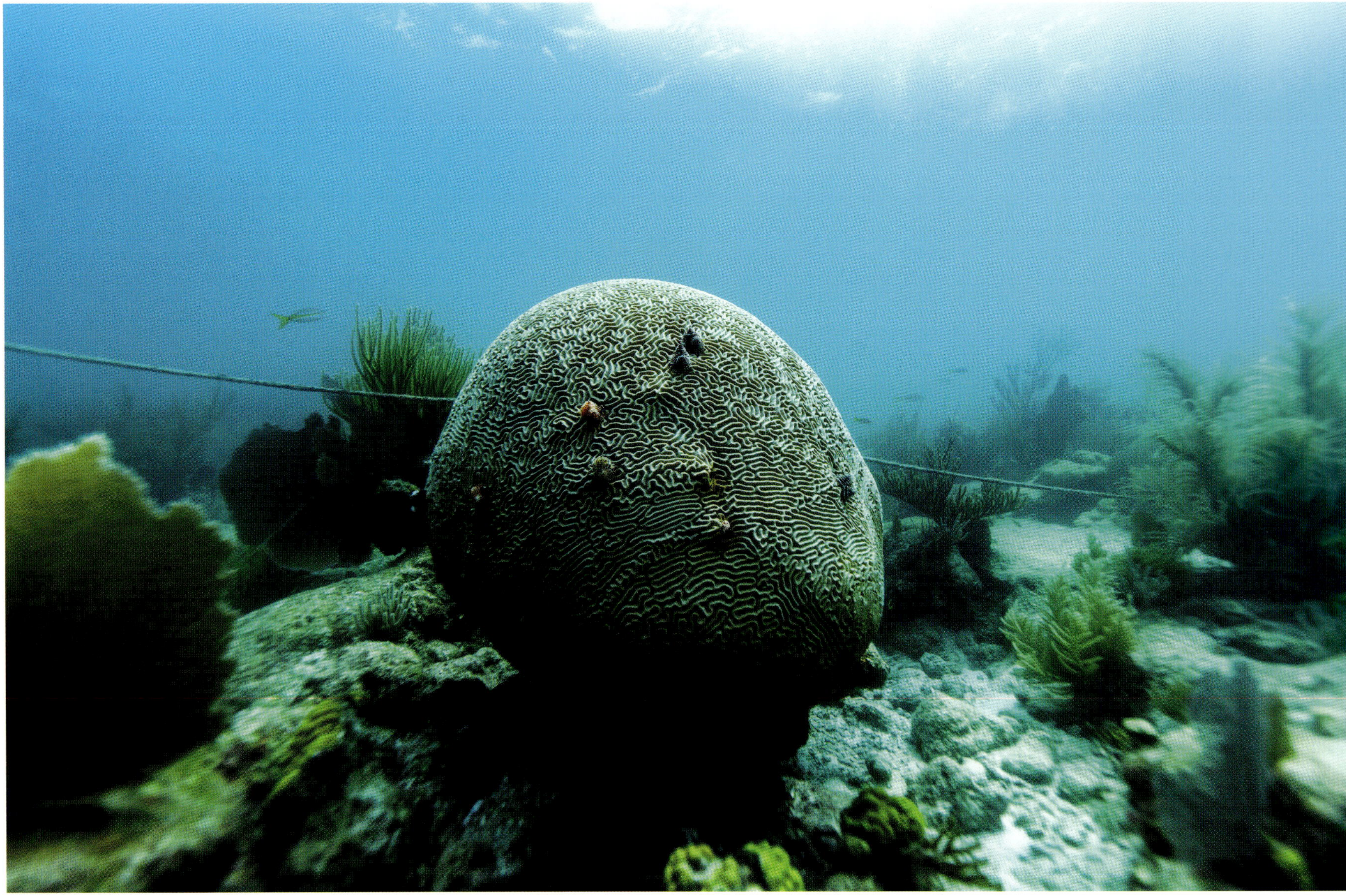

With a trapline behind it, a brain coral sits isolated in a patch reef.

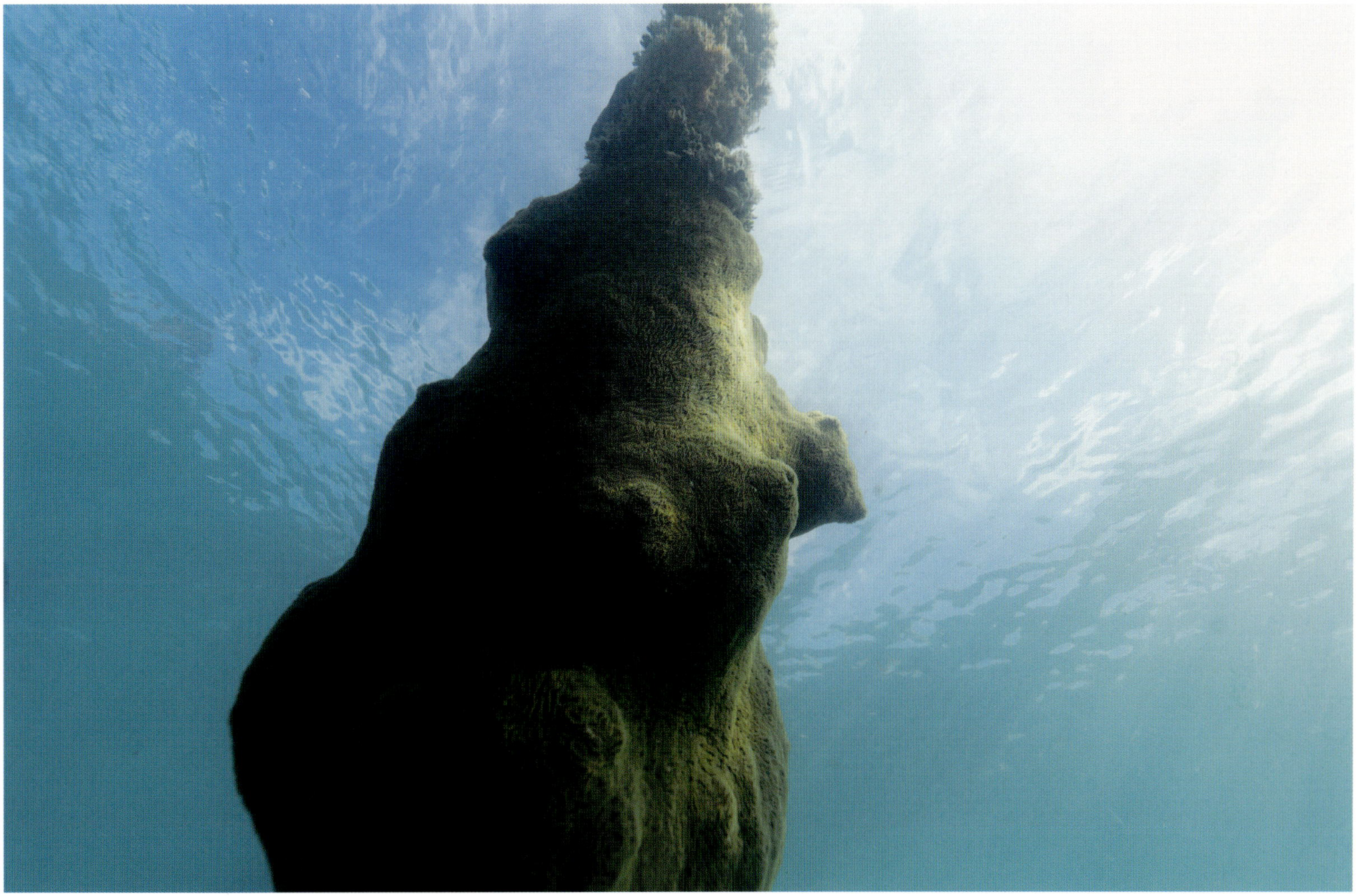

An old coal dock piling completely encrusted in coral.

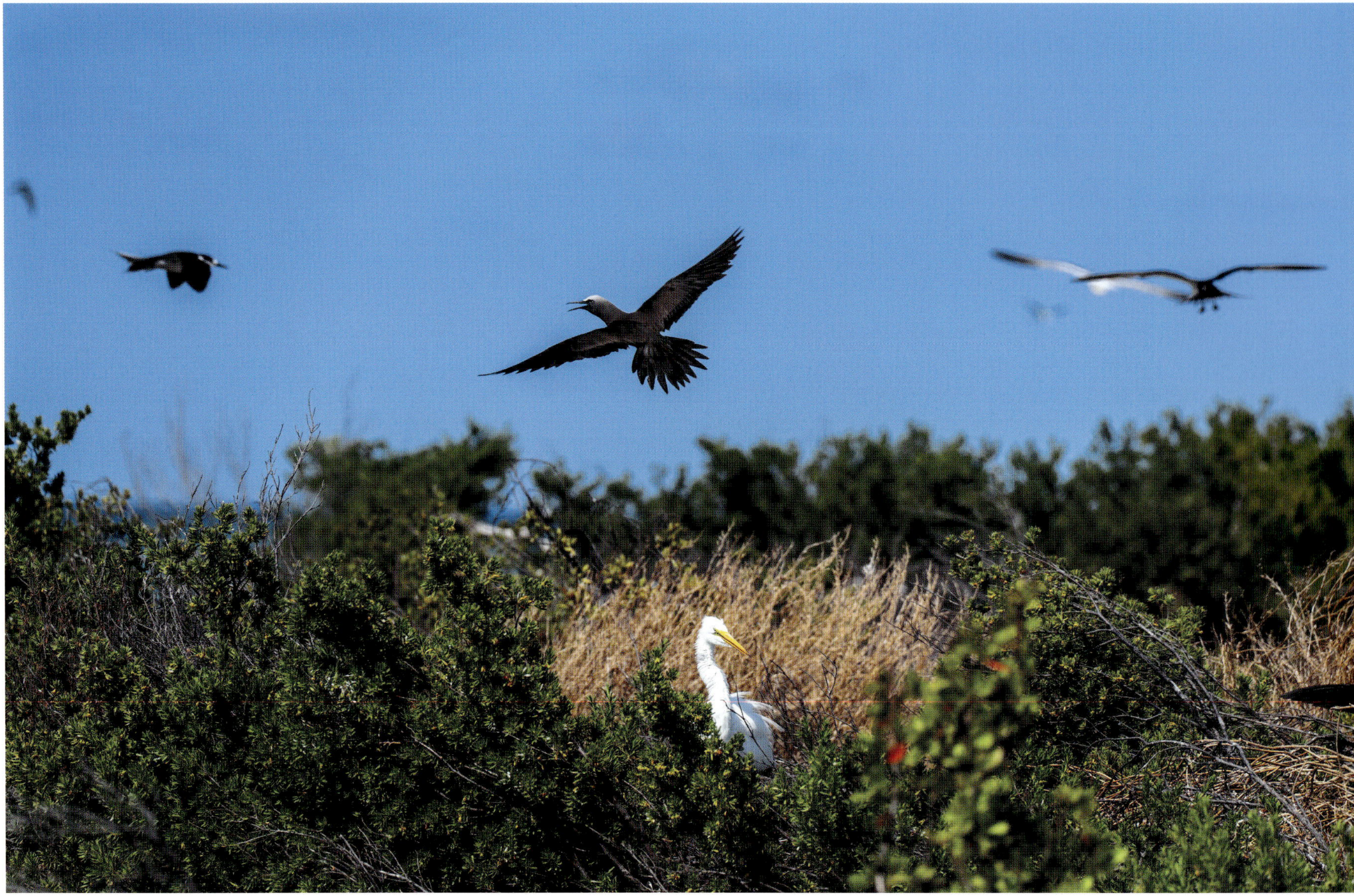

A brown noddy tries to defend its nest from a hungry snowy egret (*Egretta thula*).

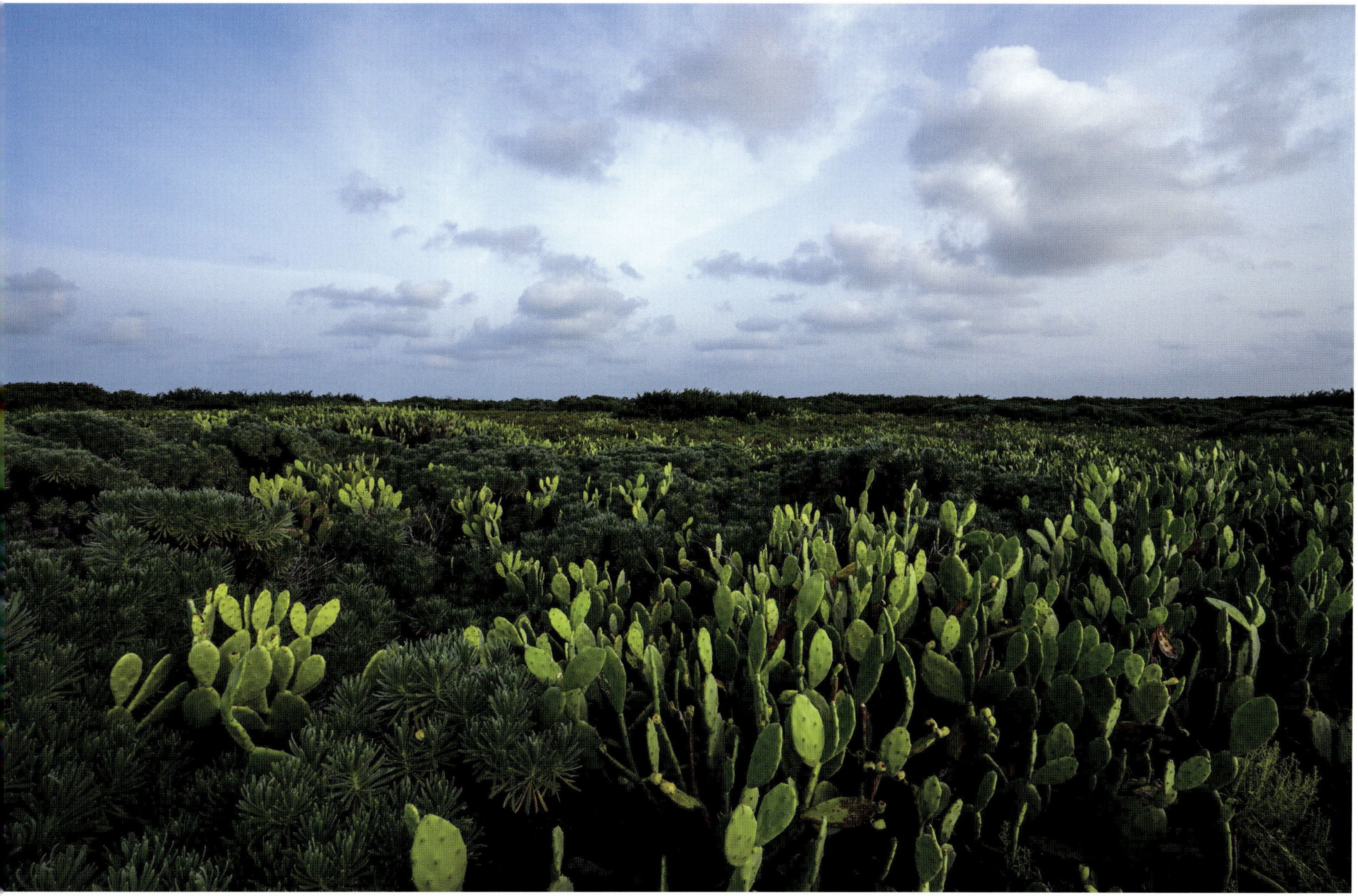

Flora of Loggerhead Key. Here, prickly pear cactus (genus *Opuntia*) is interspersed with dense stands of sea lavender (*Heliotropium gnaphalodes*).

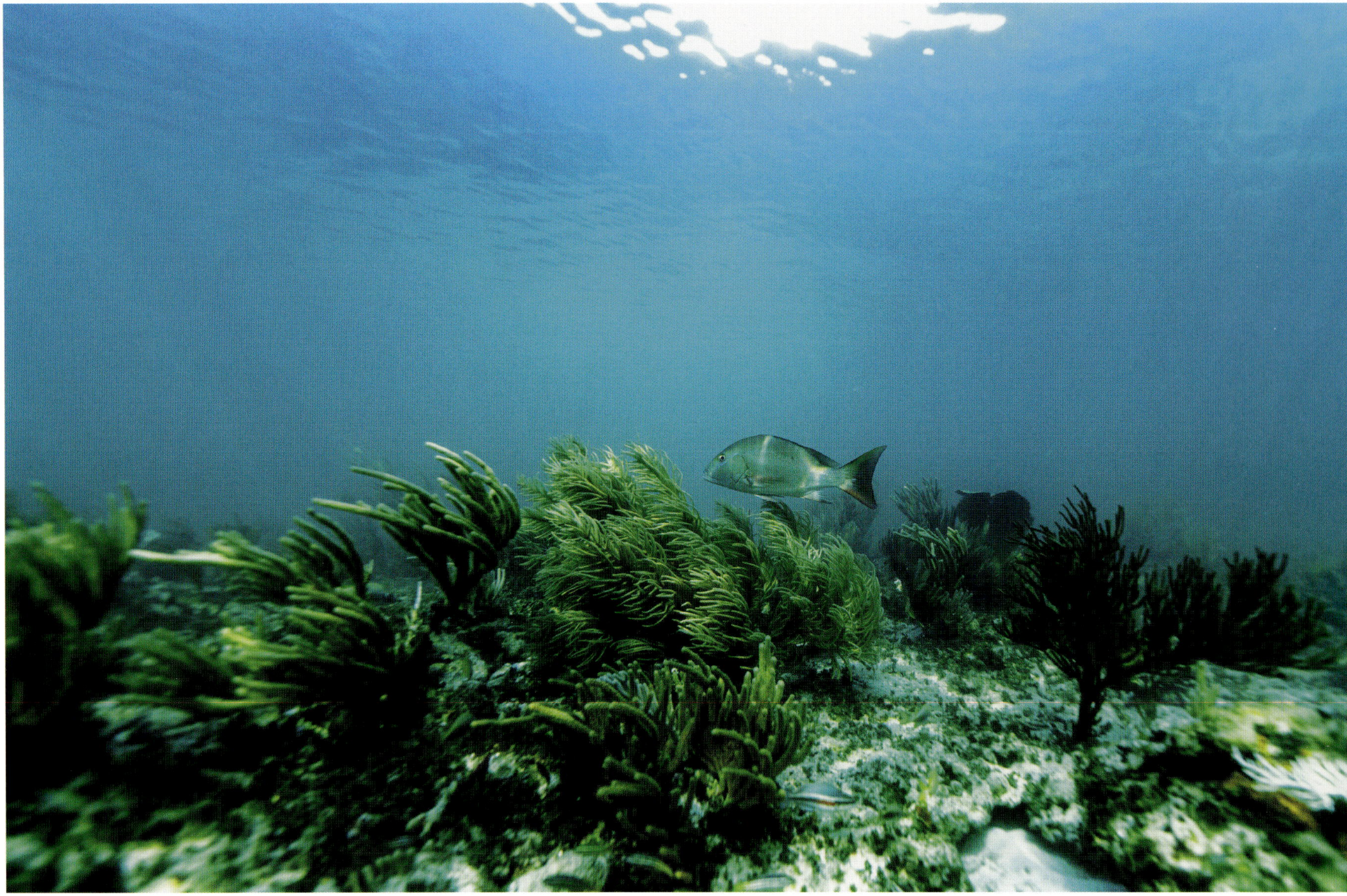

Mutton snapper (*Lutjanus analis*) on a patch reef off Loggerhead Key.

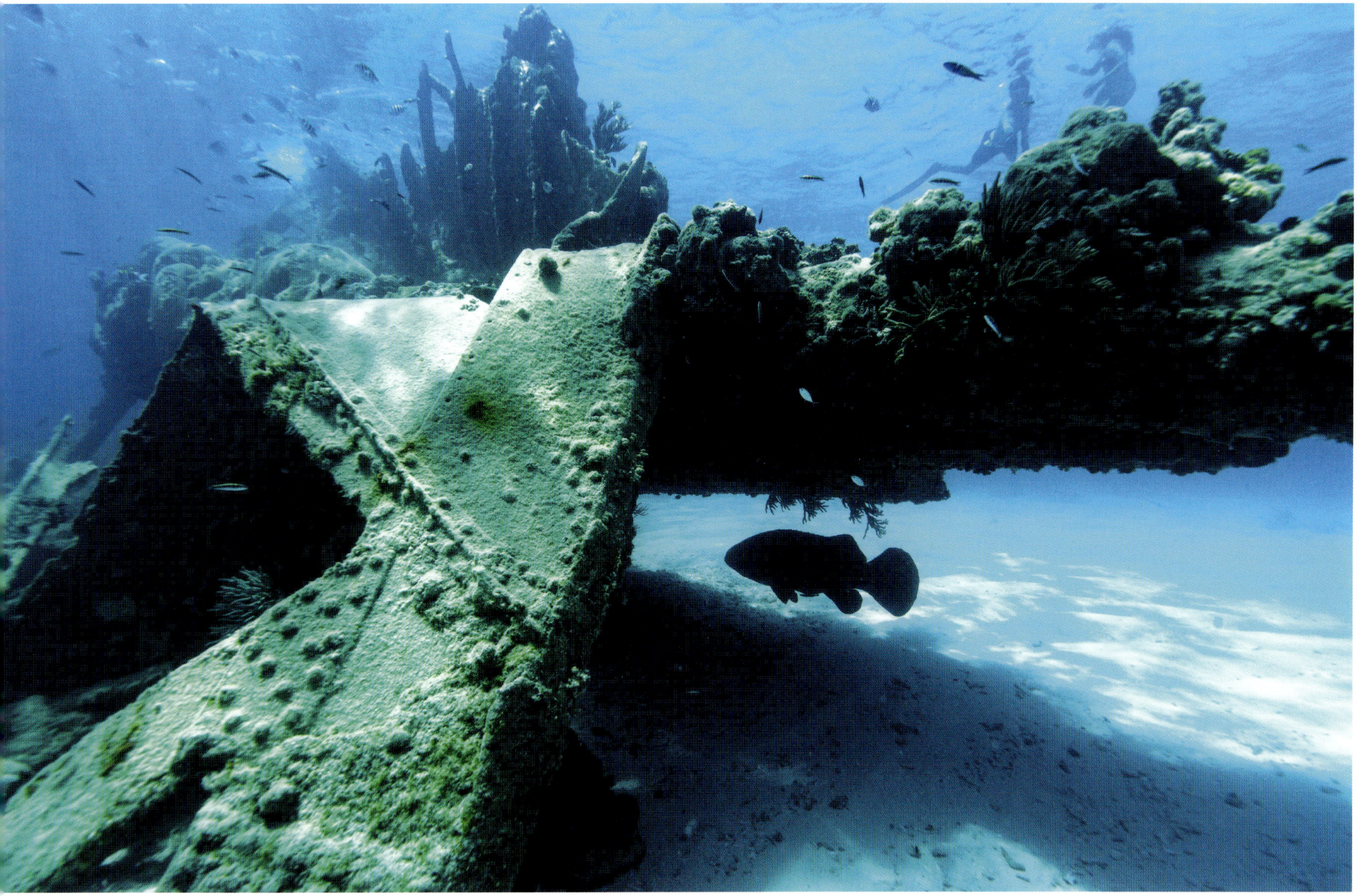

A goliath grouper beneath the Windjammer wreck, about one mile off Loggerhead Key.

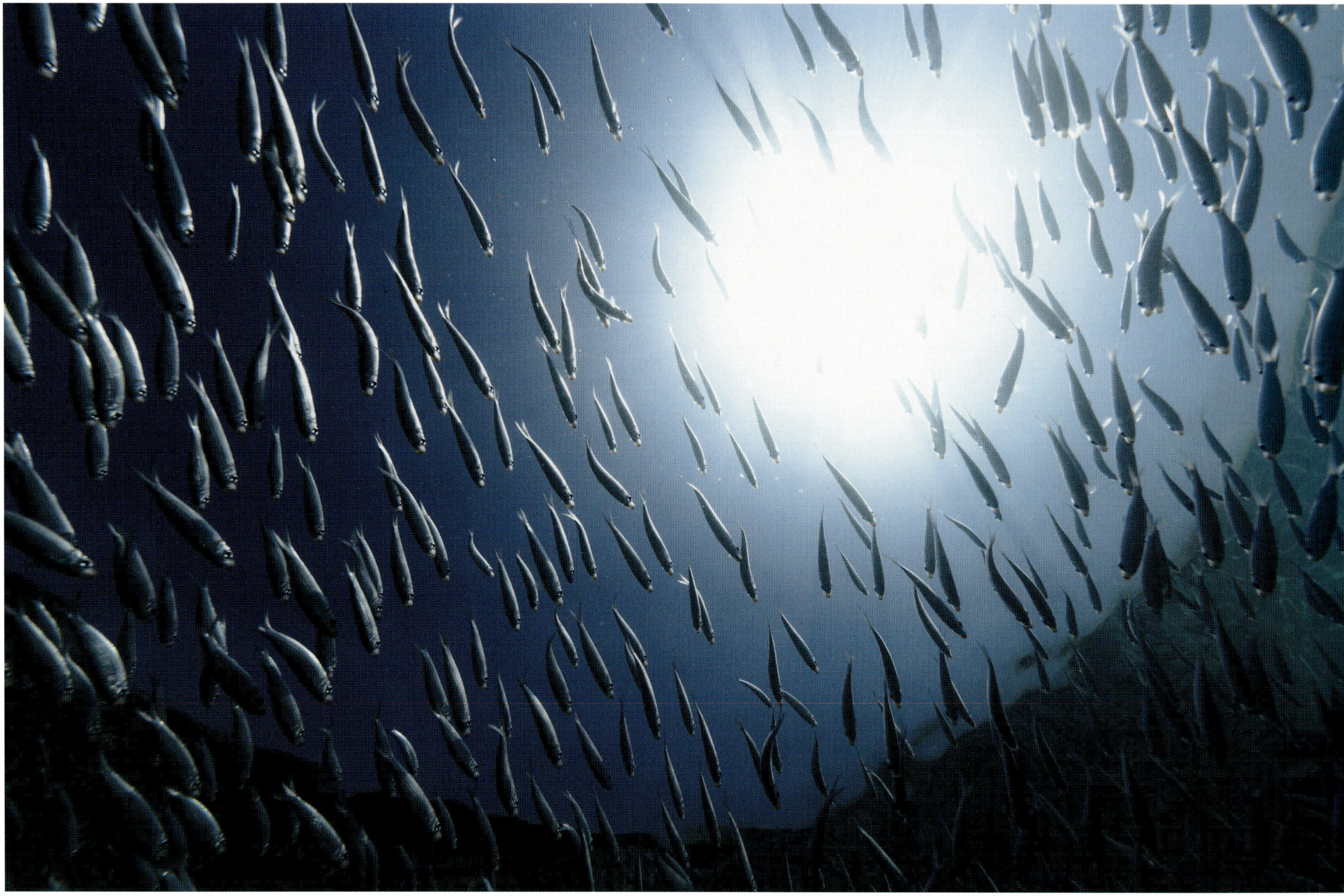

A school of pilchards viewed from below the water's surface.

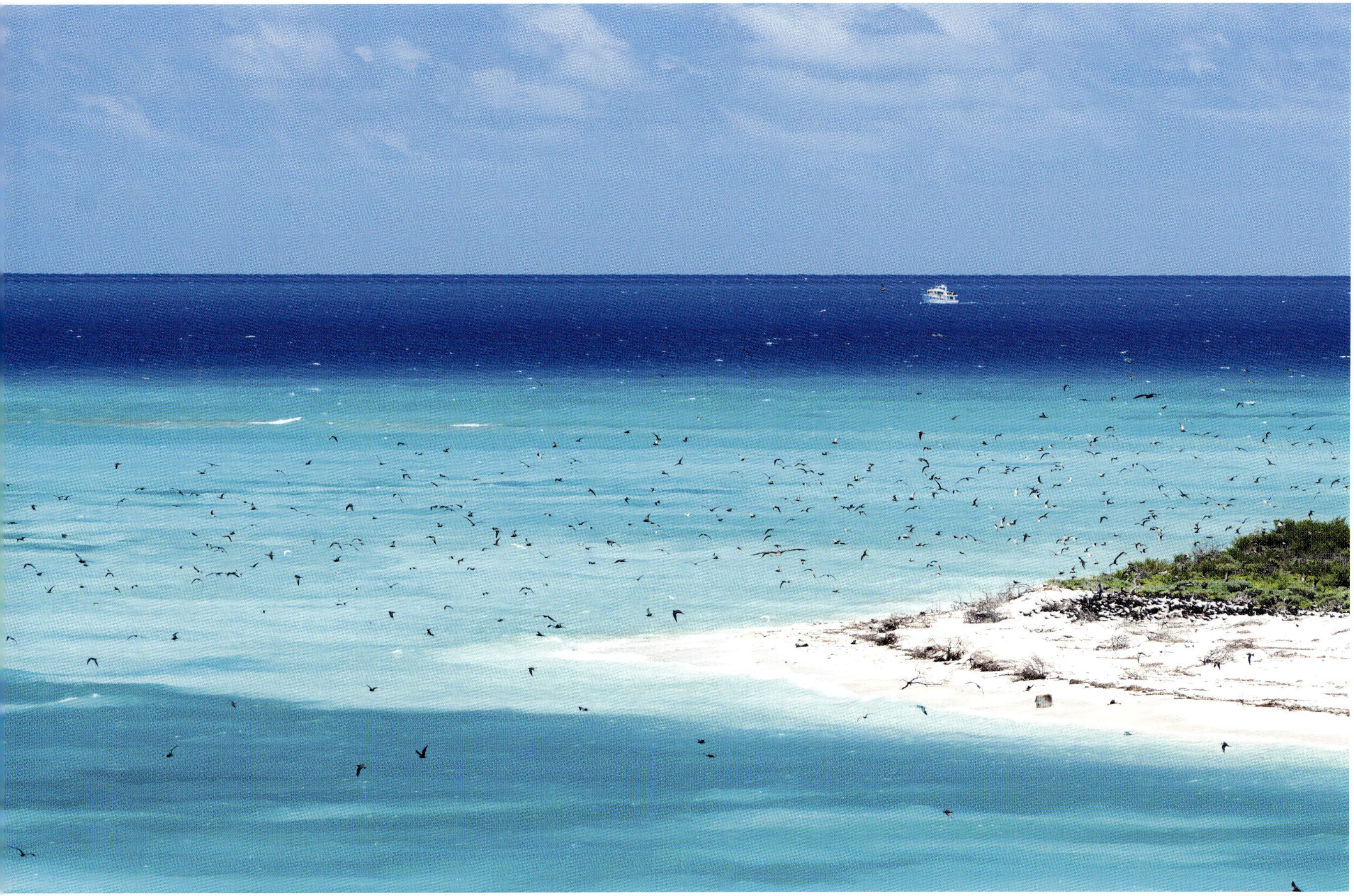

Brown noddies and sooty terns (*Onychoprion fuscatus*) off Bush Key.

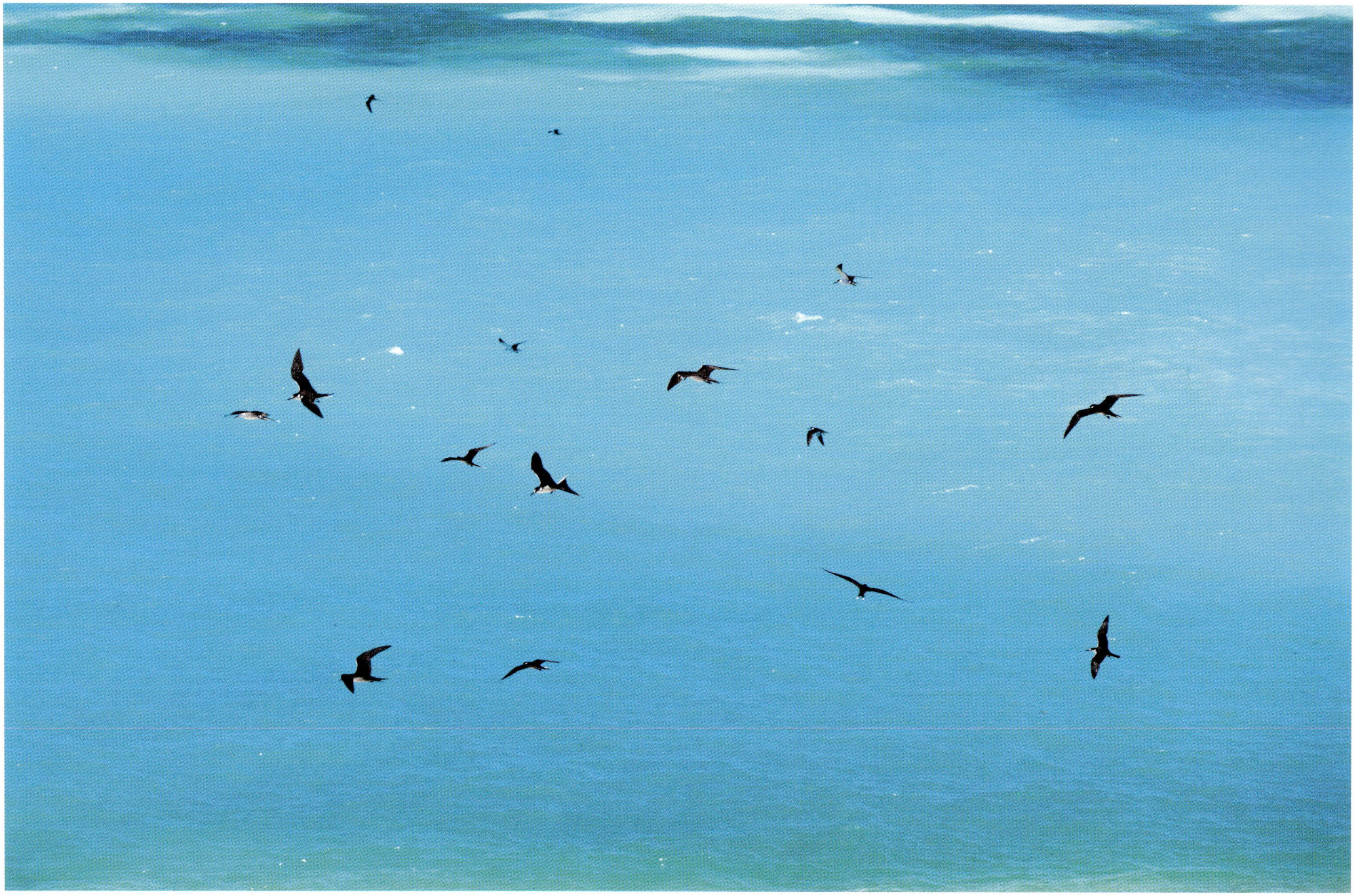

Sooty terns fly over milky blue waters.

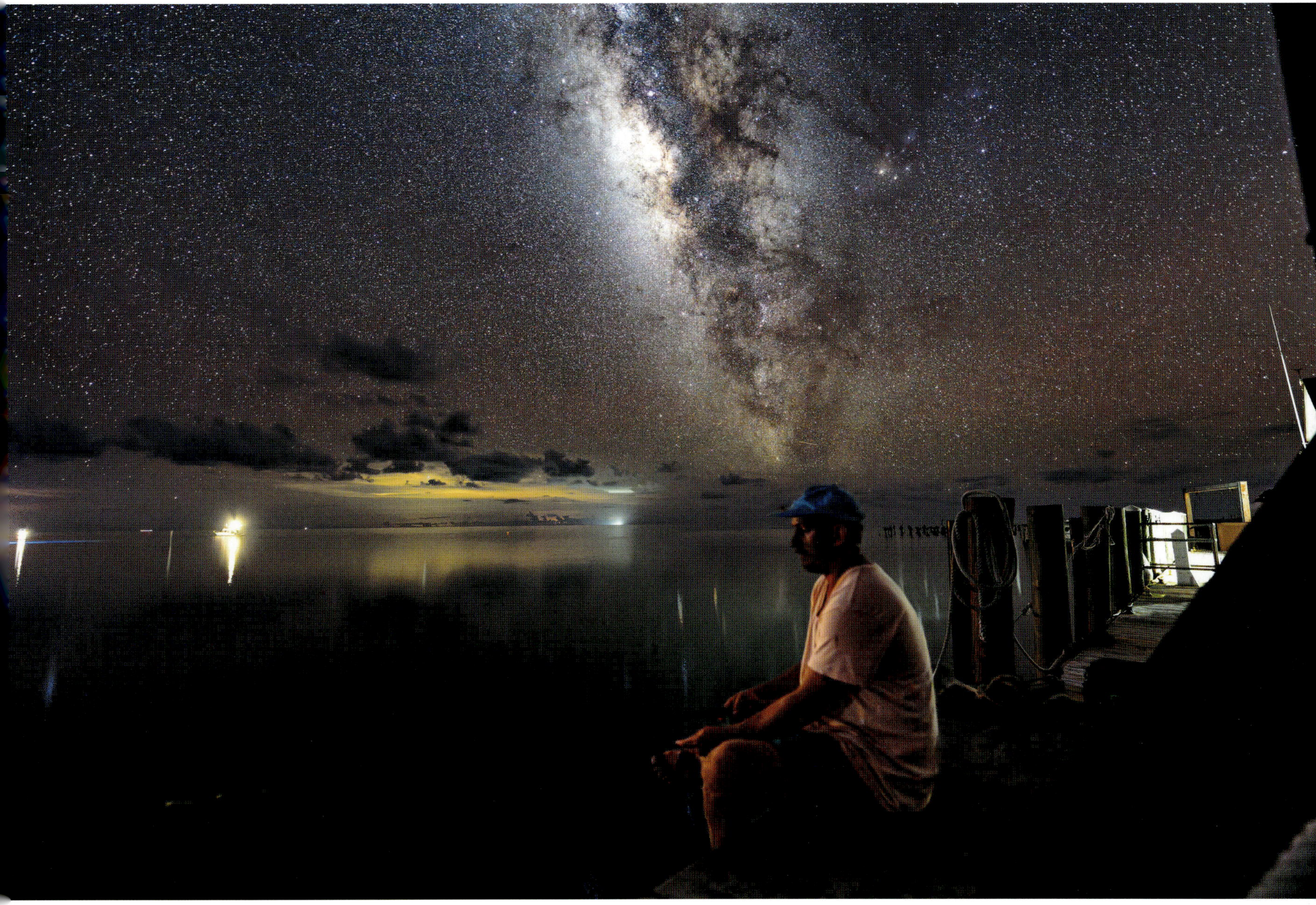

Fishing off the Garden Key ferry dock under the Milky Way.

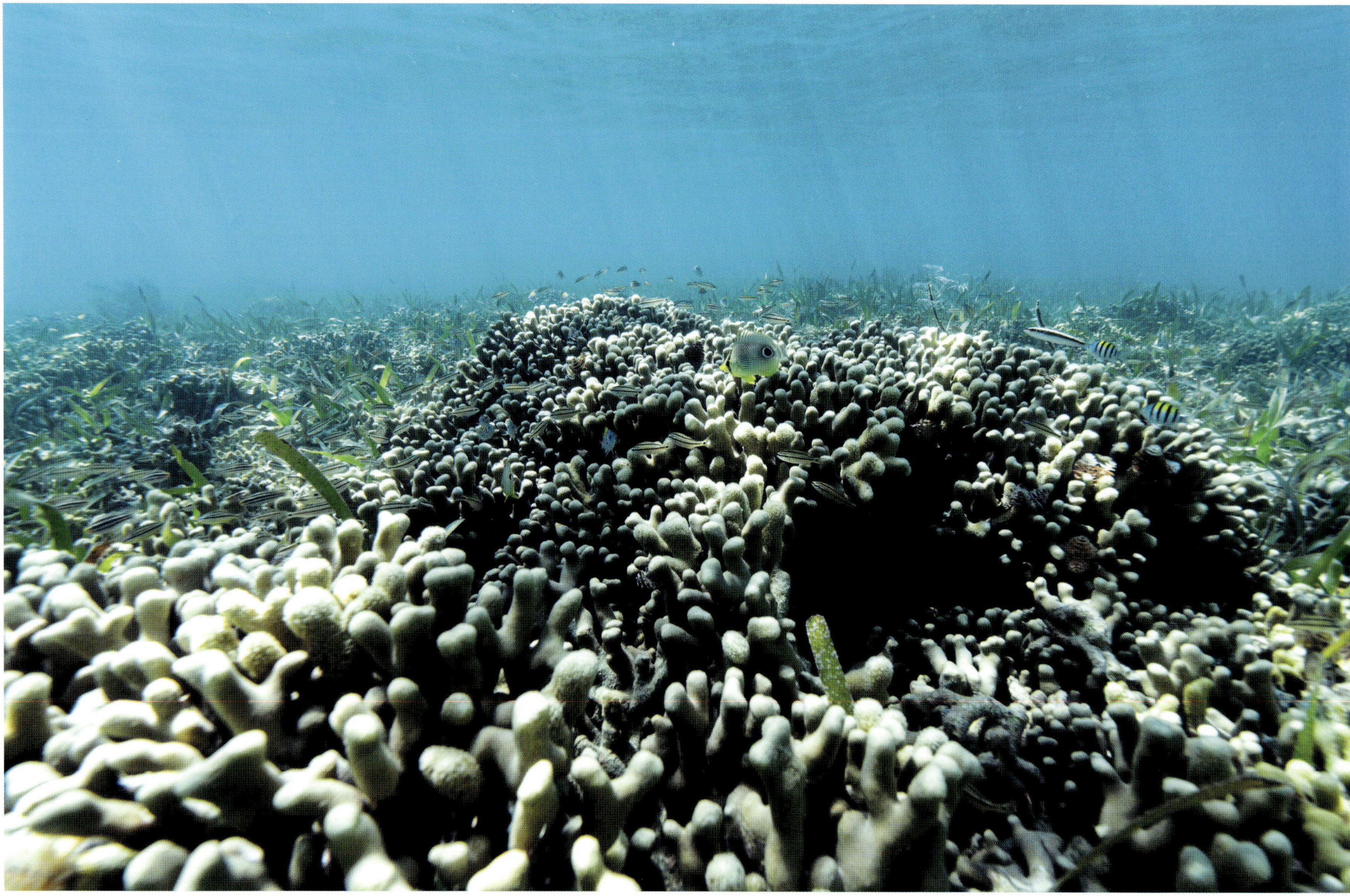

A curious foureye butterfly fish (*Chaetodon capistratus*) swims amidst a finger coral (*Porites porites*) colony off Garden Key.

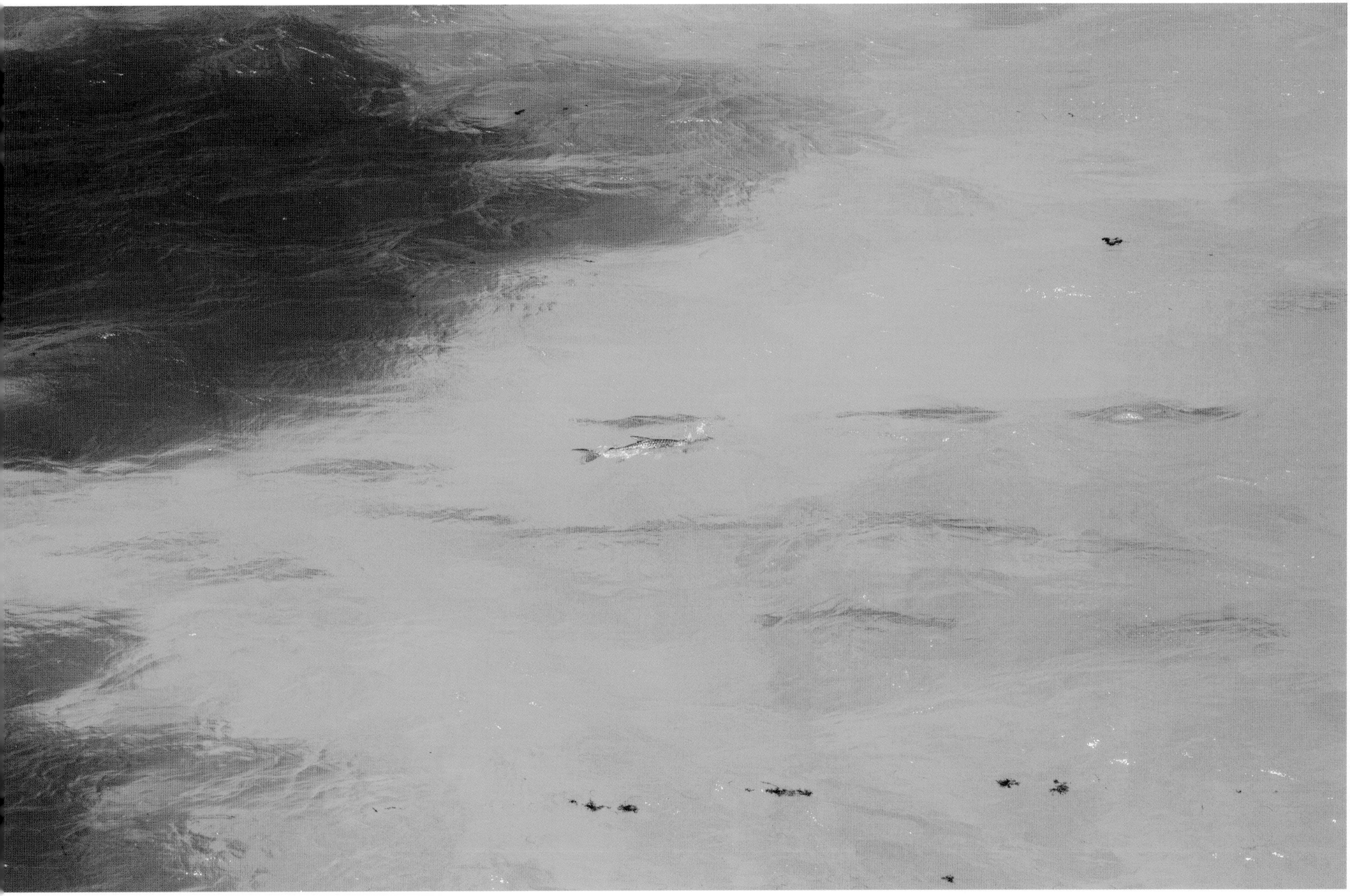

A string of tarpon as observed from the top of Fort Jefferson.

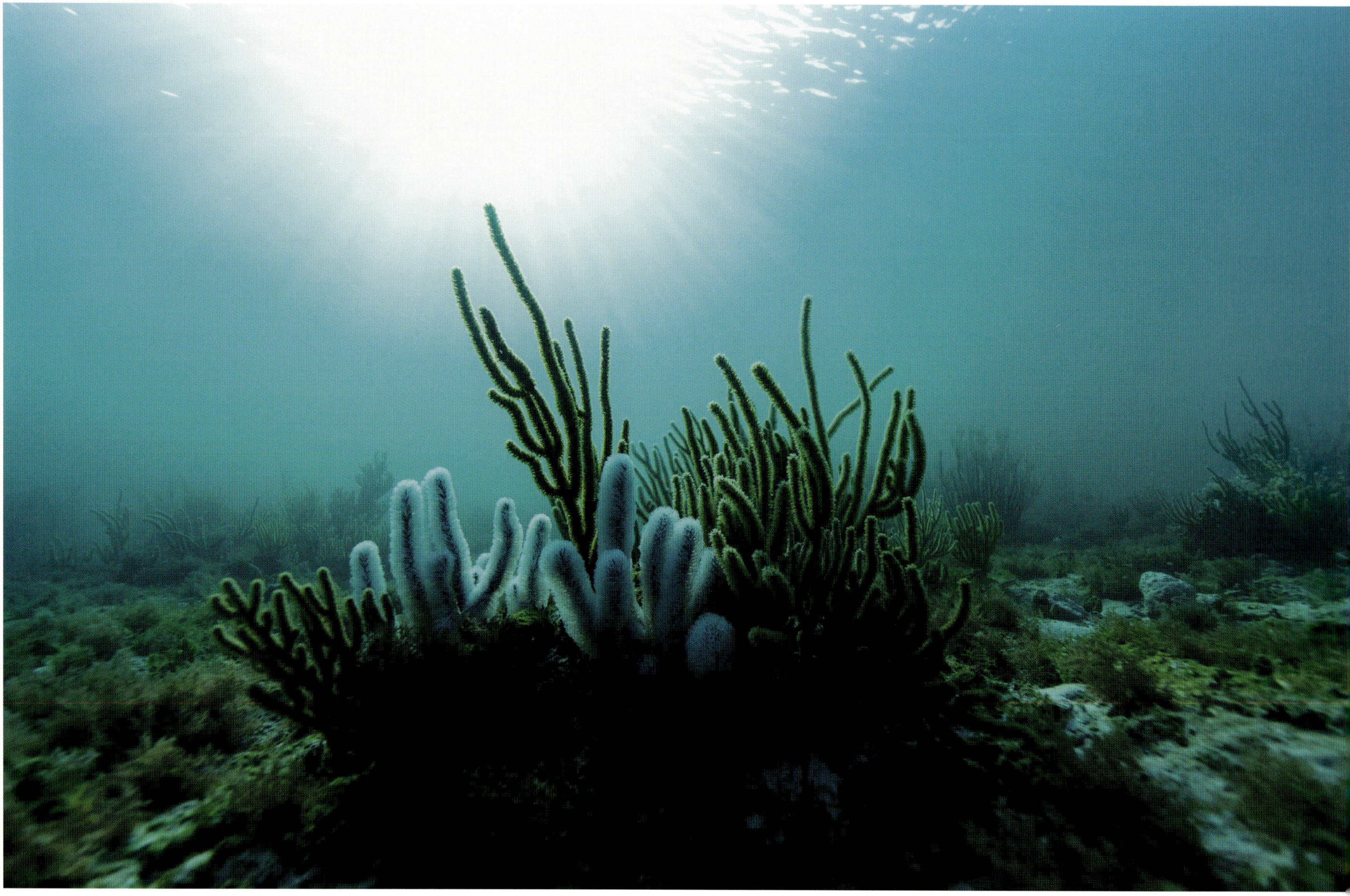

Gorgonian soft corals in the muted evening light.

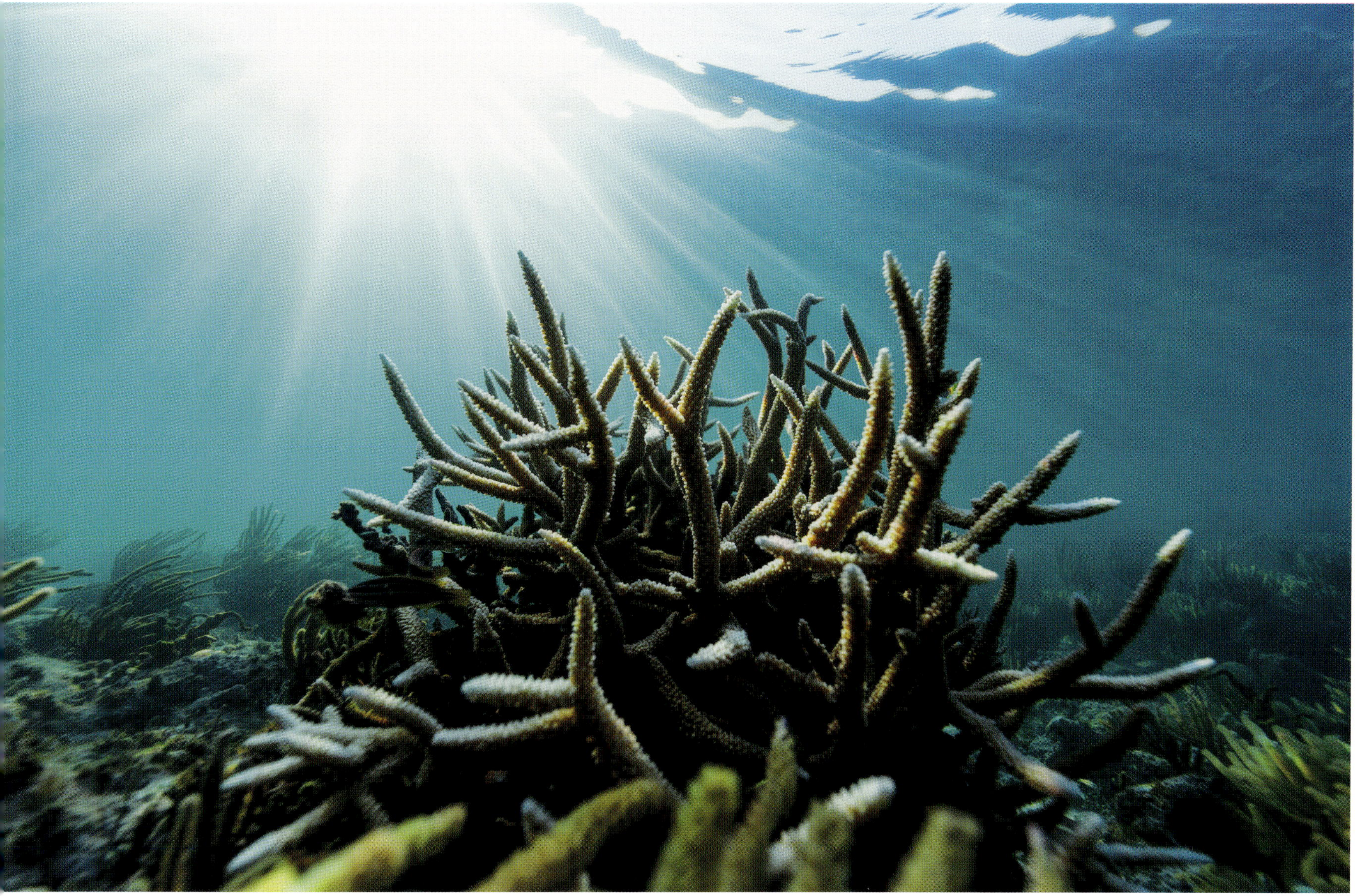

Staghorn thicket.

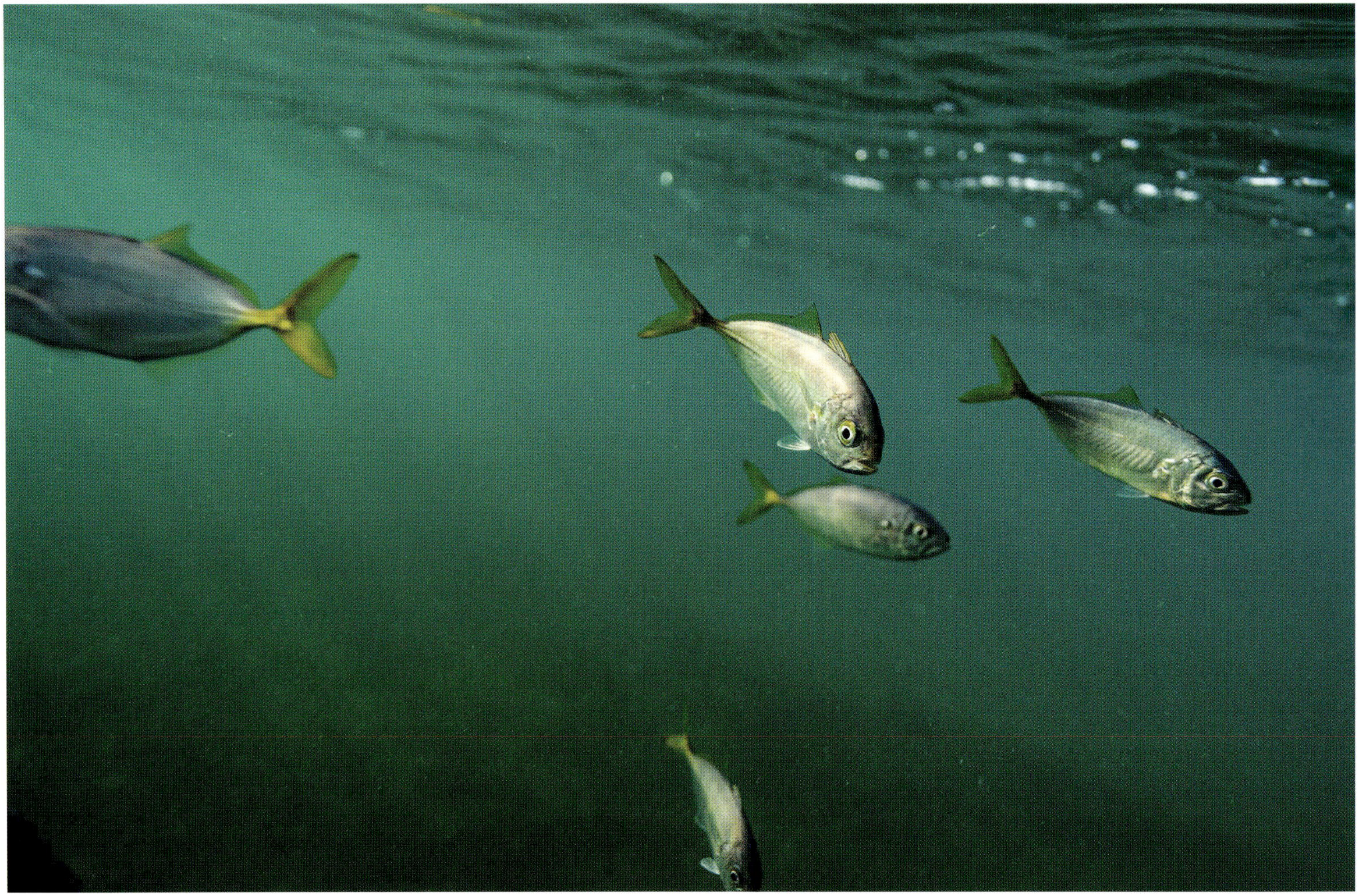

Juvenile yellow jacks brighten the waters off Loggerhead Key.

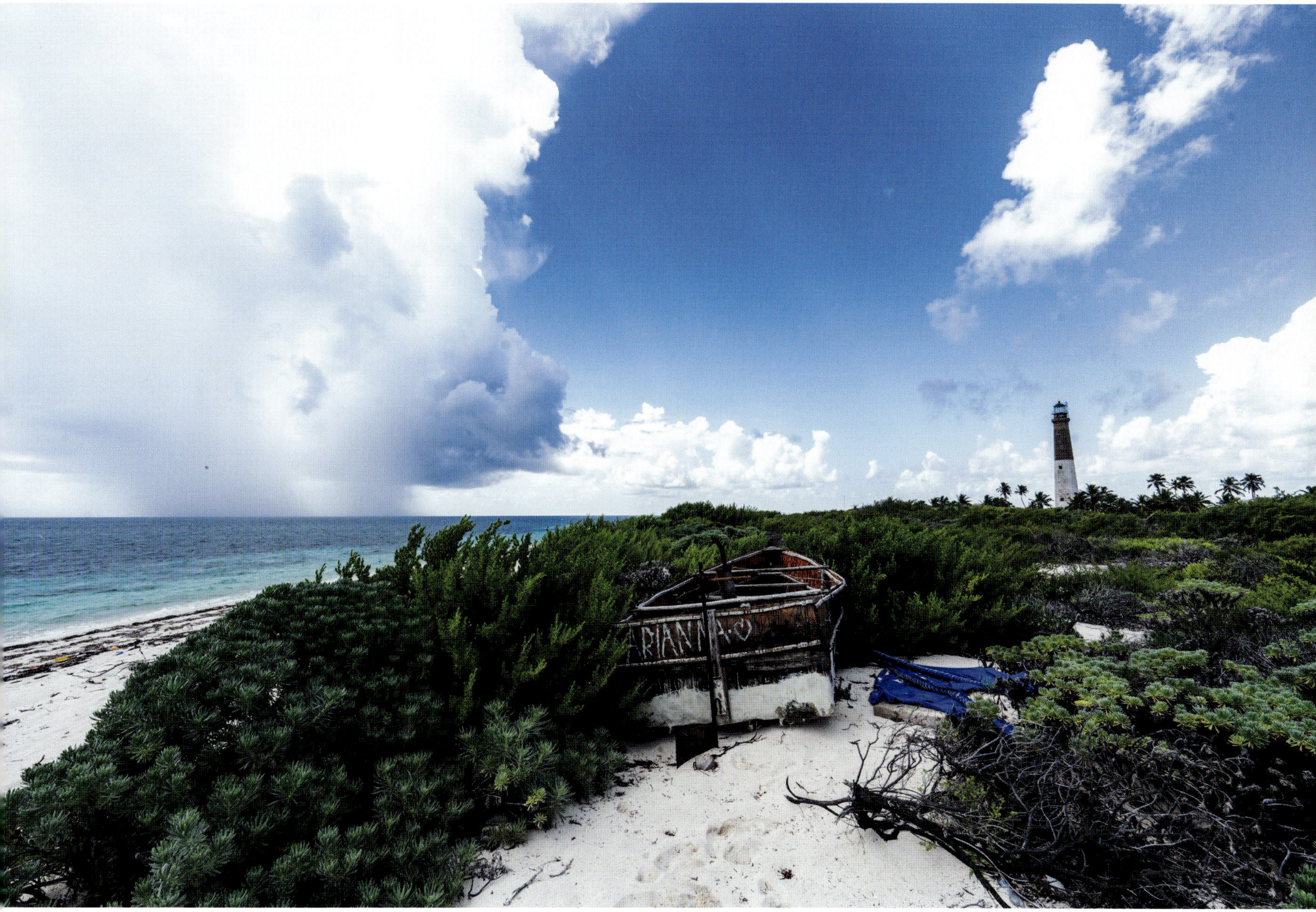

An abandoned Cuban migrant boat on Loggerhead Key.

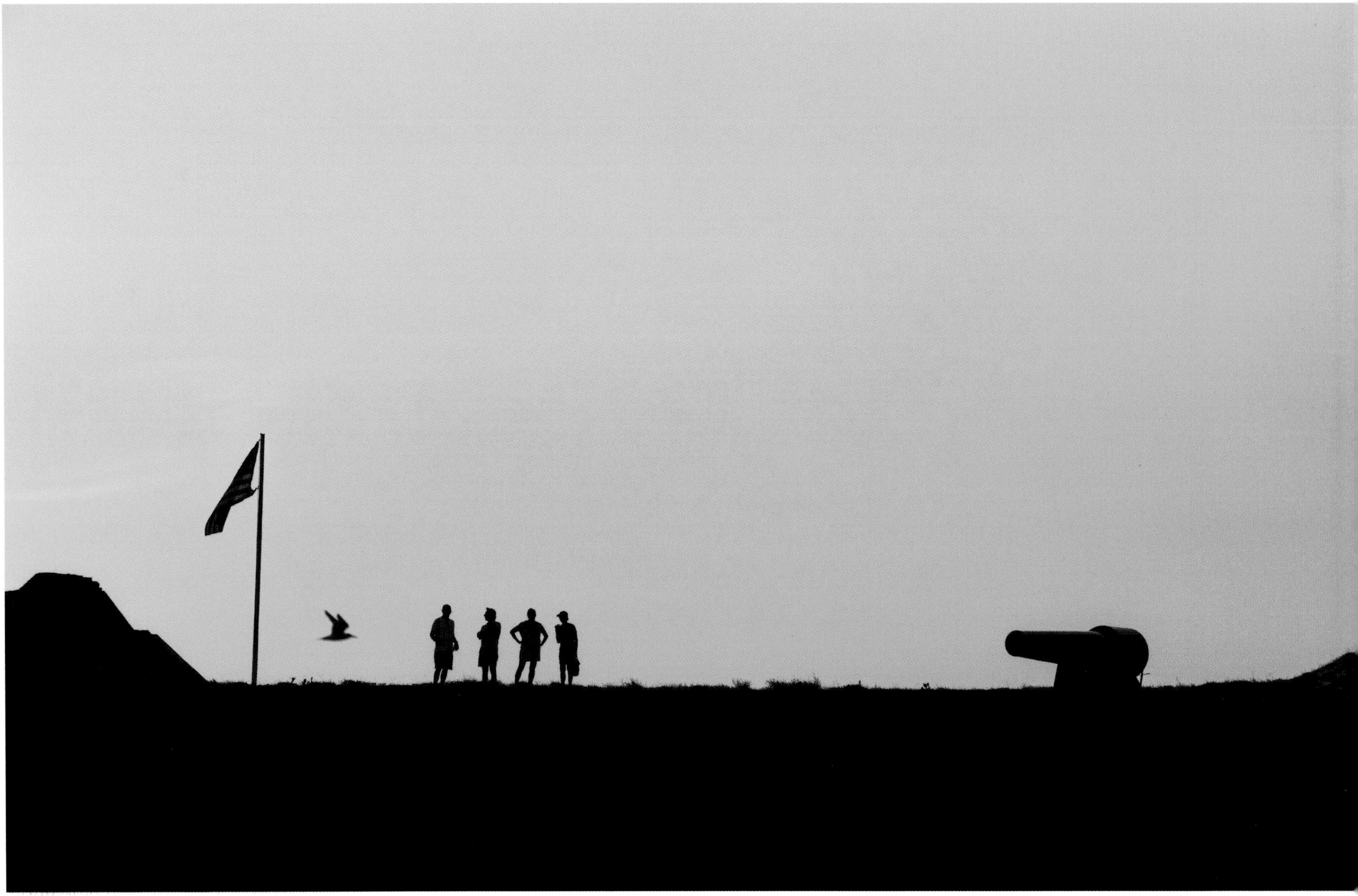

Park patrons enjoy a beautiful sunset from the top of Fort Jefferson.

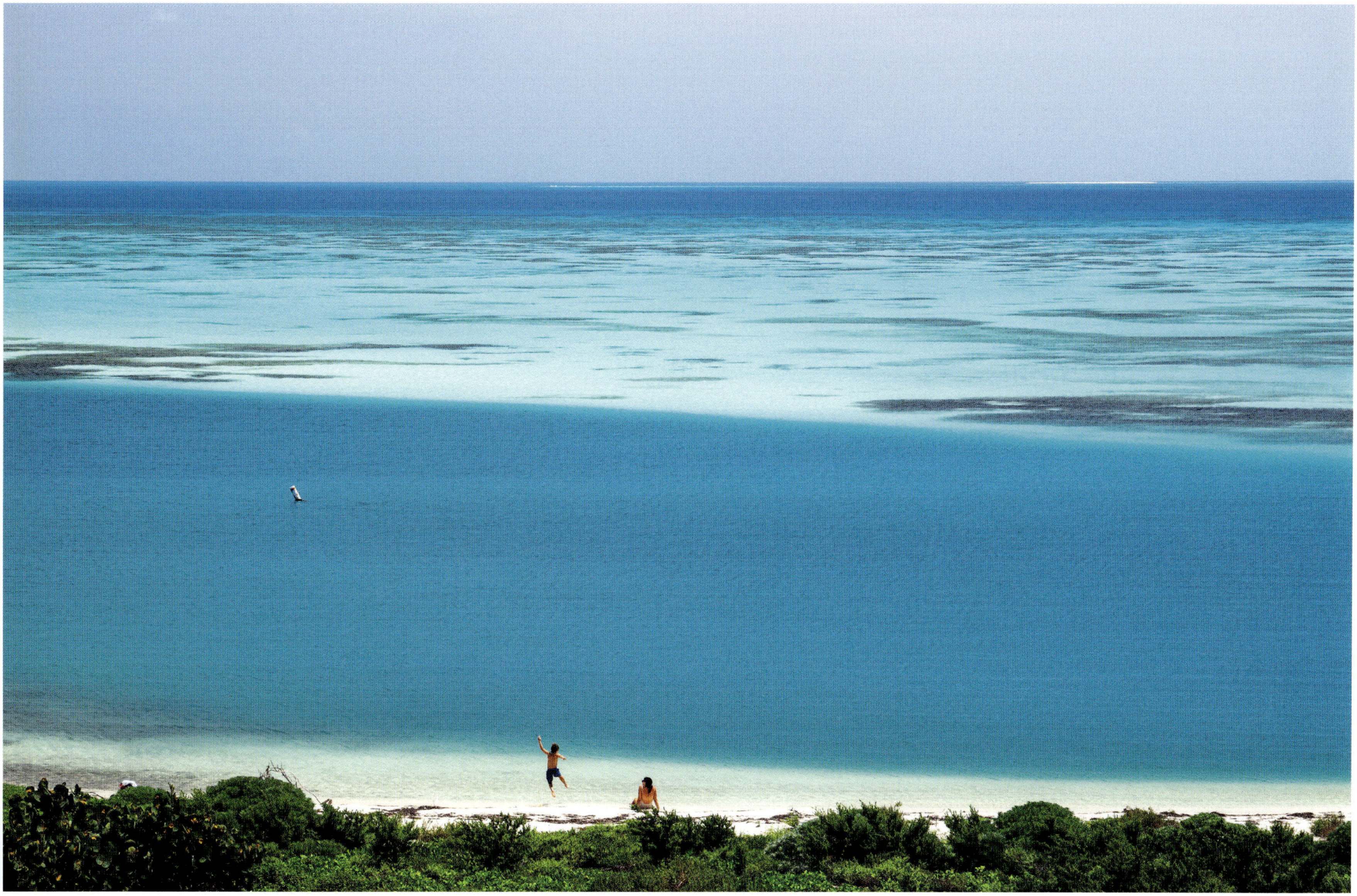

A child jumps with joy into the waters off Bush Key.

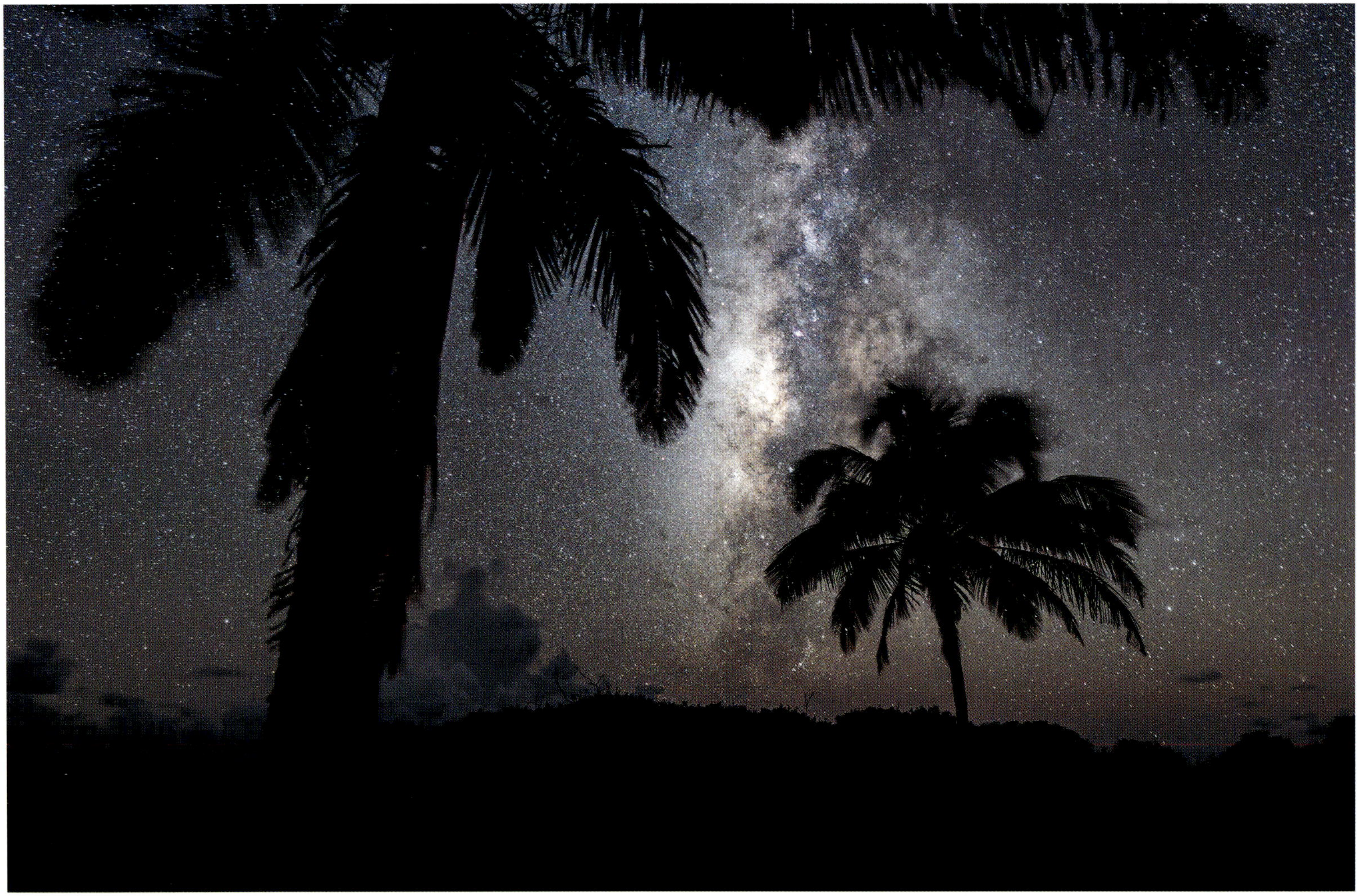

Starry night on Loggerhead Key.

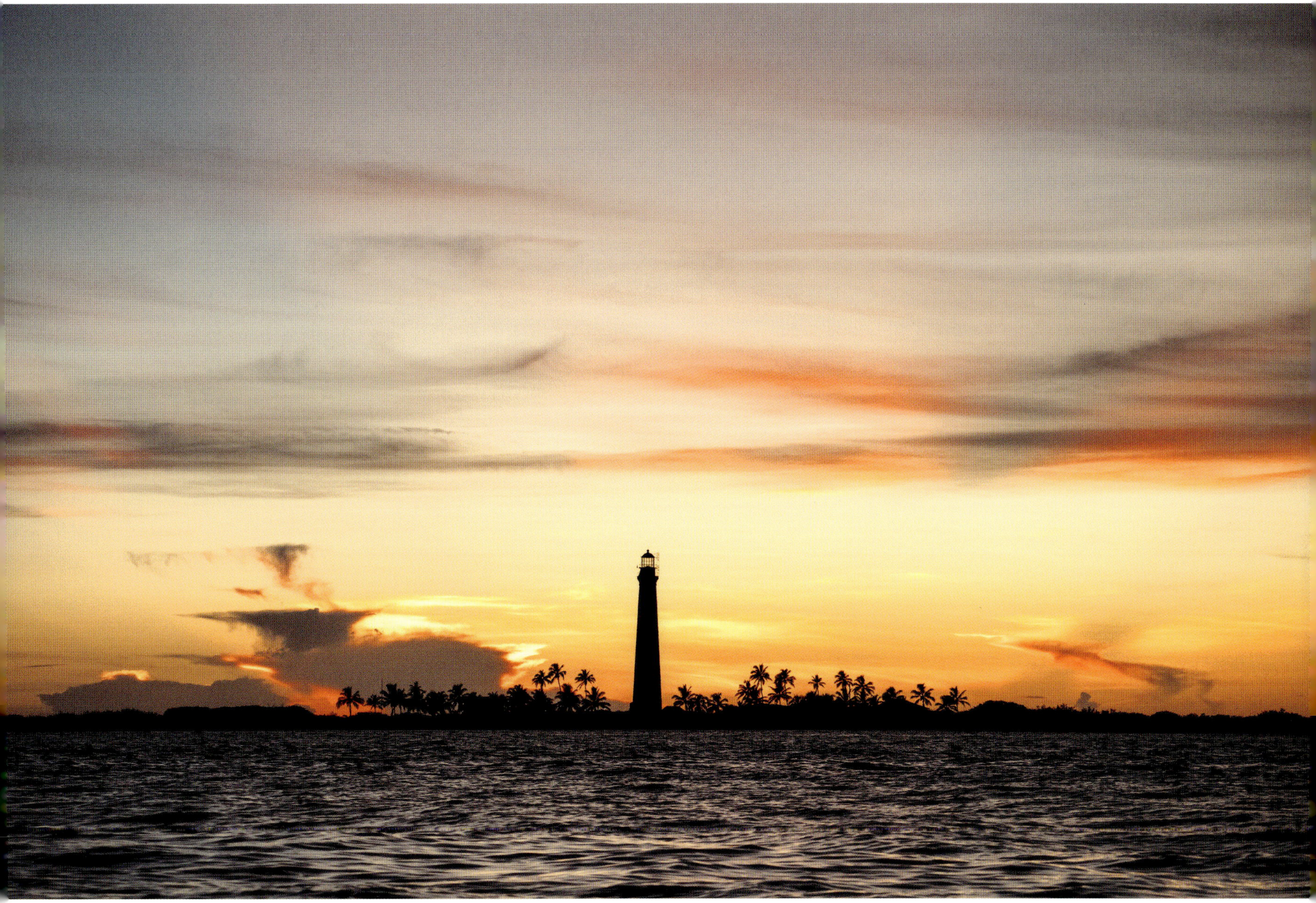

The sun descends behind Loggerhead Key.

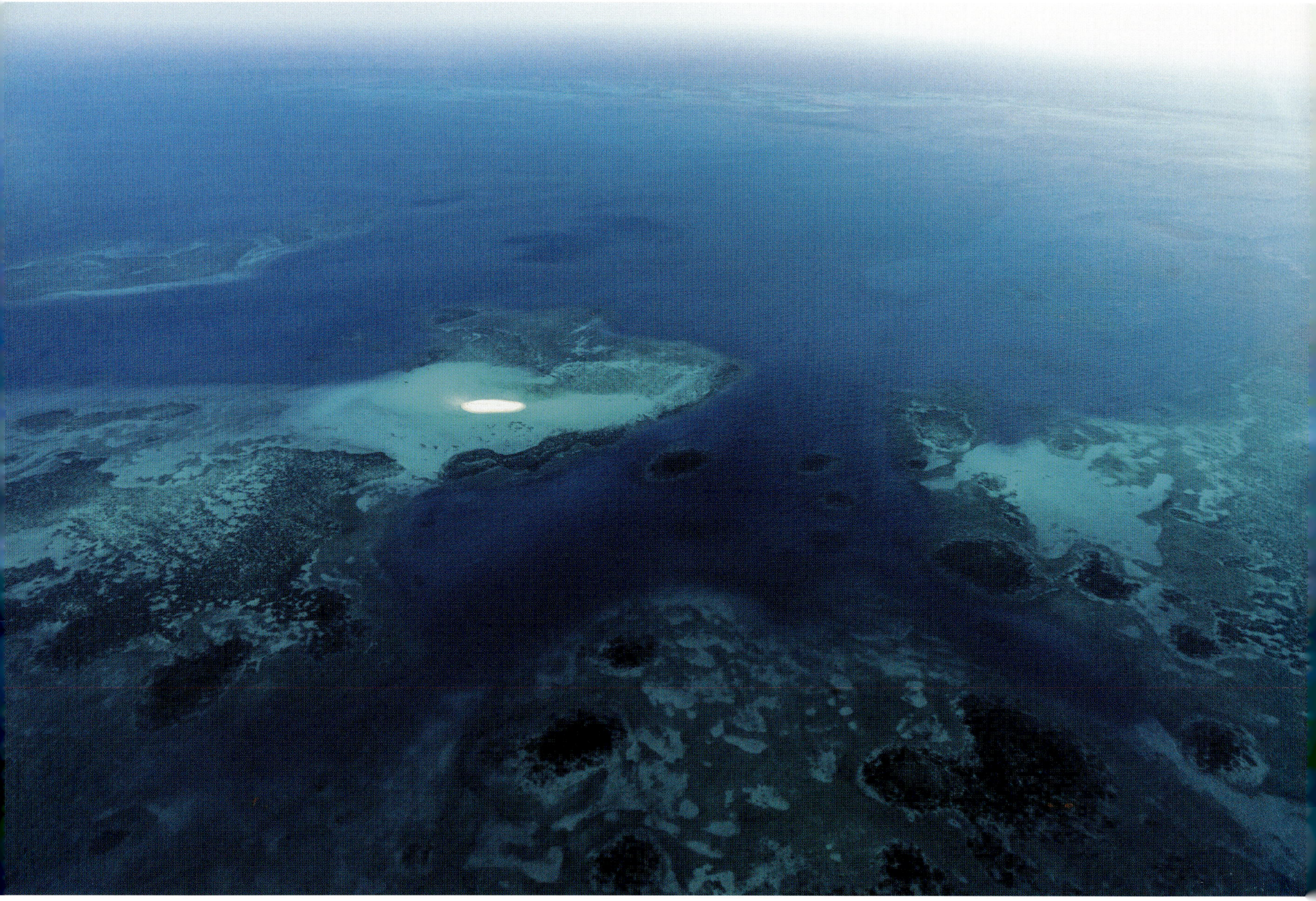

Middle Key and surrounding reefs from the air.

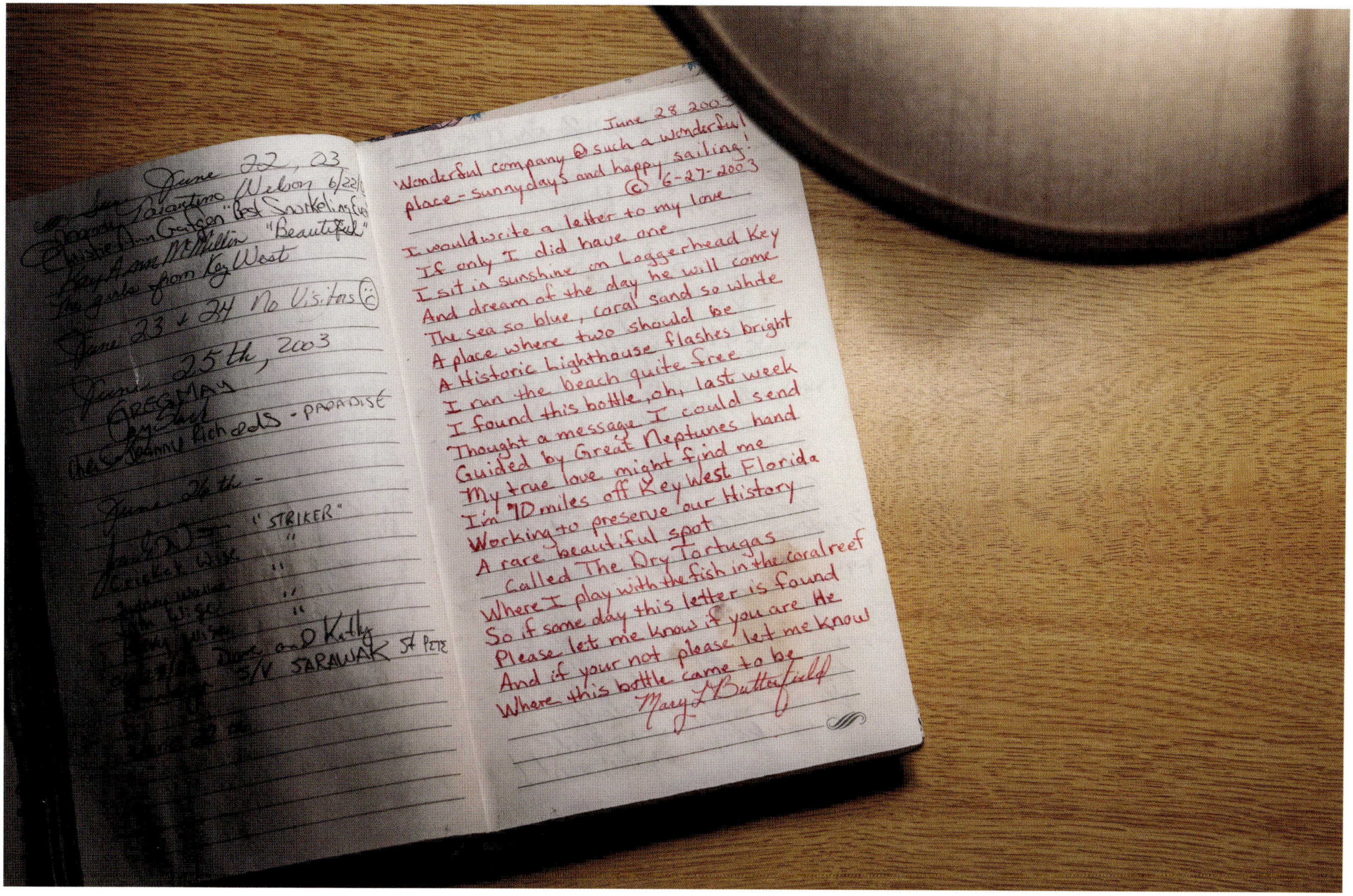

A guestbook entry from a previous visitor to Loggerhead Key.

ACKNOWLEDGMENTS

I consider myself extremely lucky to have had the support of so many over the years and wish I could list everybody who has contributed to my journey along the way. From my incredible Florida Keys community to the individuals who helped guide the art direction for this book and everyone in between: this book would not have been possible without you all, and I thank you from the bottom of my heart.

I extend my heartfelt gratitude to the following individuals and organizations whose unwavering support and contributions made this book possible.

Dry Tortugas National Park
National Park Arts Foundation
Key West Art and Historical Society
Key West Seaplane Adventures
The crew of the *Yankee Freedom*
The crew of the MV (Motor Vessel) *Fort Jefferson*
Curtis Hall
Cori Convertito
Tanya Ortega
Sarah Fangman
Nancy Klingener
Austin Armstrong
Mac Stone

This book is a testament to the collaborative spirit and dedication of these individuals and organizations. Thank you for joining me on this incredible journey of discovery and conservation.

CONTRIBUTORS

Cori Convertito is curator for the Key West Art and Historical Society as well as an adjunct instructor of American history and humanities at College of the Florida Keys. Convertito earned her PhD from the University of Exeter and specializes in eighteenth-century maritime history. She has written several book chapters and articles, including "Mending the Sick and Wounded: The Development of Naval Hospitals in the West Indies, 1740–1800" in the *Canadian Journal of History.*

Sarah Fangman is superintendent of the Florida Keys National Marine Sanctuary. Prior to this position, she worked within the National Marine Sanctuary System for nineteen years, most recently as superintendent of Gray's Reef National Marine Sanctuary in Georgia. Fangman holds a U.S. Coast Guard 100-ton master captain's license and is certified as a submersible pilot.

Curtis Hall is lead ranger for resource education at Dry Tortugas National Park, where he is also a diving supervisor for the park's underwater resources. From 1997 to 2006, he served in the U.S. Navy as a Special Operations EOD (explosive ordnance disposal) diver. Hall holds a BS in parks, recreation, and ecology from Indiana University and an MS in natural resources from Virginia Tech.

Nancy Klingener is the community affairs manager for the Monroe County Public Library. She has lived in the Keys since 1991 and worked as a journalist for the *Miami Herald, Solares Hill,* and WLRN Public Media. She is board president of the Key West Literary Seminar and has a BA in English and an MA in the humanities.

Ian Wilson-Navarro, a Florida Keys native, grew up exploring the reefs, seagrass flats, and mangrove islands off the backyard of his home archipelago. A passionate outdoorsman and advocate for conservation, he blended his deep-rooted affinity for the Keys with his fervor for adventure sports such as surfing, free diving, and fly fishing. These pursuits fostered his intimate relationship with the natural environment. His imagery has been featured in *Garden and Gun, Field and Stream,* and the *Fly Fish Journal.* And his active engagement with conservation organizations like Bonefish and Tarpon Trust underscores his commitment to the cause.